Planning and Analyzing Foreign Direct Investment Projects:

Emerging Research and Opportunities

Halil Sarıaslan
Başkent University, Turkey

A volume in the Advances in Finance, Accounting, and Economics (AFAE) Book Series

IGI Global
DISSEMINATOR OF KNOWLEDGE

Published in the United States of America by
IGI Global
Business Science Reference (an imprint of IGI Global)
701 E. Chocolate Avenue
Hershey PA, USA 17033
Tel: 717-533-8845
Fax: 717-533-8661
E-mail: cust@igi-global.com
Web site: http://www.igi-global.com

Library of Congress Cataloging-in-Publication Data

Names: Sariaslan, Halil, author.
Title: Planning and analyzing foreign direct investment projects : emerging research and opportunities / by Halil Sariaslan.
Description: Hershey, PA : Business Science Reference, [2019]
Identifiers: LCCN 2018033033| ISBN 9781522576969 (hardcover) | ISBN 9781522576976 (ebook)
Subjects: LCSH: Investments, Foreign.
Classification: LCC HG4521 .S33435 2019 | DDC 332.67/3--dc23 LC record available at https://lccn.loc.gov/2018033033

This book is published in the IGI Global book series Advances in Finance, Accounting, and Economics (AFAE) (ISSN: 2327-5677; eISSN: 2327-5685)

British Cataloguing in Publication Data
A Cataloguing in Publication record for this book is available from the British Library.

Advances in Finance, Accounting, and Economics (AFAE) Book Series

ISSN:2327-5677
EISSN:2327-5685

MISSION

In our changing economic and business environment, it is important to consider the financial changes occurring internationally as well as within individual organizations and business environments. Understanding these changes as well as the factors that influence them is crucial in preparing for our financial future and ensuring economic sustainability and growth.

The **Advances in Finance, Accounting, and Economics (AFAE)** book series aims to publish comprehensive and informative titles in all areas of economics and economic theory, finance, and accounting to assist in advancing the available knowledge and providing for further research development in these dynamic fields.

COVERAGE

- Economic Policy
- International Economics
- Fiscal Policy
- Economics of Agriculture and Biotechnology
- Borrowing and Lending
- Ethics in Accounting and Finance
- Applied economics
- Economics of Risks, Uncertainty, Ambiguity, and Insurance
- Auditing
- Accounting information systems

IGI Global is currently accepting manuscripts for publication within this series. To submit a proposal for a volume in this series, please contact our Acquisition Editors at Acquisitions@igi-global.com or visit: http://www.igi-global.com/publish/.

The Advances in Finance, Accounting, and Economics (AFAE) Book Series (ISSN 2327-5677) is published by IGI Global, 701 E. Chocolate Avenue, Hershey, PA 17033-1240, USA, www.igi-global.com. This series is composed of titles available for purchase individually; each title is edited to be contextually exclusive from any other title within the series. For pricing and ordering information please visit http://www.igi-global.com/book-series/advances-finance-accounting-economics/73685. Postmaster: Send all address changes to above address.

Titles in this Series

For a list of additional titles in this series, please visit:
https://www.igi-global.com/book-series/advances-finance-accounting-economics/73685

Handbook of Research on Microfinancial Impacts on Women Empowerment, Poverty, ...
Ramesh Chandra Das (Katwa College, India)
Business Science Reference • ©2019 • 452pp • H/C (ISBN: 9781522552406) • US $275.00

Emerging Economic Models for Global Sustainability and Social Development
Bryan Christiansen (Global Research Society, LLC, USA) Irina Sysoeva (Independent Researcher, Russia) Alexandra Udovikina (Independent Researcher, Russia) and Anna Ketova (Khabarovsk State Academy of Economics and Law, Russia)
Business Science Reference • ©2019 • 430pp • H/C (ISBN: 9781522557876) • US $225.00

Techno-Social Systems for Modern Economical and Governmental Infrastructures
Alexander Troussov (The Russian Presidential Academy of National Economy and Public Administration, Russia) and Sergey Maruev (The Russian Presidential Academy of National Economy and Public Administration, Russia)
Business Science Reference • ©2019 • 351pp • H/C (ISBN: 9781522555865) • US $205.00

Perspectives, Trends, and Applications in Corporate Finance and Accounting
Constantin Zopounidis (Technical University of Crete, Greece) Apostolos G. Christopoulos (National and Kapodistrian University of Athens, Greece) and Petros Kalantonis (Technological Education Institute (TEI) of Piraeus, Greece)
Business Science Reference • ©2018 • 354pp • H/C (ISBN: 9781522561149) • US $215.00

Microfinance and Its Impact on Entrepreneurial Development, Sustainability, and ...
Ramesh Chandra Das (Katwa College, India)
Business Science Reference • ©2018 • 385pp • H/C (ISBN: 9781522552130) • US $245.00

Maintaining Sustainable Accounting Systems in Small Business
Luísa Cagica Carvalho (Open University, Portugal & University of Évora, Portugal) and Elisa Truant (University of Turin, Italy)
Business Science Reference • ©2018 • 387pp • H/C (ISBN: 9781522552673) • US $215.00

For an entire list of titles in this series, please visit:
https://www.igi-global.com/book-series/advances-finance-accounting-economics/73685

IGI Global
DISSEMINATOR OF KNOWLEDGE

701 East Chocolate Avenue, Hershey, PA 17033, USA
Tel: 717-533-8845 x100 • Fax: 717-533-8661
E-Mail: cust@igi-global.com • www.igi-global.com

Dedicated to my grandchildren: Hazal, Helin, Halil Berhan, Umut Baran, and Serhan for living in a peaceful, free, and democratic world.

Table of Contents

Preface

During the last few decades, specifically after the end of the so-called Cold War or the collapse of the former Soviet Union at the end of 1980s, the speed and amount of international investments have increased tremendously, not to mention the proliferating number of multinational companies around the world. Furthermore, as it is clearly witnessed today, the flows of funds, capital, and goods have surpassed the physical boundaries of all countries without any hesitation and any problem at all, and thus, enormous amounts of global funds and capital spread all over the world in an unprecedented manner. Presently, just the annual flow of foreign direct investment portion of international investments is around two trillion dollars.

The essential reason for such a huge amount of foreign direct investments, undoubtedly, has been the universal acceptance of the idea of competitive market economy by almost all countries of the world. As such, all countries try to establish the competitive market mechanism with all the institutions and rules required for it. Even those developing countries work hard to deregulate their economies and privatize their state-owned enterprises to establish a competitive market economy. The simple reason for this universal trend is that the competitive market economy or the market mechanism that depends on private ownership and individual entrepreneurship has proved to be the most efficient way of allocating and utilizing scarce resources of nations, as opposed to the state owned or controlled economies which have failed to do so, as seen in the case of the former economies of the Soviet Union. The universal acceptance of the competitive market economy indicates a universal trend that is determining the economic order of the world economy in the twenty first century.

In such a new world order all individuals are considered economically as well as politically free citizens of a global world, where individual creativity and entrepreneurial skills are fostered as essential determinants of the economic and social development. In such a global world, countries cooperate easily and develop close relations since countries have much more political and economic values in common. In fact, this convergence on political and economic values has led countries to unite or integrate their economies, as seen in the case of EU (European Union), or to remove trade barriers, as in the case of NAFTA (North Atlantic Free Trade Agreement) and APEC (Asia-Pacific Economic Cooperation), in order to increase the competitiveness of their economies, not to mention the increasing number of free trade agreements among various nations as a result of the "free trade and fair trade" slogan echoing in the world within the last few decades. No doubt that this phenomenal trend of cooperation and integration of world economies and/or unification of some countries is essentially the result of the universal acceptance of political and economic freedoms of individuals in all nations as well as the efforts of creative entrepreneurs.

This internationalization process which has been called globalization is significantly being accelerated by information technologies which have made the distance between locations meaningless and that increased the speed of business transactions tremendously. In such a globalized world, as it is generally labeled, business transactions have become similar such that business is done in the same manner in almost all countries. Entrepreneurs and businessmen make their investment decisions by taking into account the potential of international markets, since their national or local markets have become export markets for others any longer. Moreover, in daily business life, for instance, the concepts like multi-national corporations, foreign capital, foreign investments, etc. are being replaced by concepts such as multi-domestic corporations, international capital, and global investments. In other words, the concept of international investment is presently widely used instead of foreign investment in the literature to refer to the business activities of firms investing in financial and physical assets in other countries.

In this study we focus on foreign (international) direct investment projects that are proposals for making fixed or real capital investments abroad. A real capital investment project is a set of interdependent activities or jobs which have to be completed within a given period of time and with a certain amount of resources. Therefore, the projects for foreign or international direct investments have to be prepared and designed in detail to determine all business activities involved in and costs associated with the investment proposals so as to appraise the value of direct investments in advance. Additionally, the rational use of resources as the essential principle of business management necessitates a comprehensive project study to rationalize or justify the investments planned, because managers always want to make prudent and rational decisions concerning resource allocation.

Moreover, since foreign direct investments are very expensive in nature, international investors usually resort to external financing. However, in cases of using external financing, financial institutions require detailed studies for investment projects in order to ascertain the ability of the projects to pay back the loans to be lent. On the other hand, most governments of foreign countries, especially those of developing countries, provide various incentives to attract international investors. Accordingly, international investors who want to take advantage of those incentives are required to submit detailed project studies to governmental authorities to prove the profitability and thus the viability of the investment projects they plan.

In sum, there are good reasons why a comprehensive and detailed project study should be conducted for an international or a foreign direct investment proposal. Thus, the purpose of this book is to explain and clarify how such a comprehensive project study could be prepared and conducted to evaluate the desirability and the feasibility of a direct investment. The details of the work and/or activities involved in preparing such a project study are elaborated in separate chapters to systematize the flow of decisions to be made regarding the evaluation of investment projects. Accordingly, a systems approach methodology is developed for conducting a comprehensive project feasibility study.

For this purpose, the book is organized in seven separate but complementary chapters in that previous chapters provide background or lay foundation for the following ones. As such, in many cases for the work to be done in a chapter, there would be a need to refer to previous sections or chapters to see what has been done. Chapters provide feedback for each other and that the previous chapter adds meaning to the content of the next one. Accordingly, all chapters together accomplish a determined common objective: How can a project manager plan and analyze a foreign direct investment project to determine whether or not it is valuable? The answer to this question is given in seven consecutive chapters.

Chapter 1 deals with the conceptual basis of international investments. At the outset two general types of international investments are distinguished from the viewpoint of investors' objectives of controlling the investment area, namely, international portfolio investments and foreign direct investments. However, since portfolio investments are not the main subject of this study, they are briefly discussed, just to complete and show the whole picture of the subject of international investments. Thus, having given a brief description of various forms of international portfolio investments, their advantages and disadvantages are discussed from the viewpoint of the receiving countries to give the reader an idea about the portfolio side of international investments. Moreover, since international portfolio investments are considered as significant flows of international funds for solving foreign currency shortages in developing countries, their advantages and disadvantages are further clarified and simplified in a systematic framework to draw attention to the risks associated with portfolio investments in the process of economic development in developing countries. However, when the subject of foreign direct investment is elaborated in the following chapters, one may see that what developing countries need as international investments is, in fact, foreign direct investments that create employment opportunities.

Later on in the chapter, in order to complete the conceptual basis of international investments, the theoretical aspects of foreign direct investments as the main subject of this book are explained to establish a theoretical background for this book. So, upon describing various forms of foreign direct investments, the reasons for international investors to invest abroad as well as the advantages of direct investments for host countries are expounded to give the reader a holistic picture about the importance of foreign direct investment for both sides. That is, the advantages of foreign direct investments are clarified both from the viewpoint host countries and international investors. Eventually, the traditional political critiques of international investments are put forth to cover all pros and cons of international investments in general and foreign direct investments in specific. Furthermore, the essential reasons for conducting a comprehensive feasibility study for planning and analyzing foreign direct investments are discussed in order to state the significance of this book.

Chapter 2 lays the foundation of the book where the methodology and steps to be followed are summarized and linked to each other. This chapter thus provides a brief review of main stages to go through for planning and analyzing foreign direct investments, namely, market analysis, technical analysis, and financial analysis. But each analysis stage is elaborated in a separate chapter to clarify the theoretical structure of the book and, thus, to provide the reader an easily seen framework of the study. In other words, this second chapter develops a framework for the whole book and defines a road map for the chapters that would follow it. However, in order to follow the road map or to go through the stages of analyses defined for a comprehensive economic study called a feasibility study for an investment project, a starting point, that is, a country for a foreign direct investment is needed. Therefore, country selection is the first step for starting a study for planning and analyzing foreign direct investments.

In other words, planning, analyzing, and evaluating a foreign direct investment project requires the existence of a country since the investment project would be appraised on the basis of the prevailing economic conditions of that country. For this reason before starting to plan, analyze, and evaluate a foreign direct investment, a country has to be determined for the direct investment project. Accordingly, a country called host country has to be selected for the contemplated direct investment. As such, factors affecting country selection in terms of opportunities and risks related to alternatives are specified and elaborated first and then put together in an example to develop a methodology for selecting a host country for the direct investment planned abroad. Country selection is based on a procedural methodology that goes through, firstly, a scanning stage that aims at identifying possible countries for investment, secondly, eliminating less desirable countries for determining possible candidates, and finally choosing the most adequate country for investment.

The following chapters are sequential stages of the methodology for planning and analyzing foreign direct investments, namely, market analysis, technical analysis, and financial analysis. Each analysis stage is given in a separate chapter so as to provide a clear and compact viewpoint for each stage of analysis. Thus, Chapter 3 is devoted to the so-called market analysis which aims at determining whether or not the market for the direct investment project is large enough. Therefore, all studies, work, and activities involved in the market analysis stage are confined to determining whether or not the target market for the product to be manufactured through a foreign direct investment is sufficient. For this purpose the essential points to be considered for analyzing the competitive market environment in terms of demand and supply conditions of the market as well as purchasing behavior of consumers are explained step by step.

On the demand side, a target market is firstly defined on the basis various socio-economic and geographic factors as well as consumer characteristics and purchasing behaviors. Then, widely used forecasting methods are explained for estimating the size of the target market. On the supply side of the target market, having determined the market structure and essential competitors, a detailed analysis of the competitive environment is discussed in terms of the degree of competition in the market, barriers to entry, and tools for competition. Finally, how a marketing strategy could be developed on the basis of the information regarding the demand and supply sides of the target market is discussed and that what possible market share might be captured is elaborated as the final point of the market analysis. In short, the market analysis involves the necessary topics to answer this specific question: "Would the product to be manufactured have a sufficient market share"?

Chapter 4 builds on the information provided by the market analysis in the sense that it explains the tasks or jobs that are required for designing a production system and/or a technical production facility. Designing a technical production facility is mostly engineering related and thus the topics concerning production design in terms of the requirements of machinery, equipment, and labor, as well as layout of facilities are not detailed, but the essential points to be taken into account when planning and analyzing an investment project are discussed sufficiently. On the other hand, the subjects such as selecting optimal technology, choosing production capacity, deciding on plant location, and preparing implementation plan are important aspects of a technical analysis that are explained in detail.

Capacity selection decision is based on the availability of technological alternatives. That is, in many cases, technological alternatives dictate a capacity level for production. As such, when the production technology chosen is not a standardized technology requiring a certain scale of production, the factors affecting and/or determining the optimal capacity selection decision are discussed to shed light on various economic aspects of capacity selection decisions. In other words, the chapter on technical analysis covers topics and discussions about technical aspects of establishing a production facility. Thus, it answers the question of whether the production of a product that is determined to be marketable is technically possible and if so, how the production facility should be designed. If the investment project is technically feasible, then an implementation plan through project programing techniques of network analysis is developed for both estimating the total cost of fixed investment and plan the establishment of the plant or factory required. Thus, at the end of the technical analysis stage, the use of project programing techniques is elaborated in a sufficient content for planning the implementation of an investment project.

Chapter 5 is confined to financial analysis of foreign direct investments and is the backbone of this book. Financial analysis generally covers three essential subjects; such as estimating the total amount of investment and financing needs, appraising or evaluating the profitability of the investment proposal, and if the investment promises profit, its risk level is analyzed for an investment decision. However, a chapter that would include these three subjects is necessarily to be very large in size and complicated in content. Therefore, to prevent this complication and have a clear theoretical structure for the chapter, the financial analysis stage is divided into three consecutive and complimentary chapters.

As such, Chapter 5 specifically deals with estimating the total amount of investment in terms of the fixed capital (fixed costs) and working capital, sources of financing, annual operating expenditures, and expected sales revenues. The essential cost items to be considered and the basic principles to be followed were expounded for preparing right financial tables for all costs and revenues associated with foreign direct investment projects. Finally, in order to put together all related costs and revenues and thus develop a base for evaluating the profitability of investment projects more easily, the subject of preparing pro forma net cash flows is discussed in detail. Pro forma net cash flows statements are the indispensible financial tables for analyzing and evaluating investment projects. Thus, this chapter provides a financial base as well as a workable framework for the following two complimentary chapters that are confined to evaluating the profitability and risk associated with foreign direct investments. That is, the remaining two chapters should be regarded as subsections of the financial analysis stage.

In Chapter 6 the methods widely used in evaluating investment projects are discussed and their advantages as well as shortcomings are highlighted. The appraisal or evaluation of foreign direct investments is explained at two consecutive stages. First, an investment project is evaluated at the host country level as an independent project at regional or national level. For this purpose, the classical evaluation techniques of simple rate of return, payback period, net present value, profitability index, and internal rate of return are elaborated. Additionally, the methods are compared and the shortcomings of each method are expounded to show the reader the weaknesses of the techniques to be aware of when using them. Later in the chapter, evaluating foreign direct investment projects from the viewpoint of the parent company is discussed in terms of profit and/or income transferred to the home country.

The same investment evaluation techniques are applied to the net cash flows transferred to the home country of the parent company. The possible income and/or dividends to be remitted to the home country of a parent company are identified and discussed so as to reflect the viewpoint of investing parent companies when planning foreign direct investments.

Chapter 7 is devoted to the analysis of risks associated with foreign direct investments with three different perspectives; namely, business (commercial) risk, political risk, and currency exchange rate risk - exposure. With regard to business or commercial risk, an economically profitable investment project is first analyzed through some well-known financial methods to determine if the investment project has commercial market risk, and then it is appraised in terms of the risk associated with it. The appraisal or evaluation methods that are based on probability distributions, including Monte Carlo simulation technique, are explained in detail for evaluating commercially risky investment projects. Computations involved in those techniques are done manually through simplified examples to get the reader grasp the techniques used in evaluating risky investment projects. In short, commercial or business risk is first identified and assessed, and then the risky investment projects are evaluated by taking into account the relevant risk level.

On the other hand, political and exchange rate risks are discussed separately. The sources and/or causes of these risks are then elaborated to point out to the significance of political and macroeconomic environments in investment evaluation. Thus, each risk factor is considered as a separate evaluation criterion. That is, an investment project may be rejected due to having a high level of any one of these three risk factors. For instance, a profitable investment proposal may not have a significant business risk but might have a high level of political risk requiring its rejection. Finally, it should be stated that risk analysis is conducted only if a foreign investment project is profitable from the viewpoint of the parent company. Otherwise, there is no need for a risk analysis since a direct investment project that does not create profit for the parent company would be rejected any way.

Consequently, when all chapters are put together, this book essentially aims at meeting the textbook needs of undergraduate college students in courses such as international capital budgeting, capital budgeting in financial management, and international business, as well as a source book for companies planning to invest abroad and specialist and/or project managers conducting feasibility studies for real capital investment proposals in general and foreign direct investment projects in specific. This book is written from a systems approach viewpoint in that all explanations and discussions are centered on the accomplishment of the objective of investment and that all analysis involved are related to each other. That is, all analyses involved are sequentially dependent on each other such that the first stage analysis provides input for the following analysis. Furthermore, all analyses together aim at measuring the profitability of a foreign direct investment project as a final objective. Thus, the fundamental tenet of the systems approach stated as the interaction of components with regard to achieving the main objective is always kept in mind. In brief, it is believed that planning and analyzing foreign direct investment projects, indeed, always require a holistic and interactive viewpoint that could only be provided by a systems approach.

Finally, I hope that this book contributes to the understanding of investors and project managers in their work for preparing direct investment projects and that help the general reader to understand the subject matter easily. The last but not the least I would like to extend my appreciation and thanks to my colleague Dr. Onur Sunal for reading and commenting on the manuscript. Furthermore, my special thanks go to our research assistants Ziya Can and Gulay Erol Boyaci in the department of International Trade at Başkent University for their help in preparing some figures and tables.

Halil Sarıaslan
Başkent University, Turkey

Chapter 1
Conceptual Basis of International Investments

ABSTRACT

This chapter provides a theoretical background for international investments in general. However, before going into the conceptual details of international investments, the concept of investment in general is clarified with respect to national economies in terms of financial and real capital or fixed investments. From the viewpoint of investors' objectives of controlling the investment area, international investments are classified in two general categories: international portfolio investments and foreign direct investments. In order to complete the conceptual basis of international investments, the theoretical aspects of foreign direct investments as the main subject of this book are discussed so as to establish a theoretical background for the book. Therefore, upon describing various forms of foreign direct investments, the reasons for international investors to invest abroad as well as the advantages of direct investments for host countries are expounded to give the reader a holistic picture about the importance of foreign direct investments for both international investors and host countries. Eventually, the traditional political critiques of international investment are given to cover all pros and cons of international investments in general and foreign direct investments specifically. Finally, the essential reasons for conducting a comprehensive feasibility study for planning and analyzing foreign direct investments are discussed in order to expound the significance of this book.

DOI: 10.4018/978-1-5225-7696-9.ch001

THE CONCEPT OF INVESTMENT IN GENERAL

The concept of investment generally refers to the expenditures made today for the purpose of making a profit in the future. In other words, investment is the spending of money to obtain financial and/or physical assets today with the expectation of earning more later on in the future either by selling or using them. From this general viewpoint the concept of investment covers wide range of investing activities; such as purchasing all kinds of financial instruments like company stocks and bonds, buying financial derivatives, foreign currencies, or real estate, acquiring and building factories or plants, etc. In all cases, the purpose of spending is the expectation of the investment made today to gain value in the future so as to make profit.

For example, consider a person who buys some IMB stocks in New York Stock Exchange (NYSE) and several Euro (EUR) currency call options in the Chicago Board of Trade (CBOT) or even a commodity importer in Turkey who foresees sharp rises in USD/TL (Turkish Lira) exchange rate in the near future and thus purchases from a bank a significant amount of USDs. The essential motive for purchasing financial instruments and foreign currency is that the stock price and exchange rates will increase in the future. No doubt that this is an expectation so that it may turn out to be a loss as well. That is, stock prices and exchange rates may not rise or might even go down. This variation is an inherent characteristic of all investments. This, in turn, means that all investments are based on expectations.

To be more specific about variations in the expectations of investors, let's assume that an individual expecting price rises in the common stocks of a popular automobile company buys some, say, 100 individual stocks each for $5, and thus pays $500 in total. Assume again that nine months later he or she was lucky enough and sold all common stocks for $750. Thus, disregarding the time value of money, we may simply say that this person made a profit of (750 – 500 =) $250 through investing in common stocks of an automobile company. Consequently, this person spent 500 dollars with the expectation of making profit in the future. Finally, nine months later, he or she was lucky enough and made a profit of $250 out of the investment of $500 in common stocks.

Notwithstanding the fact that the essential purpose of investing is the anticipation of making profit, however, the macro and micro economic conditions in the future may change and thus the investment may end up with a loss. For example, the country may go though some adverse economic conditions such as increases in inflation and interest rates, trade and budgetary deficits, or the company whose stocks were purchased may face some financial and marketing problems; thus, the investment in common stocks might result in a loss as well, if the person (the investor) was not lucky enough. Suppose that due to the negative economic and financial conditions surrounding the securities market, all acquired stocks had been sold for $400 in total. That is the profit seeking investor's expectation did not realize as it is desired. This time, one would say that the investment in common stocks resulted in a loss of (500 - 400 =) $100.

In order to earn money or make profit in the future, as indicated earlier, individuals and business firms make investments in various forms that might be divided in two general groups:

1. *Financial investments* in *financial assets* refers to buying company stocks, bonds, and other securities, precious metals like gold and silver, and even foreign exchange, etc. Investments in *financial assets* are, in fact, purchasing of financial instruments and securities of all kinds whose expected profits are obtained when they are sold, undoubtedly, if there is a profit. That is, the expected profit is realized through buying and selling financial instruments. Therefore, these types of investments might be considered as a kind of financial trading. Investors of financial assets are actually traders in the sense that they buy and sell financial instruments.

Accordingly, what is peculiar about financial investments to note is that they do not add a new value to a nation's stock of capital since they are indeed transfers, or more accurately, means for transfer of funds among individuals and business companies. For instance, the investor that purchased the common stocks of an automobile company sold them nine months later to someone else who, in turn, would probably sell it to another one and so on. No matter how many times the trading of the common stocks of the automobile company turns over, the common stocks and thus the automobile company is always the same. That is, there would be no addition to the country's stock of capital when trading occurs. For this reason, purchasing financial assets with the expectation of making profit in the future is not regarded as true "investment" in the fields of economics at macro level, since in economics investment refers to the construction capital goods.

2. *Real Capital investments* in *physical assets* include building plants or constructing factories, buying new equipment for production, enlarging existing production capacities, buying land for farming, etc. The essential features of such investments are that they are directed towards production of goods or services and thus increase the production capacity of countries where they are realized and create new jobs or employment opportunities for them. For this reason, such production oriented investments are called real capital or fixed capital investments in economics. The word "capital" in economics does not refer to money rather it means machinery, building, equipment, inventories of raw materials, etc.

To clarify the concept of real or fixed capital investment, consider an entrepreneur or a business firm that prefers an investment in textile industry to produce and sell T-shirts in order to earn money in the years ahead. In order to accomplish this investment objective, the entrepreneur will construct either a new factory or buy an existing T-shirt factory. In any case, further assume that the entrepreneur spends, let us say, an amount around $500.000 for such an investment. Accordingly, in contrast to trading based financial investments that pay expected profits right after trading activity; the profits expected from production oriented real capital investments are to be captured during the long operating period of the factory to be built or purchased. In other words, the entrepreneur spends a large amount of money today and gets profits piece by piece along the future years of the operating period of the investment.

As stated above, real capital investments aim at production of goods and services and thus create employment opportunities for people to work. As such, real capital investments are considered as the essential dynamics of economic growth at the macro level and that all countries provide various incentives to induce entrepreneurs to increase their efforts of investment in real assets. Indeed, the role and significance of real capital investments as dynamics of economic growth are perhaps best explained by the multiplier effect and acceleration principle of macro-economic theory.

In brief, *the multiplier effect* of investment, or *the autonomous spending multiplier* in another term, states that a unit of spending in real capital investment brings about a magnified increase or change in economic growth in terms of gross national product (GNP) equilibrium According to the macroeconomic theory, the multiplier effect is equal to the reciprocal of the marginal propensity to save, *ceteris paribus*. For instance, assuming that in an economy the income created is distributed between consumption and savings and that the marginal propensity to consume is 0.50, then an amount of $10 billion spending in investment or increase in investment demand leads to a rise of {10 x [1/(1 – 0.50)]} = $20 billion in equilibrium GNP.

Similarly, on the other hand, *the acceleration principle* of macro-economic theory is complementary to the multiplier effect of investment in the sense that an increase in investments accelerates new investments in the long run which, in turn, leads to further economic growth. Macro-economic theory puts forth that spending in investment creates income as profits and wages which, in turn, cause increases in consumption. Thus, increasing consumption level stimulates the demand for additional inventories as well as new products that eventually induce new investments. No doubt that the induced new investments would further lead to increases in equilibrium GNP[1].

Therefore, multiplier effect and acceleration principle together would be essential causes and dynamics of economic growth, not to mention the employment opportunities to be provided. Needless to indicate, providing jobs or employment opportunities plays a key role in maintaining social order in all countries. This reasoning, in fact, clearly explains why countries, especially developing ones, provide various incentives to induce entrepreneurs to make real capital investments.

Fixed or real capital investments in national economies are generally classified within four essential types:

1. **New Investments:** These are real capital investments for building new plants or constructing factories for producing goods and services. These investments aim at constructing completely new production facilities, such as building a new cement factory or constructing a new luxurious hotel. These investments increase directly the production capacity of national economies and create new jobs for employment. Thus, they are the most preferred type of investments for the economic growth and development of national economies. Accordingly, the incentives provided mostly by emerging economies and/or developing countries are usually designated for new investments.
2. **Enlargement Investments:** This type of fixed investments is directed towards enlarging the production capacities of existing factories or plants by increasing their production lines in terms of machinery, equipment, and labor. For example, the production capacity of a small factory may be increased to a medium-scaled level through purchasing extra machinery and hiring new labor. Such investments are also called as capacity enlargement investments. Although their contribution to

the production capacities of national economies is not as much as that of new investments, they still have significant effects on increasing production inventories to meet increasing demand for consumption of existing products.

3. **Replacement Investments:** Fixed assets such as machinery and equipment all have certain technical lives whose durations are generally determined by their producers. For instance, when a machine is purchased, its technical specifications indicate that it has a *technical life* of certain duration, let's say, 15 years. This means that this machinery could normally be used for 15 years. In another word, it will have a *useful life* of 15 years. Accordingly, when the essential machinery and equipment that form the basis of production systems complete their technical lives, they have to be replaced by the new ones if production is to continue.

In other words, replacement investments are related to renewing the old and/or worn-out machinery and equipment of production facilities to maintain the existing production capacity of a nation at macro level. Undoubtedly, manufacturing firms undertake replacement investments to continue their existence in business life at micro level. Therefore, replacement investments that enable manufacturing firms to carry on their present economic activities at micro level, meanwhile underpin national economies to maintain their production capabilities. As such, these investments just preserve the present production capacities and thus do not add new jobs to existing employment opportunities.

4. **Modernization (Technological) Investments:** These are investments that are required for keeping up with the pace of technological development. When the technological development makes out of date the existing machinery and equipment of a production facility, those obsolete ones have to be changed with those that are technically modern. Otherwise, the production process would not be efficient in the long run, since technologically new machinery and equipment are expected to be more effective in terms of production speed and/or cost reduction.

For instance, a newly developed and technologically very modern machine may be very fast, consuming less energy, and has almost no defective production. As such, a manufacturing firm would feel compelled to purchase this modern machine and change its existing machine just for economic reasons. This means that technological development ends up the *useful* or *economic life* of machinery and equipment although they may have longer technical lives. Therefore, even if the technical life of a piece of machinery or equipment is not completed yet, when it becomes obsolete technologically, it has to be changed with a modern one because it would be inefficient to use it any longer.

Consequently, technological development would possibly terminate the economic lives of machinery and equipment in specific and production facilities in general by way of making them out of date. Modernization investments that are also called technological investments are very important for business firms as well as national economies to compete. Thus, business firms that want to keep up with the pace of technological development and to improve their competitive power so as to continue their production operations have to make modern or technological real capital investments. Otherwise, they would not survive.

INTERNATIONAL INVESTMENTS AND THEIR VARIOUS TYPES

The business activity of seeking profit through investments, as explained above, may also take place in foreign countries as well. In such cases the concept of investment is labeled as *international* or *foreign investment*. However, in the last few decades, the concept of *"international investment"* is preferred to the concept of *"foreign investment"* since the later has a negative connotation. The speed and amount of international investments have increased tremendously during the last few decades, specifically after the end of the so-called Cold War or the collapse of the former Soviet Union at the end of 1980's. For instance, as will be explained shortly, just the foreign direct investment portion of international investments reached to $1.75 billion in the year 2016 (UNCTAD, 2017). The essential reason for huge increases in international investments has been the universal acceptance of the idea of competitive market economy by almost all of the countries of the world.

The competitive market economy as an economic mechanism for allocating and utilizing limited resources is presently a world-wide accepted trend that is practiced by almost all economies of the world. As such, all countries try to establish the competitive market mechanism with all the institutions and rules required for it. Even those developing countries work hard to deregulate their economies and to privatize their state-owned enterprises to establish a competitive market economy. The simple reason for this universal trend is that the competitive market economy or the market mechanism that depends on private ownership and individual entrepreneurship has proved to be the most efficient way of allocating and utilizing scarce resources of nations, as opposed to the state owned or controlled economies which have failed to do so, as seen in the case of the former economies of the Soviet Union.

The universal acceptance of the competitive market economy indicates a universal trend that is determining the economic order of the world in the 21st century. In such a new world order all individuals are considered as economically as well as politically free citizens of the a global world, where individual creativity and entrepreneurial skills are fostered as the essential determinants of the economic and social development. In other words, the world of the 21st century is envisaged to be a single globe, where competitive market economy and pluralistic democracy are complementary to each other, and that all human beings are to be considered as the global citizens of this world (Sarıaslan, 2013). In such a global world countries cooperate easily and develop close relations since doctrinaire ideologies among nations are vanishing and that countries have much more political and economic values in common[2].

In fact, this convergence on political and economic values has led some countries to unite or integrate their economies in order to increase the competitiveness of their economies, as seen in the case of EU (European Union), NAFTA (North Atlantic Free Trade Agreement), and APEC (Asia Pacific Economic Cooperation), not to mention the increasing number of free trade agreements among various nations. No doubt that this phenomenal trend of cooperation and integration of world economies and/or unification of some countries is essentially the result of the universal acceptance of political and economic freedoms of individuals in all nations as well as the efforts of creative entrepreneurs.

This process which has been called globalization is significantly being accelerated by information technologies which have made the distance between locations meaningless and that increased the speed of business transactions tremendously. In such a globalized world, business transactions have become similar and, thus, business is done in the same manner in almost all countries[3]. Entrepreneurs and businessmen make their investment decisions by taking into account the potential of international markets, since their national and/ or local markets have become export markets and that the flow of goods and capital have gone beyond national boundaries without any political problem. Additionally, in daily business life the concepts like, for instance, multinational corporations, foreign capital, foreign investments, etc. are steadily being replaced by concepts such as multi-domestic corporations, international capital, and global investments.

Accordingly, the flows of funds, capital, and goods have surpassed the physical boundaries of all countries without any hesitation and any problem at all, and thus, enormous amounts of global funds and capital spread all over the world in an unprecedented manner. This, in turn, has accelerated the integration and unification of financial markets as we have been observing recently in such cases of European and US stock exchanges, which eventually accelerated the flow of international funds worldwide. If we take into account that globalization is, indeed, a business-driven phenomenon, it can easily be inferred that the integration of world financial markets in particular and economies in general will lead to a single world market, where economic systems of the countries of the world are to be globally interdependent (Sarıaslan, 2013) as we witness today, and undoubtedly there would be no boundaries to the flows of international funds and/or investments. Despite the fact that the process of globalization is a mega-trend which is shaping a new world order in the 21st century, there is a heated debate in the literature regarding pros and cons of the globalization process and that the viewpoints are very divergent (Bende-Nabende, 2017).

The international investment activities of individuals and business firms take various forms. However, for the sake of theoretical explanations they are generally classified in two broad categories in this study; namely, international portfolio investments and foreign direct investments. Although foreign direct investments form the base of this study, a brief explanation and discussion of international portfolio investments is firstly given below to cover the complete picture of the concept of international investments in general. The remaining sections of the book would be devoted to foreign direct investments.

Portfolio Investments

These types of international investments are those business activities of international firms and/or foreign individuals that are in search of increasing their earnings through interest payments and returns on their funds invested in financial assets, such as securities of business corporations and governmental debt instruments in other countries of the world. The main motive behind international portfolio investments is twofold:

1. To obtain higher interest income or earnings on fixed income securities such as corporate and governmental bonds and savings accounts in banks,
2. To increase the returns on portfolios made of securities traded in stock exchanges of foreign countries.

Accordingly, the flow of international portfolio investments is essentially determined by the level of interest rates and the magnitude of returns that would possibly be earned on the financial assets of other countries, *ceteris paribus*. Portfolio investments have three basic types as follows:

1. **Investments in Securities Traded in Exchanges:** In this type of portfolio investments international investors buy corporate securities like bonds and common stocks in other countries for the purpose of earning a higher interest income on bonds and obtaining a larger return on stocks. For example, an American investment bank may find attractive the interest rates on Turkish corporate bonds traded in Istanbul Stock Exchange and decide to buy the bonds of various corporations to earn interest income. On the other hand, if someday the American investment bank believes that the bond prices have increased high enough in Istanbul Stock Exchange, it may also sell the bonds before they mature if it wishes, and thus, obtains a larger profit or return on bond trading.

Similarly, let us also assume that this American investment bank is interested in common stocks of Turkish corporations, believing that security prices will go up in Istanbul Stock Exchange in the near future. So it buys a large volume of stocks of various Turkish corporations. Later on, when the stock prices in Istanbul Stock Exchange go up, the investment bank will sell them and make a profit from its investment in Turkish corporate stocks. Accordingly, one may say that the American investment bank formed a good portfolio of Turkish securities composed of corporate bonds and common stocks and that it obtained a large rate of return on its portfolio investment in Turkey.

In fact, the size of the foreign portfolio investments in the so-called "emerging markets", that is, the capital markets of those developing countries which have realized greater economic progress, has increased drastically. For example, the share of foreign investors in the securities trade in Istanbul Stock Exchange is over 65%. Thus, foreign investors provide a significant degree of liquidity in terms of trading activities of purchasing and selling securities. However, trading activities are almost completely dominated by foreign investment funds such that in cases when portfolio investors, for some reason, start leaving the stock exchange by selling their securities, the financial system signals symptoms of financial disturbances reminiscent of a financial crisis.

2. **Buying Governmental Debt Instruments:** Governments all over the world are the largest and the most important players in financial markets since they issue through their institutional agencies huge amounts of debt instruments in terms of short term treasury bills and long term governmental (or state) bonds to deal with budget deficits. Interest rates on these debt instruments may attract international investors and, thus, they may buy large amounts of such instruments to earn higher interest income when compared to the returns in their domestic markets. The emerging market economies often deal with larger budget deficits because the level of national savings is not sufficient enough to handle and finance high rates of economic development. Therefore, such countries issue large amounts of different governmental bonds usually paying higher interest rates to attract foreign investors.

International investors of all kinds, such as multinational corporations, wealthy foreign individuals or businessmen, foreign monetary funds including hedge funds, securities dealers, and investment banks, form and manage large portfolios composed of governmental bonds. The revenues obtained through selling of those governmental debt instruments to international investors help issuing governments manage budgetary deficit problems, finance current account deficits, handle foreign currency shortages, bring dynamism and liquidity to financial markets. As such, governments facing budgetary deficit problems and foreign currency shortages do not wish to implement economic policies to curb the inflow of portfolio investments. In another word, those governments generally like the ease and comfort provided by foreign currencies which international portfolio investors bring in.

3. **Foreign Currency Savings Accounts:** In many countries where the inflows of foreign currency from real economic activities such as exporting of goods and services are not at a desired level and that shortages of foreign currencies often bring about problems, commercial banks are allowed to open foreign currency savings accounts which usually pay higher interest rates. No doubt, higher interest rates will motivate foreign individuals, companies, and monetary funds to open foreign currency

"time deposit" accounts in commercial banks. Even in some cases, foreign currencies are converted into local currencies and then the local currencies are invested in time deposits. Consequently, foreign currency accounts are effective financial instruments to draw foreign capital and, therefore, are considered an important type of portfolio investments.

A final point regarding foreign currency savings accounts is that they do not bear any foreign currency risk exposure since they are drawn as the foreign currency deposited without paying any exchange commission. At this point it should be added that the other portfolio instruments such as investments in corporate securities and governmental debt instruments all have foreign currency risks associated with because they are traded in local currencies. Therefore, international investors desiring to purchase of these securities they first have to convert their foreign currencies into local currency and then purchase. Later on, when they want to transfer back home their funds including profits made, they will buy foreign currency by using local currency. Thus, during this currency conversion cycle portfolio investors are subject to foreign currency risk exposure.

In conclusion, as it is clear from the above given explanations, international portfolio investments generally have no intention of controlling the areas of investment or the corporations whose securities or financial assets are purchased. The main purpose of these investments is generally to earn higher interest income and get larger returns on their capital as much as possible. In cases where the volume of common stocks bought gives a voting power to control the related company, then, this type of portfolio investment in corporate stocks is considered as a "foreign direct investment".

For instance, if a foreign investor buys more than 50% of all common stocks or shares of a Turkish company, then, this investment is called a foreign direct investment since the investor has the voting power (more than 50% of votes) to control and manage the Turkish company. Even in cases where almost all shares of a public company are widely distributed among investors so that shares less than 50% give a voting power to control a company, this portfolio investment is considered an international direct investment. Thus, the power of controlling the investment area is a distinguishing characteristic for international investments.

Another distinctive feature of portfolio investments is that of the high speed of flowing in and flowing out of countries. That is to say, the funds tied up in portfolio investments move in and out of countries very quickly. For example, let us consider a foreign corporation that owns securities of Turkish firms and that also has foreign currency savings accounts in Turkish banks. If this corporation wishes to leave Turkey, it may sell all of its securities in stock exchanges and close its bank accounts within hours. Then, of course, it may transfer its funds or capital to anywhere it desires. For this characteristic of speedy movement, portfolio investments are also called the *"hot money movements"* in the sense that large amounts of cash money flows in or out of a country within hours.

As the *hot money* flowing in through corporate securities, governmental debt instruments, and foreign currency savings accounts, international portfolio investments provide a great deal of ease and temporary comfort for the governments and companies of the issuing countries. These advantages of portfolio investments may be elaborated on the basis of four essential points as follows:

1. Helping governments to solve and manage budgetary deficits through issuing governmental (state) bonds to obtain extra budgetary funds from international investors. Thus, in countries where local savings are not sufficient, the governments facing budget deficits usually pay higher interest rates on governmental debt instruments to attract foreign capital. Similarly, short term treasury bills that are easily sold to foreign portfolio investors also help governments to pay short term debts or meet urgent cash needs of governments.
2. Financing national current account deficits as well as handling foreign currency shortages through the inflow of foreign currencies obtained from international portfolio investments. The concept of the national *current account deficit* here refers to the gap or discrepancy between all kinds of foreign currency inflows and outflows related to the balance of payments of a national economy in terms of exports and imports of goods and services as well as those associated with tourism revenues, contracting, and subcontracting services in foreign countries, even remittances of workers working abroad, etc. For example, for some emerging economies such as Turkey tourism revenues and workers' remittances from abroad are important sources to narrow down current account deficit resulting from large foreign trade deficit.

However, developing countries, mostly those of emerging economies, usually depend on foreign currency inflows of portfolio investments when they have large *foreign trade deficits* during the periods of large amounts of imports, especially, in capital goods. Accordingly, the countries facing current account deficits are always inclined to pay higher interest rates to international investors and/or funds to induce them to invest in fixed income governmental securities. In fact, as long as current account deficit is not reduced through the other foreign currency creating sources such as exporting and tourism activities, interest rates would eventually go up to attract international portfolio investments, either though market dynamics or governmental policies.

3. Enabling business corporations to get equity and debt capital by issuing and selling corporate securities to international investors, and thus, helping them finance their business activities. Moreover, this will also help local business firms to address to international investors and get to know them for further business relations in the future. This is an important contribution of international portfolio investments in terms of developing stock exchanges and thus enabling business firms to go public. As indicated earlier, international portfolio investments bring in liquidity to stock exchanges which, in turn, provide ease of raising funds for business companies by issuing various securities.
4. Finally, issuing and trading of the financial instruments involved in international portfolio investments will make local financial markets more liquid and dynamic. This, in turn, would certainly contribute to the development of financial markets in the sense of gaining depth and instrument variability. Liquidity and dynamism added to higher returns are important features for capital markets to attract national and international investors for trading corporate securities. No doubt that liquidity and dynamism in capital markets, in turn, would lead business firms to go public and issue securities to raise funds for growth. Additionally, the increasing number of firms going public in a national economy would contribute to the professionalization as well as internationalization of business companies, since public firms have to observe and obey to the rules and regulations of capital markets as well as meet the requirements of international investors.

On the other hand, despite these advantages or the ease and comfort provided for host governments, the excessive inflows of international portfolio investments have some severe disadvantages for national economies. As explained earlier, the essential characteristic of international portfolio investments is the speed of movement in the sense of inflows and outflows and, thus, international portfolio investments are also called *"hot money movements"*. Accordingly, the excessive inflow of hot money in terms of international portfolio investments into the economies of developing countries might bring about some severe macro-economic problems as explained below sequentially in a simplified manner:

1. Large amounts of inflows of foreign currencies in the form of international portfolio investments will make exchange rates move down. That is, the national currency will appreciate (gain value) and the foreign currency will depreciate (lose value) as a result of increasing supply of foreign currency to the national economy. No doubt that this will, in turn, pushes down the prices of foreign goods imported, compared to the prices of goods produced in the local economy and traded in the local currency, because of the depreciated foreign currency.
2. The decreasing prices of imported goods compared to those of the domestically produced local goods due to the depreciation of foreign currency will certainly increase the level of imports and decrease that of exports in that country. Depending on the degree of foreign currency depreciation, imports may go up to very high levels causing huge deficits in the foreign trade as well as the national current account of that country.
3. Prolongation of the increasing imports would eventually lower the pace of fixed or real capital investments, since the demand for domestically produced goods is not moving up due to the price disadvantages relative to imported goods.
4. Needless to state that if new fixed or real capital investments are not made, there would be no possibility of creating new jobs in that economy so that unemployment rate will go up as well.
5. Consequently, as the results of large amounts of inflows of hot money in terms of international portfolio investments;
    a. Appreciation or overvaluation of national currency,
    b. Depreciation of foreign currency,
    c. Increasing imports,
    d. Huge deficits in foreign trade and national current account,
    e. Diminishing levels of real capital investments, and thus,
    f. Increasing unemployment rates,

All together will make the whole national economic system vulnerable to great financial shocks and even deep financial crises.

No need to mention that bottlenecks in the inflows or, especially, the large amounts of sudden outflows of *hot money* in terms of foreign currency in such countries will always have a hidden potential to trigger financial shocks and crises. Consequently, the magnitude of international portfolio investments and their repercussions, especially in emerging economies of developing countries, should always be carefully observed and precautionary measures be taken whenever they are needed. Unfortunately, there is no easy solution once a country gets into such a hot money trap without facing some sort of financial shocks that may bring about even more problems.

Foreign Direct Investments

Foreign direct investments (FDI) are production oriented fixed or real capital investments that give the international investor a controlling power to manage and control the areas in which the investments are made. The investors engaged in foreign direct investments try to make profit through producing and then selling goods and/or services by constructing new factories or acquiring established business firms in foreign countries. Therefore, in contrast to portfolio investments, foreign direct investments give the investor a controlling interest in a foreign company and, thus, provide ownership of the company to manage and control it.

Since this type of international investments are production oriented and thus provide employment opportunities, they are preferred to portfolio investments by receiving host countries. Foreign direct investments sometimes are called international direct investments or simply "direct investments". In this study these concepts are used interchangeably. Whatever the labeling is, international or foreign direct investments are generally classified into three basic categories as explained below:

1. **Greenfield Investments (New Investments):** These are new investments in terms of building new plants or factories in foreign countries in order to manufacture goods which the investors plan to sell and maximize their profits. In another word, investors build up new physical plants with new equipment to produce goods and services to earn money in foreign countries. For example, a Turkish firm may go to Macedonia and then buy some land in a city, let's say in Skopje, and start constructing a new factory with brand-new equipment. As a second example, assume again that a German company is planning to invest in Turkey through building a new factory in the Eastern part of the capital city of Ankara.

Since greenfield investments are new investments and contribute additional capacity to a country's production capabilities and provide new jobs or employment opportunities, they are the most desired type of foreign direct investments. However, they are the riskiest type of direct investments in that they often control and operate a production facility in a foreign country all alone. Therefore, entering in a new country and operating there as planned require a great deal of due diligence and careful analysis of investment environment in terms of social, economic, and political conditions. Due to the high potential of risks related to greenfield investments, those investors that want to avoid them may prefer some type of partnership investment as in the case of joint ventures to be explained shortly.

2. **Mergers and Acquisitions:** In some cases, in contrast to greenfield investments, international investors prefer to acquire existing business firms in foreign countries rather than building new ones for various reasons as will be detailed shortly. Therefore, investors planning to make investments abroad might buy existing firms in the countries where they intend to go. For example, a French company may purchase all shares of an aluminum casting firm in Turkey. Similarly, the Turkish government decided to privatize and, then, planned to sell the Turkish Telecommunication Company which was a state-owned company. Later on, an international investor bought 56% of its shares. This was a partial acquisition; however, it gave the international investor a voting power to control the Turkish Telecom Company. Thus, this type of acquisition investment is considered as a foreign direct investment in Turkey.

In addition to acquisitions, investors desiring to go abroad may merge their business activities with those local business firms operating in the countries selected for investment as a form of partnership. For instance, a French firm operating in the metallurgical sector in France may plan to merge with a Turkish firm functioning in the same line of business in Turkey. Thus, a different firm will be established through a French and Turkish partnership. It should also be stated that acquisitions are more common in developing countries while mergers are frequently seen in the developed countries due to the level of technological development.

The contribution of mergers and acquisitions to national economies with respect to additions to national production capacity and creation of new employment opportunities is often questioned on the grounds that these investments just maintain the existing positions of host economies without adding any new capabilities. This might be partly true since it may seem at the first sight that business firms just change ownership through such investments, nothing more. However, as it will be discussed later, one of the important points to note when evaluating the effects of foreign direct investments in host countries is the so-called spillover effects of investments. These are essentially indirect effects on the surrounding socio-economic environment. The spillover effects in some cases might even be more important than the first level effects of greenfield investments.

For instance, consider an acquisition deal in which a local business firm is bought by a foreign company. For now, one may say that the local firm just changed ownership in the sense that the local firm became an international or a foreign firm any longer. However, this is not quite true if the sales revenues obtained from the acquisition deal are taken into account. For example, if the former local owners use these sales revenues in realizing a new real capital investment in their home country, the country in question, this time, would have a new national company through a foreign acquisition investment. Therefore, whatever the effects of mergers and acquisitions are to be on the production capacities and employment opportunities for national economies, the use of foreign funds obtained from these investments should be the base of evaluation from the viewpoint of national economies.

3. **Joint Ventures:** Joint ventures are a type of foreign direct investments through which two or more companies (at least one is a foreigner) share the ownership of a new company created for a specific business. These investments are generally based on business contracts that define a particular objective to be accomplished within a certain time period as well as some certain rules for managing and terminating (dissolving) the joint venture company. However, joint venture companies may continue to operate indefinitely as their objectives are redefined.

Although joint ventures are usually thought of as companies formed by two partners with equal shares of 50/50 percent, however, in practice, the number of partners may be more than two and that the partners may have unequal shares as well. That is, a partner in a joint venture may enjoy minority, equal, or majority ownership. For example, a joint venture with three partners whose shares are 25, 35, and 40 percent is possible. The managerial power and thus controlling of joint ventures is based on the contract agreement signed by partners rather than the voting power or the size of the shares of partners. Unanimous decision making is a common managerial practice in almost all joint ventures, no matter what the shares of partners are.

For this reason, the joint venture agreement is the essence such business partnerships and is of the outmost importance for the realization and operation of joint venture investments. For example, how top level boards, committees, and managers are to be selected and/or appointed, how profits would be distributed, how disputes are to be solved, which courts may be appealed to, etc. all business partnership related subjects are clarified in a joint venture agreement. As indicated above, for a joint venture to be considered as a foreign direct investment, at least one of the partners has to be a foreigner. Additionally, in daily business life when several partners, generally more than two, take part in, the joint venture is called a *"consortium"*.

Another characteristic of joint ventures is that participants would provide the partnership not only with their shares of capital but also with the managerial business skills and/or intangible assets that each partner has more than the others. For instance, foreign participants may bring in technology or finance, and local partners would help find markets and deal with legal and other administrative issues of the partnership. Indeed, joint ventures are formed to enable international companies to participate in direct investments with their essential intangible assets and/or advantages over the others. Thus, national and international companies as partners of joint ventures will bring together their advantages (superiorities of position) to realize international direct investments to compete in a globalized world. Furthermore, as it will be indicated shortly, joint ventures are preferred by international companies to overcome trade barriers as well.

From the viewpoint of host countries, joint venture investments are equally desirable as greenfield investments in that these investments are, in fact, new investments. Thus, they provide additional production capacities and new employment opportunities for host countries. Furthermore, joint ventures attract hesitant international investors through local or national partners sharing risks and helping them to deal with various problems emanating from local conditions. In other words, joint ventures are risk sharing modes of foreign direct investments. That is, a foreign investor that may not take over the perceived risk of a direct investment in a country all alone may decide to take part in a joint venture if there is an adequate local partner to help with marketing activities as well as solving legal problems. In fact, sometimes even powerful local partners convince foreign investors that have technological advantages to form a joint venture and invest together.

Aside from the above mentioned types of foreign direct investments, *strategic alliances* and *collaborative arrangements* among international business firms or multinational companies are sometimes specified as the fourth kind of direct investments in the literature on international business. Strategic alliances and collaborative arrangements among multinational companies to support each other in international business activities are important modes of international business in the process of globalization (Warner & Sullivan, 2017). However, from the viewpoint of this book which will focus on planning, analyzing, and evaluating foreign direct investment projects, strategic alliances and/or collaborative arrangements are not considered as direct investments. Accordingly, in this study, foreign direct investments are meant to be comprised of greenfield investments, mergers and acquisitions, and joint ventures, as summarized above.

Consequently, whatever the types of foreign direct investments are, choosing the appropriate type of direct investment would certainly depend on its suitability to the objectives and needs of international investors. Investors planning to go abroad for investment would prefer greenfield investments, that is, build new factories if (Daniels, Radebaugh, & Sullivan, 2015; Hill & Hernandez-Requejo, 2011):

1. There is not any desired company available to buy,
2. Buying an existing company will lead to problems in the local business community, governmental relations, or bureaucracy,
3. Valuing or pricing the existing national or local businesses is uncertain and brings about various valuation problems, and
4. Building a new plant provides ease of finance to spread costs over time during the construction and/or the operating period.
5. Furthermore, even in cases where there is an adequate firm available to buy, but if it has a large number of employees, an international investor will usually refrain from acquiring it because of not desiring to deal with the labor problems of the existing firms. Instead, a new factory is built and then the desired level of employment in terms of quality and quantity is decided as deemed appropriate for operation.

On the other hand, international investors would like to buy existing companies for:

1. Avoiding start-up problems, including bureaucratic transactions or red tape of any kind,
2. Finding a chancc of buying a company cheaper than the cost of constructing a new one,
3. Gaining the goodwill, brand identification, and access to distribution channels if buying provides such possibilities, and
4. Not desiring to add further capacity to the existing market so as not to increase competition.

In brief, international investors planning to make direct investments abroad would evaluate pros and cons of various types of direct investments and then will decide on the type of the investment they would like to make.

REASONS FOR FOREIGN DIRECT INVESTMENTS

As stated earlier, the speed and amount of international investments have increased tremendously during the last few decades, not to mention the proliferating number of multinational companies around the world. Furthermore, as it is clearly witnessed today, the flows of funds, capital, and goods have surpassed the physical boundaries of all countries without any problem at all. Thus, enormous amounts of global funds and capital spread all over the world in an unprecedented manner. Similarly, the flow of foreign direct investments has also gained speed enormously within the last decade and reached to figures stated in trillion dollars.

As seen in Table 1, after a strong rise in 2015 reaching to $1.77 trillion, the global flow of foreign direct investments (FDI) stayed almost at the same level in the year 2016 and it is estimated to increase to a level of $1.85 trillion in 2018 by the United Nations Conference on Trade and Development (UNCTAD, 2017). Nevertheless, the distribution of foreign direct investments around the world differs from region to region. In 2016 as the last year of the existing data, the share of developed economies in global FDI inflows was 59% whereas that of developing countries was 37%. FDI prospects are seen moderately positive in most regions with a sizeable increase in developing Asia. However, prospects seem stagnant in Latin America and the Caribbean, as well as developing economies.

Even though inflows were down across all developing regions, FDI still remains the largest and most constant external source of finance for developing economies. It is further believed that policy uncertainty, geopolitical risks,

Table 1. FDI Inflows by Group of Economies and Regions (2014 - 2016), and Projection for 2017 (Billions of Dollars)

Group of Economies and Regions	2014	2015	2016	2017 (Projection)
World	**1,324**	**1,774**	**1,746**	**1,670 – 1,870**
Developed Economies	**565**	**984**	**1,032**	**940 – 1,050**
• Europe	272	566	533	560
• North America	231	390	425	360
Developing Economies	**704**	**752**	**646**	**660 – 740**
• Africa	71	61	59	65
• Asia	460	524	443	515
• Latin America & the Caribbean	170	165	142	130
Transition Economies	**57**	**38**	**68**	**75 – 85**

Source: UNCTAD (2017). *World Investment Report 2017*, Geneva: The United Nations Publications.

terrorism and social instability, and tax policy changes could significantly affect cross-border investments. The other factors affecting FDI activity negatively include exchange rate volatility, increasing interest rates, and rising debt levels in emerging economies. The UNCTAD business survey of 2017 comprising multinational corporations and investment promotion agencies also points out to the following findings:

1. The outlook for global FDI activity becomes more optimistic. Most of the executives in developed economies strongly believe that the global economic development will lead to increased direct investment in the coming years.
2. Economic and technological factors bolster the development of FDI activity and the multinational corporations' intention for FDI spending is increasing gradually.
3. The most attractive industries in developed economies are information technology and professional services while those in developing economies are agribusiness.
4. China is presently the most promising source of FDI and the United States, Germany, and the United Kingdom are closely following it.
5. Attractive destinations for FDI are emerging markets and the United States closely followed by China and India.

Consequently, the prospect of the FDI activity in a globalizing world would be ever increasing in the years to come. The reasons for such a huge flow of funds for foreign direct investments are that such investments are equally desired by all parties involved in. That is, all countries and business companies around the world wish to have direct investments since such investments have significant advantages for all of them as will be delineated in the following subsections.

Advantages of Foreign Direct Investments for Host Countries

Foreign direct investments provide some important advantages for host countries although the degree of contribution to host economies may depend on the type of investment. As such, countries, especially developing ones, compete through providing various incentives for attracting more direct investment. The reasons for this competition are quite clear; namely, providing additional production capacity, creating employment, transferring technology, and paying large amounts of tax income for the host countries (Cavusgil, Reisenberger, & Knight, 2016; Daniels, Radebaugh, & Sullivan, 2015), as summarized below:

1. **Providing Additional Production Capacity:** Since foreign direct investments are production oriented, they clearly contribute to the production capacity of host countries and, thus, affect the levels of economic growth and competition in their economies. Increasing production would have varying degrees of effects at macro-economic level in receiving host countries depending on the amount and type of production. For instance, consider a greenfield or a joint venture investment that would introduce a new product or a technologically developed product to a host country. Its direct and indirect effects (spillovers) would be tremendous.

For example, in the mid 1990's Ford automobile company made a significant direct investment in Turkey that later deeply affected the automobile market in the country in many ways. First, it has increased the degree of competition in the market which, in turn, has led to a discernible quality increase and development in the automobiles produced by the existing two companies established through Italian and French partnerships with local entrepreneurs.

Later on, new competitors from Japan and Europe followed the Ford Company. Finally, the automobile market and thus its industry have made great progress so that automobile exporting presently is the number one item within the exporting activity of Turkey in terms of the amount of exports in USD.

It is believed that the Ford automobile company's direct investment in Turkey was the essential cause of this development. Interesting to note, the Turkish government at that time provided relatively significant incentives for the Ford automobile company such that many people accused the government of selling the country to foreigners. But now they are proud of their country for exporting cars to European Union and lots of Asian countries. In short, foreign direct investments through their productions would, undoubtedly, effect positively the supply, quality, and price of products in a competitive market, depending on the magnitude, type, and timing of direct investments.

2. **Creating Employment:** As stated above, production oriented foreign direct investments have the ability of enlarging production capacities of host countries and, thus, create employment opportunities for the economies of those countries. The effect of foreign direct investments on employment in terms of job creation is very important for all countries, especially, for those developing countries where the level of national savings is not sufficient to realize fixed or real capital investments. In other words, almost all developing countries including emerging economies are in need of foreign direct investments to provide employment opportunities for their citizens since they are short of fund to invest in fixed or real capital investments.

The advantage of direct investments in creating new jobs is, thus, a very much desired purpose of all developing countries where unemployment rates are usually very high. No doubt, employment not only provides continuous income but also releases social tension and, thus, helps maintain social order in all societies. For this reason, specifically developing countries provide lots of incentives to attract direct investments. Nevertheless, the employment effects of direct investments differ according to the type of investment. As explained earlier, greenfield and joint venture investments have the greatest potential of creating new jobs and, thus, incentives provided by host countries most often directly address to them.

3. **Transferring Technology:** In general, almost all direct investments are made and owned by companies from industrial countries. Therefore, the production related foreign direct investments have a very high potential of transferring technology to host countries for all managerial business activities, not just know-how for the production of goods and services. Here, we use the term technology in the largest sense of the term as the sum of all knowledge, skills, and experience available in a society, including the technical knowledge labeled as "know-how" for producing a specific product. In short, technology is not machinery and equipment or the "*hardware*" side of production; it is rather the "knowledge" or the "*software*" dimension of production. Machinery and equipment are the practical results of technology.

Thus, from the viewpoints of investment and production, technology is a broader concept that also covers technical knowledge called "know-how" in addition to all the other ways of doing business, such as marketing, packaging, accounting, consumer relations, etc. Needless to say, the transfer of technology is an indispensible factor for developing countries in the process of economic development. Technology, production, economic growth, and economic development, all are interdependent factors for countries to prosper. In other words, developing countries not only need technical knowledge to produce, but also are in lack of knowledge for managing businesses, marketing and promoting sales, developing consumer relations, etc. Accordingly, production oriented foreign direct investments from developed countries would certainly transfer such technology to developing countries if they are willing to absorb.

4. **Paying Tax Income:** Finally, the profit maximization oriented foreign direct investments create income in terms of profits for the owners and salaries paid to the employees. This income creation effect, in turn, leads to large and significant amounts of tax payments that foreign direct investments provide for the governments of host countries. Undoubtedly, the amounts of direct taxes on profits and wages as well as indirect taxes on products in terms of value added taxes, all together, as tax income provided by business firms established through foreign direct investments will certainly have significant contributions to the budgets of the host countries. Additionally, foreign companies pay their taxes on time, that is, they do not forget to pay them! Because of being in a foreign country, they always prefer not to engage in with public authorities due to skipping some rules.

5. **Balance-of-Payments Effects:** Foreign direct investments usually substitute imports of goods in host countries. That is, they often produce goods that are imported from foreign countries. Accordingly, when this substitution occurs, imports would decrease and the host country would pay less for purchasing foreign goods. Thus, there would be a positive effect on the current account of host country's balance of payments. Furthermore, in some cases, the products manufactured by foreign companies are even exported. When this happens, the effect of direct investments on balance of payment would be further improved. Needless to state, if the host country is experiencing foreign currency shortages as it is often the case in developing countries, the contribution of foreign direct investments to the balance of payments of host countries would be much more meaningful.

In conclusion, the above explained advantages of foreign direct investments are highly appreciated by developing countries so much that they provide lots of incentives for international investors to attract more direct investments. Developing countries even compete with each other in providing various incentives for inducing international investors[4]. The most common incentives include free land for construction, providing free infrastructure and related services such as water, sewerage, electrification facilities, and connection roads to main highways, customs tax exemption for imports, and corporate tax exemption for a certain period of time, etc. All these clearly indicate that developing countries consider direct investments as an important factor to combat unemployment and to trigger the process of economic development.

Despite these important advantages of direct investments for host countries and the efforts of developing countries to attract more direct investment, some long disputed negative effects of foreign direct investments with regard to developing countries are put forth by some critics who are generally oriented by their political ideologies. It is asserted that the increasing magnitude of international investments in general and direct investments in specific affect host countries both economically and politically so much that the host countries would be dependent on the home countries of investing firms in the long run.

This dependency, as contended, would eventually lead to the exploitation of developing countries by multinational corporations in terms of acquiring and using their natural resources cheaply. Consequently, multinational corporations would hinder economic development of the host countries receiving foreign capital and investments[5]. No doubt that the issue of dependency is a general peculiarity of our *global era* in which *global interdependency* is unavoidable not only for developing countries but also for all developed countries and business firms. Finally, the question to be answered by those critics is that why developing countries provide so many incentives to attract international investors!

The Advantages of Foreign Direct Investments for International Companies

Foreign direct investments have advantages for all parties involved in. In parallel to the above indicated advantages for host countries, foreign direct investments have even more advantages for the investing companies of home countries. The motives and/or reasons leading business companies to invest abroad are various (Cavusgil, Reisenberger, & Knight, 2016; Daniels, Radebaugh, & Sullivan, 2015), and may be explained as given below:

1. **Expanding Market:** One of the essential reasons or basic objectives of companies for investing abroad is to increase their sales and thus expand their market. As such, through investing and producing in foreign countries, companies expect to gain access to new markets and obtain new opportunities. Thus, investment versus trade in terms of exporting would become a rational alternative for doing business in some cases, not to mention the significant reductions in transportation costs. Undoubtedly, increases in sales through direct investments are not only expected in the local target market or country but also in the surrounding markets of other countries as well. As such, companies having excess capacity and thus start exporting, later on, when the amounts of exports and trade increase largely, will necessarily make a direct investment abroad to reduce transportation costs and keep closer relations with costumers.
2. **Overcoming Trade Restrictions or Barriers:** When business firms confront with restrictions or various tariffs and non-tariff barriers to exporting to a very attractive market or market region, they plan to invest and produce there. For example, before being a member of the World Trade Organization (WTO) in 2001 China used to create various barriers to lead international companies invest in China mostly in the form of joint ventures. Indeed, it succeeded as well since China has been an attractive market for international companies and thus many multinational companies invested in China.

3. **Reducing Negative Country of Origin Effects:** In cases where consumers in an attractive market have some prejudices and/or resistant negative feelings towards an imported product simply due to the country of origin of the product for some reasons, then, perhaps one way to overcome this problem and do a successful business in that attractive market may be to invest there. For instance, consider a successful company from an Asian country exporting to the European market. The market is very attractive and that the company managers also believe that they have a good chance to compete in the market with respect to the quality and price of their product.

However, there is one adverse factor as the "county of origin effect" in the sense that the company managers have found out that the consumers in the European market have had some negative feelings towards their country for various reasons of which some have deep roots in the history. Therefore, when consumers notice the tag or the mark on their products indicating the country of origin as *"made in (the country name)"*, they change their purchasing decision. On the other hand, since the tag *"made in (the country name)"* is compulsory on importing products, the company managers plan to invest in one of the European countries so as to have a tag *"made in (the* European *country name)"*, for example *"made in Germany"*, on their products. Meanwhile, the possibility of reducing transportation costs and establishing closer relations with local markets and customers, added to the country of origin effect, rationalized the decision to plan for an investment in a European country.

4. **Following Essential Competitors and Key Customers:** Business firms operating in oligopolistic markets or industries where few companies control an industry, companies strive for maintaining or expanding their market shares through going abroad and investing in the markets where their essential competitors or key customers operate. That is, they follow their essential competitors and thus invest in the market regions where they operate in order to prevent their competitive advantage of being alone as well as to weaken their competitive position by forcing them to engage in activities to defend their market shares. In other words, they go into a market just to compete with their essential competitors face to face and, thus, to limit their competitive advantage. For instance, automobile companies usually follow such a strategy and invest in the regions where their essential competitors operate.

A similar action is applicable for companies following their key customers abroad for not leaving them to other vendors, just as tire companies following the automobile factories which are their key customers. Here the motive is not to lose or leave the key customers to the other competitors. It is believed that multinational companies operating in oligopolistic industries and not following their essential competitors in some regions of the world would eventually leave those markets to their competitors; because of leaving key competitors completely free, not keeping up with changing marketing strategies, not establishing and developing desired consumer relations, etc. Undoubtedly, the same is valid for the case of a tire company not following its key customer as an automobile company.

5. **Acquiring Resources:** Companies may invest in foreign countries for the purpose of obtaining access to production factors such as abundant and cheap raw materials and labor. That is to say some investing companies that use large amounts of production factors such as raw materials and labor are mostly supply oriented. Therefore, the main objective to go abroad is to acquire abundant and cheap resources of host countries. Accordingly, when such supply seeking companies look for a country to invest; their essential motive is to select the country that supplies cheap production factors as much as needed.

Resource availability is also an important consideration for companies looking for vertical integration to control different stages of a product as well as for those planning to adapt to the product life cycle arrangements for moving to developing countries. As it is known, vertical integration is legally forbidden in almost all developed countries for the sake of protecting competition. Additionally, there are powerful public authorities, named such as trade commissions and market or competition boards, to observe the rules and regulations for protecting competition and preventing monopolistic tendencies in markets. However, most of the developing countries presently do not have such institutions and judicial arrangements. As such, if a multinational company from a developed country desires to maintain its competitive power by establishing a vertical integration for one of its products, a possible way might be to invest in one of those developing countries to have a hold on the abundant resources of production factors.

Similarly, as it will be explained later in the chapter on the Market Analysis, almost all industrial products have product life cycles in terms of market stages that an industrial product goes through; namely, “introduction” to the market, "growth stage", "maturity", and "decline" stage. Accordingly, if a company has an industrial product in the decline stage of the life cycle, that is a product that is about to leave the market for being replaced by another product, one of the rational ways for the company to extend the life cycle of the product is to move the production to a developing country. Needless to say, the developing country which would be chosen for investment would be one with large supplies of resources of production factors. Furthermore, in such cases, countries providing attractive and large amounts of incentives may also be chosen or preferred by international investors to invest.

6. **Minimizing Risks:** Companies investing abroad are generally from the developed industrial countries, where competition is quite severe and quality standards are very high and demanding. Therefore, the companies from such countries, which may have difficulties to keep up with this pace of severe competition, may prefer to move to developing countries where their existence would not be threatened due to severe competition. This location change would also enable them to take advantage of market imperfections in developing countries and enjoy monopoly advantages of being a company from a developed country in terms of technology, management skills, product differentiation, etc.

Furthermore, some companies, mostly multinational companies, prefer to invest in more countries in order to prevent cyclical changes in sales and supply dependency on one or few countries. The reason for diversification of places for sales and sources of supply is essentially to avoid risks associated with marketing and procurement activities of multinational firms. For instance, if a firm invests in one country for expanding its sales or for acquiring resources, and later on someday in the future, if the market conditions in that country would turn out differently, the firm may not sell its products or will not be able to procure the production factors needed.

Accordingly, multinational companies generally wish to invest in more than one country and, thus, if someday some problems occur in one country, the others will compensate for it. In fact, diversification of any kind is always considered as a general way of reducing risk in business management, such as portfolio diversification of financial assets. This refers to the general principle of portfolio theory that indicates not to put all eggs in one basket.

7. **Maximizing Efficiency:** Efficiency, in general terms, as the goal of accomplishing a company's objectives in the least costly way, is desired by all business firms so that each company tries to be as much efficient as possible in all its business activities. Therefore, any factor leading to cost reductions is taken into account when business companies plan to go abroad. Within this context, in decisions concerning "investing versus exporting", all cost reduction possibilities; such as locating production facilities near customers to decrease transportation costs, having access to abundant and cheap sources of production factors, and taking advantages of governmental incentives, are significant factors for business companies to have direct investments abroad.
8. **Obtaining Political Advantages:** In addition to the above stated reasons there some political motives that encourage business companies to make direct invests abroad. For instance, some companies, usually multinational ones, desire to develop spheres of global influence in some regions of the world and to maintain good relations with foreign governments so as to gain and keep control of supplies of strategic resources. Therefore, as long as it is profitable, such companies would prefer investing in foreign countries where they might also accomplish their political objectives. It is further believed that the governments of home countries, that is, the countries of the firms making direct investments, support such companies in various ways since these companies may help their governments establish good relations with host countries as well.

On the other hand, notwithstanding the fact that almost all ownership of direct investments is by companies from the developed industrial countries, in some cases, large companies from developing countries looking for political sanctuaries or desiring a foot in democratic and politically safe countries also invest abroad but in mostly developed countries[6]. This investment behavior of companies from developing countries perhaps stems from a safety need to take some precautions if one day political turbulences occur in their home countries. Thus, companies from countries where the rules and order of law are not maintained move some of their business operations to the developed countries where the rules of law are observed and that believed to be more democratic. Furthermore, these companies are also in the anticipation of assets gaining access to technical know-how, managerial knowledge, and other intangible available in developed countries.

CONCLUSION

In conclusion, foreign direct investments have advantages for both host countries and investing international companies. Additionally, foreign direct investments make companies more successful domestically because of providing a great deal of international experience in conducting business activities. Furthermore, companies investing abroad would eventually become multinational corporations which are regarded as prestigious firms both at home and abroad. Thus, planning, analyzing, and evaluating foreign direct investment projects require a serious work for right decisions to get the advantages of foreign direct investments. The following chapter explains how a right country is selected for starting a right foreign direct investment project.

REFERENCES

Akcaoglu, E., & Erol, C. (2011). The Race between the Czech Republic and Turkey for Hyundai's Investment in Europe. *Transnational Corporations Review*, *3*(4), 71–86. doi:10.1080/19186444.2011.11658311

Bende-Nabende, A. (2017). Globalisation, FDI, Regional Integration and Sustainable Development: Theory, Evidence and Policy (2nd ed.). London: Routledge.

Buckley, P. J., Clegg, L. J., Voss, H., Cross, A. R., Liu, X., & Zheng, P. (2018). A Retrospective and Agenda for Future Research on Chinese Outward Foreign Direct Investment. *Journal of International Business Studies*, *49*(1), 4–23. doi:10.105741267-017-0129-1

Cavusgil, T., Reisenberger, J. R., & Knight, G. (2016). *International Business: The New Realities* (4th ed.). Harlow, UK: Pearson Education, Ltd.

Daniels, J. D., Radebaugh, L. H., & Sullivan, D. P. (2015). *International Business: Environments and Operations* (15th ed.). Harlow, UK: Pearson Education, Ltd.

Hill, C. W. L., & Hernandez-Requejo, W. (2011). *Global Business Today* (7th ed.). New York: McGraw-Hill Irwin.

Huang, Y., Fischer, T. B., & Xu, H. (2017). The stakeholder Analysis for SEA of Chinese Foreign Direct Investment: The Case of 'One Belt, One Road' Initiative in Pakistan. *Impact Assessment and Project Appraisal, 35*(2), 158–171. doi:10.1080/14615517.2016.1251698

Ibeh, K. I., Uduma, I. A., Makhmadshoev, D., & Madichie, N. O. (2018). Nascent Multinationals from West Africa: Are Their Foreign Direct Investment Motivations Any Different? *International Marketing Review, 35*(4), 683–708. doi:10.1108/IMR-08-2016-0158

Sarıaslan, H. (2013). Dynamics of Globalization. In A. Koyuncugil & N. Ozgulbas (Eds.), *Technology and Financial Crisis: Economical and Analytical Views* (pp. 8–13). Hershey, PA: IGI Global. doi:10.4018/978-1-4666-3006-2.ch002

Sherman, H. J., Meeropol, M. A., & Sherman, P. D. (2018). *Principles of Macroeconomics: Activist vs. Austerity Policies* (2nd ed.). London: Routledge.

UNCTAD. (2017). *World Investment Report 2017*. Geneva: The United Nations Publications.

Warner, M., & Sullivan, R. (Eds.). (2017). *Putting Partnerships to Work: Strategic Alliances for Development between Government, the Private Sector and Civil Society*. London: Routledge.

Wild, J. J., & Wild, K. L. (2012). *International Business: The Challenges of Globalization* (6th ed.). Boston: Pearson Education.

ENDNOTES

1 More on the effects of real capital investments on economic growth for national economies, see Sherman, Meeropol, and Sherman (2018).

2 For an explanation of some universal trends envisaged for a world of 21st century, see Sariaslan (2013).

3 For more about the effects of globalization on companies and business environment, see Wild and Wild (2012), Hill and Hernandez-Requejo (2011), and Cavusgil, Reisenberger, and Knight (2016).

4 To see the importance of incentives in attracting foreign direct investments, see Akcaoglu and Erol (2011).

5 For a summary of discussions about the political ideology and foreign direct investment, see Hill and Hernandez-Requejo (2011).

6 For outward foreign direct investment behaviors of business companies from emerging economies, see Huang, Fischer, and Xu (2017), Buckley et al. (2018), and Ibeh, Uduma, Makhmadshoev, and Madichie (2018).

Chapter 2
Planning Foreign Direct Investment Projects

ABSTRACT

This chapter develops a framework for the whole book and defines a road map for the chapters that follow it. However, in order to follow the road map or to go through the stages of analyses defined for a comprehensive economic study called a feasibility study for an investment project, the starting point is to select a country for the foreign direct investment contemplated. Therefore, country selection is the first step for starting a comprehensive economic study for planning and analyzing foreign direct investments. For this reason, before starting to plan, analyze, and evaluate a foreign direct investment, a country has to be determined for the direct investment project intended. As such, factors affecting country selection in terms of opportunities and risks related to alternative countries are specified and elaborated first and then put together in an example to develop a methodology for selecting a host country for the direct investment planned abroad. Country selection is based on a procedural methodology that goes through, firstly, a scanning stage that aims at identifying possible countries for investment; secondly, eliminating less desirable countries for determining possible candidates; and finally, choosing the most adequate country for investment through a so-called opportunity-risk matrix.

DOI: 10.4018/978-1-5225-7696-9.ch002

REASONS FOR PLANNING AND ANALYZING FOREIGN DIRECT INVESTMENT PROJECTS

Investment projects are proposals for making fixed or real capital investments either at home or abroad. In other words, an investment project is a proposal for construction of physical facilities and/or acquisition of capital goods, such as machinery and equipment for production of goods and services. Moreover, an investment project is a set of interdependent activities or jobs which have to be completed within a given period of time and with a certain amount of resources. Therefore, the projects for international or foreign direct investments, just like all the other real capital investment projects, have to be planned and/or designed in detail to determine all business activities involved in and costs associated with the investment proposals so as to appraise the values of direct investments.

In fact, when intending to make fixed or real capital investments in general or foreign direct investments in specific, business companies and/or project managers have to conduct comprehensive and detailed studies and analyses to determine in advance whether or not to undertake such investment projects. Such a comprehensive project study is often called a *feasibility study* and it involves lots of interrelated studies, analyses, and decisions that will be explained shortly. There are three essential reasons why a feasibility study as a comprehensive economic study has to be planned and conducted as stated below:

1. Foreign direct investments by nature are very costly investments and thus entail large amounts of limited resources. Because business managers always want to make prudent and rational decisions concerning resource allocation, the costly foreign direct investments are to be carefully planned, analyzed, and evaluated in order to justify the expenditures to be made. In other words, the rational use of resources as the essential principle of business management necessitates a comprehensive project study to rationalize the investment planned, since such investments are very costly and, thus, require lots of resources.

Furthermore, business managers or project managers are aware of the fact that it is almost impossible to reverse or correct the wrong and/or haphazard decisions made after the direct investment is realized. For instance, consider an investor that made a greenfield investment in a country and six months later found out that the country selected was not an appropriate place for the direct investment made or bought a factory in an adequate country but discovered later that it was a wrong acquisition because the market size is not sufficient. In each case, there is not much to do in order to compensate for the mistakes made, except to take on the resulting losses. In brief, international investors have to plan, analyze, and evaluate their foreign direct investment proposals in the form of a feasibility study in order to determine in advance whether or not they are profitable, to rationalize the use of large amounts of resources, and to get shareholders' approval.

2. Secondly, again as foreign direct investments are very expensive in nature, investors usually resort to external financing from financial institutions since they cannot finance the whole project through equity or simply do not desire to do so for some other reasons. Nonetheless, in cases of using external financing, financial institutions require detailed project or feasibility studies in order to ascertain the ability of the projects to pay back the loans to be lent. That is, financial institutions would like to see if a project will operate as it is intended as well as be able to capture the level of revenues expected. In many countries the requirement of a project feasibility study for lending long term loans or providing long term project credits is compulsory either as an internal auditing rule of financial institutions or a legal rule of law imposed by financial regulators. Thus, a project feasibility study has to be prepared at least for financial institutions when external financing is sought.
3. Finally, as indicated earlier most governments, especially those of developing countries, provide various incentives to attract international investors to realize foreign direct investments in their countries. Accordingly, international investors or entrepreneurs who plan to go abroad for direct investments and also want to take advantage of such governmental incentives have to submit detailed project feasibility studies to governmental authorities to prove the profitability and thus the viability of the investment projects planned.

In other words, governmental authorities would like to be convinced that investment proposals requesting incentives would operate successfully as planned so that they would be able to provide employment opportunities as put forth and contribute to the transfer of technology as intended. Therefore, those investors that do not submit a detailed feasibility study are not given governmental incentives. Countries providing governmental incentives have special departments in charge of incentives and request specific questions to be answered by feasibility studies to be submitted. For instance, the General Directorate for Implementing Incentives in Turkey requests information regarding production capacity, breakeven point, total number of employees, technological and innovative capabilities expected, annual amount of the value added of production, effects on exports and substituting imports, rate and level of profitability, etc.

In sum, as explained above, there are good reasons why a comprehensive and detailed project study called a feasibility study have to be planned and conducted for a foreign direct investment proposal. A comprehensive and detailed project feasibility study requires lots of interrelated studies to be done and various decisions to be made at some stages. The details of the work and/or activities involved in a feasibility study are explained in the following sections of this book with respect to greenfield investments. The framework to be developed for planning and evaluating a greenfield investment proposal is quite comprehensive such that it can also be used for the other types of direct investments by simply skipping the redundant analyses.

For starting to plan and conduct a feasibility study for a foreign direct investment, that is, for a greenfield investment, a decision has to be made about where to invest since the country selected would be the base for planning the feasibility study. In other words, if a company desires to make a direct investment abroad for some reasons, then, what it has to do first is to decide in which country to make a greenfield investment. Thus, *country selection for a foreign direct investment* is the first step to plan for realizing a greenfield investment abroad. Country selection decision is indeed very important in the sense that once the right step is taken, that is, the right country is selected; the remaining work may go well. This important subject, that is, how a company evaluates and selects a country for a direct investment is dealt with in the next section.

COUNTRY EVALUATION AND SELECTION FOR FOREIGN DIRECT INVESTMENTS

For the reasons explained earlier when a company desires to invest abroad, the first step to be taken is to select a country for investment. Indeed, this first step is so important that it will definitely be the base for the success of the company to be in the future. If an international investing company chooses an appropriate country for its investment, it will most likely not encounter business problems during both the construction and the operation periods of the investment, except managerial problems inherent in business companies.

Thus, if the decision for selecting a country is a right one, the investment would probably be successful, insofar as the feasibility study conducted indicates no problems in marketing, technical, and financial aspects of the investment project. However, selecting an appropriate country for investment is, in fact, not an easy job since there are lots of factors to be taken into account when evaluating alternative countries for investment. Unfortunately, some of these factors are not measurable while some of them cannot be measured with the same measurement units. Accordingly, it is almost impossible to put together all those factors so as to develop a kind of mathematical model or some sort of quantitative approach to evaluate alternative countries and select the most optimal one.

Despite all these difficulties, some approaches are developed on the basis of the practice and experience of multinational corporations. One of these approaches which is widely used in practice is a method called *the opportunity and risk matrix* (Daniels, Radebaugh, & Sullivan, 2015). This method is based on a table containing opportunity and risk scores of countries weighted according to a specified scale. The use of *the opportunity and risk matrix* requires two specific tasks to be accomplished; namely: (*1*) *scanning and eliminating* candidate countries and then; (*2*) developing an *opportunity-risk matrix* to evaluate alternative countries and thus select the most attractive one.

Scanning aims at viewing and identifying candidate countries almost all over the world so that some possible candidates are not skipped in any region of the world. For this purpose the project manager compares almost all potential countries on the bases of his/her experience, personal knowledge, and information that is readily available. Neither any detailed analysis nor visits to candidate countries are needed. Simply, through personal knowledge, publicly available information, and search on the Internet, the project manager reviews the desirability of countries as possible candidates for his/her contemplated investment. As such, scanning may help managers refrain from examining too few or too many alternatives.

In other words, the purpose of scanning is twofold: (*1*) to prevent managers from intuitively considering the surrounding environment at first so as not to overlook possibilities in the other regions of the world and; (*2*) not to let them go into detailed analyses of too many countries and spend too much time for determining candidate countries. Therefore, for instance, a relatively careful scanning of the world map and reviewing of countries in different regions of the world and, then, identifying some possible candidates for further analysis is the basic objective at the first step.

For now, let us assume that a project manager planning a direct investment abroad identifies 12 candidate countries through the scanning procedure as stated above. However, examining and analyzing so many candidates (i.e., 12 countries) and then selecting the most promising one is a quite difficult task. Moreover, examining and analyzing such a large number of countries may also be redundant, since some of these countries will most probably have similar conditions if they are closely examined.

Therefore, at this point of the study to select a country for investment, the project manager should eliminate some candidate countries so as to limit the number of possible alternatives to few countries (perhaps 3-5) for detailed analysis. The elimination procedure requires the project manager to search for additional specific information concerning the candidate countries identified at the first step, compare similar countries, consult with his colleagues, communicate with experienced people, and even visit few countries. That is to say, the elimination procedure is a kind of close examination of those candidate countries (i.e., 12 countries in our example) on the basis of the additional information obtained and recommendations made by colleagues and experienced people to narrow down the number of candidate countries.

Let us now assume that at the end of such an elimination procedure, the project manager came up with 5 alternative countries that should be considered for direct investment. Having limited the number of alternative countries to few (in our example to 5), an opportunity-risk matrix is to be developed for those alternative countries. The development of an *opportunity-risk matrix*, first of all, requires determining the possible *opportunities* provided and *risks* created by alternative countries for the contemplated international direct investment as elaborated below.

Opportunities

As explained earlier, the objectives of international investors or the reasons for companies to invest abroad are various. Accordingly, depending on these objectives or reasons, a project manager should determine some specific opportunities that are expected from investing abroad. Basic opportunities that an investor looks for and thus may use to compare the attractiveness of alternative countries may be specified as follow.

1. **Sales Expansion:** For profit maximizing firms, the purpose of realizing sales expansion or increasing sales is the essential motive to go abroad and, thus, such firms prefer countries that provide opportunities in terms of large markets as well as possibilities to reach neighboring market areas. Therefore, countries that have large markets with high growth potential in the future and that enable companies to reach neighboring markets easily will be more attractive. However, it should immediately be added that *the existing market size* and *the potential for growth* are not sufficient per se for sales expansion.

The magnitude of the market size should also be judged in terms of the possible price of the product, degree of substitution by other products, income inequality, income per capita, income elasticity, and cultural factors such as preferences and tastes of consumers in a country. All these factors are important determinants for evaluating the level of *effective demand* for a product in a given market. Effective demand refers to the part of the existing demand that would be able and thus most likely purchase the product to be manufactured by the investment project.

That is, in a presumably large market where consumers' income level is not sufficient for purchasing the product and/or the characteristics of the product do not match with the preferences of consumers, the possible market share might not be sufficient even though the target market is large enough. Therefore, all these factors should be taken into account when trying to figure out the market size in general and the market share in specific.

2. **Resource Acquisition:** Again, as indicated earlier, another important reason for companies to invest abroad is to obtain access to production factors such as raw materials and labor. Therefore, companies that are mostly supply oriented would favor the countries which have abundant and cheap resources of *raw material* and *labor*. Needless to state that the availability of abundant and cheap resources is related to reducing costs of production. This clearly explains why well-known large textile firms of developed countries have chosen densely populated developing countries for producing various textile products.

Additionally, countries providing large amounts of *governmental incentives*; in terms of free land for construction, all kinds of free infrastructure and related services, and corporate tax exemption for a certain period of time, etc., will also be attractive for lowering operating costs. In summary, county evaluation and selection should take into account the availability of all cost reducing factors such as cheap raw materials, labor, and incentives provided.

3. **Ease and Compatibility of Operations:** Companies going abroad for a direct investment would also prefer countries which are *nearby*, have the *same languages* or *similar cultural behaviors* and *market operations*. These factors will make easy business operations as well as daily lives of companies' personnel, if they fit with the characteristics of companies. Furthermore, business companies will also feel comfortable in countries where *infrastructure* services are available, and that, especially, transportation and communication facilities are sufficient and cheap.

Moreover, there is no doubt that investors would avoid to have business operations in countries where bureaucratic barriers or *red tape* and *corruption* is widespread. Foreign companies of developing countries will always have difficulties with adapting to such local operating conditions. Accordingly, when red tape and corruption are considered widespread problems, they would be a deterring risk factor for country selection. Consequently, countries that provide ease and compatibility of operations for business companies will certainly be desired by international investors or vice versa. Reports published by international institutions such as Transparency International provide comprehensive information regarding such socio-politic problems. Transparency International even ranks countries according to their levels of transparency based on some corruption perception indeces[1].

Risks

When evaluating alternative countries for investment, business companies take into account risks that might possibly be created by the countries in consideration as well. In fact, in order to judge the desirability of a country correctly, both advantages and disadvantages in terms of opportunities provided and risks created by that country have to be considered and compared. Risks that companies generally take into account are summarized below.

1. **Competition Risk:** Some companies prefer to invest in countries, especially in developing countries, where they may not face severe competition and, thus, may enjoy monopoly advantages in terms of technology, patents, management skills, product differentiation, access

to markets, etc. In another word, they like markets or countries that competitors are not strong and that essential international competitors have not entered yet.

Ironically enough, international investors do not favor political, social, and economic factors or market environments preventing foreign companies to compete either. However, the degree of competition above a certain level creates a market risk (competition risk) for some companies. Such companies will take into consideration the degree of competitive risk prevailing in alternative countries for direct investments. For this reason, possible rival companies operating in alternative countries are closely examined in terms of numbers, brand images, reputation, market shares, and power of competition as a whole. The effects of competition on the commercial profitability of investments is delineated in section 7.1.1 under the heading "Business (Commercial) Risk Analysis".

2. **Monetary Risk:** The monetary risk is mainly conceived of *mobility of funds* such as *transfer of dividends* to home country. As known, the essential purpose of companies investing abroad is to expand sales and obtain cheap sources for maximizing their profits. Therefore, if they will encounter severe limitations on transferring their profits to their home countries, they will naturally refrain from investing in such countries. Although many countries around the world have some sort of restrictions for transferring funds out of the country, the important point for international investors is the ratio of dividends allowed to be transferred and the degree of bureaucratic red tape involved for obtaining permission of such transfers.

Another important point to be considered in relation to monetary risk is the possibility of converting dividends earned in local currencies into hard currencies when dividends are to be transferred. Accordingly, if the dividends and/or profits earned in local currencies are not converted into hard currencies (e.g., US dollar, Euro, British pound, Japanese yen, and Swiss franc) freely and cheaply, the permission of transferring funds abroad would not be meaningful. In some countries even though there seems to be no problem regarding currency exchanging, however, conversion is often made with fixed exchange rates that are officially declared by governments, usually quite below real exchange rates.

In countries where local currencies are not converted into hard currencies with adequate exchange rates or higher commissions are charged, illegal *black markets* for currency exchanges are developed. In short, *currency convertibility* is an important issue that foreign firms pay close attention to when evaluating alternative countries. Developing countries declare officially that their national currencies are convertible if they deem appropriate for their economic policies. This official declaration means that anyone may exchange any time as much as local (national) currency into hard foreign currencies with officially declared exchange rates in the Central Bank or the assigned state banks.

Additionally, in the countries where volatility in exchange rates is quite high and that currency devaluation is a common problem, *exchange rate risk*[2] is also deemed to be a significant problem when judging monetary risk in a country. Exchange rate risk will be discussed later in the chapter on Risk Analysis in Project Evaluation. In fact, all the factors indicated so far regarding the monetary risk reflect the *efficiency of financial markets*. Therefore, in countries where financial markets are functioning efficiently, problems or issues related to monetary risk in terms of transfer of funds, convertibility, and exchange rate risk may not be a matter of concern. Thus, the degree of efficiency in financial markets or that in the *financial system* as a whole reflects the level of monetary risk in a country as well[3].

Furthermore, in countries where financial systems are functioning efficiently, companies would have chances to raise funds when needed and/or invest their idle funds to get some returns on. Consequently, the degree of efficiency of financial systems and the magnitude of the related monetary risks are all significant matters in evaluating the desirability of a country for investment. The effects of exchange rate risk on business firms are explained in section 7.1.4 under the heading "Foreign Exchange Risk - Exposure".

3. **Political Risk:** The concept of political risk refers to any political change that worsens the working conditions of foreign companies. It is sometimes referred to as country risk. Political risk is specifically related to the changes in the political and/or legal systems of countries and thus covers a wide range of factors affecting business activities of foreign firms. Once seen from this point of view, the risks stated above as competition and monetary risks might even be considered as political risks since they are the results of political changes as well. However, here as a risk component in country selection decisions political risk is confined to political factors and/or conditions involve the followings:

a. Changes in political ideology and policies of governments,
b. Sharp differentiation in opinions of powerful political leaders,
c. Legal changes in laws or rules governing businesses,
d. Government intervention in business,
e. Legislative changes unfavorable to foreign firms,
f. Social and political unrest,
g. Political instability, illegal regime changes, and coup d'états,
h. Xenophobia and nationalism,
i. Animosity between the host and home countries,

Adverse changes in these political and socio-economic factors and/or conditions certainly will deteriorate the operational conditions of foreign firms in terms of raising their operational costs, forcing them to accept lower profit levels, and causing loss of sales in some market segments or even loss of the whole businesses (expropriation or nationalization). As seen, the type of political risk will be depending on the factors causing it, which are in fact numerous as indicated above[4]. However, to grasp the wide range of political risk and thus to evaluate the magnitude of its effects on a foreign direct investment, some sort of classification is needed.

In the literature on the subject, the factors and/or conditions causing political risk are categorized from varying viewpoints, but naturally all providing the similar content of political risk in general. Perhaps, a practical classification for political risk might be one that involves and distinguishes three types of political risk; namely, *operational risk, differentiating risk,* and *takeover risk* (Eiteman, Stonehill, & Moffett, 2010; Cavusgil, Reisenberger, & Knight, 2016; Daniels, Radebaugh, & Sullivan, 2015):

1. *Operational risk* encompasses legal changes in laws or rules governing businesses that affect all companies including foreign ones. It is usually the result of changes in governmental economic policies that intervene in business operations. Direct and indirect interventions that affect business operations of firms most often include increasing taxes and customs duties, restricting imports and monetary transfers, and even intervening in wages of employees of foreign companies. As such, this type of political risk in developing countries is generally related to the economic instability in terms of adherence to the rules and regulations of market mechanism as an economic system.

In some cases of developing countries, the opinions of political leaders and/or policies of political parties vary even conflict with respect to the market mechanism or market economy. Some politicians are liberal, some are in favor of a controlled economy, and even some defend a mixed economic system largely based on state-owned economic enterprises. Therefore, the degree of changes in the economic system in general and business activities in specific depends on whomever or whichever political party takes power in the government. For instance, one may privatize state-owned companies today and later another one, when takes control of government, might nationalize them.

2. *Differentiating risk* is a type of political risk that involves discrimination against foreign companies. In other words, governmental officials or governments in general treat foreign companies unfairly and differently. Changes in laws or regulations are prepared in favor of host countries. Sometimes the same laws are enforced differently with respect to foreign companies or are not enforced at all. For example, air pollution regulations may be strictly enforced on foreign companies and negligible problems are heavily fined while local firms are not even visited for controlling pollution. Furthermore, in some cases, the existing laws protecting the rights of business companies in general may just exist on paper when foreign companies are of the concern. For instance, laws and regulations regarding intellectual property such as trademarks are often not enforced or inadequately enforced.

A more common way of differentiating practices against foreign companies is protectionism. Some countries, mostly developing ones, protect their local companies in certain industries from foreign firms' competition for the purpose of creating a favorable economic environment for them to prosper. Those industries that are usually protected are the so-called "infant" industries designated by the economic policies of those countries. Even in some countries where some industries are considered as "strategic", protectionism is widely practiced in industries such as agriculture, telecommunication, defense, and so on, depending on what the politicians consider strategic. Accordingly, the governmental intervention in business life excessively with the objective of protecting "baby" and "strategic" industries would be a significant political risk for foreign companies, since foreign companies are not to be allowed to operate in such industries.

Furthermore, in some countries political thoughts and opinions related to political ideologies might work against foreign companies in some cases if they become widespread. For instance, some politicians or political parties of a country may believe that foreign companies are exploiting their national resources and that their home countries are operating against the interests of their own country as well. In such cases, when these politicians or political parties take power in the national government and/or local municipalities, they may discriminate against foreign firms in various ways to disturb them so as to have them leave the country. The reasons for such differentiating conduct against foreign firms are various; however, the basic motive is to bother foreign companies to leave the host country.

3. *Takeover risk* refers to the changes that occur seldom but end up in catastrophic consequences leading to losing the whole business and/or property completely. As a result of political changes; such as social and political unrest, illegal regime changes, and coup d'états, foreign companies might be expropriated or confiscated. In the case of expropriation, foreign businesses are forcefully transferred to the national governments of host countries by paying the values of businesses taken over; however, in cases of confiscation, no compensation is made.

Additionally, nationalization, especially in developing countries, is a more common legal threat for all businesses including foreign and local ones. Many countries have legislations enabling their governments to nationalize a whole industry in general or a personal property in specific when the public interest necessitates doing so. Therefore, in countries where the rule of law is not observed, a reason might be found out to nationalize foreign companies that are not desired by national governments! When a company is nationalized, its value is determined by the government or the public authority nationalizing it. So this procedure raises various questions whether or not the right value is paid.

With regard to political risk, what is important to note here is the fact that political risks often occur after foreign direct investments are realized. Needless to state that if project managers notice the existence of a political risk during the country evaluation study, undoubtedly, they will eliminate that country. Accordingly, the project manager's task in this case is to predict the probabilities of confronting a political risk during the operating period of the investment; that is, after the investment is realized and the operations start. Therefore, predicting political risk for a country to be selected requires carefully and neatly designed studies to gather and analyze lots of data and information regarding the political development as well as the socio-economic conditions of that country in the future.

However, at this point of the study for country selection, there is no need for detailed analyses and prolonged trips to alternative countries to predict political risk, since the economic feasibility or profitability of the contemplated investment in alternative countries is not known yet. Needless to indicate, if the contemplated foreign direct investment is determined to be feasible in one of the alternative countries, then a detailed risk analysis including prediction of political risk has to be conducted for investing in that country, including site visits and field surveys. The subject of political risk will be further elaborated in the chapter entitled "Risk Analysis in Project Evaluation" which deals with commercial (business), political, and exchange rate risk analyses.

In summary, as explained above, having scanned and eliminated candidate countries and thus determined a workable number of alternative countries for investment (5 countries in our example); the country evaluation study continues with collecting data and gathering information about alternative countries with regard to the possible opportunities and risks that might be associated with each country. Finally, on the bases of the opportunities and risks defined for each alternative country, an *opportunity-risk matrix* is developed to evaluate alternative countries and select the most attractive one.

The development of an *opportunity-risk matrix* goes through the following steps:

1. The *opportunities* and *risks* that an international investor considers important for the contemplated direct investment are specifically defined as shown in the first column of Table 1 given below. As seen in the table, the opportunities and risks shown in column 1 are defined according to their essential components. For instance, for our explanatory example, the opportunity of sales expansion is indicated by "market size" and the "market growth" potential.
2. Secondly, as given in column 2 of Table 1, the opportunities and risks items defined are weighted over a total scale of 100% (W) according to their importance attributed by the investor or the project manager for the direct investment. For example, in Table 1 below, the project manager weights "market size" and "market growth" potential by 0.30 and 0.35, respectively. In relation to risk factors, the project manager attributes a

larger weight of 0.50 to "profit transfer" item as a significant factor of monetary risks while the efficiency of financial system is overlooked and assigned a weight of only 0.05. As noticed, all opportunity and risk factors separately add up to 1 (i.e., 100%).

3. Later on, alternative countries, which are determined after the procedures of scanning and eliminating, are given scores over a specified scale to indicate the importance of each country with respect to the defined factors of opportunities and risks. For example, in our example in Table 1, a scale from 1 to 20 is chosen and then the alternative countries A, B, C, D, and E are assigned scores of importance in relation to the opportunity and risk factors identified, as shown in the related columns of the countries.

For instance, the project manager attributes 15 points (over 20) to country A and 18 points to country E for "market size", believing that country E's market size is larger than that of A. On the other hand, country A's score for "raw material" (20) is greater than the score of country E (18), indicating that country A has a greater potential for *Table 1.*

providing abundant and cheap raw material than the country E. The country with the lowest political risk is the country D with a score of 1 while the one with the highest level of political risk is the country A with 16 scores.

The scores that each country gets according to its importance in relation to the defined opportunities and risks are then multiplied by their weights (W) indicated in column 2, respectively, in order to calculate the weighted values. The computed weighted values for each country are shown in the remaining columns of the table. For example, the weighted values for opportunities provided by the country A are shown in the fourth column of Table 1 as 4.5, 5.6, 0.5, 3.0, 1.0, and 1.0 with a total of 15.6.

4. Finally, multiplication results for each country are summed up separately for both opportunities and risks to obtain the sum of weighted scores, as shown in the two rows labeled as TOTAL in Table 2.1. The totals of these weighted scores of both opportunities and risks for each country are then put on a matrix (or a grid) to evaluate the attractiveness of each country as shown in Figure 1. The horizontal axis of the matrix in Figure 1 indicates the increasing opportunity as the vertical axis shows the increasing risk levels.

Table 1. Weighted Scores of Alternative Countries

Opportunity and Risk Factors	Weights (Importance) of the Factors (W)	Alternative Countries (Scale: 1 - 20)									
		A		B		C		D		E	
		Score of Importance (A)	Weighted Value (WxA)	Score of Importance (B)	Weighted Value (WxB)	Score of Importance (C)	Weighted Value (WxC)	Score of Importance (D)	Weighted Value (WxD)	Score of Importance (E)	Weighted Value (WxE)
Opportunities											
Market Size	0.30	15	4.5	10	3.0	12	3.6	8	2.4	18	5.4
Market Growth	0.35	16	5.6	5	1.75	17	5.95	10	3.5	20	7.0
Labor Availability	0.05	10	0.5	7	0.35	15	0.75	15	0.75	20	1.0
Raw Materials	0.15	20	3.0	15	2.25	16	2.4	12	1.8	18	2.7
Incentives	0.10	10	1.0	5	0.5	15	1.5	11	1.1	16	1.6
Ease of Operations	0.05	20	1.0	10	0.5	12	0.6	5	0.25	15	0.75
TOTAL	1(100%)		15.6		8.35		14.8		9.8		18.45
Risks											
Competitive Risk	0.15	10	1.5	8	1.2	5	0.75	2	0.3	15	2.25
Financial System	0.05	5	0.25	10	0.5	12	0.6	4	0.2	12	0.6
Transfer of Funds	0.50	15	7.5	10	5.0	14	7.0	5	2.5	5	2.5
Convertibility	0.10	18	1.8	16	1.6	10	1.0	2	0.2	4	0.4
Political Risk	0.20	16	3.2	10	2.0	3	0.6	1	0.2	10	2.0
TOTAL	1(100%)		14.25		10.3		9.95		3.4		7.75

Thus, alternative countries are placed on the so-called opportunity - risk matrix according to their opportunity and risk levels just as co-ordinates on a graph (or a grid of 20x20) for the scale of importance. Consequently, according to Figure 2.1, the country with the highest opportunity is E (18.45) while D is the least risky country (3.4). However, the opportunities provided by the county D (9.8) are not large enough. That is, D is both a low opportunity and a low risk country D (9.8;3.4), respectively. On the contrary, A is a country with both high opportunity and high risk A (15.6;14.25).

Therefore, the project manager will consider the countries that have high opportunities by counter balancing with their associated risk levels, which the decision maker may be willing to take on. From this viewpoint we see in Figure 1 that the country labeled E might be the most attractive country in the sense that it has the highest opportunity with a moderately lower level of risk E (18.45;7.75), respectively.

That is, even though the country E's risk level (7.75) is not the lowest one, however, it could be considered as a tolerable level that any investor may take on. As such, a project manager selects E as the most appropriate country for the investment intended and decides to conduct a comprehensive feasibility study in this country as explained in the following sections.

At this point of the country selection study, it should be added that, in some cases, two or three countries may be very close to each other with respect to opportunities and risks associated with them in the opportunity – risk matrices developed. If such a situation with few close alternatives is encountered, the feasibility study to be conducted should involve all those close alternatives and be repeated for each alternative country. That is, in such cases, feasibility studies should be conducted for two or even three alternative countries and the selection decision should be based on the economic results of these feasibility studies. No doubt, the alternative country with the highest economic profitability rate should be chosen as the host country for the contemplated foreign direct investment if it satisfies the expectations of the investor.

Therefore, in such cases where there are two or even three close alternative countries, investment decision and country selection are made at the same time. For instance, assume that a feasibility study was conducted and repeated for three countries, such as W, X, and Y countries, to determine which country is more profitable to select. Finally, at the end of the feasibility study, it was found out that country W is the most profitable one and that its rate of profitability satisfies the expectation of the investor. As such, both the country selection decision and the investment decision would be made at the same time. That is: Make the profitable investment in country "W" as

Figure 1. Opportunity-Risk Matrix

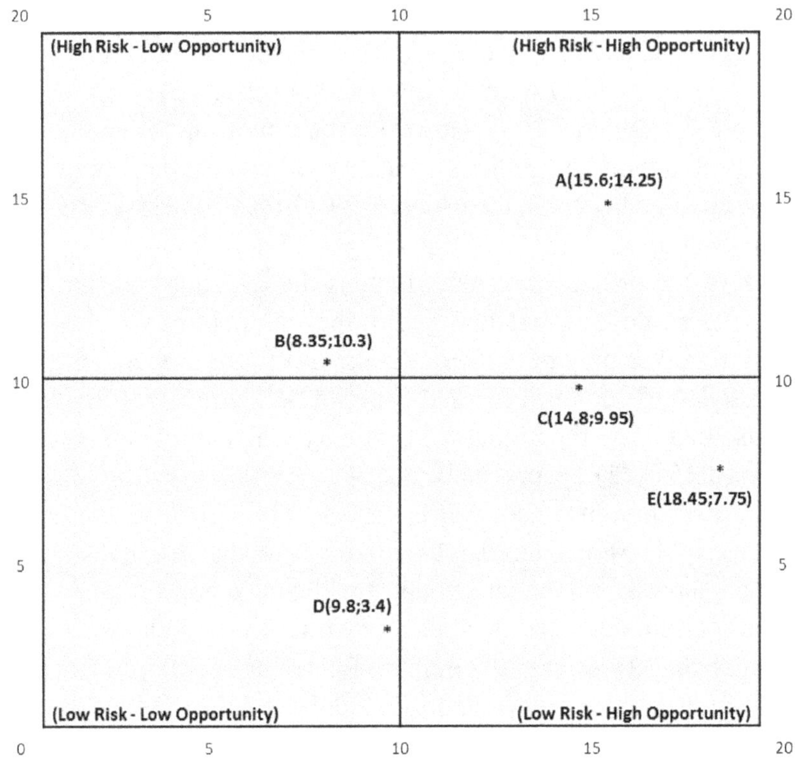

determined by the feasibility study conducted. Undoubtedly, if none of the countries seems to be profitable, then the planned foreign direct investment will not be realized and thus the idea of investing abroad will be abandoned.

PLANNING AND ANALYZING FOREIGN DIRECT INVESTMENT PROJECTS IN THE COUNTRY SELECTED

As explained in the foregoing section, having selected a country for the investment contemplated, the international investor needs to conduct a comprehensive economic study which is generally called a *feasibility study*. A feasibility study for evaluating the economic desirability of a greenfield type of direct investment requires lots of interrelated activities to be carried out and various decisions to be made. These activities and decisions may be broken down into three interrelated and consecutive basic stages; namely, market analysis, technical analysis, and financial analysis, as shown below in Figure 2. The details of the work and/or activities involved in these stages will be explained separately in the following sections of this book.

However, in order to grasp and comprehend the content of a detailed feasibility study, a brief summary of these stages is given below to understand the tasks involved in a comprehensive feasibility study. At this point it should be indicated that, as stated previously, our explanations throughout this book will be based on *the greenfield (or new) investment* type of direct investments, since the work involved in a feasibility study for a greenfield investment is both more comprehensive and also applicable to or valid for the other types of direct investments as well.

1. **Market Analysis:** The purpose of the market analysis is to determine whether or not the product, which will be produced via the investment contemplated in the country selected, will have a sufficiently large market. The market analysis is essentially information oriented and tries to gather lots of information and data regarding supply and demand conditions of a target market in order to decide if the product will be marketable. For this purpose a target market is defined on the basis of the need of consumers that the product of the planned investment intends to meet. Having defined or determined a target market, the dynamics of market operations are analyzed in terms of consumers' purchasing behaviors, demand and supply conditions, market structure, and tools of competition. Later on, the possible market share expected to be captured by the direct investment project is estimated through taking into account the forecasted market size, the degree of competition and the powers of essential competitors, and the possible marketing strategy to be followed.

If the estimated possible market share is not sufficient, that is, the product of the investment project is not marketable, and then the idea of investing in the chosen country should be abandoned (QUIT). However, in some cases, the project manager for some reasons may need to repeat some parts of the market analysis to make sure that the market is indeed not sufficient. Accordingly, when the project manager believes that the product of the investment project is certainly not marketable, the investment project has to be quit. As it is known, if a direct investment will not have a sufficient market share or a desired level of demand for its product, it will definitely not be a successful business in the future and certainly end up in a loss. Therefore, businesses with insufficient market shares should not be started. But if the product of the contemplated investment is determined to be marketable, that is, if it will

Figure 2. Flow Chart for a Feasibility Study

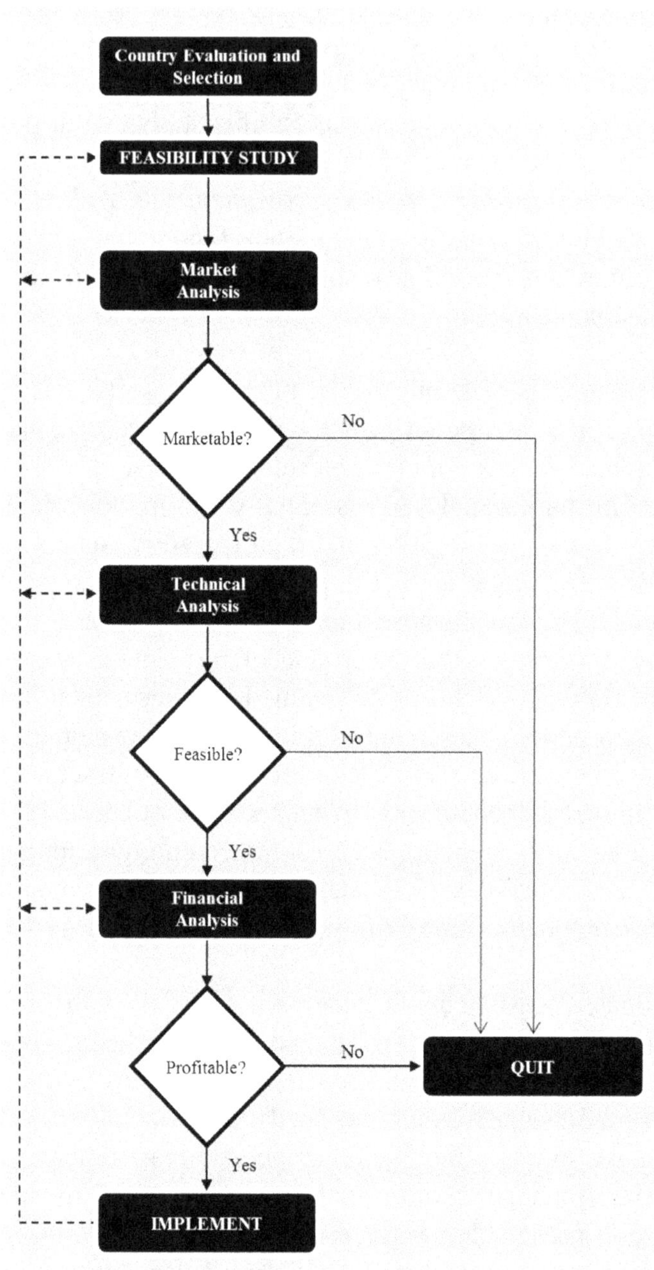

have a large enough market share, then, the feasibility study should continue with a technical analysis.

In short, the market analysis aims at identifying the target market, defining and describing the competitive market environment, quantifying the market size and the possible market share, and finally deciding whether or not the market share is sufficient. If the market share is seen large enough for the foreign direct investment to be realized, the project

feasibility study goes on with the technical analysis. Otherwise, the project study is ended and the idea of investing in the selected country is given up. Although the work and activities required in the market analysis are logically planned and would be explained sequentially in an interrelated manner, there is a feed-back loop operating all the times. That is, at any stage of the market analysis the project manager or analysts may refer or go to any stage of analyses and get the data and information needed for a decision at that point of the study. This feed-back process is working throughout the whole feasibility study including the technical and financial analyses as well.

2. **Technical Analysis:** As stated above, the general purpose of the market analysis is to determine whether the product intended to be manufactured through the direct investment is marketable or not. If the product is marketable, that is, it captures a sufficient market share, then a technical analysis is conducted to determine how the production system should be to manufacture the marketable product. Therefore, the work in technical analysis aims at determining the technical aspects of a production system for manufacturing the desired product in terms of production technology, production process, machinery, equipment, and labor needed, building requirements, plant location in the country chosen, etc. If the production technology is available for manufacturing the marketable product and that there is no problem related to the design of production facilities at all, one would say that the investment proposal is technically feasible and thus the desired product can be produced properly. Once this decision is made, that is, when the investment project is technical feasible, then, the financial analysis stage starts.

Nevertheless, if the contemplated investment proposal is not technically feasible, that is, the desired product cannot be manufactured for some technical reasons, the feasibility study should be terminated (QUIT). For instance, if there are technical problems such as licensing agreements that cannot be overcome to set up a production system, the production system cannot be designed and thus the product cannot be technically produced. Hence, the technical analysis and the feasibility study as a whole should be abandoned. However, the repetition of the technical analysis should also be checked in order to assure that the investment project which has a "marketable" product is really not feasible technically. In sum, if the project manager believes that the investment project is technically feasible, the financial analysis will then start as summarized below. Otherwise, it should be quit.

3. **Financial Analysis:** If the direct investment proposal has a marketable product and that it is also technically feasible, then, on the basis of the technical aspects of the investment, as determined at the stage of the technical analysis, the total costs of the investment should be estimated as the first step of financial analysis. Later on, how the total amount of investment is going to be financed and what revenues are expected from the sales during the operating period of the investment are important points to be determined. Financing the total amount of investment is important in the sense that foreign direct investments are costly and thus usually necessitate use of external financing. If financing needs are not met, the project study and the investment proposal should be quit since it cannot be realized due to shortages of funds. However, if there is no problem with financing of the investment project, the revenues expected from the sales of the marketable product are to be estimated.

Finally, based on the costs and sales revenues associated with the investment project, the investment proposal has to be evaluated in terms of both its profitability and risks involved in it. At the financial analysis stage the profitability of a foreign direct investment project is evaluated from two aspects:

1. The investment proposal is evaluated as a single investment project per se from the viewpoint of the economic conditions of the host country

where it is going to take place. That is, the project is appraised as if it is a national or a local project carried out by a local investor from the country selected. If the commercial profitability of the project is not at a desirable level, the investment project should be rejected as an investment proposal. This means that the investment project is not profitable according to the operating conditions of the country selected. On the contrary, if the investment proposal is commercially a profitable project from the viewpoint of the country chosen (host country); then, the investment project should be appraised from the viewpoint of the international investor, that is, the parent company planning to realize the direct investment.

2. A project that is locally profitable per se may not be profitable for the parent company due to restrictions on the amount of income and/or profits to be transferred to the home country of the parent company. Furthermore, taxation policies for transferring funds and inappropriate foreign exchange rates would also be deterring factors for remitting funds home. Therefore, a locally profitable project, that is, a direct investment project which is profitable at the host country level should then be evaluated from the viewpoint of the parent company in terms of both the profits to be transferred home and risk associated with it. No doubt that if the project is not profitable and/or too risky for the parent company, it will be abandoned (QUIT) since it is not financially feasible. There is no need to indicate that at this final stage of the feasibility study the project manager should ensure that the decision to reject (QUIT) a "marketable" and a "technically feasible" investment project is a correct and sound one. Therefore, the repetition of the financial analysis and/or evaluation procedures should be considered as a double check.

On the other hand, if the investment project is financially profitable from the viewpoint of the parent company, and that it has also a tolerable level of risk involved, the contemplated investment should be started in the country selected (IMPLEMENT) according to the details determined by the feasibility study. Broken lines in Figure 2 indicate the information flow for feedback at all stages of the feasibility study when there is a need to refer to the data and/or information provided at the other stages.

CONCLUSION

In conclusion, the subject of country selection is the base for a comprehensive economic study to plan and analyze a foreign direct investment project. Upon deciding on a country for investment, a comprehensive economic study called a feasibility study is conducted as elaborated in the following chapters. A brief summary of the stages covered by a detailed feasibility study, namely, market analysis, technical analysis, and financial analysis, is given above so as to see the tasks involved in a comprehensive feasibility study. The details of each analysis stage are explained in separate chapters as follows.

REFERENCES

Cavusgil, T., Reisenberger, J. R., & Knight, G. (2016). *International Business: The New Realities* (4th ed.). Harlow, UK: Pearson Education, Ltd.

Collins, S., Narula, R., & Rugman, A. M. (2016). *International Business* (5th ed.). Essex, UK: Pearson Education Limited.

Daniels, J. D., Radebaugh, L. H., & Sullivan, D. P. (2015). *International Business: Environments and Operations (15th ed.)*. Harlow, UK: Pearson Education, Ltd.

Eithman, D. K., Stonehill, A. I., & Moffet, M. H. (2015). *Multinational Business Finance* (14th ed.). Boston: Pearson Education Inc.

Fabozzi, F. J., Modigliani, F., & Jones, F. J. (2013). *Foundations of Financial Markets and Institutions* (International Edition). Boston: Pearson Education, Inc.

Mishkin, F. S., & Eakins, S. G. (2012). *Financial Markets and Institutions* (7th ed.). Boston: Pearson Education Inc.

ENDNOTES

1 To see country profiles in *Corruption Perception Index 2017* (www.transparency.org/country).

2 For a detailed discussion of foreign exchange rate risk, see Eithman, Stonehill, and Moffet (2015).

3 Concerning a detailed discussion of market efficiencies in financial systems, see Mishkin and Eakins (2012) and Fabozzi, Modigliani, and Jones (2013).

4 For more about the nature and sources of political risk, also see Collins, Narula, and Rugman (2016).

Chapter 3
Market Analysis

ABSTRACT

The chapter is devoted to the market analysis as the first stage of the methodology proposed for planning and analyzing foreign direct investments. The market analysis that precedes technical and financial analyses stages of the comprehensive economic study for planning and analyzing foreign direct investments aims at determining whether or not the market for a direct investment project is large enough. Therefore, all studies, work, and activities involved in the market analysis stage as explained in the chapter are confined to determining whether or not the target market for the product to be manufactured through a foreign direct investment is sufficient enough. For this purpose, the essential points to be considered for analyzing the competitive market environment in terms of demand and supply conditions of the market as well as purchasing behavior of consumers are explained step by step. Finally, how a marketing strategy could be developed on the basis of the information regarding the demand and supply sides of the target market is discussed that what possible market share might be captured is elaborated as the final point of the market analysis.

DOI: 10.4018/978-1-5225-7696-9.ch003

THE PURPOSE OF MARKET ANALYSIS AND ITS DATA REQUIREMENTS

The overall objective of the market analysis is to determine whether or not the product to be produced through the direct investment contemplated will have a sufficiently large market in the country selected. For this reason, the market analysis aims at; searching, gathering, processing, analyzing, and evaluating lots of data and information in order to determine in advance the existing and the possible future conditions of the market to be entered into. In other words, the market analysis aims at gathering and collecting information so as to find out in advance the reactions and effects of the surrounding environment where the project is going to take place in. Thus, the market analysis, on one hand, deals with the commodity market (sales market) and, on the other hand, with the factors market (procurement market). As such, it involves lots of studies and work to be done.

At the end of a detailed market analysis in terms of clarifying consumer behaviors, defining supply and demand conditions, and describing competitive environment, the project manager should be able to estimate the possible market share to be captured by the investment project. If the product to be manufactured is believed to be marketable, that is, if it will have a large enough market, then, the feasibility study should continue with a technical analysis as will be explained later. However, if the product is not marketable, that is, the market share that might be captured is not sufficient due to low level of demand and/or severe competition in the market; then the idea of investing in the selected country should be given up.

Nonetheless, before starting a market analysis, it should be indicated that since the market analysis is essentially information oriented, depending on the amount of data and information needed, it may turn out to be a detailed marketing research study. For this reason, before conducting a market analysis the needs for data and information should be determined first. Then, the search for the data and information needed should be planned through the familiar techniques known as *desk surveys* of secondary data sources and *field surveys* to obtain primary data and information through the methods of observations, questionnaires, and personal interviews as summarized below.

1. Desk surveys of secondary data sources include the search for and review of all published documents related to macro and micro economic

conditions as well as market operations of the country in question. For this purpose research reports (published by universities, public institutions such as statistical institutes, central banks, and commissions or boards for capital markets and banking, governmental ministries of Finance, Economy, Treasury, Trade, and Industry, and professional institutions like chambers of commerce, industry, and commodity exchanges, etc.) are valuable sources of information and data for market analysis. Furthermore, country reports published by international institutions such as International Monetary Fund (IMF), Organization for Economic Cooperation and Development (OECD), United Nations Industrial Development Organization (UNIDO), United Nations Conference on Trade and Development (UNCTAD), World Trade Organization (WTO), and World Bank (IBRD) may cover relevant information regarding the countries studied for the direct investment.

2. Field surveys are carried out to collect data and information if the information and data needed for evaluating the desirability of a country is neither sufficient nor available at all in the secondary data sources. Thus, the project managers collect the needed data and information through field surveys according to their own needs. The data and information collected through specific field surveys is called primary data and information since it is obtained firstly by those that needed it. The methods used in field surveys to gather the required data and information are those traditional search methods called "observation", "personal interview", and "questionnaire". In the observation method the field researchers watch or observe personally the events which they want to gather information about for an adequate time period and take notes to compile the required data and information regarding the market place in specific and the country in general. For instance, information concerning purchasing behaviors of consumers is quite often obtained in this way.

On the other hand, in the case of using the methods of personal interview and questionnaire, questions concerning the subject to be searched are prepared and the potential consumers are asked to answer them. Personal interviews could be person to person talks or through telephone conversations. However, in the questionnaire method, a questionnaire form comprised of various questions is prepared and often sent via mails (including e-mails) to the potential consumers or those that are requested to answer. The answers are then processed to obtain the information needed. The questions prepared for interviews and questionnaires may be "open-ended", "multiple choice (closed-ended)", and "dichotomous" type questions. Open-ended questions are free style questions where a general question is asked and a commentary answer is expected of the replier. In contrast, the closed-ended questions are the so-called multiple-choice questions with alternative answers and thus the replier is required to select one of the alternative answers. On the other hand, the questions with only two choices or more specifically the questions that expect "yes" or "no" answers are sometimes labeled as dichotomous type questions. For example, "have you ever traveled to Europe?" The answer is "yes" or "no"?

Needless to state that field surveys are quite expensive compared to desk surveys. Thus, they have to be well planned as well as effective in terms of what they are expected to do in terms of gathering the right data and information needed. Therefore, the content, number, and style of questions are important points to be taken into account when planning interviews and questionnaires. That is, the questions have to be clear enough and well understood as well as sufficient enough to elicit the needed information, but not too many to bother the repliers and lead them not to answer or give quick and wrong answers. For this purpose a pre-application of the questionnaire form with few consumers is usually done to test the effectiveness of the questionnaires before they are applied for field surveys.

Furthermore, field survey methods are subject to statistical sampling errors because these methods try to collect information and/or data about a large population of consumers or a large market in general from a selected and limited sample of consumers. In other words, information about population parameters is inferred from sample statistics. Therefore, in order to be able to generalize the information obtained from the sample to the whole population, the sample size should be large enough and that the selection of sample members has to be done randomly. That is, the sample should be drawn at random from the population such that every member of the population has an equal probability of being included in it. Otherwise, the information gathered through survey methods might be misleading. In other words, correct information cannot be obtained by talking to a small number of consumers that are met in a shopping center or observing the purchasing behaviors of several customers in a certain shop for a short while.

Consequently, as indicated earlier, the market analysis is a heavily information based study. Therefore, the data and information needs for conducting a market analysis have to be determined at the outset of the market analysis in order to avoid duplications and/or replications. Once the needs are determined, then, the methods for searching and gathering the data and information needed have to be planned. The content of a detailed market analysis, which aims at searching for and analyzing data to identify, describe, and quantify the market so as to determine whether or not the product of a contemplated direct investment would have a sufficient market share, covers the following studies as explained in separate subsections.

DEMAND AND CONSUMER ANALYSIS: DETERMINING A TARGET MARKET

The demand for the product of an investment project is the first and foremost essential factor to be determined since the amount of demand is the base of a market. It is quite clear that the greater the demand for a product the larger the market would be for that product because a market refers to the total amount of the demand for a product. For instance, the automobile market in a country is composed of the total number of individual and institutional consumers that would be willing to possible purchase cars. From this viewpoint the concepts of market and demand may be considered similar as the two sides of a coin, with the exception of some subtleties.

On the other hand, the demand for a product is the result of a need driven by a motive. That is, a need is a shortage which a consumer feels and desires to be fulfilled or satisfied, perhaps by purchasing a product. Accordingly, consumers demanding a certain product to satisfy their needs form a market for that product. Therefore, it could easily be stated that the concepts of "needs", "consumers", and "demand" are interrelated within the context of a market analysis. As such, in a study aiming at understanding the operations of a market, conditions determining the demand level in a market in terms of the needs, consumer's purchasing behaviors, and demand characteristics have to be clarified in details by considering the following factors:

Consumer Needs

A need is a gap or a lack felt by a consumer. Additionally, a consumer that has felt a need is, in turn, driven by a motive to satisfy that need, most possibly by purchasing a product or a service. That is to say the need and the motive behind it together lead a consumer to purchase a product to satisfy the need. Therefore, if there is no need and/or the need is satisfied in other ways, then there would be no purchasing. In other words, purchasing occurs only if there is a need to be satisfied. So, a project manager, at this point of a market analysis, has to raise such related questions to clarify the existence of a need: "what is the need for our product", "which need is met by our product", "what is the actual need of our probable consumers", "why do they have to buy or purchase our product", and "what are the motives affecting the purchasing process", etc.

Accordingly, through such similar and interrelated questions, the project manager should make sure the existence of a need to be satisfied by the product to be manufactured. Needless to indicate that if a need is not well defined and/or a product does not meet a need satisfactorily, that production facility would not be successful. In other words, no matter what the marketing activities and/or promotional campaigns of a business firm are, if the product manufactured by the firm will not satisfy the need of consumers completely, that business firm would not be successful in the long run. The business firm may survive for the first few years through intensive promotional campaigns, but sooner or later it would fail because of not meeting the need of consumers. In another word, why should consumers purchase a product if it does not meet their needs satisfactorily? Therefore, the project manager should comprehend and define clearly the need of consumers as the starting point for a market analysis.

Additionally, the motive behind the need should be also clarified as much as possible. If the motive leading consumers to purchase a product is known, then the marketing strategy required to motivate the consumers would be developed more successfully. For example, if the motive behind a need is a result of various physiological factors and that the need is vital to the existence of a human being, then, it would be easier to motivate that individual to purchase a product satisfying that need. The reason for this is quite clear since physiological needs are of vital importance for the continuity of life and, thus, have to be met any way. However, remembering Maslow's theory of the hierarchy of needs, it would be more difficult to motivate a person to purchase a product satisfying a psychological need, since those needs are felt after physiological and sociological needs are met. In brief, being aware of the needs of consumers as well as the motives driving or leading the consumers to purchase a product would be very helpful in designing a marketing strategy and developing a marketing plan, as it will be discussed later.

Types of Consumers and Market Segmentation: Defining a Target Market

As indicated above, a market (a commodity market specifically) is composed of a variety of consumers demanding a product to satisfy their needs. For example, a car market, an oil market, a wheat market, etc. Moreover, when we talk about an active market for a product, we actually speak of a market involving an *effective demand* comprised of various consumers that are willing and able to purchase that product. On the other hand, the variety of consumers of a certain product may include very different types of buyers, such as governments, institutions, business firms of all kinds, households, and various individual groups. It would, therefore, be very difficult, if not impossible, to satisfy or to meet efficiently the needs of such a large group of consumers of all kinds.

In other words, an investment project or an existing company may not be able to effectively produce a product to satisfy all expectations, desires, preferences, and tastes of such a large variety of consumers. That is, business firms would encounter a lot of problems to appeal to such a large variety of consumers whose locations, preferences, buying attitudes, and purchasing practices are varying. Therefore, market segmentation according to some specific features of consumers would be helpful to determine a certain target market for a product, which a company would prefer to serve. A company focuses either on a larger segment or few smaller segments (niches) through a *concentrated (niche) marketing strategy*. It is generally recommended that a market composed of a large variety of consumers be segmented according to some specific features of consumers such that a specific target market could be defined unless there is a clear reason not to do so. Accordingly, such market segmentation would be very effective both for designing a product suitable with consumer's needs, preferences, and tastes as well as developing an appropriate marketing strategy[1].

However, if market segmentation is not desired, an investment project may not differentiate between the preferences and tastes of consumers so that it may aim at meeting the needs of all kinds of consumers for its product through an *undifferentiated* or *mass marketing strategy*. That is, the project manager may decide to overlook the differences in the characteristics of consumers and target the whole market with one product. Moreover, if it is further desired, through a strategy called *differentiated marketing strategy* the project manager may differentiate between the preferences and tastes of consumers but will design and produce different types of the same product for each group of consumers (Armstrong, Kotler, & Opresnik, 2017).

The factors which may generally be used for market segmentation to define a target market are given below[2]:

1. **Geographic Factors:** Market segments could be defined according to some geographic areas, such as certain regions of a country, national (local) or international markets covering several nations. For instance, the market of Eagan and Mediterranean regions of Turkey, The Western states of USA, the market of Germany, the Scandinavian market covering Sweden, Norway, Finland, and Demark, the EU (European Union) Market, etc. Thus, consumers or buyers taking place in one of those geographically defined areas will constitute a target market for a product.
2. **Demographic Factors:** Demographic factors such as age, gender, race, family size, and nationality may be used for segmenting consumers of a product. For instance, a target market of baby boys below the age six, or a market of young ladies between the ages of twenty and forty, etc. Demographic factors are the most widely used factors for segmenting a market since they are easily measurable and define larger consumers groups sharing common characteristics such as preferences, tastes, and usage rates.
3. **Socio-Economic Factors:** These factors are related to the social status and economic powers of consumers in terms of level of education, occupation, personal income, social class, religion, lifestyle, etc. For instance, the rich and educated segment of consumers in several nearby countries whose monthly income is over ten thousand dollars may be considered a target market. Similarly, middle income level employees in service sector in a country would define a large market segment of consumers
4. **End-Users of a Product:** Market segmentation could be made on the basis of the final or end-users of a product such as governmental institutions, business firms, households, individuals, etc. For example, a market composed of textile firms operating in several Asian countries might be regarded as a target market.

Consequently, on the basis of the above mentioned factors a market segment could be specified and may be defined as the target market. As such, a target market refers to a set of consumers that have common and/or similar characteristics so that a company desires to serve. For now, having determined a target market and thus the potential consumers to be served and thus to be reached for marketing and selling activities, the project manager should collect as much information as possible concerning the preferences and tastes of the consumers as well as their purchasing attitudes and behaviors so as to analyze the purchasing process for developing a marketing strategy, as explained below.

Analyzing Purchasing Process

In general, the most important point in all marketing activities as well as promotional campaigns is the purchasing of the product by the targeted consumers. That is, whatever the degree of a marketing campaign is, the campaign would be considered successful only if it is ended up in purchasing. Otherwise, it will be a waste of resources. The way of getting consumers to purchase a product is, of course, to design a product suitable with their wants, preferences, and tastes as well as to be aware and comply with their purchasing behaviors. Accordingly, lots of information is needed to design a successful marketing strategy for selling a product or getting consumers purchase the product. For such information there would be a need to do a detailed field survey to collect the necessary data and information regarding the purchasing behaviors of consumers.

Purchasing attitudes and behaviors of consumers are essential in developing a successful marketing strategy. Therefore, a project manager should pay close attention to obtain relevant information to answer such questions regarding the purchasing process of consumers: “when do they purchase”, “where do they purchase”, and “in what quantity do they purchase”. Consumers may purchase seasonally or all the time whenever they need a product and go to designated places, specified markets, shopping centers, etc. Moreover, when they buy, they may purchase in small units or in large quantities. Accordingly, information or answers to these questions would help a project manager to develop a marketing strategy to make available or store as much product as consumers purchase in those places at the time when they buy. This is, indeed, the first step towards a successful marketing strategy in terms of providing a product in desired places, at desired time, and in desired quantity. More specifically, this would contribute to development of an effective distribution policy for a successful marketing strategy as will be explained later.

Additionally, "how do consumers decide to purchase" is another important question to be answered for marketing activities. Consumers may collect lots of information from different sources, get advice from other users, consult some specialists, and then decide to purchase the product in a "planned way"; or whenever they see or come across a product, they purchase it in an "impulsive way". Finally, "who is making the purchasing decision" is another crucial point to be clarified in order to determine the audience of the marketing and/or promotional campaigns. It should be indicated that purchasing decision for a product is not always made by those that need the product. In many cases the purchasing decision may be made by some others. For instance, consider baby products. The purchasing decision is made by parents although babies need the products. The same is applicable to purchasing of machinery, equipment, and tools in production facilities. It is, in fact, the engineers not the owners of production facilities who decide on purchasing. Therefore, the promotion policy of a successful marketing strategy should be directed towards those who provide information and/or give advice about purchasing as well as deciding on purchasing.

Consequently, information regarding the above mentioned questions would help project managers to develop a marketing strategy or a so-called "product mix" about designing a good product for an adequate price, with an efficient promotion campaign, and an appropriate distribution policy. That is to say, by way of clarifying the purchasing process through the questions stated above, a project manager would be able to prepare a marketing plan to adequately meet the demand of consumers at the right time and in the right places with adequate quantity. Moreover, through such information the project manager would also be able to elaborate the design of a product such that consumers may prefer it more and that an effective promotion campaign which would address those that decide on purchasing of the product could be carried out. In conclusion, as a result of all these studies concerning consumers' needs, market segmentation, and purchasing behaviors of consumers, that were explained so far, a project manager would have a good grasp of the functioning of the demand side of the target market, excluding the market size that will be dealt with later on.

SUPPLY AND ANALYSIS OF COMPETITIVE ENVIRONMENT

The supply side of a market is as important as the demand side since the availability of a market generally depends on the difference between the demand and supply conditions of a market. Supply, as the total amount of a certain product provided by all rival firms in a market, is directly related to the number and technical capabilities of rivals or competitors. Therefore, in order to see clearly the supply side of the target market in terms of its operation and the degree of competition involved, the following points have to be clarified and the necessary data and information be gathered:

Determining Market Structure

In general terms, the concept of market structure refers to the numbers of competitors operating in a market in the sense of monopolistic, oligopolistic, and competitive trends existing in the market. A monopolistic market is a market dominated and completely controlled by a single firm so that there is almost no competition in the market. If few firms control operations in a market, then, one may talk about an oligopolistic market, where competition turns out to be a game of struggle to survive for individual firms. In other words, an oligopoly is a market or an industry controlled by a limited number of large companies, such as three companies controlling 85% of a national market of a country. No doubt that if the firms operating in a market are more than few, the level of competition in the market increases as the number of competitors goes up.

At this point it should be indicated that if the market analysis of a feasibility study indicates the existence of a monopolistic or an oligopolistic market concentration, the work for the market analysis should be ended. Because it is quite difficult to enter into monopolistic and oligopolistic markets and that the strategies required to compete are different, here we assume that the market is competitive and, thus leave out the subject of monopolistic operation and oligopolistic competition.

Now assuming and considering that the target market is competitive and that there are many competitors producing the same product, the task at this stage of market analysis is to gather as much information as possible to answer the following questions:

- How many rivals or competitors are there in the target market?
- Who are the competitors?
- Which are the leading companies and/or main competitors?
- What are the possible market shares, brand images, product quality, and prices of main competitors?
- What are the possible weaknesses and strengths of the essential rivals?

Consequently, the project manager has to strive hard to collect as much information as possible to know the essential rivals in terms of their market shares, product qualities, brand images, unit prices, etc. Furthermore, if possible, information concerning technical capabilities, financial possibilities, and managerial policies of competitors would help a lot in developing strategies to compete. That is, the more information a company has about the rivals the better its position would be in the competition process. In fact, gathering information about the rivals is not an easy job since the relevant information is not published nor given to outsiders. Nonetheless, the project manager has to do his or her best to get to know the competitors as much as possible.

Bases of Competition

The second aspect that a project manager has to ascertain concerning the analysis of the competitive environment is the tools that competitors use for competing. The tools that competition for a product is generally based on are price per unit, quality, and services provided by producers after sales, mostly in case of industrial products. Higher prices will affect sales negatively, especially, if the socio-economic level of consumers in the target market is low. On the other hand, a higher quality increases the demand for and, thus, sales of a product. Actually, price and quality are closely related and go hand in hand, but operate conversely for competition. A higher quality necessitates a higher price, that is, the higher the quality the more expensive the product probably would be. However, the higher the unit price the lower the demand would be, considering all the other things remaining the same (*ceteris paribus*). Thus, this effect of price increases on demand, which is known as *price elasticity of demand,* has to be determined for establishing an optimal balance between the price per unit and product quality.

Therefore, at this point of the market analysis, the project manager has to collect the relevant data and information concerning the unit price and product quality, including brand images, of competitors' products. Then, taking into account the prices and quality of the products of the essential competitors as well as the socio-economic level of consumers in the target market, an optimal balance between the price and quality should be determined and, thus, an adequate price for the product of the planned investment should be figured out. This information would be of great value when determining a marketing strategy later on.

Finally, generally in the case of industrial products, services provided by producers after sales of a product in terms of quick repair services and cheap supply of spare parts are important factors for competition. Moreover, in some countries in order to protect consumers, governments officially require foreign companies to set up a certain number of service channels distributed over the country in order to enter into the local or national markets. For example, automobile market in some emerging economies such as Turkey has such distributional requirements in terms of service stations and spare parts distributors scattered around the country.

Consequently, price per unit, product quality, and after sales services in case of industrial products are essential tools for competition in product markets. Accordingly, the project manager has to find out the effect of each tool as the basis of competition or, conversely stating, the degree of sensitivity of consumers to each of these tools has to be ascertained. Then, these factors or tools of competition should be taken into account all together when developing an effective a marketing strategy for competing in the target market as will be explained later.

Barriers to Entry

Even though entering into competitive markets is supposed to be free; however, there are some certain factors inherent in the operation of a competitive market that create barriers to enter into a competitive market. These legal and market operation related factors are as follow:

1. **Economies of Scale:** In most of the economic sectors or industries, the principle of *increasing returns to scale* works. That is, the average unit cost of production decreases as the volume of production increases. This decrease in the average unit cost continues up to a certain production volume and, then, if the production volume continues to increase, the average unit cost starts increasing thereafter. The basic reason for this is that at the first stage of production as production volume increases, the fixed cost per unit will decrease since fixed costs which are independent of production volume are divided by the quantity produced. Thus, as production quantity goes up, the average unit cost will go down due to decreases in the fixed costs per unit. However, if the production volume continues to increase after a certain production volume, the average unit cost this time starts to increase since increasing production volume entail additional fixed costs in terms of capital investment in new machinery, equipment, and tools as well as extra managerial costs. So, the production volume at which the average unit cost reaches its minimum level is called the *optimal production quantity*.

Accordingly, the concept of economies of scale as a barrier to entry refers to the fact that in some economic sectors or industries there are some sort of determined and standardized optimal production capacities. For instance, automobile, cement, tire, sugar, petro-chemical industries, etc. are some examples for industries where production facilities have to be established with production capacities not less than certain levels of scale. Therefore, if an investor is going to invest in one of those industries requiring a standardized optimal production capacity, which is generally large and thus necessitates a very large amount of investment, the investor has to build a factory of that large capacity. However, some investors may not be able to finance such large-scaled production capacities required by economies of scale because of their limited financial capabilities. On the other hand, they cannot build a small factory either since they would not be able to compete due to higher average unit cost of production. Thus, they will not enter or invest in those industries because of not financing large enough factories to compete with rivals on the basis of the average unit cost of production. Undoubtedly, a larger average unit cost entails a higher sales price which, in turn, limits the competitive power of business firms.

2. **Absolute Cost Disadvantage:** In competitive markets, some companies may have some special cost reducing advantages in terms of a production formula, a patent, or a hidden specific know-how which add a very special attribute or a very much desired characteristic to their products. The other firms may neither have such advantages nor an opportunity to obtain them. For example, it is said that Coca Cola Company has such an absolute cost advantage as a secret production formula which gives its products a very special taste. Accordingly, the firms competing with such privileged companies have to invest large amounts of resources in research and development (R&D) activities in order to have their product get similar attributes or characteristics. Otherwise, they will have very hard times to compete.

Unfortunately, even very large amounts of spending in R&D activities will not be able to solve the problem. Therefore, competitors try to compensate this disadvantage through some other ways that will bring about additional costs, such as increasing expenditures for promotion and reducing unit prices. So, some companies may have such absolute cost advantages with regard to a competing product while the other competitors will face an absolute cost disadvantage. In such cases, a project manager should evaluate the existence of absolute cost disadvantages from the viewpoint of conditions surrounding the target market. If the ability to compete is declining too much, the investor may not enter into the market.

3. **Brand Loyalty:** Similar to absolute cost advantage but different in the sense that some successful companies may have established some good relations with their customers in the past such that the customers will get used to using their products. This usage gradually mounts to a habitual use and further the trademark of a product turns out to be the name for that product in the market. For example, the word "nescafe" in Turkey means instant coffee although it is in reality the trademark of a coffee company for its product of instant coffee. Eventually, consumers' habitual use of such products, later on, leads to the development of a kind of loyalty by consumers for those products, which is often called brand loyalty. Consumers that have developed brand loyalties will hardly switch to using the products of the other companies. Accordingly, in a market analysis study, if brand loyalties for the products of some essential rivals are observed, the project manager should be careful in assessing the potential of the target market as well as surviving in it.

4. **Vertical Integration:** Vertical integration refers to the business operations in which a company manufacturing a product also controls procurement (supply of production factors) as well as distribution activities related to the same product. In another word, a manufacturing company that owns or has the control of supply of production factors may control channels of distribution as well. Accordingly, some day when a new competitor enters into the market the vertically integrated company will do anything possible to push the competitor out of the market. For instance, the company enjoying vertical integration may not provide for or sell production factors to the incoming competitor and/or not let it use its physical distribution channels. A competitor, that is intended to be refrained from entering a market through the power obtained by vertical integration, will face lots of difficulties in the market and may be forced either to leave the market or to invest additional resources in procurement activities and even establish a distribution system for its own company. No doubt, such solutions are too costly for competitors.

However, vertical integration is illegal in many countries where competition in markets is preserved. Despite this fact, in many developing countries there are no laws preventing vertical integration. So, in some of those developing countries where production factors seem to be abundant and cheap, the production factors and/or distribution channels may be controlled by few firms. Therefore, a project manager conducting a market analysis should pay close attention to find out if there is some kind of vertical integration in the target market. If it the case, the project manager should take necessary measures to handle the matter, including the decision to give up the project study.

5. **Institutional Constraints:** In addition to the above-mentioned barriers to entry, which are indeed inherent in market operations, there are some governmental and/or institutional constraints that may create some barriers to entry. Although these constraints are applicable to all business firms, some new comers may not be able to meet them since constraints are generally elevated from the past to the present as problems increase. For example, as air pollution measurements get higher and higher, rules and regulation to control and prevent air pollution as well as to protect public health become stiffer. Eventually, such rules and regulations for protecting environment and public health may necessitate very large additional expenditures and so increase the total amount of investment to be realized. This additional cost of investment may deter new entries

into that market. Additionally, in some countries some economic policies in the name of protecting competition or preventing monopolization, controlling imports or exports, and administering product and/or raw material prices may hinder entry into such markets in those countries. Therefore, the project manager should be aware of such constrains and ascertain whether or not they will create problems for the investment project that is planned.

Product Life Cycle

The degree of competition in markets for industrial products will differ with respect to the life cycles of products. Industrial products have life cycles that go through the stages named "*introduction*", "*growth*", "*maturity*", and "*decline*" as shown in Figure 1.

1. **Introduction Stage:** An industrial product is introduced to a market upon being innovated or invented mostly in an industrial developed country. There is no competition in this entrance stage since the product has just been introduced to the market, so that there is no other company to compete with. That is, more or less, a monopolistic situation is observed in the market. However, profits are usually negative or quite low since demand is low due to consumers not being aware of the product yet. Therefore, a great deal of promotional activities requiring large amounts of expenses is to be carried out to inform consumers and have them try the product. The risk of the product staying in or leaving the market (i.e., living or dying risk) is the most important problem to be considered. If the product stays or lives in the market, indicating that consumers have accepted it, the innovating or inventing company would enjoy a monopoly power for a while but not for a long time period since the comfort in the market will induce new companies to enter the market.
2. **Growth Stage:** In the growth stage, the sales of the product would increase quickly indicating that the product is satisfying the expectations of the market. However, the growth of the market attracts new companies imitating and/or developing similar products to enter into the market. Nevertheless, the number of new companies will not be at a level causing a severe competition in the market. That is, there are few companies in the market and the market is growing significantly because new consumers becoming aware of the product are entering into the market. Production may take place in some other industrial countries as well. In brief, few

companies enjoy the ease of operation in a growing market as well as making good profits in the growth stage. Therefore, this stage of the life cycle seems to be the best time for a new company or investor to enter into a market since competition is not intense and the market is growing.

3. **Maturity Stage:** In contrast to the growth stage, competition will become very severe at the stage of maturity where the whole demand seems to be almost met and the market reaches to a saturation point. At this stage of the life cycle, there are many companies operating in the market and producing similar products. Production will take place in many countries including developing ones. However, the severe competition may lead some companies to leave the production or move it to some developing countries. That is, the product has become standardized and matured such that the products of almost all companies look alike in terms of design, quality, and price. Therefore, this is not an easy stage for a company to enter into a market since competition is quite severe and the profit margin is very small. The only way for a new company to be able to enter into and stay in such a saturated market and compete is to have a product with some additional desirable characteristics as well as some cost or price advantages.
4. **Decline Stage:** The severe competition for a standardized product during a prolonged maturity stage makes the companies in developed countries to move their production to developing countries in order to increase their sales and to acquire cheap resources to cut down costs. In fact, this is the only way for the product to survive. Thus, eventually almost all production of the product will take place in developing countries and that the once exporting developed countries will become the importing ones. Additionally, the highly standardized product leads the affluent consumers in developed countries to demand new and modified different products.

Accordingly, the decline stage of a product is the time for the product to fade away or perhaps to be replaced by a new version of it. For instance, consider black and white television sets being replaced by colored TVs which were also replaced by LCD TVs. Possibly, LCD TVs are about to be substituted by 3Ds (three dimensional TVs). Thus, if the life cycle of an industrial product is determined to be in the decline stage, then there is no reason for a new company to enter into the market and to produce that product because the product is fading out of the market. Consequently, if a project manager

Figure 1. Product Life Cycle

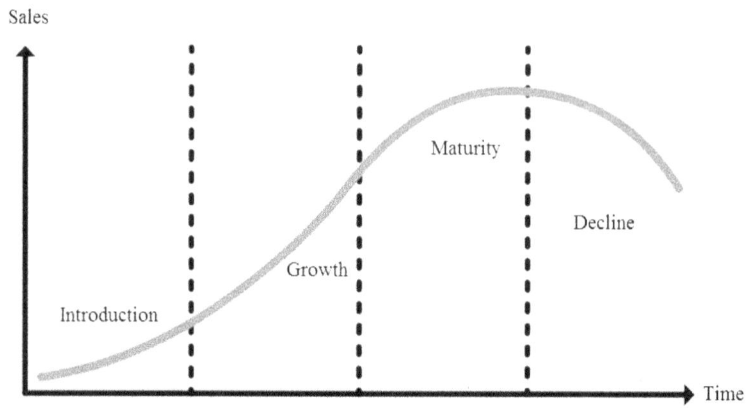

is analyzing a market for an industrial product, the life cycle of the product should be closely analyzed and the degree of competition in the target market with regard to the stage of the product's life cycle be carefully evaluated. If the target market is in the saturation stage with a mature and/or standardized product or is in the declining stage with a product fading away, the project manager should not consider it for entering.

FORECASTING THE DEMAND (SIZE OF THE MARKET)

As a result of the studies and/or analyses explained so far, the project manager must have compiled a great deal of information and data regarding the demand and supply sides of the target market. That is; a target market has been specified and defined in terms of the needs, socio-economic characteristics, preferences, attitudes, and purchasing behaviors of consumers such that a satisfactory data base must have been formed with respect to the demand side of the market. On the other hand, concerning the supply side; the market structure, competitors operating in the market, and dynamics of competition were analyzed and clarified as much as possible. Therefore, as of the supply side of the target market, lots of information and data must have been compiled about the production capabilities of competitors and the degree of competition in the market.

Now at this point of the market analysis, the project manager needs to find out the size of the existing target market as well as its growth potential in the future since the investor is expecting to capture some part of it. Therefore, the project manager has to estimate the existing market size and forecast its magnitude for the upcoming years. For estimating the size of the existing target market and its growth rate in the future years, quite many forecasting techniques have been developed. These forecasting techniques are classified in two general categories as short-term and long-term techniques. However, short-term techniques such as moving averages and smoothing techniques are not appropriate for making long run forecasts. The long-term forecasting techniques are best suited for estimating the size of a market during a certain period of time in the future.

The long-term forecasting techniques to estimate the market size or the demand for a product are numerous and usually divided in two general categories; namely, qualitative techniques and quantitative techniques. An explanation of all these techniques is beyond the scope of this book but the literature is quite rich on this subject (Montgomery, Jennings, & Kulahcı, 2016; Hyndman & Athanasopoulos, 2018). However, a brief description of these techniques is given below to remind the reader of the available long-run forecasting techniques, as well as to show the practices of the time series trend analysis and the multiple regression analysis, which are two widely used techniques in demand forecasting, are given below:

Qualitative Techniques

These forecasting techniques are judgmental ones and involve no significant mathematical computation and/or statistical analysis. Forecasts are often based on the judgmental estimates of professionals, experienced managers, and experts. In such *judgmental techniques* project managers review the past and the present data regarding the market size, may even compute the growth rates noticed in the past, and then depending on their personal knowledge and experience and/or consultation with some colleagues or professionals make estimates about the market size in the future. For instance, they may calculate the growth rate of the past data and then say that the existing market size of 2.000.000 units today will grow by 5% each year in the future so the market size would be [2.000.000x(1+0.05)] = 2.100.000 units next year, $[2.000.000x(1+0.05)]^2$ = 2.205.000 the second year, etc.

However, in cases where there is no past and present data and information regarding the size of a market and the related explanatory factors; for instance, the market for a newly discovered product, forecasting would be quite difficult. In such markets when there is no data available, *Delphi* and *Cross-Impact* techniques are recommended for making estimates. In using the *cross-impact* technique for estimating the demand for a product, forecasting or estimation is based on some other factors which have, in one way or another, some association with the market or product in question. Thus, indirect information is used for making some judgmental estimates.

On the other hand, the *delphi* technique is a sequential search procedure based on the personal estimates of a group of experts on the subject to be forecasted. The experts are not aware of each other. That is, no one knows the other members of the *delphi* group since interaction of experts is not desired as group members might influence each other if they interact. The estimates of experts are gathered upon the completion of several sequential rounds of questionnaires. At the end of each round; the lower and higher extreme estimates are discarded (about 25% - a quartile - at each side) and then the range and average of the remaining mid 50% are computed. Later on, these results including the extreme ones are sent to the experts in the delphi group for the next round.

The experts are again asked to make new estimates in the light of the information provided regarding the previous round. Experts insisting on their earlier extreme estimates are also required to send in their comments and reasons for staying with their former estimates. All these comments and/or reasons for insisting on extreme estimates are also shared with experts in the following rounds, of course not the names of experts. The process of discarding extreme answers and computation of the range and average for the mid 50% and then sending all the information about the estimates to the experts to renew their estimates, including the comments and reasons of the experts insisting on their extreme estimates, is repeated about 4 rounds. Finally, at the end of the last round the average of the mid 50% is taken as the estimate of the Delphi group. Therefore, it is expected that the experts would make up their mind regarding the estimation subject through the feedback of information loops covering the estimates of other unknown experts.

Quantitative Techniques

These techniques require the use of some mathematical methods and/or statistical techniques that analyze past data to develop a mathematical model or a statistical trend to forecast the future. There are various approaches, methods, and/or techniques in this category that might be classified into two general groups as *time series analysis* and *causal models* which are explained in separate sections in the following pages.

1. **Time Series Analysis:** This analysis is based on the series of data observed in the past years and then the trend of the past series of data is determined through a statistical technique called *trend analysis*. The determined trend is later projected into the future by using "time" as the "explaining factor (independent variable)". The classical simple regression model is the most common example of time series analysis. Additionally, the methods called *classical decomposition techniques* and *Box-Jenkins models* are some extensions of time series analysis. Nevertheless, the classical simple regression model as a method for trend analysis is the most common technique utilized for forecasting the market size since it assumes that "*time*" as an explaining variable covers various factors that may not be quantified. In cases where a linear trend is not observed in the past data series, lo-linear trends are estimated through curves such as *exponential* and *Gompertz* curves. The use of these curves in time series forecasting will also be evaluated after the explanation of the classical trend analysis in the form of simple regression analysis as follows.
    a. **The Classical Trend Analysis:** Out of the time series analysis techniques the one that is most widely used for long term forecasting is that of the *classical trend analysis* based on simple regression analysis. The reason this widely use in practice is that it assumes the "time" as an explaining variable covers various factors that may not be quantified. As an example for the trend analysis of the time series analysis, let us consider an analyst who desires to forecast the sales or demand in a market segment on the basis of the past historical data about the sales realized in the market segment.

The analyst believes that the trend of sales observed in the past will also continue in the future in a similar manner. Therefore, he or she collects the past historical data on sales (Y_i) for 12 consecutive years (X_i) as given in Table 1 and tries to determine the past sales trend through the simple regression analysis as explained below. The last two columns of the table indicate the computation values required by the methodology of the simple regression analysis.

In the trend analysis based on the simple regression, the relationship between the sales volume and the time (years) is assumed to be linear and thus the line that fits best the distribution of sales in the form of a simple regression model is stated as:

Table 1. The Amounts of Sales Volume during the Last 12 Years (000 Units of Product)

Years	Time Period (X_i)	Sales Volume (Y_i)	(X_iY_i)	X^2_i
2006	1	400	400	1
2007	2	470	940	4
2008	3	450	1350	9
2009	4	450	1800	16
2010	5	475	2375	25
2011	6	510	3060	36
2012	7	512	3584	49
2013	8	500	4000	64
2014	9	534	4806	81
2015	10	550	5500	100
2016	11	595	6545	121
2017	12	620	7440	144
n= 12 years	$\Sigma X_i = 78$	$\Sigma Y_i = 6066$	$\Sigma X_iY_i = 41800$	$\Sigma X_i^2 = 650$

$$\hat{Y}_i = a + b X_i$$

where;

$\hat{Y}_i$: denotes the dependent variable or the variable to be estimated; that is, sales forecast,

X_i: is the independent variable or the variables that explains the changes in the dependent variable. In the case of time series trend analysis it just represents the time (years).

a: is the starting value (intercept) of the line,

b: is the coefficient of the steepness or slop of the line, that is the effect of on change in the independent variable on the dependent variable.

The values of the coefficients of the linear estimation model are determined through the least square method with the following formulas:

$$b = \frac{n\sum X_iY_i - \sum Y_i \sum X_i}{n\sum Xi^2 (\sum X_i)^2} \quad (i = 1, 2, \ldots\ldots\ldots, n)$$

$$a = \frac{\sum Y_i}{n} - \frac{b\sum X_i}{n}$$

where;

Y_i: is the value of the ith observation of the sales volume, that is, the value of dependent variable,
X_i: is the value of the ith time period, as the independent variable that explains the changes in the dependent variable in the case of time series trend analysis.
n: is the number of observations. In our example n = 12.

The values in Table 1 may now be used in the formulas given above to calculate the a and b coefficients of the regression model as given below. As seen the number of observations or years considered in the example is 12 years, that is, n = 12. Thus:

$$b = \frac{12(41,800,000) - 78(6,066,000)}{12(650) - (78)^2}$$

b = 16,580

and

$$a = \frac{6,066,000}{12} - \frac{16,580(78)}{12}$$

a = 397,730

Therefore, the linear simple regression model for forecasting the sales volume would be:

$\hat{Y}_i = a + b X_i$

$\hat{Y}_i = 397,730 + 16,580 (X_i)$

Needless to state that such computations could easily be done through computer package programs like SPSS as given in Boxes 1-3.

As seen, the coefficients of the model are the same as those we computed above with a small rounding error for the coefficient of a (the constant), that is:

(Constant) a = 397, 727 or rounding to 397,730 as previously computed.

(Time) b = 16,580

$\hat{Y}_i = 397{,}730 + 16{,}580\, X_i$

Box 1.

Model Summary				
Model	**R**	**R Square**	**Adjusted R Square**	**Std. Error of the Estimate**
1	,951[a]	,904	,894	20,432

a. Predictors: (Constant), Time

Box 2.

ANOVA[b]						
Model		**Sum of Squares**	**df**	**Mean Square**	**F**	**Sig.**
1	Regression	39312,175	1	39312,175	94,165	,000[a]
	Residual	4174,825	10	417,483		
	Total	43487,000	11			

a. Predictors: (Constant), Time
b. Dependent Variable: Sales

Box 3.

Coefficients[a]						
Model		**Unstandardized Coefficients**		**Standardized Coefficients**		
		B	**Std. Error**	**Beta**	**t**	**Sig.**
1	(Constant)	397,727	12,575		31,628	,000
	Time	16,580	1,709	,951	9,704	,000

a. Dependent Variable: Sales

At this point of the analysis it should be indicated that before using the simple regression model for estimation purposes, the validity of the model has to be evaluated through the so-called hypothesis tests based on the F and t values shown in the computer output given above. The statistical evaluation of the model and/or tests of hypothesis are not dealt with here since it's out of the scope of this study[3]. Nevertheless, it may be stated that since the computed value of F = 94.165 is greater than the standard Table value of F given in Appendix 2 (with $df_1 = 1$ and $df_2 = 10$ degrees of freedom at $\alpha = 0.05$ risk level), $F_{0.05;1;10} = 4.96$, the regression model may be considered significant for estimation.

Additionally, as seen in the second part of the computer output given above, the value indicated as "R Square" (0.904) is called *the coefficient of multiple determination* (R^2). In regression analysis R Square ($R^2 = 0.904$) indicates that the independent variable (time) explains 90.4 percent of the changes in the sales volume. Accordingly, it might be inferred that the linear regression model is meaningful and explains 90.4% of changes in the sales volume at the 5 percent risk level chosen. However, in interpreting R^2 or multiple determination coefficients in times series analysis attention should be paid to the problem of "autocorrelation" which inflates R^2 value. But this is a different subject not to be dealt with here.

For now, since the model determined is significant and meaningful as a whole, let us assume that the analyst wants to forecast the sales volume for the years of 2018 and 2019. In this case, since there are 12 time periods included in the model, the values of the independent variable of X_i (time periods) would be taken as 13 and 14 in the prediction model for the years specified, respectively. Thus, the model would predict sales volume as:

For the year 2018:

$$\hat{Y}_i = 397{,}730 + 16{,}580\,(X_i)$$

$$\hat{Y}_{2018} = 397{,}730 + 16{,}580 \qquad (13)$$

$$\hat{Y}_{2018} = 613{,}270 \text{ units.}$$

For the year 2019:

$$\hat{Y}_{2019} = 397{,}730 + 16{,}580 \tag{14}$$

$$\hat{Y}_{2019} = 629{,}850 \text{ units.}$$

Finally, it should also be added that when the effects of the beginning time periods are desired to be reduced and/or those of the last time periods to be increased, the numbering of the time periods may be started from zero (0). That is, the time period number as the value the independent variable would start counting as (0, 1, 2, 3, …., 12). In any case, the number of time periods must not be less than 12 periods for an appropriate use of trend analysis. Additionally, it should be stated that before fitting the best line to the assumed linear trend of the past data series, seasonal, cyclical, and random changes and/or variations in the past data series should be viewed first and then the forecasting model must be selected (Montgomery, Jennings, & Kulahci, 2016).

b. **The Exponential Logarithmic Curve:**

As stated above, in cases where the observations values of the past data series do not reflect or show a linear trend, then, non-linear or curvilinear logarithmic models may be used for forecasting purposes. For instance, if it is believed that the past data series do not reflect a linear trend, then instead of the classical linear trend model of:

$$\hat{Y}_i = a + b\,X_i$$

an *exponential curve* in the form of a model like,

$$y = AB^x$$

may be fitted to the past data series.

where:

y: denotes sales values (Y_i) as the dependent variable,

A and B: are coefficients of the exponential curve (intercept and slope, respectively),

x: shows the number of time periods (X_i) as the independent variable.

The coefficients of the exponential model may be computed through the least square method if we take the logarithmic values of both sides of the above given equation of the model as follows:

$$\log y = \log A + x \log B$$

Now, if we define the logarithmic values as:

$$\log y = Q$$

$$\log A = a$$

$$\log B = b$$

The logarithmic equation may be stated as:

$$Q = a + b\,x$$

Therefore, we now have a linear simple regression model as explained earlier in the classical trend analysis and thus its coefficients can be computed through the least square model as given below:

$$a = \frac{\sum Q_i}{n} - \frac{b\sum X_i}{n}$$

$$b = \frac{n\sum X_i Q_i - \sum X_i \sum Q_i}{n\sum Xi^2 - (\sum X_i)^2}$$

Here in the above formulas; Q_i values are log Y_i values, that is, the logarithmic values of the past sales values of Y_i while X_i values are the numbered time periods, as explained earlier in the linear trend analysis. Thus, since we defined ($Q_i = \log Y_i$),

$$\sum Q_i = \sum \log Y_i$$

Similarly, the sum of the multiplication of $\sum X_i\, Q_i$ is;

$$\sum X_i\, Q_i = \sum X_i \log Y_i$$

Thus, once the appropriate data is provided for the above given least square model, a and b values would be easily computed for the regression equation of;

$$Q = a + b\,x$$

However, recall that the dependent variable Q was previously defined above as;

$$Q = \log y$$

Therefore, in order to estimate the sales in the year 2018 and thus give a period number equal to 9 for the independent variable x, the regression equation would be:

$$Q = a + b \qquad (9)$$

Finally, taking the antilog of the computed Q value, the sales in 2018 will be estimated, that is;

$$\hat{Y}_{2018} = \text{antilog } Q$$

However, if one desires to determine clearly the exponential with its appropriate coefficients as,

$$y = AB^{x}$$

Then we have to take the antilog values of a and b values to get the A and B coefficients of the exponential model as given below:

$$\text{antilog } a = A$$

$$\text{antilog } b = B$$

Accordingly, when we are desire to forecast the sales for a period, say, numbered 9th year, the estimate would be computed as:

$$y = AB^{x}$$

$\hat{Y}_{2018} = AB^9$

Now for the sake of providing a workable example for the exponential curve estimation, assume that the statistical past data regarding the sales volumes for a product in a certain market segment during the time period between 2009 and 2017 are as given in Table 2. If the numbering of time periods (X_i) is started from zero, that is, the year 2009 is given a zero value, the coefficients of the exponential curve are computed through Excel spreadsheet as given on the right side of the Table 2.

As seen, the forecast for the year 2018 is 11.4234 billion units, that is, 11,423,400 units. Similarly, the exponential model is:

antilog a = A

antilog b = B

A = antilog(0.7552) = 5.691

B = antilog(0.0336) = 1.08

Thus, the exponential model is:

Table 2. Sales (2009-2017)

Years	Xi	Sales (Billion Units)	log Sales (Yi)		
2009	0	4,94	0,6937	a	0,7552
2010	1	6,21	0,7931	b	0,0336
2011	2	7,18	0,8561		
2012	3	7,74	0,8887	Q= a + bX	
2013	4	8,38	0,9232	Q= 0,7552+0,0336*Xi	
2014	5	8,45	0,9269	Q= 0,7552+0,0336*9	
2015	6	8,73	0,941	Q	1,0578
2016	7	9,42	0,9741	y (antilog Q)	11,4234
2017	8	10,24	1,0103		
2018	9	11,42	1,0578		

$\hat{Y} = AB^x$

$\hat{Y}_{2018} = {}_{5.691}(1.08)^9$

$\hat{Y}_{2018}$ = 11.4 billion units (neglecting rounding errors).

c. The Gompertz Curve:

One of the widely used logarithmic trend analysis is the so-called *Gompertz curve* that is formulated as:

$$y = ka^{b^x}$$

where;

y: denotes sales (Y_i) as the dependent variable,
k, a, and b: are coefficients of the Gompertz curve. Depending on the logarithmic values of these coefficients, the curve would have concave or convex and increasing or decreasing shapes or profiles.
x: shows the time periods (X_i) as the independent variable.

The model requires the length of the past data series, that is, the number of past periods or years to be divisible by 3. Accordingly, whatever the number of past years is the series is divided by 3 and defined as cycles n_1, n_2, and n_3. Then, the logarithmic values of the past data (sales Y_i) are taken and summed up for 3 cycles. Finally, on the basis of logarithmic values of the three cycles, the values of coefficients of b, a, and k are consecutively computed. The computations involved are somewhat tedious and thus thanks computer spreadsheet programs like Excel for very quick solutions.

For example, let us estimate the sales revenues in the year 2018 on the basis of the past data series for the years between 2009 and 2017 as given previously in Table 2. On the basis of the same data in Table 2, the coefficients of the Gompertz curve are calculated through Microsoft Excel spreadsheet as given below (see Box 4).

As seen, the coefficients of the Gompertz curve are calculated as:

b = 0.7782

Box 4.

	Years	Sales (million TL)	log Sales				b^3	0,4713
							b	**0,7782**
	2009	4,94	0,6937					
n1	2010	6,21	0,7931	Sum of n1	2,3429		loga	-0,3141
	2011	7,18	0,8561				a	0,4851
	2012	7,74	0,8887					
n2	2013	8,38	0,9232	Sum of n2	2,7388		logk	1,0306
	2014	8,45	0,9269				k	10,7297
	2015	8,73	0,941					
n3	2016	9,42	0,9741	Sum of n3	2,9254		log y=log k+b^x log a	
	2017	10,24	1,0103				logy	0,9977
	2018	9,9471	0,9977				y	9,9471

a = 0.4851

k = 10.73

Therefore, the Gompertz curve model would be:

$$y = ka^{b^x}$$

$$y = (10.73)(.4852)^{(0.7782)^x}$$

This model may be stated more easily in a logarithmic form as follows:

$$\log y = \log k + b^x \log a$$

If the logarithmic values of k and a are put on the right hand side of the equation, the model would be;

$$\log y = 1.0306 + (0.7782)^x (-0.3141)$$

Consequently, in order to forecast the sales revenues in the year 2018, which would be the 9th year in the time series if the time series is numbered from 0, then the estimate of the model would be:

$\log y = 1.0306 + (0.7782)^9 (-0.3141)$

$\log y = 0.9977$ (if we take the antilog of this value we get the estimate for 2018 as)

$Y_{2018} = 9.9471$ billion units.

One may compare the estimates of the exponential and Gompertz curves and see the difference with the same set of data. Needless to say, the strength of each model should be evaluated for different forecasting objectives. Unfortunately, the evaluation of forecasting methods is out of the scope of this study[3].

2. **Causal Models:** Aim at forecasting a variable on the basis of the factors affecting it. For this purpose, at first, the possible factors affecting (determining) the changes in the variable to be forecasted are specified and, then, data (either time series or cross-section) concerning the variable to be forecasted (dependent variable) as well as the related explaining factors (independent variables) are gathered. Later on, depending on the relationship conceived between the dependent and independent variables either an existing or an econometric model to be developed is used to forecast the future values of the dependent variable.

Out of the causal models the most widely used models are linear regression models developed through *regression analysis*. In a *regression analysis* the relationship between the dependent and independent explanatory variables is assumed to linear. Once a linear trend is determined depending on the changes of values of independent variables, the forecasted values of the dependent variable are computed according to the linear trend. However, if regression analysis or the other existing methods for forecasting are not suitable, an analyst may develop his or her own *econometric model* stated, perhaps, as simultaneous equations.

Regression analysis is a widely used forecasting technique and there are various statistical computer packages to do the necessary computational analysis easily. In regression analysis, if the variable to be forecasted (dependent variable) is associated with one explanatory (independent) variable, that is, if dependent variable is tried to be explained by a single independent variable, the technique is called *simple regression analysis*. Otherwise, if more than one independent variable is used to explain the changes in the dependent variable, the analysis is called *multiple regression analysis*. In order to explain how this technique is used to make forecasts, let us assume that an analyst who wants to estimate the demand for or the sales of a product in a certain market area for the next two years by the multiple regression analysis. Moreover, the analyst believes that the changes in the sales (Y_i) are explained by the annual promotional expenses (mostly advertisement expenditures) (X_{i2}) and the annual income per capita (X_{i3}).

Therefore, he/she searches for and collects the relevant data for the last 15 years as given in Table 3. Here we hasten to add that, for the sake of simplifying the computations required by the multiple regression analysis, since a dummy independent variable labeled (X_{i1}) is included in the calculation procedure as a unit matrix, the numbering of real independent variables starts from 2 in the form of X_{2i}, X_{3i}, ..., X_{ki} as shown in Table 3.

Now, assuming a linear relationship between the sales volume (dependent variable) (Y_i) and independent variables X_{2i} (promotional expenses) and X_{3i}, (income per capita), the linear estimation model of the regression analysis with two independent variables would be stated as:

$$\hat{Y}_i = b_1 + b_2 X_{2i} + b_3 X_{3i} + e_i \ (i = 1, 2, \ldots\ldots., n)$$

where:

$\hat{Y}_i$: The value of the dependent variable (sales volume) to be estimated for the ith observation,
n: The number of observations. For our example n is 15 (i = 1, 2, 3, ..., 15),
b_1: The starting value (intercept) of the regression line,
X_{2i}: Annual promotional expenses for the ith observation,
X_{3i}: Income per unit for the ith observation,
b_2 and b_3: The coefficients of slopes of independent variables, respectively,
e_i: The portion of the dependent variable that is not explained by the changes in the independent variables, that is, the error of estimates. If the changes

Table 3. The Distribution of Promotional Expenses and Income per Capita for the Last 15 Years

Years	Sales Volume (000 tons) (Y_i)	Promotional Expenses ($ 000) (X_{2i})	Income per Capita ($ 000) (X_{3i})
2003	360	25	5.0
2004	395	30	5.0
2005	410	30	5.4
2006	405	32	5.5
2007	420	35	5.9
2008	450	38	6.0
2009	455	37	5.8
2010	440	37	6.0
2011	460	38	6.9
2012	480	37	7.2
2013	520	40	7.0
2014	455	35	6.8
2015	520	45	7.3
2016	510	45	7.0
2017	560	48	7.8
n = 15 years			

in the independent variables explain all the change in the dependent value, then the value e_i would be zero (0) the ith observation.

Compared to the computations involved in the simple regression analysis as explained earlier, calculating the coefficients of the multiple regression models is quite time consuming due to the number of independent variables. Thus, we thank ones again to computers and/or package programs such as SPSS for solving multiple regression models. The SPSS solution of our example is given in Boxes 5-7 as the output of the package program.

Therefore, the regression equation is:

$$\hat{Y}_i = 102{,}963.024 + 5.223\ X_{2i} + 25.499\ X_{3i}$$

As noticed, this model about the linear relationship between the dependent variable (sales volume) and independent variables (annual promotional expenses and income per capita) is determined on the basis of 15 past

Box 5.

Model Summary									
Model	R	R Square	Adjusted R Square	Std. Error of the Estimate	Change Statistics				
					R Square Change	F Change	df1	df2	Sig. F Change
1	,975[a]	,951	,943	13,066763	,951	116,291	2	12	,000

a. Predictors: (Constant), Income, Promotion

Box 6.

ANOVA[a]						
Model		Sum of Squares	df	Mean Square	F	Sig.
1	Regression	39711,117	2	19855,558	116,291	,000[b]
	Residual	2048,883	12	170,740		
	Total	41760,000	14			

a. Dependent Variable: Sales
b. Predictors: (Constant), Income, Promotion

Box 7.

Coefficients[a]						
Model		Unstandardized Coefficients		Standardized Coefficients	t	Sig.
		B	Std. Error	Beta		
1	(Constant)	102963,024	25063,635		4,108	,001
	Promotion	5,223	1,169	,591	4,469	,001
	Income	25,499	8,121	,415	3,140	,009

a. Dependent Variable: Sales

observations. Thus, it may be subject to sampling errors and that there might be no relationship between the variables in question. That is, the coefficients (b_2 and b_3) indicating the magnitude of the relationship may not be significantly different from zero (0 or no relationship) and that the values computed may just be because of a chance. Accordingly, before using a regression model determined to forecast a dependent variable, its level of significance and/or validity for forecasting has to be tested according to some statistical tests such as F and t tests, which would not be explained here[3].

Nevertheless, according to the statistics given above in the computer solution output, the regression model determined is significant as a whole at $\alpha = 0.05$ risk level since its computed F value is greater than the standard Table value of F (with $df_1 = 2$ and $df_2 = 12$ degrees of freedom at $\alpha = 0.05$ risk level) given in Appendix 2. That is, $F = 116.291 > F_{0.05;2;12} = 3.89$.

Furthermore, the value of "R Square" (0.951) shown in the computer output given above is defined as *the coefficient of multiple determination* (R^2) in regression analysis and it indicates that the independent variables (annual promotional expenses and income per capita) together explains 95.1 percent of the changes in the sales volume. Accordingly, it might be inferred that the linear regression model is meaningful and explains 95.1% of changes in the sales volume at the 5 percent risk level chosen. However, when time series data is used in practice, the problem of "autocorrelation" should be taken into consideration.

On the other hand, the overall significance of a regression model evaluated though F tests does not ensure that each coefficient of the model is significant per se. Therefore, each coefficient of the independent variables has to be evaluated through t tests to see whether or not they are significant at a certain risk level. However, without any further explanation, it could be indicated that since the computed t values for all coefficients of independent variables (b_i), as seen in the last part of the above given computer output, are greater than that of the standard Table value of t given in Appendix 3 (with df = 12 degrees of freedom at a two-tailed risk level of $\alpha_{/2} = 0.025$), $t_{0.025:12} = 2.1788$, the coefficients of independent variables (b_i) are significant.

Therefore, the linear estimation model may be used to forecast sales volume. For now, if we assume that the project analyst wants to estimate the size of the demand or the sales volume in a market when the promotional expenses are \$ 50,000 and the income per capita is \$ 7,500, the estimate for the sales volume would possibly be:

$X_{2i} = \$\ 50{,}000$

$X_{3i} = \$\ 7{,}500$

$\hat{Y}_i = 102{,}963.024 + 5.223\ X_{2i} + 25.499\ X_{3i}$

$$\hat{Y}_i = 102{,}963.024 + 5.223\ (50{,}000) + 25.499\ (7{,}500)$$

$$\hat{Y}_i = 555{,}355.52 \text{ tons.}$$

DETERMINING THE MARKETING STRATEGY

The foregoing studies concerning the market analysis that were explained so far must have clarified the degree of competition in terms of dimensions and tools of competition, numbers and capabilities of competitors, and trends and dynamics of market operations as well as the size of the market at present and in the future as just estimated above. Now, the project manager needs to determine a marketing strategy in order to decide in advance how the investment project is going to compete in this targeted market. Therefore, by taking into account all these factors and the related information obtained, the project manager has to develop a marketing strategy or a plan indicating how the project would compete and strive to get a satisfying market share when entered into the defined market.

Developing a marketing strategy or a marketing plan refers to the task of preparing a so-called marketing mix which requires deciding on four basic factors at the same time; namely, product, price, promotion, and place (i.e., distribution) policies of a company:

Product

In the light of the information obtained so far the project manager at this point of the market analysis should be able to make certain decisions about the sales or marketing characteristics of the product to be manufactured. These characteristics involve properties relevant with a product per se in terms of quality, physical appearance, shape, color, taste, packaging, etc. Such characteristics of a product identify the physical peculiarities of a product to appeal to consumers in the marketplace. Therefore, the information about consumers' purchasing attitudes, preferences, and tastes as well as the characteristics of the products of essential competitors in terms of quality, image, appearance, and packaging is of great value as explained and emphasized in the previous sections on demand and supply sides analyses.

In brief, as the first task of developing a marketing strategy, the final characteristics of the product to be produced are decided upon and most likely they will not be changed any more. That is to say the final quality and physical characteristics of the product are decided for determining technical requirements of the product to be manufactured later on in the stage of the technical analysis. In other words, at this first step of developing a marketing strategy, the product that is planned to be produced through the foreign direct investment is clearly defined in terms of physical appearance and marketing characteristics to appeal to consumers so that they hopefully purchase it. Otherwise, if the product to be manufactured would not appeal to the consumers in the target market and thus not purchased by them as desired, the investment would be a loss. Various new strategies are recommended for pleasing customers when designing service quality that might also be beneficial for designing products (Stewart & O'Connell, 2016).

Price

The second decision for developing a marketing strategy is to determine the price of the product whose characteristics are outlined above. By taking into account the degree of competition as well as the prices of essential rivals, an appropriate price for the product should be determined. Price is an essential tool for competition. So the project manager has to consider all influencing factors to make the right decision. Some of possible pricing strategies are as stated blow (Kotler & Keller, 2016; Austin, n.d.; Kotler & Armstrong, 2018):

- **Cost-Plus Strategy:** Is followed when a company adds a certain profit margin to its manufacturing costs. This strategy is also called *mark-up pricing* in that the ratio of profit margin is determined as a certain percentage over cost (in some cases over selling price). For instance, if the average unit cost of a product is 30 dollars and 6 dollars are added as profit margin, then the product is sold for 36 dollars and the mark-up is 20% (6/30=0.20) on cost. But the mark-up is 16.7% (6/36=0.167) on sales price. This strategy is suitable for easy markets where competition is not severe.
- **Market Price Strategy:** Is followed by business firms when they sell their products at the prices determined in the marketplace through demand and supply conditions. Thus, firms change their prices according to changing market conditions. In some cases, some companies add some extra features to differentiate their product so as

to be sold for higher prices. Thus, they increase rather than decrease prices to compete.

- **Penetration Price Strategy:** Is determining a lower price than those of competitors to enter a competitive market. This strategy is usually followed when a company plans to overcome barriers to enter a market and wishes to obtain a larger share of it.
- **Loss-Leader Strategy:** Refers to the practice of pricing a product below its cost with the intention of attracting consumers to buy the other products of the company. Thus, the loss from one product is anticipated to be compensated through the profits from the others. For a firm to practice this strategy it has to manufacture at least two types of products.
- **Price Leadership Strategy:** Is a pricing strategy based on the price of the firm leading the market. In other words, firms follow and set their prices equal or quite close to the price of the leader(s) of the market. There is no secret price agreement among companies as in price cartels or in oligopolistic competition. They do it willingly according to the market conditions. However, in countries where competition is protected by laws, public authorities may investigate the matter and if there is some sort of clandestine agreement, they all will be fined. But in most of the developing countries this may not be a problem.
- **Skimming Strategy:** Is quite different in the sense that a company following this strategy sets a higher price for skimming off or getting the richest segment of the market. This happens in marketplaces where there is almost no competition and/or the product is a new one with very unique characteristics and images. For instance, in countries where local markets are protected against imports by higher walls of customs duties, the skimming strategy may seem appropriate to follow.
- **Predatory Pricing Strategy:** Aims at wiping out competitors from the market as well as preventing new comers to enter in by setting prices significantly below their prices. This pricing strategy is aggressive and illegal in countries where competition is preserved by law and public authorities.
- **Controlled and Subsidized Pricing Strategy:** Involves the intervention of public authorities in some countries to control the prices of some products and/or to subsidize them, such as the prices of products like wheat, oil, electricity, etc. In such cases, project managers have no control over product pricing, except to follow governmental regulations and observe the market operations.

Consequently, in the light of such pricing strategies as well as the prices of competitors, the project manager should decide about the price of the product whose sales or marketing characteristics were determined in detail as stated before. No doubt that product and price are two essential factors for competition and they are inversely related with respect to marketing potential. That is, a good product would probably have a higher price that may affect sales negatively depending on the price elasticity of demand.

Promotion

For now that the project manager has decided on the final specifications or characteristics of the product to be produced and that the unit selling price is determined, the next step for developing a marketing strategy is to decide on how to promote the product. In other words, manufacturing a good product with an adequate price is not always enough for a marketing success or a desired level of sales in competitive markets because consumers may not be aware of such a product or not pay attention to it. Thus, business firms should look for some ways to have consumers be aware of their products and prices. In general, promotion involves all kinds of efforts such as advertising, personal selling, sales promotion, and public relations which aim at increasing the sales of a product. Therefore, what is needed then is to develop and plan efficient promotional activities in order to get the consumers be aware of the good product, hear about its suitable price, and see the other advantages so as to buy it.

Consequently, the project manager should search for possible ways and decide how to promote the product. That is, which *massage* should be given to which *audience* through which *channels* and with what *vehicles* are key points to be decided upon. Here, the word "massage" refers to the characteristics and advantages of the product to be transmitted, "audience" involves those who decide on purchasing of the product, and "cannels and vehicles" cover mass communication tools. This sequence of questioning the efficiency of promotional activities is supposed to be the base of designing an effective promotional campaign and that it also is considered as a golden key for a successful promotional activity.

As it might be recalled, the information needed for deciding about the key points of a promotional activity is gathered when the purchasing process of consumers is analyzed at the beginning of the market analysis. For instance, the answer to the question "who is making the purchasing decision" defines the "audience" that the "massage" of the promotional activity is to be transmitted. Therefore, at this stage of the market analysis, the project manager has to determine the promotional activities of a campaign required during the operating period of the investment project and, then, to estimate the total annual promotional expenses which will be regarded as sales costs in the financial analysis of the project.

Distribution

The basic purpose of distribution function is to make a product available to consumers at the required time, in the required places, and in the required quantity with minimum cost. As seen, distribution involves physical movement of products and thus it becomes a quite expensive function for a company to carry out. The costs of distribution do not solely involve transportation costs of products. The bulk of the costs include the cost of inventories in the sense of keeping the produced items in storage. In other words, the costs related to distribution function are as follows:

- **Transportation Costs:** Simply refer to costs of activities for physically moving products from factory to sales points.
- **Inventory Carrying Costs:** Include two essential cost items: *(1) opportunity cost* of tying up funds in inventories rather than using them elsewhere to earn income and; *(2) warehousing costs* of rent, security, energy, insurance, and maintenance such as deterioration, spoilage, breakage, etc.

On the other hand, trying to reduce inventory costs by carrying fewer inventories would lead to *shortage costs* of inventory when demand for a product is not met, in terms of the unrealized profit and especially the customers lost. Nevertheless, the most important aspect of shortage costs is that of losing customers due to not providing the required amount of products at the right time in the purchasing places. That is, if fewer inventories are carried out at selling points to reduce inventory costs, customers most likely would not find the product at the time they want to buy. Therefore, if this shortage of the product happens often, customers would eventually purchase products of competitors and thus would be lost or left to rival firms. On the contrary, if too much inventories are made available at the selling points all the time in order to prevent any customer loss due to not finding the product at the purchasing time, the inventory carrying costs would hike up. Accordingly, a project manager has to take into account all cost factors related to the distribution function and develop an optimal distribution policy.

Physical distribution or movement of products from factory to consumers is carried out through two essential ways; *direct* or *indirect* distribution as shown below in Figure 2. In *direct distribution* the producer, that is, the production factory distributes products directly to consumers and incurs all distribution costs mentioned above. This way of distribution gives a producer the chance of keeping in touch closely with its consumers so that good relations could be established to satisfy the needs of consumers as well as to minimize loss of costumers. Unfortunately, establishing an efficient direct distribution system is quite expensive with respect to the fixed costs of warehouses, transportation vehicles, and the related personnel.

On the contrary, in the case of *indirect distribution*, a producer uses the services of intermediaries to move products to the market places and make available for consumers. The intermediaries are layered at generally two levels, wholesalers and retailers. Accordingly, products are first sent to wholesalers that later distribute them to retailers. Retailers are the essential points of distributing products to consumers in direct distribution policy. Sometimes there are even no wholesalers and the producers distribute products to retailers that then sell them to consumers. That is, the length of the channel is shortened. However, in some cases, the length of distribution channel is further increased through representatives and/or distributors above the level of wholesalers. That is, producers send products to distributors or representatives which in turn distribute them to wholesalers.

Wholesalers and retailers as intermediaries take over distribution costs and function on the basis of discount commissions. For instance, consider this simplified example: if a producer decides to sell a product in the retail market for $30, the producer may sell it to wholesalers for $20 and then the wholesalers will sell it to retailers, for example, for $24. Finally, the retailers

Figure 2. Distribution Channels

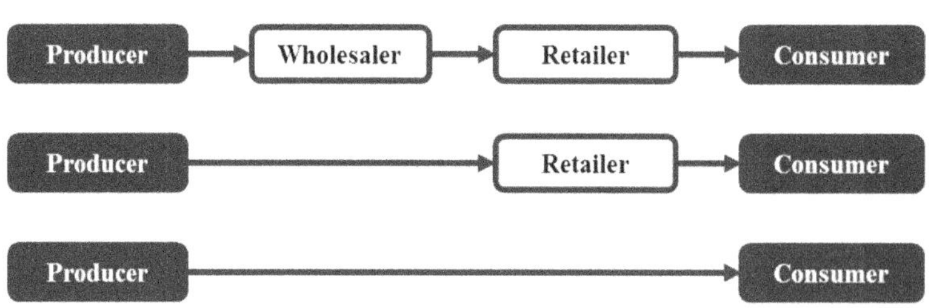

will sell the product to customers for $30. Therefore, intermediaries are paid for their distribution costs through commissions as discounts on the sales price. From the viewpoint of cost considerations, indirect distribution has lots of advantages because distribution costs are passed over to intermediaries in terms of discount commissions. However, in such a distribution system based on intermediaries, producers lose their direct relations with their consumers and, thus, if intermediaries will not function properly, loss of customers will be inevitable.

The number of levels that products move through is called a *distribution channel* and thus the length of a distribution channel depends on the levels of intermediaries. As such, direct distribution does not have any level of intermediation since a company sells directly to consumers. The most common distribution channel is one that goes through wholesalers and retailers and thus defines an indirect distribution policy. As indicated above, both the direct and indirect distribution alternatives have advantages as well as disadvantages in terms of costs incurred and relations established with consumers.

Nonetheless, selecting a distribution system or determining the length of marketing channels usually depends on some additional restricting factors which might be summarized below:

1. **Characteristics of Consumers:** The characteristics of consumers in terms of their numbers, geographical dispersion in the market, and purchasing behaviors such as how often and in what quantity they buy are all important factors that affect the decision about selecting a distribution channel. For instance, in a market where consumers are spread over a very large geographical area and that they buy the product wherever they see it, a direct distribution system would not be efficient since it will be too costly. In other words, in such large scaled cases, establishing a direct distribution system with all required warehouses, special transportation vehicles, and the related personnel for operating it necessitates a great deal of investment. Thus, an indirect distribution becomes inevitable.
2. **Characteristics of the Product:** Similarly, the characteristics of a product such as the possibility and duration of spoilage, fragility, size, and weight also restrict the selection decision for evaluating alternative marketing channels. For example, for food products which get quickly spoiled and/or lose weight significantly, direct distribution would be the most appropriate one to reduce the time for distribution.

3. **Degree of Competition:** The degree of competition in the targeted market is perhaps the most significant factor that determines the selection of a channel for distribution per se. Producers will try to use every possible distribution channel (wholesalers and/or retailers) to reach to as many consumers as possible so as to increase their sales. Therefore, the products whose characteristics are suitable and that do not create time constraints for distribution, length of marketing channels will be determined according to degree of competition in the market. For instance, in markets where consumers purchase products in an "impulsive way" whenever they see it, an indirect distribution policy based on a large number of retailers seems to be more appropriate. Nonetheless, international investors may confront with various problems when dealing with many retailers, so local wholesalers might be considered in the indirect distribution system to get them deal and develop business relations with the large number of retailers more easily.

In brief, in a market analysis at this point of the study, the project manager should consider all relevant factors and then make the right decision regarding an optimal distribution system. Suffice to say, the final decision about the length of marketing channels and the distribution policy will be made when plant location in the country selected is determined, as will be explained later in the chapter on Technical Analysis. At this point it should also be indicated that after the distribution system is determined and defined, the project manager has to estimate all fixed costs as well the as operating costs associated with the physical distribution of the product in question. As indicated earlier, the activities and thus the costs related to physical distribution of products from factories to consumers are transportation, communication, warehousing, and inventory carrying costs.

Consequently, having determined the so-called factors for determining an appropriate marketing strategy; namely, product, price, promotion, and distribution, the project manager has to consider the interaction of all these factors together and determine the optimal combination of them as the basic marketing strategy. These factors that form a marketing strategy are, in fact, contradictory to each other in the sense that when one becomes better the others become worse. For example, a product of good quality which is distributed quickly and promoted well becomes very expensive and thus it may be quite difficult to sell it. In such contradictory cases, the pragmatic framework suggested by Nonaka and Zhu (2012) would be quite helpful for shaping and solving strategic problems in a practical and creative manner.

Therefore, an optimal combination and balancing of all related factors with respect to "product", "price", "promotion", and "distribution" is an important point of consideration to determine an efficient marketing strategy. In the simplest meaning of the word, an efficient marketing strategy indicates how a company is going to compete in the target market. As it might be recalled the purchasing attitudes and behaviors of consumers as well as the degree of competition in the market are essential factors in developing a successful marketing strategy. Therefore, as stated previously, answers to the questions about the purchasing process of consumers in terms of "when", "where", "in what quantity", and "how" consumers purchase are valuable sources of information for developing a successful marketing strategy, not to mention the importance of the analysis of competitive environment of the target market.

ESTIMATING THE MARKET SHARE

Now that up to this point of the market analysis, the target market is analyzed in terms of the size, structure, determinants and degree of competition, essential competitors, their capabilities, strengths, and weaknesses; then the project manager should try to estimate the possible market share that the investment project could capture through the marketing strategy just developed. Despite the bulk of information available, unfortunately, there is no clear-cut methodology to follow for estimating the market share of a new company entering into a market. Accordingly, what is done in practice is a kind of judgmental evaluation of the information obtained so far regarding the factors specified above.

This judgmental evaluation procedure for estimating the market share that a new company may capture in the targeted market involves the following steps:

1. The starting point is the size of the target market at present and in the future years. Therefore, as explained previously, the size of the target market along the operating years of the direct investment project has to be estimated through a reliable forecasting technique in specific terms. For example, for an automobile market in a country the estimates may be: (900,000 cars) in the year 2019, (980,000 cars) in 2020, (1,100,000) in 2021, …….., and (2,125,000 cars) in 2028.
2. The market shares of the essential competitors at present and the possibility of continuing in the future years should be estimated as much as possible on the basis of: (a) the present sales, brand images,

strengths, and weaknesses of essential competitors; (b) the possibility of competitors maintaining, increasing, or losing their present market shares in the future years, and; (c) the possible marketing strategy of essential competitors at present and the most likely strategy that they may follow in the next years. For instance, let us assume that in the automobile market indicated above there are three essential manufacturing competitors with market shares estimated to be around 30%, 25%, and 15% and also several other companies sharing the remaining market through exporting cars to the country in question.

3. To get a feeling concerning the potential market share of the investment project, the possible share of each essential competitor and a close approximation for all the remaining other exporting competitors should be added up to find out the total market share that is most likely captured by all competitors. This total market share of competitors may be compared with the estimated market size in the future through a judgmental evaluation such as this: For instance, as stated above, in the targeted car market there are three essential competitors with estimated possible market shares of 30%, 25%, and 15%. Additionally, the other rival companies sharing the remaining market through exporting cars are thought to have a total share of 20%. Therefore, all together 90% of the market seems to be captured by the existing companies and that the remaining 10% of the target market is left as if free, although it is filled by varying rivals as well as several other imported brands.
4. At this point, the project manager would review the availability of the remaining market share of 10% and the possibility of capturing it through the marketing strategy developed for the direct investment project. If this 10% share of the target market does not seem to be sufficient, and even the project manager believes that some existing competitors will capture some portion of it through an aggressive marketing strategy; then the market analysis should be ended and the investment planned in the selected country should be abandoned as well. In such a case, there seems to be no chance to establish a profitable business since the market share expected is not enough.
5. However, let us assume that the project manager believes, for example, at least 80% of the remaining market share of 10% not captured by the competitors, that is, (80% x 10% =) 8% of the whole target market would most likely be obtained through the marketing strategy developed for the investment project. Then, he/she may look for the possibility of obtaining some additional share from competitors. The project manager may even

modify the marketing strategy developed already; for example, reducing the unit price by 5% and increasing promotional expenditures by 10% in the first year of the operating period. Finally, the project manager is convinced that through such a change in the marketing strategy an additional market share of 4% in total would possibly be obtained. Thus, it is believed that the most plausible market share to be seized by the investment project would be (8% + 4% =) 12% on the average. That is, according to the data of the above given car market, (900,000 x 0.12 =) 108,000 cars in the year 2019, (980,000 x 0.12 =) 117,600 cars in 2020, (1,100,000 x 0.12 =) 132,000 cars in 2021, ..., and (2,125,000 x 0.12 =) 255.000 cars in 2028.

Consequently, if this most likely market share of 12% is still considered to be small or not enough for the direct investment project planned, the market analysis and thus the investment planned in the country selected should be given up because the product of the contemplated direct investment is not marketable, that is, would not capture a large enough market share. However, if the 12% market share is thought to be sufficient enough, the market analysis will be completed after preparing a sales report as indicated below and the feasibility study for the direct investment project will continue with the technical analysis.

PREPARING THE SALES (MARKETING) REPORT

As the last step of the market analysis, once the market share is estimated and considered to be sufficient, the most plausible market share to be captured (i.e., 12% as above) should be reviewed again by taking into account the most likely marketing strategies of competitors as well as that of the direct investment project to be followed in the years ahead. If the project manager is still convinced that the market share estimated is realistic and that it would be sufficient in the years to come; then, the possible sales volume of the investment project in the future years are computed simply through multiplying the size of the target market forecasted earlier by the market share to be captured, as done above. Thus, a sales report summarizing the possible sales in the future years during the operating period of the direct investment project should be prepared as given in Table 4.

Table 4. Estimated Sales and Promotional Expenditures

	t_{m+1}	t_{m+2}	t_{m+3}	-------------	t_{m+n}
Sales Volume (Units)[a]	108,000	117,600	132,000	--------------	255,000
Sales Expenditures (EUR)[b]	E_1	E_2	E_3	--------------	E_n

m: Duration of the establishment period.
n: Duration of the operating period.
(a) Sales are in units such as 108,000 cars.
(b) Sales expenditures are in Euros and shown by symbol E, as such E_1 is the amount of promotional expenditures in the first year of the operating period.

Additionally, as seen in the second row of the Table 4, the sales report should also include the expenses planned for promotional activities and the other related marketing campaigns as sales expenditures in the relevant years. The sales expenditures would later be added to operational expenditures of the investment project in the financial analysis. The other costs associated with the distribution policy are not shown in the sales report since the operational costs of distribution are incurred throughout the operating period of the project and thus are taken into account together with the operational expenditures. Moreover, the costs of distribution for fixed assets such as constructing warehouses and buying transportation vehicles will be considered during the establishment period of the project and are included in the fixed costs of direct investment.

CONCLUSION

In summary, the sales report is the final output of the market analysis indicating the most likely sales volume that the foreign direct investment project would possibly realize and that it is regarded by the project manager and/or investor as large enough to continue with the investment project.

REFERENCES

Armstrong, G., Kotler, P., & Opresnik, M. O. (2017). *Marketing: An Introduction* (13th ed.). Boston: Pearson Education, Ltd.

Austin, J. E. (n.d.). *Agroindustrial Project Analysis*. Washington, DC: The World Bank.

Doane, D., & Seward, L. (2010). *Essential Statistics in Business and Economics* (2nd ed.). New York: McGraw - Hill, Inc.

Hyndman, R. J., & Athanasopoulos, G. (2018). Forecasting: Principles and Practice (2nd ed.). OTexts.com.

Keegan, W. J., & Gren, M. C. (2017). *Global Marketing* (9th ed.). New York: Pearson Books.

Kotler, P., & Armstrong, G. (2018). *Principles of Marketing* (17th ed.). Boston: Pearson Education, Inc.

Kotler, P., Kartajaya, H., & Setiawan, I. (2017). *Marketing 4.0 - Moving from Traditional to Digital*. John Wiley & Sons.

Kotler, P., & Keller, K. (2016). *Marketing Management* (15th ed.). Boston: Pearson Education, Inc.

Montgomery, D. C., Jennings, C. L., & Kulahcı, M. (2016). *Introduction to Time Series Analysis and Forecasting* (2nd ed.). Wiley.

Nonaka, I., & Zhu, Z. (2012). *Pragmatic Strategy: Eastern Wisdom, Global Success*. Cambridge, UK: Cambridge University Press. doi:10.1017/CBO9780511736568

Silvia, J. A., Swanskoski, K., Watt, S., & Bullard, S. (2014). *Economic and Business Forecasting: Analyzing and Interpreting Econometric Results*. Wiley.

Stewart, T. A., & O'Connell, P. (2016). *Woo, Wow, and Win: Service Design, Strategy, and the Art of Customer Delight*. New York, NY: Harper Collins Publishers.

ENDNOTES

1 For more on market segmentation, see Armstrong, Kotler, and Opresnik (2017) and Keegan and Gren (2017).

2 For a variety of variables or factors for segmenting markets, see Kotler, Kartajaya, and Setiawan (2017).

3 For more about evaluating forecasting models, see Doane and Seward (2010) and Silvia, Swanskoski, Watt, and Bullard (2014).

Chapter 4
Technical Analysis

ABSTRACT

A comprehensive feasibility study should continue with a technical analysis if the market analysis, as explained in the chapter, defines a sufficiently large market share for the product to be manufactured through a foreign direct investment project. The technical analysis as the second stage of a feasibility study aims at determining whether or not the production of the marketable product is technically feasible in terms of what the production technology will be, how the production process is to be designed, and where the production site would be located in the country selected. This chapter covers topics and discussions about technical aspects of establishing a production facility. Thus, it answers the question of whether the production of a product that is determined to be marketable is technically possible and, if so, how the production facility should be designed. If the investment project is technically feasible, then an implementation plan through project programing techniques of network analysis is developed for both estimating the total cost of fixed investment and planning the establishment of the plant or factory required. Thus, at the end of the technical analysis stage, the use of project programing techniques is explained for planning the implementation of an investment project.

DOI: 10.4018/978-1-5225-7696-9.ch004

DETERMINING TECHNICAL DESIGN OF THE PRODUCT

Technical design of a product refers to defining technical specifications of the desired product for production. In the simplest sense of the term, at this first stage of the technical analysis an important engineering work is going to be carried out to determine how the marketable product as defined in the market analysis would look like technically. In other words, as it is often witnessed in practice, the technical specifications that engineers figure out or plan may not fit to the marketing characteristics of the product defined and described for the marketing strategy. Therefore, everything possible should be done to fit technical specifications to marketing characteristics so as to produce a marketable product just as defined in the market analysis. Otherwise, the product decided to be marketable may turn out to be an uncompetitive product. For this purpose, the technical specifications for a marketable product should be examined from the following two aspects:

1. **Functional Specifications:** In general, a product that is going to be produced has first to perform what it is expected to perform. Otherwise, there is no reason to purchase it. Likewise, the essential function of a product is to meet the need for which it is conceived. Therefore, a product has to be so designed that it should fulfill the need which it is expected to satisfy. Otherwise, whatever the other specifications are the product would not be successful in the market since a product is essentially bought for meeting a need. Furthermore, in fact, for any product that is to be purchased for satisfying a need, the degree of satisfaction, that is, the degree of accomplishing its function is indeed a promotional factor per se. In other words, the higher the degree of accomplishing its function the higher its competitive power in the market would be.

Accordingly, functional specifications of a product have to be determined clearly as the technical standards and requirements of the product to be produced. For instance, if the marketable product of an investment project is a refrigerator, the functional properties showing that this refrigerator would hold in a certain amount of various kinds of foods, such as cheese, eggs, meat, vegetables, fruits, drinks, etc. as well as keep them cool properly have to be clearly determined first of all. That is, buyers should be convinced that the product will accomplish its essential objective of meeting the need for which it is purchased.

2. **Sales Specifications:** A product which has a functional design indicating that it will accomplish its objective should also have some attractive features to appeal to consumers as well. Otherwise, it may not be sold. For instance, if the refrigerator given above as an example is functionally well designed but its physical appearance is not attractive enough for consumers, it would certainly not be a successful product in the market. In other words, a product must have some marketing or sales specifications which appeal to the preferences and expectations of consumers. As it was explained earlier in the market analysis section, the first factor to determine in developing a marketing strategy is the sales or marketing characteristics of the product to be produced in terms of quality, physical appearance, shape, color, taste, packaging, etc. These characteristics identifying the peculiarities of a product to appeal to customers are decided in the market analysis stage as a strategy to compete in the market.

Therefore, when designing a product, the marketing or sales specifications of the product that were defined and described in the market analysis stage should be combined with those functional specifications and, thus, the final design of the product for production has to be completed. Needless to indicate at this point that the attention and care shown for fitting or harmonizing the sales specifications with functional specifications should also be given to cost considerations in the production process. Sometimes in practice during the technical design of the product, engineers may design products that might be well beyond the standards defined through the marketing strategy, as of very high quality with attractive peculiarities. Such designs would certainly conflict with the marketing strategy developed for the investment project. Therefore, when confronting with such conflicts, the problem must be resolved right away at this stage of analysis. Otherwise, it would be too late.

On the other hand, if there is going to be some changes in the technical design of the product, then the compatibility of the marketing strategy with the product design must be secured. That is to say the technical design of a product has to be suitable with the marketing strategy developed already. If not, the market analysis would be meaningless since the purpose of the market analysis in a sense is to define a marketable product. Therefore, the design and then the production of a product must be realized as it is defined by the marketing strategy or the market analysis in general.

Technical design of a product is in fact a preparation for producing that product in terms of detailed drawings showing how it would be made. It is, in fact, an engineering activity based on marketing information. In some cases, physical models or even prototypes of the product are developed to assure that the product would be produced as it is desired.

CHOOSING THE OPTIMAL PRODUCTION TECHNOLOGY

After the technical design of a product is completed, then a search for alternative technologies should be started in order to determine how the product designed would be manufactured. In general, *technology* refers to the total of *knowledge*, *skills*, and *experience* available in a society for producing a good or a service. Within this general context, the concept of technology is sometimes regarded as *the state of the art* of a society in terms of its production capabilities. In contrast to this general definition, however, in practice, technology is often used in a narrower sense of the term indicating the technical knowledge needed to produce a product. For this reason, technology is usually defined in practice as *know-how* to indicate the technical knowledge required for manufacturing a product. This narrower meaning of the term is also preferred in this book. Accordingly, once the technical design of a product is completed, the appropriate technology (know-how) needed to produce that product should be looked for.

In order to determine or to choose the appropriate technology one has to be aware of the available alternative technologies. Therefore, a search for alternative technologies should be started in order to find out what alternatives are available for producing the product just designed. This search should be considered as a research activity for determining all existing alternative technologies for production. As such, project managers should not restrict themselves with limited alternatives they know; rather look for all new developments in the related field of production. As stated earlier, especially at this point of the technical analysis, there is definitely a need for the service of an engineer. So, through the help and support of engineers, the project manager should search for alternative technologies to produce the marketable product whose design is completed. In fact, such decisions are usually made simultaneously and there is always a feed-back loop functioning throughout all studies. The possible alternative production technologies that are searched for are generally available in three possible ways:

Exclusive Technology

The technological alternative could be a new and *exclusive technology* developed by the investor specifically for production of the product in question. Thus, the investing company has all license and pertaining patent rights. However, in this case, the validity of the exclusive technology has to be proven in the sense of its ability and efficiency in producing the product according to its technical design. Perhaps, the so-called pilot-runs of production are recommended actions to ensure that the exclusive technology is indeed effective.

Generalized Common Technology

The alternative technology could be a general technology that may be used by any company to produce a certain product. That is, any engineer in the field of production could design a production system so as to manufacture the product without any problem. The product of such generalized production systems is more or less standardized but companies may add some extra features to the product without any technical restriction if they can. For example, iron casting operation can generally be done by any metallurgical engineer. However, some engineers might have developed some additional special methods for more efficient production in terms of quality, production speed, defective production rate, etc. It should also be added that when technology to be used for production is a generalized common one, the possible ways of developing it further or any additional contribution to it should be searched for so as to make sure that the production technology to be used is not behind the level of those used by competitors.

Licensed Technology

Another technological alternative could be a *licensed technology* usually developed by multinational companies from the developed industrial countries. Such licensed technologies are, in fact, not many so the owners of such technologies may enjoy a quasi-monopolistic power in the market. Furthermore, licensed technologies are the intellectual properties of big multinational companies, which may be obtained or transferred only through a *license agreement*. A license agreement is a legal and binding contract between a *licensor* (the one providing know-how) and a *licensee* (the one obtaining know-how), which necessarily requires a license fee to be paid. The license fee is called *royalty* and it is generally paid in two ways: A *lump-sum royalty* paid at once in total when the license agreement is signed and a *running royalty* which is paid either as a percentage of the value of the production or the sales realized along the operating period of a project.

The licensee would often insist on a running royalty to be paid as a percentage of the sales realized in order not to face liquidity or cash problems in case sales drop. On the contrary, the licensor request a running royalty as a percentage of the value of production such that dropping sales would not affect license fees. Naturally, this deal will depend on the bargaining power and the ability of the licensee. The content of a license agreement contract is quite comprehensive and could involve some very important restrictions that prevent a company from carrying out its production and marketing activities freely. Therefore, in transferring a licensed technology through a license agreement, a licensee has to be very careful and must take into account the following important factors regarding the technology to be transferred as well as additional requirements associated with license agreement:

1. The licensor should have experience either as a producer in manufacturing of similar goods, and/or as a technology owner dealing with license agreements. Moreover, the ability of the licensor to provide technical support in case needed should also be considered. Choosing the right licensor is quite important when there are few alternatives. It should be kept in mind that some multinational companies produce technology just as a service package and then sell it for a license fee, usually in the form of "turnkey projects". A turnkey project is a contract agreement through which a multinational company completely plans, builds, and equips a production system and then when it is ready for operation, turns it over to a purchasing firm for an agreed amount of payment. Such companies may not have experience in manufacturing and thus lack of providing technical supporting services along production activities.
2. The amount of royalty should not exceed those of the other license agreements made previously. In other words, the licensee should try to make a kind of "most favored customer" contract agreement in the sense that the licensee would pay a royalty as much as what the licensor's most favored customer pays. Additionally, if the licensor is a foreign

company, how and in what foreign currency the royalty is to be paid should also be clarified. In case of transferring running royalties to licensor's home country, if there would be any additional tax payments, such as withholding and/or value added taxes involved in, the license agreement should clarify this point of controversy when the contract is signed.

3. The licensor should try to have the "right of exclusivity", if possible; that is, to be the only one to use the technology in a market. This is a significant point to pay attention when operating in a foreign country with a technology license agreement from a multinational company. Otherwise, a foreign firm may lose its competitive power later on if a rival firm producing with the same licensed technology enters into the same market. Thus, a firm that would operate in a foreign country should insist on having the "right of exclusivity".
4. The duration of the license agreement should be adequate so that the technology and/or know-how could be absorbed and that of the pertaining patent rights should be matched with it as well. In almost all channels or methods of transferring technology the ultimate objective is to absorb the technology or know-how transferred after a certain period of time. Although absorbing and then using licensed technologies is not possible without any license agreement, nonetheless, the duration of license agreement should be long enough at least to realize production efficiency.
5. The licensee should be able to sell its products anywhere desired. Conversely, the licensor should not restrict, especially, the exporting activities of the licensee. This is a very important point to dwell on when license agreements are negotiated. It is indeed not uncommon to notice that some license agreements prevent licensee firms to export to surrounding countries. Nevertheless, this is a negotiable and bargaining matter of license agreements that may also depend on the right of exclusivity in a very large market. For instance, should a foreign firm accept a license agreement giving the right of exclusivity in China but restricting selling or exporting to other surrounding countries?
6. The "confidentiality" of the know-how is an essential subject in license agreements and thus licensors try to include lots of restrictions to secure the confidentiality. Therefore, attention should be paid to those restrictions and/or terms that might create severe problems, and if possible, not include them in the contract.

7. The licensee, if possible, should avoid binding contract terms to buy spare parts and/or semi-finished products from the licensor. In other words, licensors usually include binding contract terms forcing licensees to purchase the machinery and equipment required by the technology transferred as well as the tools and spare parts used during production operations. In such cases, license fees are made attractive to get licensees approve agreements with the idea that the technology is cheap! However, if such binding agreements have to be made, the pricing practice should be clarified.
8. The license agreement should include some "*force majeure*" terms to protect the licensee in case of not fulfilling contract terms due to some uncontrollable events such as natural disasters. Since the life cycle of real capital investments in general is quite long, undesirable events and natural disasters such as earthquakes, floods, nation-wide general strikes, wars, civil wars, etc. may interrupt the business operations so that the licensee may not pay license fees on time. Thus, license agreement should include terms to watch over the licensee in such cases.
9. Furthermore, the licensee has to be careful about the legal aspects of the license agreement in terms of the language to be used in writing the agreement, the procedure to end the agreement, the court to apply in case of some disputes and disagreements regarding the implementation of the license agreement, and the appointment of referees for international arbitration if disputes are not settled through negotiations.

Whatever the type of technology in general or know-how in specific is, the essential point in search for selecting technology is to make sure that project managers are aware of all technological alternatives including the possibility of new developments as well. That is to say, the investment project should keep abreast with the technological development concerning the production process. All existing technological alternatives including those on the way to be introduced to the market must be identified and then carefully evaluated. In order to evaluate the existing technological alternatives, relevant information regarding the following points should be gathered for each alternative:

1. The state of being obsolescence in terms of the essential technical and quality specifications as well as the present and the potential future use of the alternative technology.
2. In case of evaluating licensed technology alternatives, as much information as possible about the previous license agreements with other companies.

3. The requirements of alternative technologies in terms of raw materials, semi-finished products, and skilled manpower.
4. The size of the production scale or the production capacity necessitated by each alternative, keeping in mind that each alternative technology is generally efficient for a certain amount of production.
5. The costs of machinery and equipment required for each alternative technology as well as those costs of maintenance including spare parts. The cost of machinery and equipment should not be taken into account just as of purchasing costs but rather to be considered as a kind of life cycle costing in terms of purchasing, operational, maintenance, and replacement costs.
6. The estimates of the overall cost of royalty payments for each alternative licensed technology.

Consequently, having determined the available alternative technologies and gathered the necessary information concerning each alternative as stated above; the existing alternatives should be compared on the basis of the information gathered and the optimal technology should be chosen. When evaluating alternative technologies to choose the optimal one, a classical question often comes to mind is: "should the technology be *labor intensive* or *capital incentive*?" The answer to this question in the past was that "*technology should be labor intensive if labor is abundant and cheap*". However, presently in a global world where competition is so severe, products are mostly standardized, and that production systems are heavily automated, such answers are meaningless any longer. Therefore, the degree of competition would impose the degree of density in labor or capital.

Therefore, the essential point in selecting the optimal technology is that of the ability to compete in global markets and to keep up with the pace of technological development. Unfortunately, there is no analytical approach available to use for evaluating alternative technologies and to choose the optimal one, since there are lots of economic, social, political, and even legal factors to be considered simultaneously. For this reason, from the viewpoint of the country selected for investment, a judgmental evaluation of alternative technologies is made on the basis of the following factors summarizing the information gathered as explained above:

- Capital cost requirements.
- Requirements for scarce skills.

- Suitability with local or regional raw material resources.
- Need for imported equipment.
- Energy requirements.
- The state of obsolescence.
- Suitability with the production capacity to be determined.
- Contribution to employment for obtaining governmental incentives.
- Environmental effects.
- Safety and health hazards.

Finally, considering the existing conditions of the country selected for investment as well as the marketing strategy and/or the marketing policy determined for the investment project, each technological alternative should be evaluated on the basis of the above listed factors separately and then a decision should be made about selecting the optimal technology.

DESIGNING THE PRODUCTION PROCESS

Production is the process by which goods and services are created through a production technology. Hence, once the technology is chosen to produce the product whose technical design is determined, then, developing or setting up a production process is necessary for production to start. The production process is determined on the basis of the technology chosen and covers various decisions to be made as detailed in the following subsections.

Selecting the Production Capacity

The design of a production process, first of all, requires a decision to be made about the amount of production. That is, how large the scale of production or the production capacity should be is the first point to be decided here. In the context of real capital investment projects, the concept of capacity generally refers to the amount of production realized by a factory during a certain period of time, usually a year. For instance, one may say that the production capacity of a car maker company is 25,000 automobiles per year. Nevertheless, in some cases, the production capacity is measured by the amount of the production factors (inputs) processed. Sugar industry is such an example and the capacity of sugar factories is measured by the amount of sugar beet processed during a year. For example, one may say that sugar company X has a production capacity of processing 100.000 tons sugar beets per year.

There are several measures or types of the capacity concept; such as *design (technical or theoretical) capacity*, *effective (practical) capacity*, *actual capacity*, and *optimal capacity*. *Design capacity* which is sometimes also called *technical* or *theoretical capacity* refers to the production level realized by an existing company without any downtime and/or disruption in the production process due to failure, defect, and malfunction of machinery and equipment. That is, design capacity is the maximum output that can be attained under ideal operational conditions. In contrast, *effective capacity* that is also called *practical capacity* refers to a production volume that considers normal or regular disruption in the production process for maintenance and common breakdowns in machinery and equipment. Effective capacity is less than design capacity owing to the reasons stopping production process, such as periodic maintenance of machinery and equipment, scheduling problems, and so on.

On the other hand, *actual capacity* is the amount of production that is actually realized at the end of the production process in a given period of time. It is generally less than effective capacity due to the unexpected shortages of materials and/or breakdowns of machinery and equipment, etc. However, *optimal capacity* is an ideal goal in the long-run and means a desired scale of production that minimizes average unit cost of production or maximizes profit of a company in the long run. Optimal capacity is a strategically ideal goal that each company strives to realize in the future.

Accordingly, the production capacity for an investment project should be determined such that the average unit cost of production is minimized and thus the profit of the investment is increased as much as possible. This states that the production capacity to be selected for an investment project should be the optimal one among its possible alternatives on the basis of the market share as determined in the market analysis. That is to say, even if the market share is very large, the production capacity should not be larger than the optimal capacity because of the decreasing returns to scale as explained in Figure 1.

For example, let us assume that in a project study there are three possible capacity alternatives, namely, A, B, and C with short run average unit cost curves SAC_A, SAC_B, and SAC_C, respectively, to select among for establishing a production system for an investment project. Let us further assume that the relationships between alternative capacities and the average unit cost of

Figure 1. Short and Long Run Cost Curves

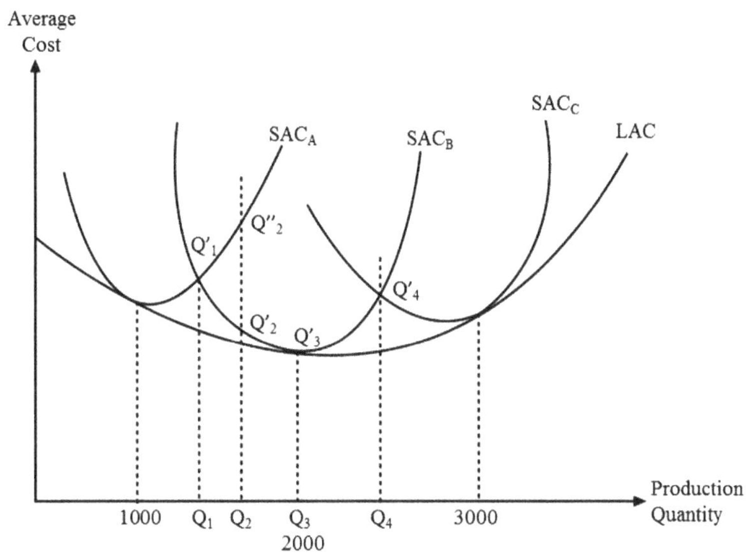

production are as given in Figure 1. Alternative capacities of A, B, and C might also be considered as a "small" factory, a "medium" factory, and a "large" factory, respectively. The average unit cost curve for each capacity alternative in the figure may be considered as *the short run average unit cost curve* (SAC) since, once a capacity alternative is selected, the average unit cost of production would be determined by the cost curve of that selected capacity alternative. Thus, SAC_A denotes short run average unit cost curve for capacity alternative A, SAC_B for alternative B, and SAC_C for alternative C. Additionally, the production quantity that makes the average unit cost minimum (optimal) in the short run is 1,000 units for the capacity alternative A, 2,000 units for B, and 3,000 units for alternative C.

On the other hand, the curve which encompasses short run average unit cost curves of alternative capacities and that touches them on their minimum points is *the long run average unit cost curve* LAC. The curve LAC, which is also named as *the envelope curve*, is formed on the basis of the assumption that there are infinite numbers of alternative short run curves. So, infinite numbers of minimum points of alternative capacities define a curve called the long run average unit cost curve (LAC). According to the curve LAC the production quantity that makes the long run average unit cost minimum is 2,000 units (point Q3), that is, capacity alternative B is the optimal capacity in the long run. Therefore, the capacity alternative B should be selected as the base for designing the production process or system if possible. As will shortly be explained, there are some important factors restricting the capacity selection decision. However, the estimated market share or the demand size of an investment project is the basic factor which affects the optimal capacity selection. For instance, according to Figure 1:

- If the possible market share or the demand size for an investment project is estimated to be *less than* Q1, the capacity alternative for the investment project has to be alternative A with the production quantity of 1,000 units since the average unit cost is the lowest at this point.
- However, if the demand size is *equal to* Q1, both alternatives of A and B are equally possible since the average unit costs of capacity alternatives A and B are equal at the intersection point of Q'1. However, if the capacity alternative A is selected, the firm would operate over the optimal capacity of 1,000 units. But, if the capacity alternative B is selected, the firm would operate under the optimal capacity of 2,000 units.
- On the other hand, if the possible market size or the amount of demand estimated is between Q1 and Q4, the optimal production capacity, without any hesitation, is the alternative B with the production quantity of 2,000 units since the average unit cost is lower than all the other alternatives within this range. For instance, at the production point Q2 the average unit cost for the alternative capacity B (Q2Q'2) is lower than that of A (Q2Q''2) by a margin of (Q'2Q"2).
- If the demand is 2,000 units at Q3 point, the alternative capacity B is the optimal capacity for both the short run and long run. Therefore, this capacity level of 2,000 units is the ideal one and thus should be selected as the optimal production capacity for the investment project. Up to the production point Q3, as it is seen, the long run average unit cost curve (LAC) indicates a situation of *increasing returns to scale*.
- Interesting enough, if the demand size is estimated to be greater than the amount of the optimal point of Q3 (2,000 units), the larger capacity alternative C would not be an appropriate one since the average unit cost in the long run would be greater than that of the optimal capacity of 2,000 units of alternative B. The envelope curve (LAC), that is, the long run average unit cost curve indicates a situation of *decreasing returns to scale* for alternative capacity C. This means that if the amount of production increases further, the average unit cost will go up and the profitability of the investment will diminish.

As a consequence of the explanations regarding the above given example in Figure 1, in a project feasibility study, even if the demand or the possible sales volume for the product of the investment project is larger than the optimal capacity level (2,000 units in our example), the production capacity that should be selected still has to be the optimal one (i.e., 2,000 units). That is, there is no need to meet all the possible demand for the investment project since the average unit cost would increase. In such cases of larger demand, a company may plan to work overtime rather than establishing a larger production capacity than the optimal one.

Furthermore, it should also be pointed out that, as stated earlier, the optimal capacity is theoretically an ideal capacity level that all companies in the same industry or economic sector try to realize in the long run. In practice when selecting or designing a production system, the establishment of such an optimal production capacity, however, may create problems in terms of financial resources needed and the demand level required. For instance, in Figure 1 given above, what should the project manager do when the demand level for the investment project is 1,500 units compared to the optimal capacity level of 2,000 units? Or, what if the investing company by no means can afford to establish a large production capacity of 2,000 units? The answer to these questions is twofold:

1. If the optimal capacity is a standardized production scale defined by the market conditions of the target market in question and that the demand for the investment project is lower than this defined optimal capacity, the investor should not enter into such markets. The reason is quite clear: The investment project cannot compete since the average unit cost of the investment project would be larger than the existing competitors operating at the optimal capacity level. In this case, the standardized optimal capacity and thus the economies of scale in terms of increasing returns to scale becomes a barrier for entry. That is to say investors planning to enter into such standardized industries or markets will either establish a production capacity of that size or not enter at all since they cannot compete in the market due to a higher average unit cost. Cement, sugar, petro-chemical, steel and iron industries are such standardized economic sectors or markets.
2. If the optimal capacity is not distinctly standardized and that the degree of returns to scale is not that much significant, the production capacity may be designed and established according to the existing conditions surrounding the investment project. In such cases, the conditions or

factors that affect the selection of an appropriate production capacity may be summarized as follow:

a. **Demand:** The magnitude of the demand for the product of an investment project is the most important factor that determines the production capacity to be selected. Since the demand for a product indicates the possible sales volume, the production capacity should be determined such that the demand is met. Accordingly, the lesser the demand the smaller capacity would be. Similarly, the greater the demand the larger the production capacity is going to be. But it should not be a very large scale to meet all the existing large demand, rather up to a certain production scale that might be appropriate. However, if the demand is indeed quite large and that the investor does not want to miss it, he/she may establish two companies with appropriate production scales in different places of the country selected.
b. **Financing Needs:** The financial ability of a firm is the second most important factor that affects capacity selection. Companies may be forced to establish small scale production systems and plan to enlarge them later on because of not having sufficient financial resources available at present time. However, in cases of standardized capacity levels required in some economic sectors, if investors are not be able to finance such large production systems, they will not enter into those markets or economic sectors. That is, in such cases, investors would not establish small scale production systems because they would not compete in the market with respect to their larger average unit cost, as explained earlier.
c. **Technology:** In the industries where technological alternatives are limited, the existing few alternatives may inevitably require a certain level of production capacity. So, if one of such technologies is going to be used to produce a product, a production scale of the size required by that technology has to be established. For example, the existing technologies in the petro-chemical industry necessitates certain and large production scales or capacities. Moreover, automated production systems also require certain production capacities. Therefore, whatever production capacity is required by the technology selected, the production system has to have a production scale of that size. As notice, here the focus is on the technological requirement rather than the optimal capacity defined by economies of scale. The technological requirement

sometimes may be overlapping with that of the economies of scale. For instance, the technology for petro-chemical industry necessitates certain and large production systems that eventually provide advantages of economies of scale.

d. **Raw Materials and Manpower Requirements:** The quantity and quality of raw materials and manpower needed for production certainly will affect the scale of the production system or the production capacity for an investment project. Production systems that necessitate processing large amounts of raw materials naturally or employment of much labor have to be large-scaled any way. For this reason, in regions or countries where shortages or bottlenecks in the supply of these production factors create problems, the production capacity should be determined according to the degree of the availability of them. Otherwise, if large capacities are selected, idle capacity would be a chronic problem to face during the operating period of the investment project. This will certainly require an adequate analysis of factor markets in the country selected. Moreover, if raw materials are going to be imported from other countries tariff and nontariff barriers have to be taken into account. The subject of the availability of production factors in terms of raw materials and labor would also be dealt with when a decision is to be made for plant location, as will be explained later. With relation to the plant location decision it should be pointed out here that plant location is also a significant factor that has to be considered when determining a production capacity, since advantages provided by plant location may become meaningless due to raw materials and manpower requirements. For this reason, in designing investment projects, capacity selection should be decided simultaneously with plant location decision.

e. **Economic Policies:** Economic policies such as taxation, incentives provided for direct investments, and foreign trade policies that are implemented by governments will certainly affect the capacity selection decision of investment projects or the establishment of new firms. For instance, a company that plans to import three main machines and operate with two shifts may buy several machines and decide to operate with a single shift, if the government of that country declares that it will remove the customs tariffs for such machinery. Therefore, the investor will select a larger production capacity.

In conclusion, capacity selection decision has to be made systematically in light of all the restricting factors summarized above, since selecting an optimal or a right production capacity is an essential subject that affects the whole operation of a business firm, including the profitability level as well. Selecting the right capacity will prevent business firms from either expensive capacity enlargement investments or facing idle capacities during the operating period in the future. As such, it will help companies to take advantage of economies of scale as much as possible.

Determining the Type and Flow of the Production Process

The production process, in the largest sense of the term, refers to identifying the activities, work, moves, and inspections required by a determined production technology to convert raw materials into finished goods. Production processes could be either of a "*continuous*" or an "*intermittent*" type and/or a mixture of both types (*mixed*) depending on the volume of production, variety of products to be produced, and the degree of repetition of the same work. Continuous types of production processes are highly adequate for large volumes of standardized products. Manufacturing a single product such as a chemical or a petroleum product requires generalized continuous production systems. However, continuous processing systems are also set up for manufacturing products in discrete units that are highly similar but not identical. Such production systems are sometimes referred to as semi continuous processing systems[1]. In continuous and/or semi continuous production processes, as in the case of television production, sequence of operations are defined and described step by step. For instance, assembly lines of a continuous production process (a mass production process) define clearly the sequence of the operations, work, moves, and control done for producing a product from the very beginning to the last stage where the final product is packed.

On the other hand, when a variety of processing activities are required for production, an intermittent type of production processing is set up. The operations and/or work required for producing a product according to a selected technology are grouped in terms of similarities of activities and/or jobs involved. Groups of similar activities or clusters of similar jobs are organized and all similar activities and/or jobs are done in the same manner. This form of intermittent production process is also known as "batch" processing. When a greater variety jobs are to be done, as in the case of an auto repair shop, the intermittent production process is labeled as "job shop" processing. Additionally, the mixed type of production process is a combination of both continuous and intermittent types in which a group of similar activities involved in manufacturing a product are done in a batch process and then the production continues along a certain assembly line, and so forth.

The type of the production process and the related flow of work are determined according to the production technology and capacity selected. Once the production type is determined, then, the flow of work and job design for the whole production process has to be defined and described sequentially step by step. This delineation of the flow of work and description of jobs sequentially is very important for estimating machinery, equipment, and labor necessary to do the work defined for production. In practice, the so-called *flow process charts* or *process charts* are prepared by engineers to detail the flow of work required by the type of production process and, thus, to determine the need for machinery, equipment, and labor for the production at the desired capacity level (Stevenson, 2015; Nahmias, 2014).

A flow process chart shows a complete process in terms of all the elements of work. More specifically, a flow process chart illustrates the sequence of the flow of all activities/jobs involved in the production of a product with appropriate symbols. On the other hand, a process chart is a graphic means of representing the activities that occur during a manufacturing job. There are several types of process charts. However, those which are used to record a process sequence in terms of series of events in the order in which they occur are quite helpful to estimate the need for machinery and equipment. A flow process chart is similar to an operation process chart in that it uses special symbols defined as "operation", "transportation", "inspection", "delay", and "permanent storage". The operation times and distances moved are also recorded along the symbols side.

These charts have three basic types labeled as "man", "machine" and "material" flow process charts that show the activities involved in the process from the viewpoints of man/worker, machine, and material, respectively. For example, the machine type flow process chart shows the activities from the point of view of machines involved in the production process and thus helps a project manager determine the need for machinery and equipment. Consequently, based on the technology selected, the type and flow of the production process has to be determined through both flow process charts and process charts so as to estimate the needs of machinery, equipment, and labor for an investment project. That is to say flow process charts together with process charts are indispensible and essential tools for estimating the machinery, equipment, and labor requirements of a direct investment project.

Determining Production Schedule and Selecting Machinery and Equipment

The production type and the related flow of work as indicated above is a good starting point but not sufficient per se to estimate correctly the machinery and equipment required for the production capacity selected. The operation of a production process may not be smooth or balanced for the whole production period. In some cases, it might be changing according to seasonal variations of sales and inventory requirements. Thus, whichever production type is determined, then, the next decision should concern the production schedule to show whether or not there are seasonal variations in terms of the demand for the product. The production schedule is a specific manufacturing program that aims at meeting seasonal variations in sales as well as inventory requirements in terms of raw materials, semi-finished and finished products, and safety stocks. Accordingly, production schedule helps project managers to make more correct estimates of machinery, tooling, and material handling equipment required for the production process.

Accordingly, once the need for machinery, tooling, and material handling equipment is determined, the next step is to decide how to select them among various alternatives since there might be many firms producing similar machinery and equipment. The selection process entails a systematic analysis and evaluation of various alternatives from different viewpoints as follows:

- Output (production) capacity of alternative machinery and equipment.
- Quality and purchasing cost of each alternative.
- Raw material, manpower, and energy requirements of alternatives.
- Costs of maintenance and set-ups.
- Technical life and scrap values.
- Risk of obsolescence.
- Safety hazards.
- Local or imported.

All alternatives of machinery and equipment needed should be analyzed and evaluated from the viewpoints of the above given information and finally an optimal decision should be made accordingly. In many cases, decisions concerning the selection of the essential machinery and equipment of the production process are made through using the so-called *capital budgeting techniques* to compare alternatives from a *life cycle cost* point of view. Life cycle costing requires cost considerations in terms of purchasing, operation, maintenance, and replacement costs. Capital budgeting techniques will be dealt with later on in the chapter on Evaluating Foreign Direct Investment Projects.

Estimating Manpower Needs

An important aspect that has to be decided about the production process is to estimate the amount of manpower needed. The manpower needs should be considered in three categories, namely, unskilled labor, skilled labor, and administrative or managerial personnel. The need for skilled and unskilled labor is estimated according to the activities, operations, and work or jobs defined by the process charts, especially through "man" flow process charts of the production process. However, in the case of estimating the amount of skilled labor, the skills that employees must have for every activity, operation, and work should be determined first according to activity definitions and/or job descriptions involved in flow process charts or process charts. Then, the number of employees of different skills is estimated on the basis of the amount of work to be done in the production process.

On the other hand, the need for administrative or managerial personnel is more easily estimated through an approximated or a tentative organizational chart for the company to be established. For this purpose, at this point of the technical analysis, a tentative organizational structure for the direct investment project is determined and thus an organizational chart for the company to be established is depicted. The organizational chart that indicates the hierarchical structure of the contemplated business organization will certainly help project managers to correctly estimate the number of managerial personnel in terms of directors, managers for, such as production, marketing, procurement, accounting, finance, human resources departments, etc., vice-managers, specialists, assistants, secretaries, etc. Organizational charts are also very helpful tools for estimating office and service space requirements.

Consequently, the total amount of manpower needed is an important element of the cost of production during the operating period of the investment project that has to be estimated in the financial analysis stage of the feasibility study.

Layout of Physical Facilities and Determining Building Needs

The final step of designing the production process is to estimate the space requirements for production activities (work stations and storage areas), offices (for general management as well as production, marketing, financial, accounting, and personnel functions), and supporting services (such as heating, air conditioning, electricity, lunchrooms, dormitories, showers, restrooms, etc.). The preceding analyses and decisions, especially those related to capacity selection, production type, work or process flow, estimates of machinery, equipment, and manpower, and tentative organizational structure will provide valuable information regarding the estimates of space requirements. However, for more correct estimates a preliminary layout of machinery, equipment, and the other related physical facilities should be made by engineers to visualize the space requirements for production activities, offices, and supporting services. The field of production management provides a huge amount of knowledge regarding layout of physical facilities and engineers are indeed good at laying out physical facilities in specific and designing production systems in general[2].

The layout arrangements are made according to either the functions of production units (*functional* or *process layout*) or the sequence of production activities for a specific product (*product layout*). In the functional or process layout, the machinery, equipment, materials, and employees are gathered according to their functions in the production process. This arrangement is used when the type of the production process selected is intermittent. On the other hand, in the case of product layout, the production type is continuous as in the assembly lines of mass production systems, and that the machinery, equipment, materials, employees, and other production inputs are gathered together according to the sequence of operations and/or activities required to produce the specific product. Additionally, *mixed* arrangements or *combination* of these two types and some special *fixed-position* types of layout arrangements in cases of constructing ships, power plants, and bridges are also possible (Stevenson, 2015).

Layout of physical facilities in any case helps project managers to make correct estimates of space requirements. Various charts, models, and techniques such as drawings, charts, space allocation diagrams, physical models, etc. are utilized by engineers to arrange layout of facilities. After the space requirements for production activities, offices, and services are determined and estimated, then the building needs should be determined in order to complete the design of a production system. The building needs will differ according to the specifications of production processes and material handling requirements. Moreover, the following points should be taken into account when building needs are determined:

- Preparing special floors for operations of heavy machinery and equipment.
- Possibility of multi-story buildings to take advantage of gravity in the flow of materials.
- Preparation for overhead material handling such as cranes and hoists.
- Construction of soundproof walls.
- Adequate space for free movements of materials, products, and workers.

In summary, the space requirements in terms of square meters (m^2) and the specific building needs for constructing a whole new factory should be determined in order to estimate construction costs of the direct investment project.

Selecting the Plant Location

Having determined the production process including the space and building requirements to realize the investment project, the next step of the technical analysis is the selection of the location for the production facility. The plant location decision is so important that once a location is selected and the factory is constructed, then there is almost no way to change the location of the investment if a mistake is noticed with regard to the plant location. In other words, if a mistake is made in selecting plant location, later on, during the operating period of the investment project two things would happen: (1) The factory will either stop its operation because of the losses incurred due to the wrong location or; (2) The cost disadvantages will stay as a hunchback or an overload over the operation of the company such that the existing foreign company would only try to survive. Furthermore, it would be even quite difficult to liquidate such businesses that were not correctly located.

Accordingly, plant location decision is very important and, in fact, it requires lots of factors to be taken into account in order to make the right decision for an optimal plant location. At this point it should also be indicated that the decision for plant location within the country selected should be viewed from two aspects; first selecting the general location and then selecting the building site. The factors that have to be considered for selecting a general plant location in the country selected might be summarized as follow:

Economic Factors

In spite of the fact that all affecting factors are economical in essence, nevertheless, the factors considered in this category are specifically related to the minimization of transportation costs. Transportation costs are viewed in two aspects: First, the costs of moving finished goods to sales points in the market place and, secondly, the costs of transporting raw materials from raw material sources to the production location as defined below.

Market Place Factors

Minimization of transportation costs for moving products from the factory to sales points requires that the plant location should be close to market place. In other words, in order to minimize transportation costs of sending goods to the sales points, the plant location should be nearby the market place. Thus, distance to move products and the availability of transportation facilities are significant points to take into account since the longer the distance the larger the transportation costs would be. Furthermore, there are some additional conditions that necessitate plant location to be near to market place. One of these factors is the *product perishability*. If products to be produced are easily perishable, then plant location should be close to market place because perishable products have to be moved to sales points as soon as possible through specially equipped transportation vehicles. Similarly, the *degree of fragility* of a product to be produced also necessitates a plant location nearby market place since fragile products need special transportation facilities that might be costly. Therefore, in order to reduce the risk of fragility and avoid the cost of specially equipped transportation vehicles as well as special packaging expenditures, the plant location needs to be close to consumers in the target market. Furthermore, it should also be kept in mind and thus taken into account that distribution of perishable as well as fragile products usually require a direct distribution policy rather than an indirect distribution which enables transferring a significant part of distribution costs to intermediaries.

Finally, another factor to be taken into account when dealing with minimizing transportation costs is the volume and/or weight of a product. In brief, if a product increases in volume or weight during production process, plant location has also to be close to market place since transportation costs of such bulky or heavy products would be very high. Consider a product that is manufactured through combining lots of inputs piece by piece such that at the end of the production process a very heavy product is formed. Moving such heavy and/or voluminous products to the target market would certainly cost a lot. Thus, producing such products nearby the market place seems to be a more logical decision. Needless to say, if the output of a production process is a kind of service, then the production place has necessarily to be located near consumers in the market place. The reason for such a decision is quite clear because service cannot be stored and thus moved to consumers or, conversely stating, all consumers cannot be moved to the plant location. So, the right decision is to move production place to where consumers are.

Raw Material Sources

Just opposite to the above given reasons for the market place factors, similar factors related to raw materials necessitate plant location to be close to raw material sources in order to minimize the costs of transporting raw materials to the production place. Here again, as in the case of market place factors, if raw materials are easily perishable, plant location is required to be chosen close to raw material sources in order to decrease the transportation costs of raw materials. Otherwise, moving easily perishable raw materials through specially equipped transportation vehicles to a production place where they are also stored until production time would cost more. As seen, the focal point here is to prevent perishability of raw material before they are put into production process. The costs of protecting raw materials through special transportation and storage facilities depend on the degree of the pace of perishability of raw materials and the characteristics of the vehicles required. This means that transportation costs to be considered for plant location are not just related to the length of distance to travel.

On the other hand, a very important characteristic of raw materials forcing the plant location to be close to raw material sources is that of raw materials losing volume or weight during production process. That is, as it is the case for iron and steel factories, in production systems where raw materials decrease in volume and/or weight significantly, the plant location should definitely be close to raw material sources. For example, iron and steel factories are situated nearby rich coal mines since coal is an essential input in the production process and that it is totally burned out (lost) during the production process. Therefore, selecting a plant location nearby the source of such a voluminous input would certainly save a lot of transportation costs that otherwise would be incurred if the plant is located close to market place. As stated above, the reason for locating iron and steel plants close to rich coal mines is thus to avoid large costs of transporting huge amounts of coal to possibly long distance plant locations. In some cases, iron and steel plants are located near sources of iron ore too. The reason for this is similar in that iron ore loses a great deal of weight in production as well. Thus, sometimes together with some other factors, the sources of iron ore attract plant location more than coal mines.

Transportation Facilities

Availability of transportation facilities in terms of rail ways, high ways, sea ways, and air ways as well as the unit costs of transportation associated with these facilities are also important factors to be considered for plant location. Needless to say, the availability of such facilities is essential for transporting raw materials and finished goods. Therefore, locations where such transportation facilities are not available should not be considered as potential alternatives since the first objective is to transport raw materials and products. How materials and products would be moved if there is no reasonable transportation facility. So availability of transportation facilities is a necessity for plant location. However, the availability of various transportation facilities is not enough per se since the unit cost of transportation is the essential factor to be taken into account for minimizing transportation cost. Unit cost of transportation is especially of great importance when very large volumes of raw materials or products are to be often transported. For instance, railways and seaways are desired alternatives if transportation of very bulky and/or heavy materials is in question. Thus, in such cases, plant location should be in regions where easy access to railways and seaways is possible. In short, when selecting a plant location in a foreign country or a region only those places where transportation facilities are available should be considered as possible alternatives, but the one with the lowest unit transportation cost should be selected depending on the effects of the other related factors.

Consequently, each of the three factors specified above as market place, raw material, and transportation facility is considered for reducing transportation costs related to moving materials and products. However, as might be noticed above, there seems to be a dilemma for the effects of factors of the market place and raw material sources in terms of minimizing transportation costs. That is, when plant location is selected close to market place, the transportation costs of moving raw materials to the plant location for production would increase. Nevertheless, if plant location is selected nearby raw material sources, in this case, costs of transporting products to the market place would increase. On the other hand, the coexistence of the market place and the raw material sources in the same location is almost not possible or is an extreme case. As such, similar cost factors of market place and raw material sources would pull the possible plant location towards two opposite directions. Needless to indicate, the solution to this dilemma is to take into account the total costs of both transporting raw materials and finished goods for each plant location alternative.

Finally, the optimal plant location would be that alternative location where total costs of transporting raw materials to the plant and those of produced goods to the market place are minimized. That is, each alternative plant location is evaluated on the basis of its total transportation costs of raw materials and finished products. Although minimization of the total transportation costs is the main purpose of selecting the optimal plant location, there are some very important but not measurable additional factors which have to be considered when deciding on the optimal plant location. These factors are specified and elaborated below.

Manpower Factors

Labor and/or manpower resource availability is another essential factor to be considered when selecting a plant location. It is quite clear that an adequate plant location should meet the needs of the production system for the skilled and unskilled labor as much as desired. No doubt, in addition to the labor abundance with regard to the skills required, the labor costs should also be minimized in an appropriate plant location. Thus, one may say that a plant location that provides the labor and/or manpower needed with low wages is regarded as an attractive alternative.

It should also be stated that location regions, where labor attitudes and union militancy create problems, are not desired since international business firms do not want to deal with local labor problems. In brief, quantity, quality (skills) and wages of labor are significant manpower related factors to be considered in selecting plant location. For example, textile firms prefer location regions where labor is abundant and wages are low since their production systems and/or technologies are labor intensive. On the other hand, high-tech firms prefer locations where well-educated and skilled manpower is available and good research centers and/or universities are present.

Socio-Cultural Factors

As a general rule of thumb, it may be stated that an adequate plant location should satisfy the social and cultural needs of employees. Such needs are the result of a certain level of social development that covers a variety of needs ranging from recreational needs to educational ones. Some examples are; the needs for theaters, cinemas, sports facilities, all kinds of other recreational facilities, good restaurants, shopping centers, educational institutions especially at elementary and secondary schools levels for the employees' children, etc. The social and cultural needs become indispensable for well-educated and skilled employees since their socio-cultural needs are at their peak level due to high levels of education, income earned, the working conditions enabling them to get in touch with different cultures, and personal motives of self-realization, etc. Additionally, high skilled and well-educated workers earn relatively high income and thus are economically able to meet their socio-cultural needs as well. Thus, when they have time, they would like to satisfy their needs.

However, if the region or the city where the plant location is situated in does not provide possibilities to meet such needs, the skilled and educated workers would leave the region and/or their work in the future for a place where they find opportunities to satisfy their needs. In other words, employees with high skills and good education and thus earning high wages would not want to work in locations where they do not have sophisticated living habitats endowed with good restaurants, theaters, indoor-outdoor sports facilities, shopping centers, and so on. Even if they would be paid high salaries to work in such places, they may work only for a while. However, later on when the time comes, for instance, to send their children to good elementary schools but if there are not good schools around, they would leave their jobs and move to other places or cities where they meet their socio-cultural needs. Accordingly, project managers have to pay close attention to such needs and thus consider regions or cities providing opportunities for satisfying such needs if they are going to have high skilled manpower employed. This point of socio-cultural factors is especially important for plant location decisions in developing countries where socio-economic development is not the same in all regions of a country.

In cases where a plant location that does not meet socio-cultural needs of employees has to be selected for other economic reasons, for instance, minimizing transportation costs, then, the investment plan should include some arrangements for providing facilities to satisfy such needs of employees within the vicinity of the plant location. For example, there are many examples of companies with modern technologies requiring high skilled labor that were established in the rural regions of Turkey because of being close to the essential sources of raw materials. Unfortunately, these companies have experienced lots of high skilled personnel turnover problems since skilled and well-educated employees always have the opportunity of getting jobs somewhere else. Even though some companies pay rather high wages compared to the wage standards in the related industries, these companies still face turnover problems that affect significantly their productivity levels. Eventually some companies provide some facilities on their own to meet the social and cultural needs of their employees; such as tennis courts, basketball and volleyball fields, modern lunchrooms, the so-called social recreational facilities, kindergartens, and even elementary and middle schools for employees' children, etc. For example, elementary schools are constructed and furnished by companies and then are transferred to the Ministry of National Education to be used for education.

Natural Factors

The geographical region where the plant location is going to take place should be suitable for its climate, geographic structure and topography of the land, and the natural water resources. Therefore, for production systems that necessitate a certain degree of heat and humidity, the climate becomes a significant factor to be considered since maintaining the heat and humidity requirements artificially would be very expensive. Similarly, in industries, such as paper manufacturing, where very large reservoirs of natural water are required the availability of natural water resources is an essential requirement for plant location. No doubt, the adequacy of the structure and topography of the geographic region for the plant location is important not only just for construction and transportation activities but also for earthquake dangers.

For instance, the terrible earthquake of 1999 that hit the Marmara Region of Turkey devastated the country's industry since the Turkish business community in that region was not aware of the fact that the Marmara Region, which was the most attractive geographic region for the Turkish industrial companies, was on the famous North Anatolia Earthquake Zone. Therefore, the topographic structure of the geographic region considered for the plant location should be examined in order not to face similar problems in the future, or at least to be aware of the fact and take necessary measures in advance. What is peculiar about the natural factors to point is that if a wrong decision is made concerning these factors, then after investment is realized, there is almost no chance to correct or compensate for it. So, project manager have to pay due attention to natural factors when selecting a plant location. Fortunately, information about natural factors regarding most regions of countries is easily available or regional authorities provide it upon request, since such geographical and topographic studies, at least presently, are made by governmental institutions in almost all countries, including developing ones.

Economic Policies of the Country Selected

Some countries, mostly emerging market economies, implement economic policies and provide various specific incentives to attract real capital investments to some underdeveloped regions of the country to increase employment and maintain social order. Such special investment incentives are just for inducing local as well as international investors to invest specifically in underdeveloped regions of the country and, thus, are different from the general incentives given to foreign direct investments. These special investment incentives in terms of free land, tax exemption, subsidized energy, etc. may sometimes be so significant to consider such underdeveloped regions of a country for plant location. For instance, there are some very attractive incentives only for fixed capital investments to be made in the Eastern region of Turkey and even some local provinces provide infrastructure services freely. In other words, when selecting a plant location in developing countries or emerging economies, such regions with significant incentives should be regarded as potential alternatives for plant location.

Furthermore, in some developing countries, mostly emerging economies, central governments together with local municipalities establish in some provinces of the country the so-called *organized industrial zones* with fully completed infrastructure and ready for business companies to realize their investments. For instance, in Turkey these industrial zones are quite attractive because all necessary physical and geographical infrastructure services in terms of sewage facilities, electrification, water, connection roads, etc. are provided and made ready for investors just to start building their factories. As such, local or national and international investors prefer these organized industrial zones when they plan to invest in those parts of a country and, eventually, these zones become gathering places for industrial firms in some parts of a country. Undoubtedly, this gathering of industrial firms in a designated region also creates external benefits for new investors, such as ready and nearby customer firms and/or procurement centers for easily purchasing inputs. However, such gathering of industrial firms in an organized zone would also have some negative effects for new comers in terms of increasing competition, turnover of employees, and some social problems such as traffic and crime. Therefore, project managers should be aware of the possibility of such opportunities and evaluate their attractiveness as alternative plant locations when they select emerging economies for direct investments.

Consequently, as explained in the preceding pages, the factors affecting plant location decisions are various and all are important determinants for selecting a general plant location. Thus, they must be taken into account explicitly when making a decision. However, as seen, some of these factors are not measurable and even further some of those that are measurable cannot be defined in monetary units. Accordingly, it is almost impossible to put them all together and develop a kind of analytic approach to determine the optimal plant location. Nevertheless, despite of all such difficulties, in practice two simple general approaches are utilized selecting an appropriate plant location in the country selected for direct investment.

The Methods for Minimizing Transportation Costs

The first approach is completely based on minimizing the total transportation costs of moving raw materials to the production place and finished products to the market place. The total transportation costs associated with each alternative plant location are estimated as indicated by the following equation:

$$C = \sum_{i=1}^{n} T_i.Q_i.M_i \text{ (i = 1, 2, ..., n)}$$

where;

C: The total transportation costs of raw materials and finished products,
n: The total number of transportation points for raw materials and finished goods, (i = 1, 2,.............., n).
T_i: The unit cost of transporting one unit load to one unit distance between the factory and i'th transportation point (for example, the unit cost of transporting 1 ton or 1m^3 load – raw material or finished goods - for 1 km),
Q_i: The total amount to be transported between the factory and i'th transportation point,
M_i: The distance between the factory and i'th transportation point.

In the method the total number of transportation points is the sum of the procurement points of raw material sources plus selling points in the market place. For example, if raw materials are procured or obtained from 2 sources and finished products are distributed to 8 wholesalers or distributors, the total number of transportation points would be (2 + 10 =) 10. Similarly, the distance between the factory and a transportation point (M_i) in kilometers (km) or miles for each point of raw material sources and selling points. Additionally, raw materials and products to be transported are measured in the same units either as volume (meter cubes, m^3) or weight (kilogram – kg – or ton).

For example, let's assume a very simple explanatory example in which a project manager is planning a direct investment in a country and considers three cities such as X, Y, and Z for plant location. Data and information related to city X is as follows:

- For a full production capacity of 20,000 units approximately 300,000 kg are materials are procured from 1 source that is 150 km away from the location conceived in city X. Thus, Q_1 = 300.000 kg and M_1 = 150 km.
- Products produced in city X are to be distributed to 3 selling points that 20, 50, and 70 km away from the production place. Thus, M_2 = 20 km, M_3 = 50, and M_4 = 70 km. (Remember that transportation points are added up). Out of 20,000 products produced 8,000 units are to be

transported to the first selling point, 7,000 units to the second selling point, and 5,000 units to the third selling point. A unit product weighs about 18 km. Thus, Q_2 = (8,000x18=) 144,000 kg, Q3 = 126,000 kg, and Q_4 = 90,000 kg.

- The cost for transporting 1,000 kg (1 ton) load to a distance of 1 km is \$0.25. Thus, T_i = 0.25 USD.

Therefore, the total costs of transportation related to city X would be:

$$C = \sum_{i=1}^{n} T_i.Q_i.M_i \text{ (i = 1, 2, 3, 4)}$$

C = (0.25x300x150) + (0.25x144x20) + (0.25x126x50) + (0.25x90x70)

C = 15,120 USD.

The same computation procedure would be carried out for cities Y and Z to calculate the related transportation costs.

Therefore, after computing the total transportation costs for each alternative location, the alternative with the least cost is considered for selection. However, the final decision is given upon a second evaluation in the light of the other location factors explained above; namely, manpower availability, socio-cultural and natural factors, and economic policies of the countries. No doubt that if the least costly country has significant disadvantages with respect to the other factors, it is eliminated and the second less costly country is considered for selection and so on. In other words, the minimization of the total transportation costs is the essential purpose in this method, but the other factors are taken into account as well. That is, the alternative location with the least transportation costs, which also fulfills other considerations at least moderately, should be selected as the appropriate plant location.

At this point of the plant location decision, it should also be indicated that the well-known "*transportation model*" and "*linear programming technique*" of the field of quantitative analysis could not be used here for determining an optimal plant location or an optimal distribution policy minimizing transportation costs. The reason is that although the transportation and linear programming models are robust quantitative techniques used for finding optimal solutions to transportation problems; however, they are solely used for the cases when there are multiple sources of supply and demand destinations.

More simply, these models are used only when there are multiple factories (at least two) producing the same product. So, they cannot be used here for selecting a plant location for a single factory. In cases where there are at least two supply sources (factories), that is, if the investing company has some other factories producing the same product and serving the same market area, supply and demand constraints may be formulated and the optimal solution that minimizes the total transportation costs for all factories could easily be found [3].

The Scale of Importance Method

The second approach for selecting plant location for a single plant is a method based on the scaled importance of factors affecting plant location decision as indicated above. The method is implemented as summarized in Table 1. According to this approach, first of all, the factors affecting plant location decision are specified and then each factor is assigned a score over a defined scale, such as between (1 - 10), indicating its importance in determining plant location for the investment project in question. For the example given in Table 1 the most important factor is seen to be the market size and thus is assigned 10 points over the scale of (1 – 10). Availability of raw materials and manpower is considered to be the second most important factor by the project manager and each is assigned 9 points. However, incentives given by governments are seen as the least important factor and so 2 points are given to it.

On the other hand, there are three alternative location regions or provinces in the country selected, namely, A, B, and C. Each alternative plant location is given scores over the same scale according to its importance from the viewpoint of each factor. In the example given in Table 1, alternative B is considered as the most attractive location with respect to market size and thus 8 points are attributed to it while location A is seen as the least attractive place with only 2 points. However, location A is in a region that has attractive incentives and thus has the highest points (8 points) among alternatives. Thus, each alternative location is assigned scores for each factor according to its significance in the affecting factors. Finally, the scores of each alternative location are multiplied by the scores of importance for each factor and then are summed up to compute the total scores for each alternative. Table 1 exemplifies these computations. The alternative location with the highest scores is assumed to be the optimal plant location for the investment project.

Table 1. Weighted Scores of Location Factors

Affecting Factors	Scale: 1-10 Scores of Importance (X)	Alternative Plant Locations					
		A		B		C	
		Scores (A)	(X x A)	Scores (B)	(X x B)	Scores (C)	(X x C)
Market Size	**10**	2	20	8	80	5	50
Raw Materials	9	7	63	4	36	5	45
Transport. Facilities	7	5	35	6	63	7	49
Manpower Availability	9	6	54	8	72	9	81
Climate	**6**	8	48	5	30	6	36
Geographic Structure	6	9	54	6	36	8	48
Water Resources	8	7	56	5	40	9	72
Energy	**8**	4	32	5	40	7	56
Incentives	**2**	8	16	3	6	5	10
TOTAL			378		403		447

In brief, according to the results of Table 1 the most attractive location is alternative C with 447 points and B comes next with 403 points. Therefore, alternative C is assumed to be the optimal plant location for the planned investment project. At this point it should be added that in practice companies sometimes use this method to find out the most attractive few alternatives and then evaluate them in terms of their total costs of transportation and some other measurable monetary costs such as labor costs.

Before concluding this subsection on selecting the plant location, it should be once more repeated that the plant location decision discussed so far relates to the selection of a general geographic region such as a province or a city within the country selected for investment. Accordingly, once geographic region or a province is selected, then the building site should be determined within that geographic region. For instance, if the province of Ankara is selected as a plant location for a direct investment in Turkey, the second question to be answered is, then, "where in Ankara"? The factors that should be taken into account when selecting a building site are of two groups: The first group of factors is related to the *size factors* of the land necessitated by space requirements in terms of building requirements (e.g., one building or several buildings), expansion plans, parking facilities, isolation requirements, landscaping objectives, etc. The second group relates to the *site location factors*; such as energy requirements (e.g., gas, electricity, etc.), waste disposal, city transportation, water, local taxes, topography and soil analysis, proximity to suitable residential areas, sewage (sanitation) facilities, cost of land, etc., are important factors to be considered for choosing an appropriate building site.

Finally, with regard to selecting an optimal building site, there are some general points that a project manager should always keep in mind. These leading points are:

1. The factors affecting selection of a general plant location and/or a building site may change over time. Therefore, when evaluating the effectiveness of those factors in making a decision regarding location, the possible changes that might take place in the future should be thought of as much as possible. For instance, a plant location for a new company presently may be in a foreign country rather than the home country necessarily. Thus, a Greek entrepreneur may establish his or her first company in Serbia rather than in Greece.
2. In some economic sectors or industries companies are gathered over time in some regions or sites for various economic reasons. Silicon Valley for the computer firms in USA and the city of Istanbul in Turkey for industrial firms are such examples. The advantages and disadvantages of such gathering of firms in large numbers should be evaluated in terms of competition, environmental pollution, and some other social problems such as traffic jams and crimes. Accordingly, in the long run to escape from such problems, firms begin to move to some other locations. All these are important and costly industrial problems that should be considered when making a location decision for a new business firm.
3. Whatever the factors considered for selecting a plant location are, it should be kept in mind that the final location chosen has to be the most appropriate place for achieving the objectives of the investment project during the operating period as a business firm. Moreover, in cases of business expansions in the future years, the selected plant location should have the ability of being enlarged and/or expanded. Thus, the plant location or the site should have the potential of being expanded in the future.

Preparing the Implementation Plan

The basic purpose of the technical analysis is to determine and design how the production system and thus the factory to manufacture the marketable product should be. Therefore, once the plant location decision is made regarding where to establish the required plant or factory, the final step of the technical analysis is to prepare an implementation plan in order to determine when to start and what to do for establishing the production facility determined or constructing the factory required. The implementation plan involves scheduling the sequence of related activities required to complete the establishment of a factory on the basis of the decisions made along the technical analysis. The purpose of such a plan or a program is three fold:

1. To determine the sequence of the related activities so as to make sure that no activity is left out;
2. To estimate the time required to complete each activity and thus the total time needed to complete the whole project, and;
3. To make correct estimates of the cost for each activity and thereby to compute the total establishment cost of the investment project. The implementation plan will also be utilized as an essential device to follow up the completion of the activities required in order to control whether or not they are on schedule and there is any bottleneck in the flow of activities.

There are well known project programming techniques, such as *CPM (Critical Path Method)* and *PERT (Project Evaluation and Review Technique)* that project managers may use for preparing an implementation plan or programming project activities. These two techniques are quite similar in the sense that they both require the whole project to be broken down into essential work components whose required activities are sequentially related to each other. Later on, the time required for completing each activity is estimated and then the total estimated time for the completion of the whole project is computed.

In estimating the time required for each activity of the project the two techniques differ. CPM requires just one normal estimate of time for the completion of each activity while PERT requires three different estimates of time for each activity; namely, *optimistic time (a), most likely time (m),* and *pessimistic time (b).* Optimistic time is the time duration needed to complete an activity if everything goes smoothly and no problem is faced in practice while pessimistic time refers to the time estimate related to a situation where almost everything may go wrong. The most likely time estimate, on the other hand, describes a realistic situation where modest delays may happen for some normal reasons. The reason for different time estimates of the two techniques is that CPM is used for the projects for which there is more experience and historical time records while PERT is used for new projects that do not have any historical background to make good estimates of time.

In using PERT, once the three different time estimates are made for each activity, the expected time (t_e) for that activity is computed according to the formula given below. This formula, in fact, computes the arithmetic mean of the beta distribution since it is assumed that the probabilities of these three time estimates resemble a *beta distribution*:

$$t_e = \frac{a + 4m + b}{6}$$

where;

t_e: is the expected time,
a: is the optimistic time,
m: is the most likely time,
b: is the pessimistic time.

In both techniques the whole project work is broken down into essential activities and the related activities are sequentially arranged and shown as a network (see the example in Figure 2 in the next page). *Activities* in a network are indicated by arrows. The beginning and the end of each activity is shown with a circle which is called an *event*. In other words, events (circles) are numbered points in time to specify the sequence of activities through showing the beginning and the end of activities. The time estimate for each activity is shown above the arrow indicating that activity. All events and activities describe a *network* indicating the sequential flow of activities involved in a project as shown below in Figure 2. Naturally, each network starts with a *beginning event* and ends with an event labeled as *the end event* which shows the completion of the project. Two activities cannot start with and end in the same events. If this becomes a necessity, the second activity is then shown as a *slack activity* in the network.

Now, for an example, let us assume that the essential activities involved in realizing an investment project and the related time estimates for those activities (either as a single estimate of CPM or a weighted average of three time estimates according to PERT) are as given in Table 2. The construction of the investment project starts with the beginning event of purchasing land (event 0) and when purchasing is completed in event 1, that is, activity (0 – 1) is ended, three activities are started at the same time with event 1; namely, starting to prepare technical projects (engineering project) for construction (activity 1 – 2), preparing the purchased land for construction (activity 1 – 4), and starting to order machinery and equipment needed for production (activity 1 – 3).

Accordingly, all the other activities required for establishing the desired factory are sequentially determined and scheduled. That is, when one activity ends, the other(s) starts. Finally, after promotional announcements (activity 7 – 9) and opening ceremonies (activity 8 – 9) are completed in event 9, the project ends. This means that the established factory starts its operation. The related network based on the information indicated above is given in Figure 2. Event numbers inside of the circles indicate the beginning and the end of events. The time required for completion of each activity, as hypothetical example, is given in the last column of Table 2. The time estimates for activities may be made either through CPM or PERT methods. If PERT is used, the expected

Table 2. Activities and the Related Time Estimates

Event Numbers	Definition of Activities	Completion Time
0-1:	Purchasing land	15 days
1-2:	Preparing technical projects for establishing project	30 days
2-6:	Recruiting personnel needed for establishment	25 days
1-4:	Preparing land for construction	20 days
1-3:	Ordering machinery and equipment	30 days
2-4:	Preparing construction projects	50 days
4-5:	Construction of buildings	240 days
3-5:	Receiving machinery and equipment from customs	45 days
5-6:	Installing machinery and equipment	60 days
6-7:	Announcements of the project for starting	10 days
6-8:	Testing production	20 days
7-9:	Promotional activities to announce the opening	15 days
8-9:	Opening ceremonies for the factory	7 days

time (t_e) is computed as indicated by the formula given above. For instance, if the time estimates for purchasing land (activity 0 – 1) are optimistically 9 days ($a = 9$), most likely 16 days ($m = 16$), and pessimistically 17 days ($b = 17$); the expected time (t_e) is:

$$t_e = \frac{9 + 4(16) + 17}{6} = 15 \text{ days.}$$

As seen in Figure 2, there are 8 paths in the network. That is, there are 8 possible ways to go from event 0 to 9. These are:

Path I: (0,1)→(1,2)→(2,6)→(6,7)→(7,9)

Expected time: 15 + 30 + 26 + 10 + 15 = 96 days

Path II: (0,1)→(1,2)→(2,6)→(6,8)→(8,9)

Expected time: 15 + 30 + 26 + 20 + 7 = 98 days

Path III: (0,1)→(1,2)→(2,4)→(4,5)→(5,6)→(6,7)→(7,9)

Expected time: 15 + 30 + 50 + 240 + 60 + 10 + 15 = 420 days

Path IV: (0,1)→(1,2)→(2,4)→(4,5)→(5,6)→(6,8)→(8,9)

Expected time: 15 + 30 + 50 + 240 + 60 + 20 + 7 = ***422 days***

Path V: (0,1)→(1,4)→(4,5)→(5,6)→(6,7)→(7,9)

Figure 2. Network Analysis for Establishing an Investment Project

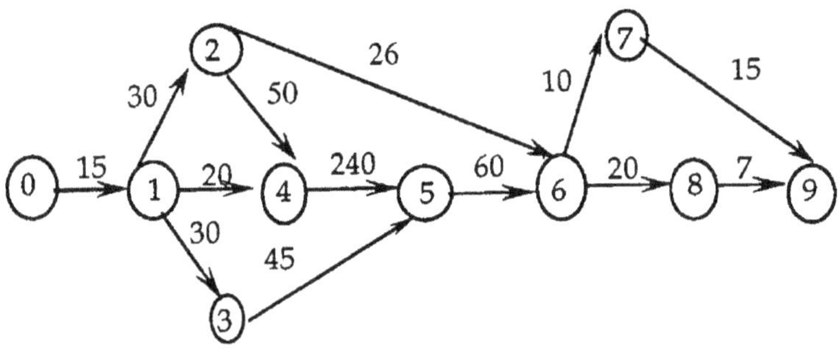

Expected time: 15 + 20 + 240 + 60 + 10 + 15 = 360 days

Path VI: (0,1)→(1,4)→(4,5)→(5,6)→(6,8)→(8,9)

Expected time: 15 + 20 + 240 + 60 + 20 + 7 = 362 days

Path VII: (0,1)→(1,3)→(3,5)→(5,6)→(6,7)→(7,9)

Expected time: 15 + 30 + 45 + 60 + 10 + 15 = 175 days

Path VIII: (0,1)→(1,3)→(3,5)→(5,6)→(6,8)→(8,9)

Expected time: 15 + 30 + 45 + 60 + 20 + 7 = 177 days

The longest path of the network, which is called the *critical path,* takes 422 days. This is the expected time required to complete all activities of required by this project. In other words, this project would be completed in 422 days and then the factory starts its operation for production. Moreover, such a network analysis for preparing an implementation plan through either CPM or PERT also help project managers make correct cost estimates for the activities required to realize the project or to establish the plant desired. As stated earlier, it will also help project managers to follow up the implementation and realization of interrelated activities during the establishment period and thus control whether or not the construction activities are on schedule. Therefore, CPM and PERT are useful methods for estimating costs of projects as well as powerful techniques for managing and controlling projects. In fact, they are well-known project management techniques in the literature on the subject[4].

CONCLUSION

In conclusion, if the technical analysis as a whole does not reveal any technical problem for establishing the required factory for producing the marketable product of the investment project in terms of:

- The production technology or know-how required,
- Labor, machinery, and equipment needed, and
- Plant location and construction for realizing the investment project,

Then, one would say that the production system is technically feasible. In this case, the implementation plan in the form of a network analysis would be a quite valuable guide for constructing and/or establishing the plant desired. Undoubtedly, the implementation of the project would be possible only if the technically feasible project would also prove that it is profitable with a moderate level of risk, as will be explained in the next chapter labeled as Financial Analysis. Needless to state that if the project is not technically feasible, for instance, the production technology may be licensed and a license agreement may not be possible, then, the feasibility study and thus the investment project should be quit.

REFERENCES

Anderson, D. R., Sweeney, D. J., Williams, T. A., Camn, J. D., & Cochran, J. J. (2011). *An Introduction to Management Science: Quantitative Approaches to Decision Making*. Mason, OH: Cengage Learning.

Hillier, F. S., & Hillier, M. S. (2013). *Introduction to Management Science*. New York: McGraw-Hill Higher Education.

Information Resources Management Association (IRMA). (Ed.). (2016). Project Management: Concepts, Methodologies, Tools, and Applications (Vols. 1-4). Hershey, PA: IGI Global.

Larson, E. W., & Gray, C. F. (2017). *Project Management: The Managerial Process* (7th ed.). New York: McGraw-Hill Education.

Nahmias, S. (2014). *Production and Operations Analysis* (6th ed.). New York: McGraw-Hill/Irwin Series.

Powell, S. G., & Baker, K. R. (2013). *Management Science: The Art of Modeling with Spreadsheets* (4th ed.). New York: John Wiley and Sons, Inc.

Stevenson, W. J. (2015). *Operations Management* (12th ed.). New York: McGraw-Hill Education.

Taylor, B. W. III. (2018). *Introduction to Management Science* (13th ed.). Boston: Pearson Publishers.

ENDNOTES

[1] For more about production processing system, see Stevenson (2015).

[2] For more about layout of production facilities, see Stevenson (2015) and Nahmias (2014).

[3] For detailed explanations of the transportation and linear programming models, see Taylor (2018) and Anderson et al. (2011).

[4] For more about CPM and PERT as project management techniques, see Hillier and Hillier (2013), Powell and Baker (2013), and for details about project management work, see Larson and Gray (2017) and Information Resources Management Association (IRMA, 2016).

Chapter 5
Financial Analysis

ABSTRACT

The market and technical analyses aim at finding out whether or not the conceived product of the investment project is marketable and that its production is technically feasible. If the product is marketable and the investment project is technically feasible, then a detailed financial analysis is required. The basic purpose of the financial analysis as the final stage of a feasibility study is three fold: (1) to compute the total amount of the investment needed for realizing the project and decide how it would be financed, (2) to estimate the total amount of annual manufacturing costs for the production process as well as the total amount of annual sales revenues expected during the operating period, and (3) to evaluate the profitability of the investment on the basis of the costs and sales revenues associated with the investment project. If the investment project is profitable, then a risk analysis is conducted to evaluate its riskiness so as to decide about its desirability. Accordingly, the financial analysis stage is the backbone of this book. However, a chapter that would include these three subjects must necessarily to be very large in size and complicated in content. Therefore, in order to prevent this complication and provide a clear theoretical explanation for the final stage of a feasibility study, the financial analysis stage is divided into three consecutive and complimentary chapters on the basis of the objectives stated above. Thus, this chapter is confined to the first objective in the sense of computing the total amount of investment in terms of the fixed capital (fixed costs) and the working capital, determining sources of financing, and estimating annual operating expenditures and expected sales revenues.

DOI: 10.4018/978-1-5225-7696-9.ch005

COMPUTING THE TOTAL AMOUNT OF INVESTMENT

The total amount of investment refers to the amount of expenditures to be made for establishing a factory or a plant for production and making it ready to start and continue its operation smoothly. These expenditures and/or costs for realizing real capital investments are classified within two general categories; namely, fixed costs (or fixed capital) and working capital as explained in the following subsections.

Estimating the Total Amount of Fixed Costs

The fixed costs or fixed investment include the expenditures required to establish or build physically the factory needed for production. As it might be recalled, during the technical analysis the details of the production system were determined in terms of the production capacity, machinery and equipment needed, space and/or land requirements, and building needs. Later on, an implementation plan was developed through the project programming techniques called CPM and PERT to define the essential activities which are required to establish the factory needed. As such, on the basis of the information provided by the technical analysis, the essential fixed cost items are defined and then the related costs are estimated through some market researches for more accurate prices.

The fixed cost items for establishing a new factory or a plant are almost generalized in some standard forms as shown in Table 1 below. The total of all the estimated fixed costs is referred to as the amount of the fixed investment needed. Needless to indicate that fixed costs are made along the establishment period according to the activities required to build a factory as defined by the implementation plan developed at the end of the technical analysis. As might be recalled, the duration of the establishment period for constructing a factory is estimated by finding out the "critical path" of the network analysis made for preparing the implementation plan. In other words, the length of the establishment period is *the critical path* of the network of the implementation plan prepared in the technical analysis. In Table 1, the duration of the establishment period of the investment project is denoted by the symbol (m). Depending on the length of the establishment period, the number of years would count as ($i = t_0, t_1, t_2, \ldots, t_m$). A brief explanation of the fixed cost items given in Table 1 follows:

Table 1. Fixed Cost Items during Establishment Period

Cost Items	Base Year		
	t_0	t_1	.... t_m
1. Project Preparation Expenditures			
2. License and Patent Fees			
3. Cost of Land			
4. Preparing Land for Construction			
5. Construction Expenditures 5.1. Factory Buildings 5.2. Supporting Facilities 5.3. Administrative Buildings 5.4. Social Facilities			
6. Transportation Facilities			
7. Machinery, Equipment, and Tools			
8. Transportation and Insurance Costs of Machinery and Equipment			
9. Customs Duties			
10. Installation Expenditures			
11. Transportation Vehicles			
12. General Expenditures			
13. Start-up Costs			
14. Miscellaneous			
Total Fixed Costs			

1. **Project Preparation Expenditures:** These are the costs of conducting a feasibility study for an investment proposal including all kinds of marketing research studies, field surveys for data and information search, engineering projects, consultancy services, and the other related venture initiation costs. As stated earlier, a feasibility study is a comprehensive study and thus it usually requires a team work and a significant amount of expenditures in terms of wages and/or salaries of analysts conducting the related studies, expenses for field surveys and engineering reports, etc. The reason for considering project preparation expenditures as fixed costs is that taxation laws of almost all countries view the total cost of conducting a feasibility study as a kind of fixed costs that may be depreciated for tax purposes, that is, for paying less tax.

2. **License and Patent Fees:** These include the total amount of the *lump-sum royalty* that is to be paid for technology licensing contracts when determining the production system or establishing the factory. Thus, the cost of using technology or know-how in the form of a lump-sum royalty is regarded as a depreciable fixed cost. However, if there is no lump-sum royalty payment, then there would be no such cost in the establishment period of the project. The license fees to be paid during the operating period of an investment project (i.e., *running royalty*) are regarded as manufacturing (operational) expenditures, as will be explained later. Multinational companies generally charge their investment projects in foreign countries (subsidiaries) a certain percentage of their sales as a license fee (running royalty) for the "know-how" the parent company provides. Therefore, in such cases, although the license fees are a cost item for the investment project per se, they are, in fact, a revenue source for the parent company as a whole. This different viewpoint with regard to license fees would be taken into account when evaluating a foreign direct investment project.
3. **Cost of Land:** The cost of the total square meters of the land to be bought for constructing or establishing the whole factory. The amount of this cost item is estimated according to the space requirements determined during the layout of facilities in the technical analysis stage. However, when the fixed costs of an investment project are depreciated for tax purposes, the cost of land is deducted since the land purchased for construction does not lose value. In contrast, it may gain a great value at the end of the operating period when the factory is liquidated. For example, consider the value gained by a plant location which has stayed inside of a developing city years later. Hence, when evaluating an investment project, the estimated liquidation value of the land is added to the salvage value of the plant at the end of the operating period.
4. **Preparing Land for Construction:** All costs pertaining to preparing the land for construction, such as the estimated cost of excavation work.
5. **Construction Expenditures:** The cost of constructing all buildings including production, administrative, and social facilities as determined in the technical analysis.
6. **Transportation Facilities:** The cost of connecting production facilities to highways and/or railways. The costs of transportation vehicles needed are not included in this cost item. These costs are taken into account in a separate cost category as defined below since they have different depreciation charges.

7. **Machinery, Equipment, and Tools:** This cost item covers the purchasing costs of all machinery, equipment, material handling devices, and tools needed according to the technical analysis. If some of these capital assets are imported, their *FOB (Free-On-Board)* prices should be taken as their costs since freight (transportation) and insurance expenditures are not depreciated for tax shield effects. However, if the import price is a *CIF (Cost Insurance and Freight)* price that includes transportation and insurance costs, then there would be no transportation and insurance costs for machinery and equipment as indicated below.
8. **Transportation and Insurance Costs for Machinery and Equipment:** This cost item includes transportation and insurance costs of the machinery, equipment, material handling devices, tools, and transportation vehicles to be imported.
9. **Customs Duties:** All relevant taxes paid at customs for the imported machinery, equipment, tools, etc.
10. **Installation Expenditures:** The cost of setting-up or installing the machinery and equipment purchased.
11. **Transportation Vehicles:** The estimated cost of transportation vehicles to be purchased for transporting raw materials and finished products as determined by the marketing plan and plant location decision. The operational costs of the vehicles, such as gas and maintenance expenditures, during the establishment period are included in the cost category of general expenditures as indicated below. However, the costs of transportation vehicles incurring during the operating period are added to the manufacturing or operational costs of the investment project.
12. **General Expenditures:** All the other expenditures incurred during the establishment period are labeled as general expenditures. Some of these expenditures are general administrative expenses, lighting, heating, air-conditioning, energy, gas, communication, traveling, etc.
13. **Start-Up Costs:** A newly constructed factory whose machinery and equipment has been just installed cannot operate smoothly during the first days or weeks of its operating period. There would always be some initial difficulties at the beginning of the operating period. Tackling such difficulties requires a trial production (pilot runs) period to adjust and harmonize the functioning of all machines. However, this process takes time and also results, to a larger extent, in defective production. Thus, it would lead to additional costs in terms of scrap, rework, overtime, training of workers, and other expenses resulting from inefficiencies in production. Therefore, considering the duration of the adjustment period

and the magnitude of the pilot runs, an approximate cost estimate should be made.

14. **Miscellaneous:** It can easily be put forth that a comprehensive technical analysis and thereby a detailed production process as well as a systematic implementation plan would be an essential source for making correct estimates of fixed costs. However, in spite of all these efforts, there still might be some mistakes in the estimates made for various reasons. Additionally, forgetting and/or omitting some costs items are always possible. Finally, the estimates made may soon change right after the investment decision due to some unexpected reasons. For all such reasons, a cost item labeled "miscellaneous" is added to the fixed costs of the project to stand for the unexpected, forgotten, and bad estimated costs.

As a rule of thumb, the "miscellaneous" costs are estimated approximately as 10% of the uncertain fixed costs of the investment. That is, the fixed cost items that are presently certain are not included since they are known for sure. For instance, costs of machinery and equipment are more or less certain, even bids may be requested from the sellers if a correct cost estimate is desired. At this point it should also be added that price increases in the fixed costs due to inflation are not considered here since it is believed that the inflation effect should be taken into consideration separately, if it is a problem.

Notwithstanding the fact that defining the above given cost items for an investment project does not bring about any significant problem; however, measuring them in monetary units does lead to some problems in the case of foreign direct investments. In practice, when investing in emerging economies or developing countries, some of the cost items, for example, machinery, equipment, and tools are generally imported and thus measured in hard currencies such as USD and EURO, while the other costs would be in local currencies. Accordingly, exchanging foreign currencies is an important issue to be considered when estimating the costs and revenues associated with a direct investment. Undoubtedly, the similar exchange rate problems are faced with when profits earned in local currencies of host countries would be transferred to home countries of the investing companies in hard currencies like USD or EURO. This subject matter will be dealt with in details later.

Now, as a working example, let us assume that a German company named WGMBH is planning a new direct (greenfield) investment in the province of Ankara, Turkey. Further assume that the studies completed so far provides the following information and data related to our hypothetical example of the WGMBH's investment in Turkey:

1. According to the critical path of the network analysis made for preparing the implementation plan in the technical analysis stage, the establishment period for the WGMBH's direct investment project is 2 years. That is, the investment will be completed and thus the factory will be ready to start its operation in two years.
2. The total amount of the fixed capital required is estimated to be 150,000,000 Euros of which 100,000,000 Euros would be invested in the first year (base year t_0) and 50,000,000 Euros in the next year (t_1) as indicated in Table 2.
3. Fixed costs in foreign currency (Euro - EUR) in the base year (t_0) are converted to local currency (Turkish Lira -TL) by using present exchange rate which is 1 EUR = 3.80 TL, that is, 3.80TL/EUR. Thus, fixed costs in local currency are (100,000,000 EUR x 3.80 =) 380,000,000 TL, as seen in Table 2. The fixed costs in Euros in the next year (t_1) are converted to local currency by estimating the next year's exchange rate through Purchasing Power Parity (PPP) method[1] as:

$$S_{t+1} = S_t \frac{(1+E_{TR})}{(1+E_D)}$$

where:

S_{t+1}: Next year's estimated exchange rate,
S_t: Present exchange rate,
E_{TR}: Annual inflation rate in Turkey,
E_D: Annual inflation rate in Germany (Deutschland) .

Now, assuming that inflation rates will be 12% and 3% in Turkey and in Germany, respectively, the exchange rate for the next year (S_{t+1}) is estimated to be;

$$S_{t+1} = 3.80 \text{ x } \frac{(1+0.12)}{(1+0.03)}$$

$$S_{t+1} = 4.13$$

Thus, the investment of 50,000,000 EUR in the next year would amount to (50,000,000x4.13=) 206,000,000 TL. Estimating exchange rates by Purchasing Power Parity (PPP) method will further be explained when evaluating the investment project later on.

Estimating the Amount of Working Capital Required

Working capital is an important but often a neglected initial cost of investment projects. Perhaps, the best way to explain the need for working capital investment with respect to real capital investment projects would be through an example. Consider the realization of a new investment project called CHEMI in chemical industry to manufacture a desired acid. First of all, a certain amount of fixed capital (e.g., 5,000,000 USD) is required for financing the fixed costs of constructing the chemical plant as explained above. Now suppose that this amount of the total fixed costs was financed and the physical plant is constructed. In addition to the fixed costs for constructing the plant or the factory, the total amount of annual manufacturing or operational costs for producing the desired acid is estimated to be, for example, 1,000,000 USD per year. Further assume that this amount is also available for purchasing the necessary production factors (inputs) to start production.

Now, one may think that there would not be any *financial* problem for this new chemical firm during its operating period for production, since the factory is established and that the funds are ready to purchase all the necessary production factors or inputs for manufacturing. This judgment is theoretically correct because the total costs of the fixed investment (5,000,000 USD) and all the necessary manufacturing costs (1,000,000 USD) for annual production are financed and ready. However, this reasoning would not be correct in practice since a firm would face some common market operations that would necessitate additional financing. These common market operations are summarized as follow:

Table 2. Total Amount of the Fixed Costs (000 EUR) (000 TL)

Cost Items	Foreign Currency		Local Currency	
	t_0	t_1	t_0	t_1
1. Fixed Capital	100,000	50,000	380,000	206,500
Total Annual	100,000	50,000	380,000	206,500

1. Sales are not always made in cash and, thus, a significant amount of funds are tied up in receivables (e.g., about 60 days as of average collection period), as such creating a need for extra cash money.
2. The products may not be sold right after the end of the production process and thus a considerable amount of finished inventories would be piled up and stored in warehouses (e.g., 25 days on average). Thus, sales revenues may decline and the need for extra funds would eventually increase.
3. There is always a need for a certain level of raw material inventory to be made ready so as to meet the production requirements until the ordered raw materials are received (raw materials inventory holding time, e. g., 20 days). This, of course, necessitates additional funds for raw material inventory.
4. An operating company may confront with various unexpected problems in practice that might interrupt the production system for a certain period. Thus, extra funds (cash) have to be made ready for such emergency cases (e.g., funds to finance business operations for about 5 days on average).

Consequently, there would always be a need for some extra funds or cash money to be used for dealing with these operational problems effectively. Therefore, in order for a newly constructed factory to operate smoothly without any interruption and delay, that is; not to wait for receivables to be collected, product inventories to be sold, and ordered raw materials to come in to continue its operation, there is definitely a need for a certain amount of additional funds to finance the production process. That is, extra funds are required to finance receivables, inventories of finished goods and raw materials, and unexpected expenditures during the emergency cases, as explained above. This means that for our above given example of the CHEMI project, some additional funds must be made ready to finance production operations for (60+25+20+5=) 110 days as stated above. In other words, the estimated amount of the fixed capital of 5,000,000 USD together with the annual manufacturing (operational) costs of 1,000,000 USD would not be enough for the chemical plant to operate or work smoothly without any interruption due to lack of funds.

Accordingly, an extra amount equal to the amount of funds required to finance operational expenditures for 110 days of business operation is further needed and must also be ready to start the production process. Otherwise, the investment project would not be a successful business because it will always confront liquidity problems and cash shortages that may interrupt and delay its production operations. This average length of time of 110 days is called as a firm's *operating cycle*. That is, operating cycle refers to the length of time between the time a firm originally purchases its raw materials and the time it sells the products and receives the cash back. A concept closely related to operating cycle is the *cash conversion cycle* which denotes the length of time difference between the operating cycle and the "accounts payable" days (Berk, DeMarzo, & Harford, 2012; Berk & DeMarzo, 2016). For instance, let us assume that in our above given example when the CHEMI project is realized, the company may purchase raw material on credit and pays about, on the average, 45 days later. That is, cash payments occur 45 days later. Thus, the cash conversion cycle is (110 – 45 =) 65 days. However, for the moment, it is assumed that there is no such opportunity of purchasing on credit.

In summary, the amount of the extra funds needed for financing the production process to run smoothly, such as the amount for 110 days as in the above given example, is called as the *working capital* need of an investment project. In other words, *working capital* represents the portion of investment that circulates from one form to another in the ordinary conduct of business over operating years. Therefore, the amount of the working capital needed has to be estimated and then added to the amount of the fixed capital to find out the total amount of the investment required for realizing a successful business. Working capital is the cash that is needed to run the business firm smoothly on a day-to-day basis. It is not excess or idle cash. It is a form of capital that circulates from one form to another; that is, sometimes in the form of raw materials, sometimes in inventories, and sometimes in the form of receivables.

For the moment, just as a starting example, let's assume that the amount of working capital that the CHEMI project needs to finance the production process for the above given example of 110 days of operating cycle is 314,286 USD, as will be explained shortly. Therefore, the total amount of the investment needed to realize the CHEMI project, as the sum of the fixed costs (fixed capital) and the working capital is thus (5,000,000+314,286=) 5,314,286 USD, not just 5,000,000 USD of fixed costs. This total amount of investment including the working capital need will be called as *initial investment*, as it is often referred to in feasibility studies. In another word, the *initial investment* is defined here as the sum of the fixed capital plus the working capital. In cases where the establishment or the set-up period of an investment project is longer than a year, working capital is added to the part of the initial investment to be made in the last year of the establishment period since working capital is a source of fund which should be ready before the operation starts.

The amount of working capital that is needed depends on the duration of financing the production process required for a smooth operation. For the CHEMI project, as explained above, this duration was 110 days, as the operating cycle, and the total amount of the working capital needed to finance the production process for those 110 days was assumed to be 314,286 USD. Now let's explain how we arrived at these figures. The *annual operation period* for the CHEMI project, that is, the actual *days* that the plant or factory will normally work for production in a year, is assumed to be 350 days. This means that the plant will not work (365 – 350 =) 15 days of a year for annual maintenance and holidays. On the other hand, recalling that the total manufacturing costs for the annual production was 1,000,000 USD, the cost of the daily production over the operation period would simply be (1,000,000/350 =) 2,857.143 USD. As such, the extra amount of financing or the working capital for 110 days would be (2,857.143x110 =) 314,286 USD. At this point it should be indicated that the *annual operation period,* which shows the number of *actual days* that a plant or factory will normally work for production in a year, is different from the overall *operating period* of an investment project which represents the total number of years during which an investment project produce and sells goods.

In fact, from the view point of manufacturing companies, the amount of working capital represents the current assets of a company in terms of receivables, inventories of raw materials and finished goods, and cash in bank accounts. Accordingly, the duration that the funds are tied up in those current assets is the so-called *operating cycle* of the current assets (in the above example 110 days). That is, funds are tied up in current assets for 110 days and then are converted back to cash. Then again, cash funds are invested in current assets and 110 days later converted back to cash; and so on the cycle repeats itself. This means that the working capital as the amount of current assets is in fact a revolving fund with an operating cycle that repeats over the operating period of the project. For this reason, when the revenues of the investment project in the last year of the operating period are estimated, the amount of working capital computed at the beginning of the operation period is added to the revenues of the last year. At this point it should be once more stated that operating cycle should not be confused with cash conversion cycle. As indicated above, cash conversion cycle refers to the length of time as the difference between the operating period and days of accounts payable (i.e., the days of purchasing on credit).

Now, on the basis of the explanations given above, in order to show clearly the number of operating cycles repeated during an operating period, a meaningful computation procedure for the amount of working capital required may be systematized as follows:

1. Compute the *operating cycle* of current assets. The operating cycle for the above given example of CHEMI project was computed to be 110 days. That is; the average collection period is 60 days, finished products wait in warehouses (carrying inventories) on the average for 25 days, raw materials inventory holding time is 20 days, and a 5 day- self-sufficiency period for the unexpected problems interrupting the production system is deemed appropriate.
2. Estimate the *"annual operation period"*. That is, the number of actual days per year that the factory normally will work for production. In the example above, it was assumed to be 350 days in a year. That is, the factory will not operate 15 days per year for maintenance and minor repair work of machinery and equipment.
3. Estimate the amount of the average annual operating expenditures or manufacturing costs as will be explained shortly. In the example for the CHEMI project given above, the average annual operating costs were assumed to be 1.000.000 USD.
4. Divide the operation period by the operating cycle to find the coefficient of the operating cycle, that is, the number that the operating cycle is repeated in an annual operation period. Thus, for the above given example, the coefficient of the operating cycle (COC) is;

COC = (Annual Operation Period) / (Operating Cycle)

COC = (350) / (110) = 3.18182

This means that the operating cycle is 3.18 times repeated in an operation year. That is, working capital is tied up in current assets and then received back 3.18 times in a year.

5. Divide the average annual operating costs by the coefficient of the operating cycle (COC) to get the estimate of the working capital. Accordingly, for our example;

Working Capital = (Average Annual Operation Costs) / COC

Working Capital = $(1,000,000)/(3.18182)$

Working Capital = 314,286 USD.

As seen above, the amount of working capital depends on the duration of the operating cycle which is, in turn, affected by various economic conditions surrounding business firms (Titman, Keown, & Martin, 2011; Gitman & Zutter, 2014). These factors that generally affect the amount of working capital may be explained as follow:

1. **The Possibility of Obtaining External Financing:** Business firms that are able to find external financing, such as short term commercial loans, may not keep more funds ready as working capital, since they have the opportunity of obtaining funds whenever they need. In fact, business firms usually establish good relations with financing institutions such as working with the same bank(s) for years. Thus, both sides get the chance to know the other quite well and then eventually they rely on each other. This type of long term relations with banks definitely provides opportunities for companies to get short term loans whenever they need. So, such companies will need less working capital.
2. **Purchasing and Selling Practices in the Market:** In markets where purchasing and/or selling is customarily done in cash or on credit will definitely affect the amount of working capital. For instance, there would be less need for working capital if it is customary to purchase raw materials in the factor markets on credit, for example, to pay 30 days later (a trade credit term of Net 30 days). This is a trade credit that a firm is extending to its customers. On the contrary, if the practice of sales on credit (trade credit) is more common in the product market, the need for working capital would increase. However, if the trade credit is practiced in factor markets then the need for working capital would decrease.
3. **Inventory Policy and Inventory Turnover Rate:** If inventory policies requiring larger levels of inventories are to be implemented for providing consumers' satisfaction so as to maintain the market share or not to lose customers, the need for working capital would certainly increase. No doubt that increasing inventory level means larger amounts funds

to be tied up in inventories. On the other hand, the companies whose inventory turnover rate is high, that is, the speed of selling or finishing the existing inventories and replenishing them with new ones is high, would need less working capital. The reason for this is quite clear since the amount of funds to be tied up in inventories would be less due to the short period of carrying inventories.

4. **Production Duration:** In industrial companies, the longer the time needed to convert material inputs into finished goods the larger the amount of working capital required would be. That is to say that if the production duration is long, the funds would be tied up in the material inputs for a long period of time and, thus, the need for working capital would increase. In other words, if the production time is long, converting material inputs back into cash would take long time and, thus, more working capital would be needed compared to companies with shorter production duration.
5. **Production Capacity and Unit Cost of Production:** It is quite clear that in business companies where production capacities are large and the cost of production per unit is high, the amount of working capital needed would be large as well. That is, large funds would be tied up in the production process as well as the inventories of costly products.
6. **Type of Business Activity:** The amount of working capital needed also depends on the type of the industry or the business activity that business firms are engaged in. For instance, manufacturing firms need more working capital than firms in tourism sector.
7. **Degree of Competition in the Market:** In a market where competition is severe companies would need more working capital due to either financing sales on credit (financing receivables) to compete or making more funds available to be ready for the times of starting promotional activities. In other words, under sever competitive conditions firms may practice sales on credit to attract consumers. So, this indicates that firms would tie up more funds in receivables. Furthermore, firms would need additional funds to promote sales through various promotional campaigns.
8. **Other Unexpected Factors:** Unexpected changes in the product or factor markets, such as increasing difficulties in collecting receivables, decreasing values of inventories due to falling prices, arising difficulties in finding external financing, etc., would affect the need for working capital. Therefore, depending on the probabilities of such plausible cases, companies would like to increase the level of working capital in

terms of the need for cash money ready in bank accounts or financial instruments with high degrees of liquidity.

As a conclusion of the foregoing two subsections, it should be once more repeated that the total amount of the investment required for realizing a real capital investment project in general or a foreign direct investment project in specific is comprised of two essential cost categories; namely, fixed capital and working capital. This total amount of the investment, that is, the sum of the fixed and working capital is called *initial investment*. Thus, from now on, the term initial investment refers to the total of both fixed and working capital unless otherwise specified. Therefore, recalling the figures stated in the foregoing pages, the total amount of the initial investment needed to realize the CHEMI investment project is (5,000,000+314,286=) 5,314,286 USD as explained above.

Financing the Total Initial Investment

For now, having explained the basis of the concept of working capital and the way how it is computed through an example named the CHEMI project, let us return to our previous example of the German company WGMBH's investment project in Ankara, Turkey, as a working example to be continued. Recall that, as given earlier in Table 2, the total amount of the fixed capital (costs) estimated for the WGMBH's investment project was 150,000,000 EUR of which 100,000,000 EUR would be invested in the first year (base year t_0) and 50,000,000 EUR in the next year (t_1). For the meantime, let's furthermore assume that the working capital need for the WGMBH's investment project was estimated to be 50,000,000 EUR as indicated in Table 3. Thus, the total amount of the initial investment required for this project will be (150,000,000+50,000,000=) 200,000,000 EUR.

Once the total initial investment as the sum of the fixed and working capital is estimated, the next question to be answered is: "could this amount be financed and if so, how would it be financed"? The first part of the question relates to the possibility of financing the whole investment project. In cases where financing the total amount of investment required exceeds the financial ability of the investor, that is, if the investment project could not be financed any way, then, the only alternative becomes to quit the investment proposal. In other words, if the investor is unable to provide funds to finance the investment project, the investment project has to be abandoned simply because there are not enough funds available to invest in the project. For instance, as seen in Table 3, the WGMBH Company may just say that financing a direct investment of a size of 200,000,000 EUR is very much beyond our financial ability. Thus, they have to give up the investment project because of being unable to finance it.

However, in cases where the owners' equity is not sufficient to finance all of the initial investment, depending on the attractiveness and thus the envisaged profitability of the direct investment project, the investor may search for alternative ways of external financing. There are various methods of financing an investment project through external sources; such as, business partnerships including joint ventures, raising funds through capital markets, venture capital financing, leasing capital assets, and term loans or long term credits from commercial institutions[2]. Accordingly, if there are possibilities of obtaining external financing, then, the investor should decide about the capital structure of the investment project. The capital structure refers to the combination of sources of funds in the sense of using internal or external funds. Therefore, an optimal combination of internal and external funds should be determined such that the overall cost of capital of the investment project would be at its minimum level. In other words, when there are possibilities of external financing as indicated above, the project manager should first identify alternative sources of funds and then determine the percentage combination of them that would make the weighted average cost of the initial capital minimum.

Upon deciding on the capital structure of the project, a financial plan should be prepared in terms of when and how much external financing (debt) will be used as indicated in Table 3. Such a simple financial plan indicating the amount of financing needs for the years of the establishment period ($t_i = 0$,

Table 3. Capital Structure of the Investment Project (000 EUR) (000 TL)

Cost Items	Foreign Currency		Local Currency	
	t_0	t_1	t_0	t_1
I. Initial Investment				
1. Fixed Capital 2. Working Capital[(a)]	100,000 ----	50,000 50,000	380,000 ----	206,500 206,500
Total Annual	100,000	100,000	380,000	413,000
II. Financing				
1. Owners' Equity 2. Long Term Loan	100,000	---- 100,000	380,000 ----	413,000

[(a)]Working capital is required at the end of the last year of the establishment period to be made ready for the beginning of the operating period.

1, …, m) may best be prepared on the basis of the network analysis made for preparing the implementation plan. As may be recalled, the critical path of the network analysis that is found through CPM or PERT techniques shows the detailed timely sequence of essential work activities. Thus, when the cost of each activity is estimated, the time that the funds are needed could also be specified and, thus, a simple financial plan or program would be developed on the basis of the critical path.

Now, let us resume with our working example of the German company (WGMBH) planning a new direct (greenfield) investment in the province of Ankara in Turkey:

1. As assumed previously, the establishment period is 2 years; the total amount of the fixed capital is 150,000,000 EUR of which 100,000,000 EUR would be invested in the base year (t_0) and 50,000,000 EUR in the following year (t_1), as it was indicated earlier in Table 2 and repeated in Table 3.
2. Moreover, as indicated earlier, the need for working capital is estimated to be 50,000,000 EUR. Therefore, the total amount of the initial investment needed is (100,000,000+50,000,000+50,000,000=) 200,000,000 Euros as shown in Table 3. As will be explained later, for project evaluation purposes, the total amount of initial investment is also stated in local currency. Therefore, the cost figures in Euros (EUR) are converted to Turkish Lira (TL), just as it was done previously in Table 2 through Purchasing Power Parity (PPP) method. Needless to state, in practice when cost estimates are made, some prices (import prices) are stated in foreign currency and the others in local currency. As such, cost items in foreign currency are converted into local currency and vice versa. Thus, cost tables for the initial investment involve two estimates, one in foreign currency and the other in local currency.
3. The investor (WGMBH) believes that there would be no problem with financing of the investment such that 100,000,000 EUR would be financed through equity in the base year (t_0) and the remaining 100,000,000 EUR in the next year (t_1) would be easily financed with a 5 year term loan with an annual interest rate of 10% as shown in Table 3. Therefore, the capital structure of the investment project was determined to be 50% equity and 50% debt. As will be explained later, investors or parent companies generally provide term loans to their direct investment projects as their subsidiaries.

4. The term loan which would possibly be obtained from the parent company is to be paid back in 5 equal installments including interest payments. For cost considerations, the equal annual payments (principal + interest) of the 5 year term loan of 100,000,000 EUR with 10% interest rate are computed as follows:
   a. The equal annual installments (A) are computed according to the following formula:

$$A = \frac{AmountofLoan}{\sum_{t=1}^{n} \frac{1}{(1+k)^t}}$$

The denominator in the above given equation is called the Present Value Interest Factor of an Annuity (PVIFA) and is easily computed for any given time period (n) and interest rate (k) as formulated below. That is:

$$\text{PVIFA}_{k,n} = \sum_{t=1}^{n} \frac{1}{(1+k)^t} = \frac{1 - \frac{1}{\left(1+k\right)^n}}{k}$$

where;

n: Term period (number of years, t=1, 2, …., n),
k: Interest rate.

Hence, the equal annual installment (A):

$$A = \frac{AmountofLoan}{PVIFA}$$

As such, in our example of WGMBH's direct investment project in Ankara, Turkey, since k = 10% and n = 5 years;

$$\text{PVIFA}_{10\%;5} = \frac{1 - \frac{1}{(1+0.10)^5}}{0.10} = \frac{1 - \frac{1}{1.61051}}{0.10} = \frac{0.37908}{0.10}$$

PVIFA = 3.7908

Thus, the amount of the equal annual installment (A) for paying back the term loan of 100,000,000 EUR is:

$$A = \frac{100,000,000}{3.7908}$$

A = 26,380,000 EUR.

Annual debt payments would start in the first year of the operating period when the production starts. However, in order to see the cost of using 100,000,000 EUR term loan in terms of interest payments, the principal and the interest portions of each equal installment computed above should be separated as given in Table 4.

Computations for Table 4 are based on the following simple procedure: For each year the interest is computed on the basis of the outstanding or remaining debt and then the computed interest is subtracted from the equal installment to find the amount of the principal. Later, the principal is subtracted from the amount of remaining debt to find the amount of debt for the next year; and so on computations are repeated until the end of the time to maturity. For example:

Year t_{m+1}:

Interest: 100,000 x 0.10 = 10,000

Principal: 26,380 - 10,000 = 16,380

Remaining Debt: 100,000 - 16,380 = 83,620

Table 4. Principal and Interest Payments of the Loan (000 EUR)

Loan Payments	Operating Period							
	t_{m+1}	t_{m+2}	t_{m+3}	t_{m+4}	t_{m+5}	----	----	t_{m+n}
1. Interest	10,000	8,362	6,560	4,578	2,398			
2. Principal	16,380	18,018	19,820	21,802	23,982			
Total (1+2)	26,380	26,380	26,380	26,380	26,380			

[a]The operating period starts after the establishment period (t_m) in the year t_{m+1} and ends in the t_{m+n}, thus, continues (n) years.

[b]The payments of the loan in terms of the principal and interest will take place in the first 5 years of the operating period since the term loan is obtained in the last year of the establishment period and payments start one year later in the year (t_{m+1}).

Year t_{m+2}:

Interest: 83,620 x 0.10 = 8,362

Principal: 26,380 – 8,362 = 18,018

Remaining Debt: 83,620 - 18,018 = 65,602

Year t_{m+3}:

Interest: 65,602 x0.10 = 6,560

Principal: 26,380 - 6,560 = 19,820

Remaining Debt: 65,602 - 19,820 = 45,782

and so on.

In order to see the cost of the term loan of 100,000,000 EUR in terms of the local currency, the principal and interest payments of the term loan in Euros (EUR) in Table 4 should be converted to the local currency, Turkish Lira (TL), as given in Table 5.

in the future years, since equal installments in EUR are converted to the depreciated TL values.

Table 5. The Principal and Interest Payments of the Loan in Both Currencies (000 EUR and TL)

Years (Operating Period)	**1**	**2**	**3**	**4**	**5**
Principal (EUR)	16.380	18.018	19.820	21.802	23.982
Interest (EUR)	10.000	8.362	6.560	4.578	2.398
TOTAL (EUR)[a]	26.380	26.380	26.380	26.380	26.380
Exchange Rate TL/EUR = 3.80	4.13	4.49	4.88	5.30	5.76
Principal (TL)	67,649	80,901	96,722	115,551	138,136
Interest (TL)	41,300	37,545	32,013	24,263	13,812
TOTAL (TL)[a]	108,949	118,446	128,735	139,814	151,948

[a]As seen, due to the high inflation rate expected in Turkey equal installments in TL are not equal

b. The exchange rates for TL/EUR during the duration of the term loan (5 years) are estimated according to the Purchasing Power Parity (PPP) method as indicated previously.

That is:

$$S_{t+1} = S_t \frac{(1+E_{TR})}{(1+E_D)}$$

where;

S_t = the base (existing) exchange rate of TL/EUR.
S_{t+1} = the exchange rate for one year later.
E_{TR} = expected inflation rate in Turkey.
E_D = expected inflation rate in Germany (Deutschland) (the lending country).

The Base Exchange rate for TL/EUR is taken as 3.80, that is, $S_t = 3.80$TL/EUR and the expected inflation rates for Turkey and Germany are assumed to be $E_{TR} = 12\%$ and $E_D = 3\%$, respectively. Accordingly, the estimated exchange rates are given in Table 5. For example, the exchange rates for the first two years are computed as given below:

$$S_{t+1} = 3.80 \times \frac{(1+0.12)}{(1+0.03)}$$

$$S_{t+1} = 4.13$$

$$S_{t+2} = 4.13 \times \frac{(1+0.12)}{(1+0.03)}$$

$$S_{t+2} = 4.49$$

$$S_{t+3} = 4.49 \times \frac{(1+0.12)}{(1+0.03)}$$

$S_{t+3} = 4.88$

:

and so on.

ESTIMATING THE ANNUAL OPERATIONAL EXPENDITURES

Operational expenditures, in general, refer to the manufacturing costs incurred by a company to produce a product at a certain level of production. For instance, consider an investment project with a production capacity of 50,000 units. When the investment is completed and that the new factory starts its operation to manufacture 50,000 units of the product as it is planned, lots of production factors (inputs) such as raw materials, various supplies, labor, energy, etc. are needed to produce the required quantity. The expenditures to be made for obtaining all such production factors or inputs to produce 50,000 units in a year of the operating period are labeled as annual operational or manufacturing costs of the production system. Needless to state that in a new investment project operational costs are incurred after fixed costs are made, that is, initial investment is completed. So, there would not be any operational costs in financial tables during the establishment period of the project.

The essential items of operational costs for an investment project in manufacturing industry are quite clear and may be defined as follow:

1. **Raw Materials:** Include the costs of all direct material inputs needed for production. Raw materials are essential inputs and are processed in the production system for conversion into finished products.
2. **Indirect Materials and Supplies:** Refer to the costs of auxiliary materials used in production but not measurably identifiable with production units and those of components utilized in production.
3. **Energy:** The costs of electricity and fuels consumed in a year for production and related supporting facilities. In other words, these costs include both energy costs of operating machinery and equipment as well as lighting and heating production facilities including supporting units.

4. **Labor:** The compensation of labor in terms of wages, salaries, etc. for all qualified and unqualified labor as well as administrative personnel. As indicated earlier in the technical analysis stage, the needs for qualified and unqualified labor are estimated through flow process charts when designing production process while the estimates of administrative personnel are made through tentative organizational charts.
5. **Licensing Fees (Running Royalties):** Payments made during the operating period for using a technology (know-how) for production. Multinational companies generally charge a certain percentage (generally between 2% and 4%) of the sales of the investment project as a license fee to their subsidiaries in foreign countries for providing "know-how". Moreover, the transfer of license fees to the home country of the parent company does not involve significant taxation problems as dividends do. However, in any case, if the license fee is a lump-sum fee paid during the establishment period, it is considered as a fixed cost item within the total amount of the initial investment.
6. **Maintenance:** The purpose of these expenditures is to increase the productivity of machinery, equipment, tools, and the other production facilities. As in the case of repair services and the need for spare parts, estimating maintenance costs is not an easy task since the demand for maintenance services is very uncertain. In practice, when manufacturing firms attempt to forecast the maintenance costs, they usually considered the demand for maintenance as a stochastic process and then try to forecast the related costs through various probability distributions. However, in project feasibility studies, project managers generally estimate them as a rule of thumb between 3 and 5 percent of the total costs of machinery, equipment, tools, and the other production facilities (Turkish Development Bank, 2015).
7. **General Expenditures (Overheads):** This cost item includes all other expenses for general administrative services; such as communication, security, insurance, training, janitorial services, and so on. In practice when there are difficulties to estimate general expenditures, some practitioners take about 2% of the fixed costs as the approximate amount of general expenditures (Turkish Development Bank, 2015).
8. **Promotional Expenditures:** These are the marketing or sales expenditures determined for the marketing strategy to promote the product during the beginning years of operating period. As explained in the market analysis stage, promotion is a significant component of a firm's marketing strategy or plan. Thus, when the market share for the

direct investment project is estimated at the end of the market analysis, the promotional activities and/or campaigns are determined as a part of the marketing strategy and the related promotional expenditures labeled as "sales expenditures" were estimated and planned in the sales report of the market analysis.

9. **Depreciation Charges:** These are charges made annually that represent the costs of investments made in earlier periods in machinery, equipment, tools, and production facilities. In other words, depreciation is a way of recognizing that buildings, machinery, and equipment wear out and thus become less valuable. As such, it represents recovery of investment. However, depreciation charges are not direct cash outlays for companies. They are computed and deducted from gross operating profits just like the other operational costs for the purpose of paying less tax. That is, depreciation charges are tax deductible and thus they have a tax shield effect since they reduce the firm's taxable income. For this reason, depreciation charges are separated from operational costs in financial tables for tax purposes. It should also be noted that depreciation charges are computed according to the taxation laws of the country selected for investment.

For instance, business firms in USA may choose one of these three depreciation methods called "straight line", "double declining balance", and "the sum-of-the years' digits" methods. Similarly, but a bit in a different way, in Turkey, according to the Turkish Taxation Law, capital assets such as machinery, equipment, transportation vehicles, and buildings have varying depreciation rates while land is not depreciated, that is, its depreciation rate is zero. Moreover, firms are allowed to use either the so-called "normal" method or "declining balances" method, which are, in fact, the same as the straight line and double declining balance methods, though named differently. The sum-of-the years' digits" method is not used in Turkey. In sum, depreciation charges are computed according to the taxation laws of host countries. In practice, when conducting project feasibility studies, depreciation charges are usually computed as an annual weighted average of depreciable assets since depreciation rates generally vary for different fixed assets. Finally, it should also be added that fixed assets purchased at the beginning of the establishment period are depreciated only when they are used in the operating period. That is, fixed assets are not depreciated if they are not in use. So, there would not be any depreciation charge during the establishment period in the financial tables prepared for financial analysis.

In conclusion, the operational or manufacturing costs as defined above should be estimated for each year of the operating period of the investment project according to the production capacity selected in the technical analysis. For instance, in a project feasibility study if the production capacity is determined to be 50,000 units, then, the question to be answered is "how much would it cost, in terms of the operational expenditures, to produce 50,000 units of the product in question in a year"?

For now, with regard to estimating annual operating costs as well as annual sales revenues that will be discussed shortly, it should be pointed out that since investment analysis is future related and thus creates forecasting problems, two practical approaches and/or assumptions are necessarily adopted for estimation purposes as stated below:

The Length of the Operating Period

The length of the operating period, that is, the number of years during which production takes place and thus revenues are expected is based on the "*technical life*" or the "*useful life*" of the essential machinery and equipment that form the basis of the production system. In general, the "technical life" of machinery and equipment is, in fact, determined by producers when they are manufactured. That is, when machinery and equipment are purchased, producers will state what the duration of their technical or useful life would possibly be or how many years they would probably be used for production. For example, when the essential machinery is purchased, its technical specifications may indicate that its *technical life* is 14 years. This means that this machinery can normally be used for 14 years. Therefore, since production technology defines the requirements for machinery and equipment which, in turn, determine the base of the production system, the technical life of the main or essential machinery and equipment is generally taken as the duration of the operating period, unless otherwise decided.

However, technological development may make the existing essential or main machinery and equipment that form the base of production systems obsolete. Therefore, when technological development makes out of date the main machinery and equipment of a production facility, they have to be replaced with technically modern ones even though they still have some technical life remaining. Otherwise, the production would not be efficient and may eventually be terminated since it would not keep up with the pace of competition. This is to say that technological development may terminate the *technical life* of main machinery and equipment and, thus, requires the renewal of the existing production facility in general. Therefore, in industries where technological obsolescence is a common or plausible phenomenon, the length of the operating period for real capital investment projects is based on the duration of the expected "*economic life*" of the essential machinery and equipment, not that of the technical life. That is, technical life is not economical any longer as far as technological obsolescence is concerned.

The economic life in this sense refers to the duration that the main machinery could possibly be used economically or efficiently by taking into account the pace of technological development. Accordingly, the length of the operating period for a new investment project should be based on the possible economic life of the essential machinery and equipment. For instance, let's assume that in a feasibility study the technical life of the essential or main machinery and equipment determining the base of the production system is, on the average, stated to be 15 years by their manufacturers. However, the engineers taking part in the feasibility study think that the pace of the technological change or development in the industry in question is significantly increasing and thus believe that a 9 year economic or useful life is much more appropriate. Therefore, the length of the operating period for the project is decided to be 9 years. Therefore, in such cases, the expected duration of the economic life of the main machinery and equipment as an average value should be taken as the length of the operating period for an investment project. That is, the length of the operating period for this project should be determined as 9 years.

In practice, an alternative to the above stated approach for computing the length of the operating period is to divide the fixed costs of the investment after the value of land by the annual weighted average of depreciation charges as follows:

$$\text{Length of Operating Period} = \frac{FixedCosts - CostofLand}{AverageDepreciatonChar.}$$

The cost of purchased land is subtracted from the fixed costs because the land is not depreciated, that is, its depreciation rate is zero (0). Additionally, in the numerator of the above given equation the concept of the annual weighted average depreciation charge refers to the fact that depreciation rates vary according to the types of fixed assets in many countries. For instance, in Turkey depreciation charges for "lump-sum" royalty, machinery and equipment, construction, and transportation vehicles are 0.20, 0.10, 0.04, and 0.15, respectively. Therefore, computing an annual weighted average of depreciation charge would be an appropriate procedure for computation purposes. Accordingly, the above given equation may be a reasonable approximation for the length of the operating period.

For example, for the sake of explaining the computations involved in the above given equation, let's assume that in a project study the total amount of fixed costs is estimated to be 160 million Turkish Liras (TL) and the cost of each fixed asset together with the related depreciation rates are as given in Table 6.

In summary, as seen in Table 6:

The total amount of fixed cost = 160,000(000) TL,

The cost of land = 15,000(000) TL, and

The total of annual weighted average depreciation charge = 14,660(000) TL.

Therefore;

$$\text{Length of Operating Period} = \frac{160,000,000 - 15,000,000}{14,660,000}$$

Length of Operating Period = 9.89 years.

Table 6. Weighted Annual Depreciation Charges for Fixed Assets

Depreciable Fixed Assets (Fixed Cost Items)	Cost (000 TL)	Depreciation Rate	Annual Depreciation Charge (Cost x Rate)
Project Preparation Expenditures	5,000	0.20	1,000
License and Patent Fees	10,000	0.20	2,000
Cost of Land	15,000	--	--
Construction Expenditures	25,000	0.04	1.000
Transportation Facilities	1,000	0.06	60
Machinery and Equipment	100,000	0.10	10,000
Transportation Vehicles	4,000	0.15	600
TOTAL	160,000		14,660

Finally, before concluding the subject on computing the length of the operating period, it should also be pointed out that, in practice, as it is the general case in the World Bank projects, when the technical and/or economic life of the essential machinery and equipment is very long, such as 20 or 25 years, or may be more as in the iron and steel industry, the duration of the operating period is just taken as 10 years. The reason for this limitation is that estimating costs and revenues after 10 years for an investment project with no past data might be difficult or even meaningless in terms of the time value of money. Undoubtedly, if the technical and/or economic life of the essential machinery is less than 10 years, then, whatever the duration of the technical/economic life is, it is taken as the length of the operating period. For example, the economic or useful life of high-tech digital machinery and equipment is often less than 10 years due to high risk of technological obsolescence. Therefore, the length of the operating period would be less than or around 10 years in investment projects whose know-how requires high-tech digital machinery and equipment.

Full Capacity Utilization

When estimating annual operational costs in practice, production during the operating period is generally assumed to be at full capacity. Otherwise, if it is believed that the project would not operate at full capacity, then there is no need to establish a large production scale or capacity. Accordingly, on the basis of this assumption, the operational costs for a year are estimated at full capacity and then are generalized for all the remaining years of the operating period assuming full capacity utilization rates in all years. However, this assumption of full capacity utilization rate in all years and even generalizing it for the first years of the operating period is questionable, since for a new company the possibility of operating at full capacity right after its establishment is very low. This reasoning is quite plausible, especially, in the case of greenfield investment projects that would operate in foreign countries. Truly, it would most likely take some time for a new international company to adapt to the local market conditions of a foreign country so as to operate at full capacity or reach a close rate to 100% capacity utilization rate.

For this reason, in practice, lower capacity utilization rates are estimated for the first and the second years of the operating period, for instance, a 60% capacity utilization rate for the first year, an 85% for the second year, and then 100% full capacity utilization rates are assumed for the remaining operating years. Later on, as indicated in Table 7, first of all, the operational costs are estimated at the full (100%) capacity utilization rate for a year and then the costs items are classified as fixed (F) and variable (V) costs. Finally, the variable costs for each year are computed proportionately according to the capacity utilization rates on the basis of the variable cost items (labeled V) estimated for the full (100%) capacity, while the cost items labeled (F) as the fixed costs are fully taken for all the years of the operating period.

For example, let us consider our previous example of the German WGMBH company's direct investment project planned in Ankara, Turkey, and assume that the optimal production capacity is determined to be 50,000 units of product per year in the technical analysis stage. Additionally, the annual operational costs at full (100%) capacity utilization for manufacturing 50,000 units per year are estimated by engineers as given in the third year (t_{m+3}) of Table 7. Furthermore, the project manager believes that when the project is realized, it will operate at 60% of its optimal production capacity in the first year of the operating period (t_{m+1}), at 85% in the second year (t_{m+2}), and then will reach to 100% (full) capacity utilization rate in the third year (t_{m+3}), and continue so in the remaining years.

Table 7. Operational Costs for Different Capacity Utilization Rates (CUR) (000 TL)

Operational Costs (TL)		Operating Period (Years)			
		t_{m+1} CUR = 60%	t_{m+2} CUR = 85%	t_{m+3} CUR = 100%	t_{m+4} CUR = 100%
Raw Materials	(V)	60,000	85,000	100,000	100,000
Indirect Materials & Supplies	(V)	9,000	12,750	15,000	15,000
Energy	(V)	6,000	8,500	10,000	10,000
Labor	(F)	35,000	35,000	35,000	35,000
Licensing Fees	(V)	9,000	12,750	15,000	15,000
Maintenance	(F)	5,000	5,000	5,000	5,000
General Expenditures	(F)	25,000	25,000	25,000	25,000
Promotional Expenditures	(V)	1,200	1,700	2,000	2,000
Depreciation Charges[a]	(F)	20,000	20,000	20,000	20,000
Total		150,200	185,700	207,000	207,000

m: denotes the length of the establishment period and thus the operating period follows as m+1, m+2, ...

([a]): *Depreciation charges* for fixed capital assets excluding land are assumed to be 20 million TL for five years of the operating period.

Operational cost estimates are made in the local currency (TL) of the host country and later on will be converted to Euros (EUR) for evaluation purposes. Moreover, operational cost items are classified as fixed (F) and variable (V) cost items in Table 7 according to their nature or characteristics of changing with the amount of production. Therefore, the fixed costs (F) are the same for all capacity utilization rates since they do not change with the level of production. That is, fixed costs are independent of the size of production. They are the same at all capacity utilization rates. However, variable costs (V) are proportionately reduced according to the capacity utilization rates for lower levels since they are assumed to be unit costs increasing linearly with the amount of production. For instance, since the capacity utilization rate in the first year of the operating period (t_{m+1}) is assumed to be 60%, then, the variable costs for this year are taken as 60% of the variable costs computed for the full (100%) capacity in the third year (t_{m+3}).

For example, in Table 7, the cost of raw materials in the third year (t_{m+3}) at full (100%) capacity is estimated to be 100,000,000 Turkish Lira (TL) and, thus, in the first year of the operating period (t_{m+1}) with the assumption of 60% capacity utilization rate, the raw materials cost would be (100,000,000x0.60=) 60,000,000 TL. Similarly, variable costs in the second year (t_{m+2}) are taken as 85% of full capacity costs, (100,000,000x0.85= 85,000,000 TL). However, the variable costs for the fourth year (t_{m+4}) of the operating period are 100% of all the variable costs in the third year (t_{m+3}) since full capacity is assumed in the year (t_{m+4}). On the other hand, the fixed costs are the same in all operating years since they do not change with the amount of production. No doubt that such a procedure for estimating annual operational costs is preferred just for practical reasons. If it is desired, annual estimates for all years of the operating period may be made separately. Even further, if classifying operational costs in two categories as fixed and variable costs is not accepted, then, operational costs may be divided into three categories as fixed, semi-variable, and variable costs.

ESTIMATING THE ANNUAL SALES REVENUES EXPECTED

The opposite side of the costs associated with an investment project is the sales revenues expected from the investment project. In fact, the costs are incurred for the sake of receiving more revenues. Therefore, all expected revenues that might be related to a new investment project should be computed and compared them with the costs incurred so as to see if the investment project satisfies the expectations. The expected annual sales revenues of an investment project are computed through simply multiplying the price per unit by the amount of the products to be produced and sold each year in the operating period. At this point it has to be indicated that in project feasibility studies "the products which are produced are always assumed to be totally sold". That is, if a certain amount of products are produced in an operating year, it is assume that they are sold and thus sales revenues are obtained in that operating year. This means that a product produced would be sold any how and thus brings in a revenue equal to price per unit any way. In practice, this general assumption may bring about some liquidity problems in terms of net cash flows. However, if there would be any hesitation regarding liquidity problems, then, a liquidity analysis, as will be explained later, should be conducted and the need for working capital should be revised.

Now, for our example of WGMBH's investment project in Turkey, let us assume that the price per unit was determined to be 15,000 TL when developing the marketing strategy in the market analysis stage. Additionally, as indicated above, the production capacity is decided to be 50,000 units and that the capacity utilization rates are believed to be 60% for the first, 85% for the second, and 100% for the remaining years of the operating period. For the sake of simplicity, let us further assume for the moment that the length of the operating period is 5 years.

Therefore, annual sales revenues (R_t) for The WGMBH's investment project during its operating period of 5 years are computed below and given in the second row of Table 8 (recall that the establishment period was two years (t_0 and t_1) and thus operating period goes as t_2, t_3, …., t_6).

According to the assumption made above, annual Sales Revenues (R_t) are computed as:

t_2: (50,000 x 0.60) x 15,000 = 450,000,000 TL

Table 8. Expected Annual Sales Revenues (000 TL)

Revenues	t_0	t_1	t_2	t_3	t_4	t_5	t_6
1. Sales Revenues	-	-	450,000	637,000	750,000	750,000	750,000
2. Surplus Value[(a)]	-	-	-	-	-	-	962,500
Annual Total	-	-	450,000	637,000	750,000	750,000	1,712,500

[(a)]It is assumed that the project has a very long useful technical life as explained below.

t_3: (50,000 x 0.85) x 15,000 = 637,000,000 TL

t_4: (50,000) x 15,000 = 750,000,000 TL

t_5: (50,000) x 15,000 = 750,000,000 TL

t_6: (50,000) x 15,000 = 750,000,000 TL

As seen in the last column of the third row of Table 8, a second revenue item is the so called *surplus* value in the last year of the operating period. This is the value estimated at the end of the operating period for the residual or the remaining part of the investment not covered by the revenues during the operating period. No doubt, as a potential company, when an investment project ends its operation at the end of its operating period, it will have a *residual value* as explained below. Thus, this value has to be estimated and added to the revenues in the last year of operating period. The residual value is taken into account either as a *salvage value* or as a *surplus value* as follows.

Salvage Value

When the *useful life* of a factory ends, the remaining old machinery, equipment, tools, and all other production facilities would have a value called salvage value. That is, salvage value is the liquidation value of all capital assets at the end of operating period upon physical deterioration of the plant and equipment. Therefore, this scrap or the remaining value of the old plant and equipment called the salvage value should be estimated and thus be added to the last year's revenues. Moreover, two additional revenue items must be included into this scrap or salvage value as extra revenues in the last operating year:

1. The first one is the *value of land*. The land purchased for establishing the desired factory or plant would definitely have a value at the end of the operating period when the plant is liquidated upon completion of its technical or useful life. Most likely, the land would gain value. Thus, whatever the value of the land would be at that time, whether gaining value or not, that value of the land should be estimated and added to the last year's revenues of the project. Nevertheless, at least, the purchased cost of the land should be considered as a revenue item in the last year, if not sure about the final value of the land.

2. The second extra revenue item is the *working Capital*: As explained earlier, the amount of working capital for an investment project represents the current assets of a company in terms of receivables, inventories of finished goods and raw materials, and cash in bank accounts for unexpected events interrupting the operation of a firm. This means that the working capital as the sum of current assets is, in fact, a revolving fund with a conversion cycle that repeats over the operation period of the project. For this reason, when the revenues for the last year of the operating period are estimated for an investment project assumed to be liquidated, the amount of the working capital computed in the establishment period as a part of the initial investment should be added to the revenues of the last operating year since the current assets would be converted into cash next year.

Surplus Value

As it was stated earlier, the duration of the operating period is determined by the length of the technical or useful economic life of the essential machinery and equipment. However, when the technical life of the essential machinery and equipment is very long, the duration of the operating period, in practice, is limited to 10 years since estimation after ten years may be meaningless or very difficult. In such cases, as in the example of steel and iron factories, when the very long useful life of a company is limited to 10 years for practical estimation reasons, a significant residual or surplus value of the company may be omitted. This surplus value which is sometimes called *terminal* or *continuation* value represents the market value of the flow of sales revenues from the project at all remaining future dates.

Therefore, for the investment projects where the operating period is longer than 10 years, the *surplus* or *continuation* value should be estimated and then added to the revenues of the last year of the operating period. As it is noticed, *the salvage value* is estimated for the projects whose technical lives are covered by the operating period while *the surplus value* is estimated for those projects having longer and useful lives that are not totally included in the operating period. In Table 8, a surplus value is estimated for our example of the WGMBH project since a longer useful life is assumed.

In order to compute the surplus value of an investment project two methods are frequently used. The first one is the so-called *infinite perpetuity* model that assumes continuous and zero growth of sales revenues in the infinite future as given below (Gitman & Zutter, 2014):

$$\text{Surplus Value} = \frac{(NCF_n)}{r}$$

where;

NCF_n: denotes the amount of the net cash flow in the last year (n) of the operating period. (The concept of the net cash flow will be explained shortly.)
r: is the average cost of capital that will be explained later.

On the other hand, the second method which is also called *Gordon's growth model* assumes continuous but a constant growth rate of sales revenues in the infinite future as follows (Gitman & Zutter, 2014):

$$\text{Surplus Value} = \frac{(NCF_n)(1+g)}{(r-g)}$$

where; "g" stands for the constant growth rate in sales revenues in the infinite future. All the others are the same as before. In computing surplus value through this formula, when it becomes difficult to estimate the value of "g", the economic growth rate of the national economy of the host country may be taken as an approximation value for "g". However, since the growth rate in sales revenues beyond the operating period are uncertain, the base net cash flow is not increased by the growth rate and, thus, the above given model is more frequently utilized as:

$$\text{Surplus Value} = \frac{(NCF_n)}{(r-g)}$$

At this point it should be indicated once more that when the surplus value is computed through one of the above given models, there would be no need to add the values of land and working capital to the salvage value and, thus, to the last year's revenues any longer, since surplus or continuation value takes into account a continuing business value. For our example of the WGMBH project the surplus value given in Table 8 is computed according to the last form of the above given model by assuming that the net cash flow in the last year (n) of the operating period and the average cost of capital, for the moment, are:

NCF_n = 115,500,000 TL

r = 12%

g = 0 (no growth is expected).

Thus; the surplus value shown in the last column of Table 8 is computed below as:

$$\text{Surplus Value} = \frac{(115,500,000)}{(0.12-0)}$$

Surplus Value = 962,500,000 TL.

As seen in this simple example, a longer technical life brings about a larger surplus value since it is assumed that the project has a longer useful life that goes beyond the length of the operating period for infinity. However, if a moderate technical life is accepted the computed surplus value might be reduced to a practical value as a judgmental approximation. For example, if the useful technical life is thought to be around 15 years then the above given surplus value may be taken as 650,000,000 TL as a judgmental approximation. Needless to say that if the useful technical life is wholly covered by the operating period, then there would be no need to compute a surplus value. Of course, in this case, consideration should be given to the salvage value, the value of land, and the working capital as explained above.

COMPUTING ANNUAL NET CASH FLOWS OF THE INVESTMENT PROJECT

Computing annual net cash flows of an investment project requires preparing a pro forma financial statement which combines all estimates of the revenues, costs, expenditures, and expenses associated with the investment project.

It thus provides all related possible cash outflows (costs and expenditures) and inflows (revenues) together in the form of a table so as to compare and evaluate the desirability of an investment project. For this purpose, once the duration of the establishment and operating periods of the direct investment project are determined, then;

- All sales revenues of the investment project in the operating years, including the surplus value in the last year,
- The initial investment including the working capital in the last year of the establishment period, and
- All direct operational expenditures together with depreciation charges in the related years of the operating period are shown in a financial table, as will be developed soon.

However, the computation of net cash flows on the basis of these cash inflows and outflows somehow differs depending on the attitudes of project analysts towards risk. In some cases interest expenditures are not deducted from the sales revenues to find gross profit or taxable income. That is, the so called - EBIT - earnings before interest and tax are computed (Eithman, Stonehill, & Moffet, 2015). Having computed the earnings before interest and tax (EBIT) for each operating year, corporate tax is paid to find the annual net income or profit, as formulated below. Finally, depreciation charges are added back to the net income or profit to calculate the annual net cash flows.

$$NCF_t = (R_t - I_t - C_t - D_t)(1 - V) + D_t$$

where;

t : Year in the life cycle of the project ($t = 0, 1, 2, \ldots, n$),
NCF_t: Net cash flow in year t,
R_t : Revenues in year t,
I_t : Initial investment in year t (investment is completed in the establishment period),
C_t: Operational expenditures in year t during the operational period, excluding depreciation charges and interest payments,
D_t : Depreciation charges in year t (in the operating period when equipment is in use),
V : Corporate tax rate in the host country where investment is made.

As seen, depreciation charges are first deducted from revenues to pay less tax and then are added back to the operating profit since they are not direct cash outlays. Thus, as it might be noticed, the first part of the equation on the right side indicates net operational profit per year (P_t), that is;

$$P_t = (R_t - I_t - C_t - D_t)\,(1 - V)$$

On the other hand, when a project is evaluated on the basis of the net cash flows computed as indicated above, the net cash flows are discounted by the weighted average cost of capital which includes the after tax cost of debt, K_d (1 - V). That is, the tax deductibility of interest payments is considered when the firm's cost of capital is calculated. Therefore, since the discount rate includes the after tax cost of debt or considers the tax shield effect of the interest rate, interest expenditures are not subtracted from taxable income in order to avoid double counting, as formulated above.

However, in contrast to the above stated procedure for computing net cash flows, some risk-averse analysts who view interest expenditures (F_t) as operational costs subtract them from gross profit and, then, compute corporate tax to find earnings after interest and taxes (net income or profit). Finally, depreciation charges are added back to the net income to calculate net cash flows as shown below:

$$NCF_t = (R_t - I_t - C_t - F_t - D_t)\,(1 - V) + D_t$$

As noticed, in this case, the interest payments (F_t) as the cost of debt are directly deducted from revenues to pay less tax. Later on, when a project is evaluated on the basis of these net cash flows, the net cash flows are discounted by the weighted average cost of capital which includes the interest rate (K_d) as the cost of debt, not the after tax cost of debt as K_d (1 - V). Thus, the tax advantage of interest payments is obtained by directly subtracting interest expenditures from sales revenues.

Consequently, in order to prepare a pro forma net cash flows statement for our example of the WGMBH's direct investment project in Turkey, first of all, we should remember and put together the necessary data given in the following tables:

- The sales revenues expected during the operating period, including surplus value in the last year (Table 8),

- The total amount of initial investment over the establishment period as the sum of the fixed and working capital (Table 3), and
- The operational costs during the operating period and the relevant depreciation charges for the fixed capital assets (Table 7),

Then, on the basis of these tables, Table 9 showing "pro forma net cash flows by years" is prepared as given below. That is, the entries of Table 9 are taken from the related Tables of (3), (7), and (8) prepared in previous sections. As seen, the net cash flows of our example given in Table 9 are computed according to the first approach and thus we do not deduct interest expenditures from sales revenues to compute corporate taxes. Using the data given in the first four rows of Table 9 and taking into consideration that the corporate tax rate (V) in Turkey is presently 20 percent (V=20%) and would not change in the short run, the net cash flows (NCF_t) throughout the life cycle of the project can be computed through the following formula for each year of (t):

$$NCF_t = (R_t - I_t - C_t - D_t)(1 - V) + D_t$$

Table 9. Pro Forma Net Cash Flows by Years (000 TL)

	Life Cycle of the Investment Project (Years) (Establishment Period + Operating Period)						
	t_0	t_1	t_2	t_3	t_4	t_5	t_6
1. Sales Revenues (**R**)	-	-	450,000	637,000	750,000	750,000	1,712,500
2. Initial Investment (**I**)	380,000	413,000	-	-	-	-	-
3. Operational Costs (**C**) (Interest and depreciation charges are not included)	-	--	150,200	185,700	207,000	207,000	207,000
4. Depreciation Charges(*) (**D**)	-	-	20,000	20,000	20,000	20,000	20,000
5. Net Operating Profit (**P**)	-	-	223,840	345,040	418,400	418,400	1,188,400
6. Net Cash Flows (**NCF**)	-380,000	-413,000	243,840	365,040	438,400	438,400	1,208,400

(*) Depreciation charges are not included in operational costs since they are dealt differently for taxation purposes.

As seen in the formula, depreciation charges are first deducted from revenues (or gross profit) to pay less tax and then are added back to the operating profit to get the net cash flows since they are not direct cash outlays.

NCF_t computations for few years are given below as examples and all results are shown in the 5th and 6th rows of Table 9.

NCF_0 = (0 - 380,000 - 0 - 0) (1 - 0) + 0 = -380,000 TL (no tax since there is no profit).

:

NCF_2 = (450,000 - 0 - 150,200 - 20,000) (1 - 0.20) + 20,000

NCF_2 = 223,840 + 20,000 = 243,840 TL

:

NCF_4 = (750,000 - 0 - 207,000 - 20,000) (1 - 0.20) + 20,000

NCF_4 = 418,400 + 20,000 = 438,400 TL

:

NCF_6 = (2,400,000 - 0 - 207,000 - 20,000) (1-0.20)+20,000

NCF_6 = 1,188,400 + 20,000 = 1,208,400 TL

As it is seen in the 6th row of Table 9, the net cash flows (NCF_t) clearly show the summary of revenues, costs, and expenditures spread over years. That is, in contrast to scattered revenues and various types of costs throughout the life cycle of the direct investment project, now it is clearer to see net cash flows in that the negative values indicate net cash outflows while the positive ones show net cash inflows. More specifically, in the first two years of the investment project some net *cash outflows* are made in order to receive a series of net *cash inflows* in the future years.

CONCLUSION

In conclusion, at this stage of the financial analysis, the question to be answered is: "*is this investment project with the net cash flows computed above a profitable one or not*?" In other words, "*should the investor accept it or reject it*"? The answer to this question, however, requires a detailed analysis of cash flows and a careful evaluation of the profitability of the direct investment project. Therefore, evaluating investment projects deserve special attention such that a detailed analysis is made in a separate chapter that follows. Furthermore, profitable foreign direct investment projects have also to be evaluated from the viewpoints of various risks associated with them for operating in foreign countries. Accordingly, in addition to evaluating foreign direct investment projects in terms of their profitability as it is done in the following chapter, risks related to them will also be elaborated in another chapter entitled as "Risk Analysis in Project Evaluation" in the remaining pages of this study.

REFERENCES

Berk, J., & DeMarzo, P. (2016). *Corporate Finance* (4th ed.). Boston: Pearson Education Limited.

Berk, J., DeMarzo, P., & Harford, J. (2012). *Fundamentals of Corporate Finance* (2nd ed.). Boston: Pearson Education Limited.

Eithman, D. K., Stonehill, A. I., & Moffet, M. H. (2015). *Multinational Business Finance* (14th ed.). Boston: Pearson Education Inc.

Gitman, L., & Zutter, C. (2014). *Principles of Managerial Finance* (14th ed.). Boston: Pearson Education, Inc.

Hubbard, G. R., & O'Brien, A. P. (2012). *Money, Banking, and the Financial System*. Boston: Pearson Education Limited.

Moosa, I. A. (2010). *International Finance: An Analytical Approach* (3rd ed.). Boston: McGraw-Hill.

Titman, S., Keown, A. J., & Martin, J. D. (2011). *Financial Management: Principles and Applications* (11th ed.). Boston: Prentice-Hall.

Turkish Development Bank. (2015). *Preparing Investment Projects*. Ankara: Turkish Development Bank. (In Turkish)

ENDNOTES

1 More on Purchasing Power Parity (PPP) method, see Moosa (2010).

2 For more about alternative financing techniques, see Hubbard and O'Brien (2012).

Chapter 6
Evaluating Foreign Direct Investment Projects

ABSTRACT

As explained in the foregoing chapter, once the relevant cash outflows and inflows associated with a foreign direct investment project are estimated so as to calculate the net cash flows, the desirability of the investment project should then be determined in terms of its economic profitability. Therefore, in this chapter the methods widely used in evaluating investment projects are discussed and their advantages as well as shortcomings are highlighted. Later in the chapter, evaluating foreign direct investment projects from the viewpoint of the parent company is elaborated in terms of profit and/or income transferred to the home country. The same investment evaluation techniques were applied to the net cash flows transferred to the home country of the parent company. The possible income and/or dividends to be remitted to the home country of a parent company are identified and discussed so as to reflect the viewpoints of investing parent companies when planning foreign direct investments. This two-level evaluation approach is generally followed in practice to make sure that direct investments are profitable at both host and home country levels, since an investment project that is not profitable at host country level would not be profitable at home country level either or a project that is profitable at host country level may not be profitable at home country level.

DOI: 10.4018/978-1-5225-7696-9.ch006

EVALUATION OF INVESTMENT PROJECTS AT HOST COUNTRY (PROJECT) LEVEL

A direct investment project, above all, is a proposal for establishing a company in a selected country (host country) and then expecting it to operate within the surrounding conditions of that country. Accordingly, its profitability should first be evaluated from the viewpoint of the host country just like a local investment proposal per se. In other words, evaluation at host country level is an appraisal of the investment project per se within the socio-economic and political conditions of the country selected for investment. If the investment project is determined to be profitable at host country level in the sense that it creates profit worthwhile for local investors in case of selling it in the future; then it would be evaluated in terms of income to be transferred to the home country of the parent company to see if it fulfills the investor's expectations. The reason for this consecutive evaluation is that some of the profit may not be allowed to be remitted to the parent company at home. This two level evaluation is generally accepted in the literature (Eithman, Stonehill, & Moffet, 2015; Van Horne, & Wachowicz, 2009).

For evaluating a direct investment project at the host country level, all cash outflows and inflows should be denominated in the local currency of the country selected for investment. Thus, cash flows in foreign currency must be converted into national or local currency. In fact, most of the cash flows would possibly be denominated in the local currency since purchasing production factors and sales would most likely be through the local currency. However, when there are cash flows denominated in foreign currencies, they should be converted to the local currency through appropriate exchange rates. There are several classical methods that are widely used to evaluate investment projects at local country level. These methods are explained in the following subsections step by step.

The Method of the Simple Rates of Return

This method aims at calculating a rate of return which is simply the ratio of the average annual profit to the total initial investment made during the establishment (set-up) period. However, in practice, rather than computing the average annual profit over the operating period, the method simply considers the annual profit in a so-called "*normal year*", which represents the operation of the project best; that is, a year in which neither revenues nor costs are extremely larger or smaller. That is, the method assumes the profit in the selected normal year as the average annual profit of the investment project. The reason for this is that, as indicated below, the method is a quick and practical evaluation measure that aims at checking the profitability of an investment project at a first glance without going into detailed analysis. This method is also called basic or accounting rates of return method since it just averages annual net operating profit (P) over the total initial investment (I). From this viewpoint the method shows a kind of rate of return on assets.

In short, the simple rate of return on the total investment (SRR_T) is:

$$SRR_T = \frac{P}{I}$$

Similarly, if desired, a simple rate of return on equity per se may also be computed as the ratio of the annual net profit in the normal year to the amount of equity invested in the investment project as follows:

$$SRR_Q = \frac{P}{Q}$$

where;

SRR_T: The simple rate of return on the total investment.
SRR_Q: The simple rate of return on equity.
P: The annual net profit in the *normal* year.
I: The total initial investment in the establishment period ($\sum$ I).
Q: The amount of equity invested in the project.

In evaluating an investment project, in order to consider a project as a profitable investment proposal, the project should have an SRR_T greater than or at least equal to the overall cost of capital is tied up in the investment. Similarly, from the viewpoint of the equity invested, SRR_Q should be greater or at least equal to the cost of equity. Furthermore, when choosing among alternative investment projects, the project with the greatest simple rate of return should be regarded as the best alternative, of course, if its SRR_T is greater or equal to the cost of capital. On the other hand, the cost of capital tied up in a direct investment project as a yardstick for evaluation is, in fact, the minimum rate of return that an investor expects from the investment project. Thus, an investment promising profit is the one that has a simple rate of return at least equal to or greater than the cost of capital is tied up in it.

Accordingly, when evaluating investment projects, the cost of capital is an important subject to be considered. This subject would be dealt with in detail when the method of net present value is discussed later on. Nevertheless, for the sake of completing our explanations regarding the method of the simple rate of return, let us assume for the moment that for our previous example of the WGMBH's investment project in Ankara, Turkey; the overall cost of capital for the investment project is 12% ($k_0 = 0.12$) and that of the equity is 14% ($k_e = 0.14$). Additionally, the pro forma net cash flows computed for the WGMBH's investment project in the foregoing chapter in Table 1 are given below again to recall.

Now, assuming that the year t_4 is considered to be the "*normal*" year, the simple rates of return will be calculated as follows:

$$SRR_T = \frac{418,400}{380,000 + 413,000}$$

$$SRR_T = 0.53$$

Additionally, recalling from Table 3, that the total amount of equity financing is decided to be 380,000(000) TL (or 100,000 EUR), then the simple rate of return on equity (SRR_Q) in terms of TL will be:

$$SRR_Q = \frac{418,400}{380,000}$$

$$SRR_Q = 1.10$$

Therefore, since the simple rate of return on the total investment is by far greater than the overall cost of capital, that is,

$$SRR_T = 0.53 > k_0 = 0.12$$

and also the simple rate of return on equity is by far larger than the cost of equity, that is,

$$SRR_Q = 1.10 > k_e = 0.14$$

Table 1. Pro Forma Net Cash Flows by Years (000 TL)

	Life Cycle of the Project (Years) (Establishment Period + Operating Period)						
	t_0	t_1	t_2	t_3	t_4	t_5	t_6
1. Sales Revenues (**R**)	-	-	450,000	637,000	750,000	750,000	1,712,500
2. Initial Investment (**I**)	380,000	413,000	-	-	-	-	-
3. Operational Costs (**C**) (Interest and depreciation charges are not included)	-	-	150,200	185,700	207,000	207,000	207,000
4. Depreciation Charges(*) (**D**)	-	-	20,000	20,000	20,000	20,000	20,000
5. Taxes (R – I – C – D) T			55,960	86,260	104,600	104,600	297,100
6. Net Operating Profit (**P**) (R – I – C – D) (1 – T)	-	-	223,840	345,040	418,400	418,400	1,188,400
7. Net Cash Flows (**NCF**) (R – I – C – D) (1 – T) + D	-380,000	-413,000	243,840	365,040	438,400	438,400	1,208,400

(*) Depreciation charges are not included in operational costs since they are dealt differently for taxation purposes.

the investment project *seems* to be profitable.

Here, the word "*seems*" is used purposefully since the computational results of the method of the simple rate of return are not much reliable. There are basically two reasons for this. The first is that this method does not take into account the time value of money in the sense that the value of a Turkish Lira (TL) or a Euro (EUR) in the year t_0 and that of the one in the year t_4 is considered to be the same. No doubt that this assumption is not true since "the bird in hand is not the same as the one in the bush", as will be explained later. Secondly, selecting a normal year for the sake of simplicity is judgmental and might change from person to person. For instance, if t_3 is selected as normal year instead of t_4, the results would be computed differently. Consequently, no project manager accepts or rejects an investment only on the basis of using the simple rate of return method.

However, despite these shortcomings, this method is very widely used by project managers when evaluating investment projects since it is simple and provides a starting base for further analysis. In other words, when evaluating investment projects in practice, a project manager firstly computes quickly the simple rate of return through picking up a *normal* year without going into the details of net cash flows for all the operating years. Then, if the project shows a relatively large and attractive rate of return, the project manager goes on to make further analyses through various other reliable methods so as to decide about the acceptance of the project. As such, when an investment project does not promise a satisfactory level of profit, then, there is no need to go into detailed analysis by using other methods for further analysis.

However, if the project shows a lower or even a moderate rate of return, the project manager stops evaluation procedure and quite the project. Because this method is not so much reliable for the reasons indicated above, it is just taken as a signal for further analysis only if it shows higher rates of return. That is, this method is regarded as a kind of checking-up procedure to see whether the investment project deserves further analysis for appraising. Accordingly, for the rates of return that do not attract the attention of the project manager, the evaluation procedure is ended and the project is rejected as an investment proposal. However, as our example above points out, a larger rate of return is taken as a signal for further analysis. Thus, we may go into detailed analyses by using other methods as follow, since our example of the WGMBH's investment project points to higher returns.

The Payback Period Method

The payback period refers to the number of years for which the project pays back its initial investment through its expected net profits or net cash flows during the operating period. If the payback period is shorter than the period which the investor or the project manager desires, the project is accepted as an investment proposal. Otherwise, if the payback period is longer than what the investor requires, the project is rejected. In other words, a project is accepted only if it pays back its initial investment in a shorter duration than that required by the investor. In case of equality, that is, when the payback period is equal to the period required, the investor may accept it since the project is recovering its initial investment at least within the period required by the investor.

The payback period (PBP) may be computed on the basis of either annual operational net profits as;

$$\sum_{t=0}^{m} I_t = \sum_{t=m+1}^{n} P_t$$

or net cash flows as;

$$\sum_{t=0}^{m} I_t = \sum_{t=m+1}^{n} NCF_t$$

Thus, the number of years satisfying these equations is considered as the payback period (PBP) for the investment project.where;

t: Denotes the years in the life cycle of the project (t = 0, 1, …, m, m+1, m+2, ..., n),
m: The number of years in the establishment period (t = 0, 1, .., m),
n: The last year of the operating period that counts as (t = m+1, m+2, …, n),
P_t: Annual net operating profit in year t,
NCF_t: Annual net cash flow in year t.

The most important point in the method of the payback period is to determine the duration of the payback period required or desired by the investor (M). This required duration is then compared with the duration computed through the above given formulas (PBP). The duration required or desired by the investor is a reflection of the judgment of the investor regarding the riskiness of the investment project with respect to the socio-economic and political conditions surrounding the investment in the country selected. If the investor regards the socio-economic as well as the political environment instable and thus risky, he or she will require a shorter payback period depending on the level of instability or riskiness. The reason for this is quite clear since the investor desires to get back his or her initial investment tied up in the investment project as soon as possible. Otherwise, the existing socio-economic and political conditions of the country selected may change over a longer term period and the initial investment may be lost.

Thus, for instance, the required payback periods for the countries like Iraq, Iran, Egypt, Venezuela, Turkey, Brazil, Holland, Sweden, and USA will be quite different for international investors. For some of these countries, for instance, Holland, Sweden, and USA, a payback period may not be required or determined either since the socio-political and economic environment in these countries is quite stable and would probably stay so for a long period of time. Therefore, no risk would be anticipated by the investor. That is, in such countries the economic profitability of the investment will be the only concern for international investors. If the investment project is profitable, it will pay back its initial investment any way whatever its payback period would be. However, for the countries like Iraq and Syria perhaps no investor will plan investing under the existing conditions of 2018. In other words, the required payback period would be so short that no investment would meet it and, may be, trading would be the only concern.

In computing payback period, investors or project managers use either annual net profits or net cash flows depending on the riskiness of the business environment. If the investment environment seems relatively risky, investors on one hand require a shorter payback period and on the other hand use annual net profit figures for computations. Since the net profit figures do not include depreciation charges but the net cash flows do, the payback period computed would be longer than that of using net cash flows. Accordingly, a shorter payback period required by an investor compared with a longer payback computed through annual net profits; altogether, make the acceptance of a project difficult in a risky environment. Thus, investors using annual net profit values for computing payback period double check and balance the riskiness of the business environment. Otherwise, when investors consider the country in question moderately risky, they use annual net cash flows to compute the payback period for evaluating investment projects. No doubt that the required payback period is determined by investors or project managers according to the risk conditions surrounding the country selected for investment.

For our example of the WGMBH's direct investment project in Turkey, the annual operational net profits and annual net cash flows given in Table 1 are stated below to recall. Payback computations based on both the annual operational net profits and cash flows are given in Box 1.

Now, assuming that the payback period required by the WGMBH's management is 3 years (M = 3), the payback period (PBP) on the basis of annual operational net profits is found as follows:

380,000 + 413,000 < = > 223,840 + 345,040 (profits of 1+1= 2 years),

793,000 < = > 568,880 (not equal in 1+1= 2 years),

The remainder;

793,000 - 568,880 = 224,120 (to be paid from the profit in the 3rd year),

Box 1.

5. Net Operating Profit (**P**)	-	-	223,840	345,040	418,400	418,400	1,188,400
6. Net Cash Flows (**NCF**)	-380,000	-413,000	243,840	365,040	438,400	438,400	1,208,400

and this is,

(224,120) / (418,400) = 0.54

of the 3rd year's profit.

Therefore, the payback period (PBP) is:

1 + 1 + 0.54 = 2.54 years.

Since the payback period is shorter than the required payback period, that is,

PBP = 2.54 < M = 3

so the investment project is acceptable.

Similarly, the payback period using net cash flows is:

380,000 + 413,000 < = > 243,840 + 365,040 (NCFs of 1+1= 2 years),

793,000 < = > 608,880 (not equal in 1+1= 2 years),

(793,000 - 608,880) / 438,400 = 0.42 years.

Thus, the payback period is:

1 + 1 + 0.42 = 2.42 years.

Again, the project is acceptable because;

PBP = 2.42 < M = 3.

Notice that the project pays back its initial investment in a shorter period of time when using net cash flows data (2.42 < 2.54).

The method of the payback period is quite widely used by international investors for evaluating direct investments projects, especially, in developing countries since it considers the overall riskiness of the country selected in terms of socio-economic and political changes. For this reason, the method is also regarded as a method for risk analysis. Thus, rather than going into the detailed commercial and political risk analyses for risky investment projects, international investors and/or multinational companies simply try to determine an appropriate required payback period on the basis of risky conditions prevailing in the country in question and, then, evaluate their investment projects according to that period as a risk indicator. That is to say, all risk factors altogether are bundled up in a factor labeled the "duration" of the payback period.

The method of the payback period is criticized on two basic grounds:

1. First, the classical use of the method, as explained above, does not take into account the time value of money. That is, the value of money in the establishment period is assumed to be the same as that one in the payback period. However, this criticism may be removed by discounting the related values used in computing payback period with an adequate rate for the cost of capital (r) as stated below:

$$\sum_{t=0}^{m} I_t / (1+r)^t <=> \sum_{t=m+1}^{n} P_t / (1+r)^t$$

where:

I_t: Initial investment in the year t in the establishment period.
m: Duration of the establishment period.
r: Denotes the rate of the overall cost of capital as a discounting factor. The subject of the cost of capital and discounting will be explained shortly.
P_t: Net annual operational profit in the year t in the operating period.
n: Duration of the operating period.

2. The second criticism is that the payback period does not consider profits or net cash flows after the payback period. For instance, in the above given example annual operating net profits after 2.54 years and cash flows after 2.42 years, that is, generally after 3 years, are not considered when evaluating the investment project. In other words, the evaluation focus is only on the profits or net cash flow values obtained in the payback period and, thus, those after the payback period are neglected. This shortcoming of the method may lead to rejecting the profitable industrial investment projects that will actually need time to penetrate into competitive foreign markets. Entering into a foreign market, competing, and finally capturing the expected market share and thus making profits to payback the initial investment actually take longer times for new

foreign companies. In fact, it is quite likely that international companies in foreign countries will spent their first few years trying to get to know the new business environment, develop desired costumer relations, and capture the targeted market share.

Moreover, larger profits may follow the payback period once a foreign company captures its expected market share. Therefore, when such an investment project is just rejected because of not paying back the initial investment in a required period of time, the investor may miss quite profitable business opportunities. Accordingly, as it is asserted, evaluating investment projects just on the basis of a required payback period would under value and thus lead to the rejection of profitable investment projects. No doubt that all these are logical and true objections. Nevertheless, the basic purpose of the method of payback period is to recover the initial investment due to the risky conditions surrounding the business environment before they get worse. Thus, profit making does not have the first priority in the evaluation process. Priority is given to getting the initial investment back as soon as possible depending on the level of risk. As such, this is not a drawback for the method but the essence of the methodology followed.

The Net Present Value Method

The net present value is the sum of the net cash flows discounted by the cost of capital over the life cycle of the investment project. Thus, the formula for computation is:

$$\text{NPV} = \sum_{t=0}^{n} NCFt \, / \, (1+r)^t$$

where;

NPV: The net present value,
n: The number of years in the life cycle of the project (t = 0, 1, 2, ……, n),
NCF_t: Net cash flow in year t,
r: The discount rate as the average cost of the capital invested in the project.

If the computed NPV is positive, the investment project is accepted, meaning that the sum of the discounted cash inflows is greater than that of cash outflows. On the contrary, when NPV is negative, the investment project is rejected since the sum of the discounted cash inflows in this case would be less than that of cash outflows. That is, when:

NPV > 0 the project is accept and

NPV < 0 the investment project is rejected.

A project with a net present value equal to zero (NPV= 0) may also be accepted if the project manager finds it beneficial for the investor because of some other reasons, since such a project earns at least a rate of return equal to the average cost of capital. That is, it does not incur a loss any way. Accordingly, if an investment project serves some other purposes for the investing company, it may be accepted when its NPV is equal to zero, (NPV = 0). For instance, a direct investment project whose NPV is zero may be accepted for following an essential customer investing in a foreign country, not leaving a powerful rival alone in an international market, entering into a developing market before the other rival firms and thus may be refraining them to enter, etc.

In addition to evaluating investment projects per se for acceptance or rejection decisions, the NPV method is also used for ranking alternative projects according to their profitability and thus helps project managers select the most desirable project among various alternatives. For example, let us consider four alternative investment projects with the following NPVs computed:

A = $ 35,000,000
B = $ 52,000,000
C = $ -5,000,000
D = $ 14,000,000

According to these values the best project is project B since it has the largest NPV. Therefore, if one project is going to be selected, that would be project B. However, if the alternative projects are not mutually exclusive, that is, the acceptance of one project does not necessarily require the rejection of the others; projects A and D may also be accepted for investment as the second and the third investment projects, respectively, since they have positive NPVs. Thus, if funds for investment are available and that the investor can handle few projects at a time, projects A and D may be accepted in addition to project B. Project C is rejected in any case because it has a negative NPV. But if the alternative projects are mutually exclusive so that only one project is to be selected, then project B is the best choice for having the largest NPV.

Following these general explanations, the NPV for the WGMBH's investment project in Turkey may now be calculated. However, the calculation of NPV, as indicated above, necessitates the estimation of the average cost of capital to discount the net cash flows (NCF_t) associated with the investment project. Furthermore, it should also be pointed out that when evaluating an investment project at the host country (project) level, the cost of capital has to be estimated according to the conditions of the host country as well, not to those prevailing in the home country. That is to say a local rate for the weighted average cost of capital should be estimated on the basis of the sources of financing the investment project.

The Cost of Capital at Host Country Level

In our example of the WGMBH's investment in Turkey, the total initial investment was estimated to be 200,000,000 EUR and 50% of it, that is, 100,000,000 EUR is to be financed by a term loan with a 10% annual interest rate. Therefore, in order to estimate the overall cost of capital for the total investment, firstly, the cost of debt (term loan) and equity denominated in euros (EUR) has to be calculated separately in terms of Turkish Lira (TL) according to the economic conditions of Turkey and then the overall average cost of capital may be computed. This, indeed, is not an easy task to be overlooked. Despite the complexities involved in it, this subject matter is generally tackled in practice in two specific ways (Eithman, Stonehill, & Moffet, 2015):

1. In the first approach, the cost of debt denominated in foreign currency is first computed and then the cost of equity is estimated through it. That is, the cost of equity is based on the cost of debt. For this reason, to compute the cost of debt, *debt payments* including principal and interest in foreign currency (EUR) are computed separately and then converted to local currency (TL). As it might be recalled, this computation and conversion operations were done in an earlier section using purchasing power parity (PPP) method and the results were shown in Table 2, which is now repeated below to see how the figures are used in computing cost of debt. The total annual debt payments for paying the principal and interest to repay the debt of 100,000,000 EUR over five years are

shown in TL values in the last row of Table 2, as equivalents of EUR values.

On the other hand, the total amount of the original debt of 100,000,000 EUR is also converted into Turkish Lira (TL) as indicated below. As it might be recalled, the exchange rate in the base year t_0 was taken as 1 EUR = 3.80 TL, that is, 3.80TL/EUR. Since the debt of 100,000,000 EUR is used in the second year of the establishment period, the next year's exchange rate is estimated through Purchasing Power Parity (PPP) method assuming that inflation rates will be 12% and 3% in Turkey and Germany, respectively. Accordingly, the exchange rate for the next year (S_{t+1}) is estimated to be,

$$S_{t+1} = 3.80 \text{ x } \frac{(1+0.12)}{(1+0.03)}$$

$$S_{t+1} = 4.13$$

Thus, the equivalent of the original debt of 100,000,000 EUR is;

100,000,000 x 4.13 = 413,000,000 TL.

For now, on the basis of the total debt payments (principal + interest) denominated in TL values in the last raw of Table 2, one may consider the debt of 413,000,000 TL (equivalent of 100,000,000 EUR) as a *financial investment* that gets annual returns of:

Table 2. Principal and Interest Payments of the Loan in Both Currencies (000 EUR and TL)

Years	1	2	3	4	5
Principal (EUR)	16.380	18.018	19.820	21.802	23.982
Interest (EUR)	10.000	8.362	6.560	4.578	2.398
TOTAL (EUR)	26.380	26.380	26.380	26.380	26.380
Exchange Rate TL/EUR = 3.80	4.13	4.49	4.88	5.30	5.76
Principal (TL)	67,649	80,901	96,722	115,551	138,136
Interest (TL)	41,300	37,545	32,013	24,263	13,812
TOTAL (TL)	108,949	118,446	128,735	139,814	151,948

(*) Computations involved in Table 5 from Chapter 5 were explained in Section 5.1.3.

+108,949(000) + 118,446(000) + 128,735(000) + 139,814(000) + 151,948(000) TL.

Therefore, the internal rate of return, that is, the discount rate that makes the sum of the discounted values of these annual returns equal to the value of the investment (debt) might be considered as the cost of debt in TL. That is, the rate of return of this financial investment in a debt instrument (loan) would be the cost of the term loan for those that use it. The internal rate of return (IRR) of the financial investment stated above is;

$$413,000 = \frac{108,949}{(1+IRR)^1} + \frac{118,446}{(1+IRR)^2} + \frac{128,735}{(1+IRR)^3} + \frac{139,814}{(1+IRR)^4} + \frac{151,948}{(1+IRR)^5}$$

IRR = 0.16

Hence, the cost of using a loan of 413,000,000 TL as equivalent of 100.000.000 EUR in a direct investment project in Turkey is 16% before tax. That is, with our previous notation, the cost of debt before tax (k_d) is:

$k_d = 0.16$

Once the cost of debt is estimated as explained above, project managers review the socio-economic and political conditions of the host country and figure out a risk premium for using equity capital in the investment project. For instance, if a risk premium of 5% is deemed appropriate, then the cost of equity is estimated at:

$k_e = (16\% + 5\%) = 21\%$.

Having estimated the costs of debt and equity as stated above, the weighted average cost of capital to be invested in the project would be computed as follows (remember that the weights or ratios of debt or term loan and equity were 50% each and the corporate tax rate in Turkey is 20%):

$k_o = w_e k_e + w_d k_d (1 - V)$

where:

k_o: The weighted average cost of capital,
w_e: The portion or weight of equity in the total investment (50%),
w_d: The portion or weight of debt in the total investment (50%),
k_e: The cost of equity capital (21%),
k_d: The before tax cost of debt (16%),
V: The corporate tax rate (20%).

Thus, the weighted average cost of capital is:

$$k_o = 0.50(0.21) + 0.50(0.16)\ (1 - 0.20)$$

$$k_o = 0.17$$

As seen, the computation of the cost of equity and thus the weighted average cost of capital in this approach is based on the cost of debt in the local currency. The reason for this is that this approach implicitly assumes that debt in foreign direct investments is usually provided by the parent companies in the form of a term loan. Thus, once the cost of debt is calculated, then the overall cost of capital is easily estimated if an appropriate risk premium is figured out for investing in the country selected.

2. The second approach to estimate the cost of capital denominated in foreign currency in terms of local currency is to take the interest rates on the long term governmental bonds of the host country as a base value. So, in this case, the debt to be invested in a foreign direct investment project is considered as an international portfolio investment. Accordingly, the interest rate on long term governmental bonds is assumed to be the cost of debt capital. Since governmental bonds are considered risk free instruments in the country selected, a risk premium for an international investment is added to the interest rate on bonds to find an estimated cost of equity. For example, if the interest rate on long term governmental bonds of the host country is 14% and a risk premium of 6% is thought to be adequate for the host country, then the cost of equity might be assumed at (14% + 6%) = 20%. Therefore, the weighted average cost of capital would be estimated as:

$$k_o = 0.50(0.20) + 0.50(0.14)\ (1 - 0.20)$$

$$k_o = 0.156$$

Needless to indicate that the difference in our hypothetical examples of the weighted average cost of capital for two approaches is due mainly to assuming different interest rates on the loan provided by the parent company and the bond issued by the host government. In fact, there would always be such differences simply because the interest rates in question always vary. Thus, the subject of which method to be chosen for computing the overall cost of capital from the viewpoint of host country's economic conditions is a matter of financing and the risk premium conceived for the host country.

One may question the reliability of these approaches on the ground that estimating a risk premium involves a great deal of judgmental evaluation regarding the socio-economic and political conditions of the host country. This is true to a certain extent. However, it should be stated that the purpose of the project evaluation at the host country level is not to decide about accepting or rejecting the investment proposal, rather it is a search for determining whether or not the investment project has a potential of economic profitability in the host country. If the project per se is profitable at the local (host country) level, then the final decision regarding the acceptance of the project is going to be made at the parent company (home country) level. Otherwise, if the project is not profitable at the host country level; then there would be no need to go further for an evaluation at the home country level. Consequently, judgmental determination of risk premiums in estimating the cost of capital is not a serious problem at host country level. Project evaluation at host country level is a kind of first level evaluation or checking-up procedure based on a logical judgment for further analysis at parent company level which is based on more correct data.

Computing Net Present Value at Host Country (Project) Level

Now, assuming that the weighted average cost of capital for the WGMBH's investment project in Turkey is estimated to be r = 17% as computed above, the net present value of the project can be calculated as shown in Box 2 (remembering that the net cash flows of the investment project are as given below):

Box 2.

6. Net Cash Flows (**NCF**)	-380,000	-413,000	243,840	365,040	438,400	438,400	1,208,400

$$\text{NPV} = \sum_{t=0}^{n} NCFt \,/\, (1+r)^t$$

$$\text{NPV} = \frac{-380,000}{(1+0.17)^0} + \frac{-413,000}{(1+0.17)^1} + \frac{243,840}{(1+0.17)^2} + \frac{365,040}{(1+0.17)^3} + \frac{438,400}{(1+0.17)^4} + \frac{438,400}{(1+0.17)^5} + \frac{1,208,400}{(1+0.17)^6}$$

NPV = -380,000 – 352,991 + 178,128 + 227,922 + 233,951 + 199,964 + 471,074

NPV = 578,048(000) TL.

Since NPV > 0, the project may be an acceptable investment proposal, depending on the evaluation at the parent company (home country) level. That is, the final decision would be based on the evaluation at the parent company level as will be explained later. However, for the moment, the investment project is profitable at the host country level. That is, the investment project is a profitable investment proposal from the viewpoint of the host country.

The method of the net present value (NPV), as the sum of the net cash flows discounted by the average cost of capital over the life cycle of an investment project, is a robust evaluation model. It is widely used in evaluating investment projects since it takes into account all related cash flows throughout the life cycle of the investment project as well as the time value of money in the sense of discounting cash flows by the cost of capital. As such, the NPV method is regarded as a reliable method for both evaluating an investment project per se and ranking alternative investment projects.

For example, let us assume that the GMBH Company considers two additional countries for investment, namely, Austria and Ukraine. The feasibility studies repeated in these countries computed net present values for Austria as NPV_A= 2,980,000.50 EUR and for Ukraine as NPV_U= 200,500,000.00 EUR. As such, as ranked below, since the investment in Ukraine would have a larger NPV than the other alternatives, Ukraine should be selected for investment. Note that NPV in Turkey is converted to EUR with the present exchange rate of 3.80 TL/EUR as (578,048,000/3.80 =) NPV_T = 152,117,894.74 EUR.

NPV_U = 200,500,000.00 EUR

NPV_T = 152,117,894.74 EUR

NPV_A = 2,980,000.50 EUR

Notwithstanding the fact that the NPV method is a reliable methodology in evaluating investment projects because of taking into account of all related cash outflows and inflows as well the time value of money; however, it also has some essential shortcomings that decision makers should be aware of, as stated below:

1. The computation of NPV requires the cost of capital to be determined and used as a discounting factor along the life cycle of the project. As such, NPV computation is quite sensitive to the cost of capital and thus requires a correct estimation of it as much as possible. However, this is generally not possible due to lack of precise data. Accordingly, companies usually estimate their cost of capital in the form of intervals such as something between 12 and 15 percent (12% – 15%). In cases of such necessarily large intervals or ranges of the cost of capital, the results of NPV computations may change depending on the values in the range for the cost of capital. For instance, NPV may be positive with a cost of capital of 12% but if the cost of capital is taken as 15%, NPV might be negative. Unfortunately, at present, it is not possible to calculate the cost of capital precisely. Thus, project analysts have to pay close attention to precision issue in estimating the weighted average cost of capital when using the NPV method for evaluating investment projects.
2. In computing NPV, once an average cost of capital is determined anyhow, this rate is used as a *constant* discounting rate throughout the life cycle of the investment project, assuming that the cash inflows created during the life cycle are reinvested with a rate equal to the average cost of capital. Nonetheless, the cost of capital or the discounting rate may change along the life cycle of the project, which is usually long. Thus, in cases where such changes are considered plausible, the changing discount rates should be taken into account to ameliorate the solution.
3. In practice, investment projects with NPV = 0 are rejected as if they were not profitable. In fact, this is not correct since these projects earn

a rate of return equal to the average cost of capital. Therefore, investors should consider acceptance of such investment projects; especially if these investments serve some other purposes for their business firms. For example, as stated earlier, to be the first firm in the target market, to follow essential customers such as tire companies following automobile factories, and not to leave main competitors in the market alone, etc.

4. Finally, the NPV method does not provide for decision makers a specific profitability rate rather than a magnitude of discounted net cash flows such as NBD = 578,048 TL. Nevertheless, investors often require a specific rate of return such as 25% to decide about an investment. In other words, the NPV method does not provide any specific information concerning the unit profitability of an investment project while decision makers generally need a specific profitability rate for comparing and selecting a project. This drawback may even lead to incorrect decisions when comparing alternative investment projects with significantly varying sizes of initial investments.

For instance, consider the following two alternative investment projects A and B whose initial investments (I) and NPVs are given below:

I_A= 120 (000,000) TL

NPV_A= 41 (000,000) TL

I_B= 70 (000,000) TL

NPV_B= 26 (000,000) TL

According to our explanations made so far, project A should be selected since it has a larger NPV than project B, that is, 41 million TL > 26 million TL. However, this is not a correct decision in terms of the rate of profitability. If we try to find out a kind of profitability measure or a *profitability index* (PI) through dividing NPVs of the projects by the amounts of initial investments consecutively, we will find out that, contrary to the first decision stated above, project B has a greater profitability index than that of A, as indicated below:

$$\text{Profitability Index} = \left(\frac{NetPresentValue}{InitialInvestment}\right)$$

$$PI_A = \left(\frac{41}{120}\right) = 0.34$$

$$PI_B = \left(\frac{26}{70}\right) = 0.37$$

Therefore, project B is the correct choice in terms of profitability since its profitability index is larger than that of A; that is, $PI_B = 0.37 > PI_A = 0.34$. Needless to indicate that projects with PI > 0 are only considered for evaluation since PI < 0 means a negative NPV and requires a rejection decision. Here, it should also be pointed out that sometimes in some text books the profitability index is regarded as a benefit/cost ratio. In this case, the profitability criterion is required to be greater than one (> 1) since benefits include only positive net cash inflows, excluding the initial investment in the establishment period. As such, a "Benefit/Cost" ratio larger than one (1), in fact, means a "NPV/ Initial Investment" ratio larger than zero (0). Needless to state that the larger the profitability index the better the investment project would be. In short, in comparing investment projects with varying sizes of investments the NPV method may lead to incorrect choices. Thus, a complementary approach similar to a profitability index is needed.

The procedure explained above to compensate for the deficiency of the NPV method for not providing specific information related to the profitability of an investment project is called *the profitability index* method. This index is used as an additional method to compare alternative investment projects in terms of the profitability ratios of their computed NPVs. More specifically with our previous notations, the profitability index (PI) as a complementary method to the NPV method is computed as follows:

$$PI = \frac{\sum_{t=0}^{n} NCF_t / (1+r)^t}{\sum_{t=0}^{m} I_t / (1+r)^t} \quad (t= 1, 2, \ldots, m, m+1, m+2, \ldots\ldots, n)$$

or,

$$PI = \frac{NPV}{\sum_{t=0}^{m} I_t / (1+r)^t} \quad (t= 0, 1, .., m)$$

As noticed, the denominator in the above given formulas indicates the discounted value of the initial investment during the establishment period. Accordingly, when comparing alternative investment projects with significantly varying sizes of initial investments, the alternative with the positive and highest profitability index should be selected.

The Method of the Internal Rate of Return

The internal rate of return is the discount rate that makes the net present value of initial investment equal to the sum of the discounted net cash flows over the life cycle of the investment project. More clearly, with respect to the net present value method, the internal rate of return (IRR) is the discount rate that makes the net present value (NPV) of the investment project, that is, the sum of the discounted net cash flows, equal to zero. So, it may be formulated as:

$$\sum_{t=0}^{n} NCFt / (1+IRR)^t = 0$$

where;

n: The number of years in the life cycle of the project (t = 0, 1, 2, ……, n),
NCF_t: Net cash flow in year t,
IRR: The internal rate of return as the discount rate to be found.

As seen, according to a given discount rate, the left side of the equation would compute an NPV value for the investment project. Therefore, if we try many discount rates, the discount rate that would make the left side of the equation (NPV) equal to zero is called the internal rate of return (IRR). The IRR value is found through a trial and error method. That is, a discount rate is tried in the equation and if the computed left side of the equation is positive, meaning that IRR is larger, the discount rate is increased. In the next trials if the left side becomes negative, indicating that IRR is smaller, then, the rate is decreased. This trial procedure of increasing and decreasing discount rate continues until the left side of the equation becomes zero. Interpolation method may be used to decrease the number of trials to find the internal rate of return through several trials.

However, on a computer with the Excel program, the solution takes less than a second of time. For instance, the IRR of the WGMBH's investment project in Turkey with the net cash flows given below is (Box 3):

$$\frac{-380,000}{(1+IRR)^0}+\frac{-413,000}{(1+IRR)^1}+\frac{243,840}{(1+IRR)^2}+\frac{365,040}{(1+IRR)^3}+\frac{438,400}{(1+IRR)^4}+\frac{438,400}{(1+IRR)^5}+\frac{1,208,400}{(1+IRR)^6}=0$$

IRR = 0.36

This means that when all the net cash flows given above are discounted by 0.36, the total value would be zero. IRR defines a specific profitability rate for an investment project. That is, IRR = 0.36 means that the profitability rate of this project is exactly 36 percent. Such clear and specific information is quite helpful for investors to make a decision regarding the profitability of an investment project. Recalling that the weighted average cost of capital for the WGMBH's investment project was assumed to be r = 17%, then one can easily say that this investment project is quite profitable at the national level since the internal rate of return is by far greater than the overall cost of capital, that is, IRR = 36% > r =17%. The method of IRR can also be used in ranking alternative projects and choosing the most profitable one. For example, if an investor whose cost of capital is 17 percent has alternative investment projects with internal rates of return of 35, 16, and 42 percent and that he/she is going to choose one of them (i.e., mutually exclusive projects), the project with 42 percent rate of return should be chosen as the most profitable one. The project with the internal rates of return of 16 percent is rejected in any case since its rate of return is lower than the cost of capital. In sum, IRR indicates a clear measure of unit profitability that is easily used for comparing alternative investment proposals.

Box 3.

6. Net Cash Flows (**NCF**)	-380,000	-413,000	243,840	365,040	438,400	438,400	1,208,400

Advantages of the Internal Rate of Return Method

The IRR method compensates the shortcomings of the NPV method in the sense that it provides a specific or a percentage profitability rate for an investment project. That is, it does not need any additional profitability index to give an idea about the profitability rate of an investment project. Thus, IRR may be compared with the cost of capital on the same basis of measurement. Additionally, compared to the NPV method, the IRR method is not sensitive to the computation of the cost of capital because it does not use the cost of capital as an input in computations. It just searches for a profitability rate as a discount rate and when it is found, it is compared with the cost of capital and then the reject or accept decision is made. Depending on the magnitude of IRR, the difficulty of estimating the cost of capital and thus measuring it in an interval does not create any problem in computing IRR as it does in NPV.

For instance, let us assume that the weighted average cost of capital for our example of WGMBH's investment project is not 17% exactly but something between 16 and 18% and that the internal rate of return is found to be 36% as stated above. As such, there would be no problem in evaluating the investment project since its IRR = 36% is greater than any value of the cost of capital between the range of 16-18%. That is, it does not make any difference whether the cost of capital is 16%, 17%, or 18%. The investment project is by far a profitable proposal anyway. However, this does not mean that the IRR method does not require computing the cost of capital for an investment project since it does not use it in finding out IRR as opposed to NPV. It is true that the IRR method does not use the cost of capital as an input in finding out the IRR value, yet to make a decision through the IRR found or calculated, the cost of capital is definitely needed. Otherwise, a decision could not be made. Therefore, there is no way to escape computing the appropriate cost of capital. The advantage of IRR over NPV with respect to the cost of capital is that the IRR computation is not affected by the cost of capital whereas that of NPV does.

In addition to compensating the shortcomings of the NPV method, the IRR method also has all the advantages of the NPV method as well. In other words, just like the NPV method, the IRR method considers the whole life cycle of an investment project including all related cash inflows and outflows, as well as taking into account the time value of money by discounting the net cash flows. Accordingly, when compared with the NPV method in terms of evaluating investment projects, the method of IRR is generally preferred by decision makers for the reasons stated above. Studies indicate that about two-thirds of business firms use the IRR method when evaluating investment projects.

Shortcomings of the Internal Rate of Return Method

Contrary to all the advantages indicated above, the IRR method has a drawback that comes up when evaluating investment projects which do not have *normal* or *conventional* net cash flows. *Normal* or *conventional* net cash flows mean that the net cash flows associated with an investment project are negative during the establishment period and positive along the operating period of the project. This is, in fact, an expected form of net cash flows. During the establishment period there are no revenues since the factory or plant is being set up and thus initial investment expenditures will make net cash flows negative. On the other hand, during the operating period there are no more investment expenditures and that production is continuing. Therefore, sales revenues flow in and the net cash flows would be positive. Consequently, net cash flows are *normally* expected to be negative during the establishment period and positive during the operating period of the investment project.

Nevertheless, in some cases the net cash flows may not be *normal* or *conventional* for various reasons. That is, the annual cash inflows (revenues) during the operating period may be less than cash outflows (operational expenditures) for some reasons and thus the net cash flows might be negative for some years in the operating period. In such cases where the net cash flows are not *normal* (*conventional*), there will be either more than one IRR or no IRR at all, for some pure mathematical reasons related to the solution method. Accordingly, in such cases, the method of IRR would not make any sense.

For instance, let us consider the following famous oil pump investment project (Mao, n/a) whose cost of capital is 10% and that has the computed net cash flows as given in Table 3.

According to the net cash flows given above, there are two internal rates of return, specifically, 25% and 400% that make the sum of the discounted cash flows equal to zero (0) as calculated below:

Trial I with 25%:

$$-1600+\frac{10000}{(1+0.25)^{1}}+\frac{-10000}{(1+0.25)^{2}}=0$$

Table 3. Unconventional Net Cash Flows

	Net Cash Flows (USD)		
	t_0	t_1	t_2
NCF	-1.600	10.000	-10.000

(*)The cost of capital is 10%.

$$- 1600 + 8000 - 6400 = 0$$

IRR = 0.25

Trial II with 400%:

$$-1600 + \frac{10000}{(1+4)^1} + \frac{-10000}{(1+4)^2} = 0$$

$$- 1600 + 2000 - 400 = 0$$

IRR = 4.

Since the cost of capital is 10%, one may say that each IRR is by far greater than the cost of capital and thus the investment project should be accepted whatever the rate is taken. However, if the net cash flows are discounted by the cost of capital of 10% to compute NPV, as given below, NPV is found to be negative:

$$NPV = - 1600 + \frac{10000}{(1+0.10)^1} + \frac{-10000}{(1+0.10)^2}$$

NPV= - 773.55 USD

Therefore, in this case, the project should be rejected since it has a negative NPV. As seen, the project which seems to be profitable by 25 or even 400 percent is incurring a loss of 773.55 USD at 10 percent cost of capital. Here, IRR and NPV methods are contradictory and that the problem is associated with IRR since the net cash flows of the investment project are *not normal*. That is, the net cash flows are not *conventional* and changes sign (becomes negative) in the year t_2 and as such the project has two IRRs. Hence, IRR is not a reliable method in such cases where net cash flows are *not normal*; that is, when they are *unconventional*. Accordingly, the investment decision should be made on the basis of NPV. That is to say this project should be rejected because it has a negative NPV. In brief, when the net cash flows are not normal or conventional, the IRR method should not be used, instead the decision should be made on the basis the NPV method.

Furthermore, in evaluating *mutually exclusive* investment projects, where selecting one project necessarily requires the rejection of all the other alternatives because they become redundant, IRR and NPV methods may conflict if the length of the life cycles of alternative projects, the sizes of initial investments, and the magnitudes of net cash flows are significantly different. For example, let us consider two mutually exclusive investment projects C and D whose net cash flows are given in Table 4. The cost of capital (r) is 0.03 and the computed NPV and IRR values for alternative projects are given in the last two columns of the table (Mao, n/a).

As seen, both projects have positive NPVs and IRR values larger than the cost of capital of 0.03. Therefore, two projects may be accepted. However, since the investment projects are mutually exclusive, only one of them is to be selected. As such, the NPV method recommends selection of project D since it has a larger NPV value while the IRR method does project C because of having a higher IRR. In other words, there is a contradiction between the two methods. In such special cases, as it will be explained shortly, the decision should be based on the NPV method. That is, the project with the highest NPV (i.e., project D) should be selected.

The reason for such a contradictions lies on the assumptions of the methods regarding the reinvestment rate of cash inflows created during the operating period. This type of contradictions with regard to the selection of mutually exclusive investment projects are seen *only if two conditions are simultaneously met*:

Table 4. Net Cash Flows ($) for Mutually Exclusive Projects C and D

	t_0	t_1	t_2	t_3	t_4	t_5	(r)	NPV	IRR
C	-3790	1000	1000	1000	1000	1000	0.03	789.71	0.10
D	-3790	200	600	600	1000	2800	0.03	822.61	0.08

(r)The average cost of capital.
Contradiction: $NPV_D = 822.61 > NPV_C = 789.71$ select project D?
$IRR_C = 0.10 > IRR_D = 0.08$ select project C?

1. If there is a discount rate that makes the net present values (NPV) of mutually exclusive projects equal to each other – this discount rate is sometimes referred to as "the Fisher's rate of return over cost" by some authors (Mao, n/a) – and additionally,
2. If the average cost of capital is smaller than this discount rate (Fisher's rate of return over cost or intersection point).

Otherwise, that is, when there is no discount rate equating the NPVs of both projects to each other (no Fisher's intersection point) or there is an equating discount rate but this rate is larger than the average cost of capital, there would be no contradiction between the two methods with regard to selecting mutually exclusive investment project. In brief, if these two conditions are not observed or met simultaneously, the methods of NPV and IRR would require the selection of the same investment project without any contradiction.

For example, as shown in Figure 1 given below, when there is no Fisher's intersection point, that is, no discount rate equating the NPVs of the mutually exclusive investment projects X and Y as seen in the first graph (I), there would be no contradiction between the two methods. In another word, both NPV and IRR would select the investment project Y since it has a larger NPV profile at any discount rate as well as a greater IRR than that of X (i.e., $r_y > r_x$). Here the concept of NPV profile refers to the shape of the NPV curve or line according to the changing discount rates (r). Therefore, when the NPV profiles of the projects X and Y are zero (0) at the points on the horizontal axis, that is, the NPVs are equal to zero, then, r_x and r_y indicate the IRRs for alternative projects, respectively.

Now let's consider the second graph (II) and assume that the NPV profiles of two projects simply touch each other (or Y is tangent to X) at a certain point. In this case, both projects would have equal NPVs at this point (Fisher's intersection point). However, there still would be no contradiction between the two methods. The NPV method would recommend selection of Y because it would have a larger NPV profile than that of X at all the other discount rates. Similarly, the IRR method would also select the project Y since it would have a greater IRR, that is, $r_y > r_x$.

However, as seen in the third graph (III) given in Figure 1, when the NPV profiles of the alternative projects X and Y intersect or are equal at a discount rate named Fisher's intersection point (R_f), there could be a contradiction between the two methods if, and only if, the cost of capital (r) is less than the Fisher's intersection point (R_f); that is, ($r < R_f$). Otherwise, there would be no contradiction between the NPV and IRR methods. The reason for this

Figure 1. NPV Profiles of Alternative Investment Projects X and Y

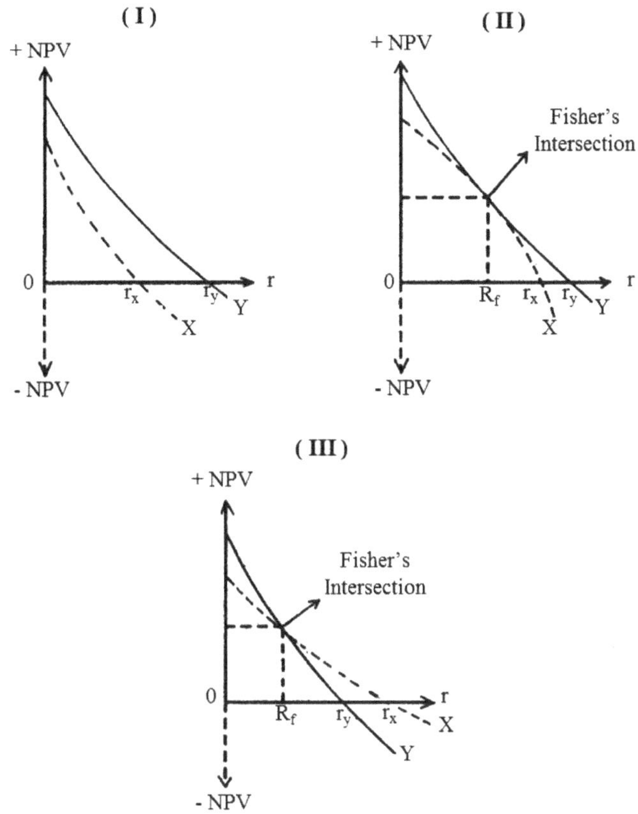

contradiction when $r < R_f$, lies at the NPV profiles of the projects X and Y. As noticed in the last graph (III) in Figure 1, the project Y has a larger NPV profile than that of X at discount rates less than the Fisher's intersection point ($r < R_f$). That is, at discount rates up to the Fisher's intersection point (R_f), the project Y will be selected by the NPV method. But the IRR method, on the contrary, will recommend the selection of the project X since it has a higher IRR than that of Y (i.e., $r_x > r_y$).

In contrast to this conflict, after the Fisher's intersection point (R_f), that is, at discount rates greater than the Fisher's intersection point (R_f), there is no contradiction between the two methods. The NPV method suggests the selection of the project X because it has a larger NPV profile than Y and that the IRR method similarly recommends the selection of X since it has a higher IRR than that of Y; that is, $r_x > r_y$. In short, there will be a conflict if the cost of capital as a discount factor is less than the Fisher's intersection point, but no conflict if the cost of capital is greater than the Fisher's intersection point.

Consequently, in evaluating mutually exclusive investment projects the methods of NPV and IRR do not always conflict. They contradict each other if, and only if, the NPV profiles of the two projects intersect, that is, when there is a discount rate equating the NPVs of both projects (a Fisher's intersection point) and furthermore the cost of capital is less than this equating discount rate (the Fisher's intersection point). In other words, if the NPV profiles of mutually exclusive investment project do not intersect or they intersect but the cost of capital for the investor (r) is greater than the discount rate at the intersection point (R_f), that is, if $r > R_f$, there would be no contradiction since the NPV and IRR methods would recommend the selection of the same project.

Liquidity Analysis

The purpose of the economic evaluation of investment projects through the methods explained hitherto is to appraise investment proposals in terms of their costs and revenues and thus to determine whether or not they are profitable or create profit. If an investment project creates profit it is accepted. Otherwise, it is rejected. However, a profitable investment project might not be viable, that is, may not continue its operation due mainly to some liquidity problems. Liquidity in this sense refers to the cash needs of a business firm and it is related to the cash balance of a firm. If the liquidity problems faced during the operating period of the investment projects are not solved or the cash needs are not met through various short term financing methods, the project may interrupt or even stop its operation.

Therefore, having determined that a direct investment project is profitable, a liquidity analysis should be made to find out if the project would face any liquidity problems in the future and, if so, to take necessary measures in advance. In other words, liquidity analysis aims at determining if a profitable investment project would continue its operation smoothly without confronting any liquidity shortages during its operating period. Such an analysis is especially important for multinational corporations in that dividend and/or income transfers to the parent company will depend on the availability of cash funds. Therefore, if a profitable foreign direct investment project would not pay dividends due to liquidity problems, the parent company's investment decision may be reevaluated. In another word, international investors may not accept foreign direct investments that would not pay the expected dividends and income.

The reasons for a profitable investment project to face possible liquidity problems are that the net cash flows which form the base for profitability evaluation do not cover all cash outflows and inflows; they just include cash flows that affect the profitability of the investment project. For instance, the term loans or debts used in an investment project are included into the total amount of the initial investment costs and thus payments for principal and interest are not considered as expenditures in the profitability analysis. Otherwise, they would be double counted since debt is taken into account as the cost of initial investments. Liquidity analysis should be made on the basis of the related annual cash flows denoted in the nominal values of the local currency of the host country since the operation of the investment project is evaluated in the selected host country. Consequently, in order to determine in advance whether or not a profitable investment project would confront any liquidity problems, a liquidity analysis has to be made by taking in to account all net cash inflows and outflows as *sources and uses of funds*, that is:

- Sales revenues,
- Surplus or salvage value,
- Separate accounts of equity and debt,
- All operational expenditures,
- Principal and interest payments,
- Dividend payments, and
- Tax payments.

For now, as an example for a liquidity analysis, let us consider our working example of WGMBH's direct investment project in Turkey and recall data entries in Tables 3, 5, and 9 from Chapter 5, which were developed previously. On the basis of the data in these tables the liquidity analysis statement is developed and shown in Table 5. All figures are available in the tables mentioned, except dividend payments that were computed in the next section in Table 9 as 70% of the annual net operating period. Additionally, license fees during the operating period (running royalties) are included in the operating costs and the surplus value is added to the last year's revenues as before when the net cash flows of the project were computed. Thus, Table 5 involves all related cash inflows as sources of funds and cash outflows as uses of funds.

The computation procedure for the liquidity analysis in Table 5 is quite simple. *The cash balance* for each year is computed as the difference between the cash inflows and the cash outflows in that year. The cash balance of each year is also noted as the cash difference within that year to calculate cumulative values. Then starting from the first year (base year) the cash balance at the end of the year is carried to the following year and termed as the cash balance at the beginning of the year. Finally, this beginning cash value of the year is added to the cash balance or the cash difference within the year to find the cash flow at the end of that year. Thus, there are three cash items for each year labeled as the "beginning of the year", "difference within the year", and the "end of the year" values that consecutively show the cumulative cash balance along the operating years of the investment project, as indicated in the last row of Table 5.

As seen in the table the investment project faces cash shortages in the first two years of the operating period. Although there is no cash shortage at the beginning of the first operating year (t_2), however, the year ends with a shortage of 21,797,000 TL. The following year t_3 begins with this shortage, but due to a positive cash balance 5,066,000 TL created within the year, the cumulative cash balance at the end of the year decreases to 16,731,000 TL. Nevertheless, this shortage is met in the next year t_4 which ends with a positive cash balance of 54,000,000 TL. The investment project does not confront any liquidity or cash shortage problems during the other years.

Table 5. Liquidity Analysis (000 Turkish Lira - TL)

	t_0	t_1	t_2	t_3	t_4	t_5	t_6
I. Cash Inflows							
1. Sales Revenues[1] 2. Equity 3. Debts (Loans)	- 380,000	- 413,000	450,000	637,000	750,000	750,000	1,712,500
II. Cash Outflows							
1. Initial Investment 2. Operating Costs[2] 3. Principal Payments 4. Interest Payments 5. Taxes 6. Dividend Payments	3800,000	413,000	150,200 67,649 41,300 55,960 156,688	185,700 80,901 37,545 86,260 241,528	207,000 96,722 32,013 104,600 292,880	207,000 115,551 24,263 104,600 292,880	207,000 138,136 13,812 297,100 831,880
III. Cash Balance							
(I - II)	0	0	-21,7 97	5,066	16,785	5,706	224,572
Cumulative Cash Balance							
IV. Beginning of the Year V. Within the Year (I-II) VI. End of the Year	0 0 0	0 0 0	0 -21,7 97 -21,7 97	-21,7 97 5,066 -16,731	-16,731 16,785 54	54 5,706 5,760	5,760 224,572 230,332

[1]Include surplus value in the last year (t_6).
[2]License fees (running royalties) are included as before.
[3]Dividends are assumed to be 70% of annual net operating profit.

On the other hand, as seen in Table 5, it is clear that the cash inflows in the years t_2 and t_3 cover all operating costs, loan payments, and taxes without any problem. The cash shortages in these years are related only to the dividend payments. Therefore, the project manager has to find a solution in advance for handling cash shortages in the years of t_2 and t_3. For instance, one possible solution might be to convince the WGMBH's management to receive fewer dividends during these two years Perhaps another solution might be to look for the possibility of arranging loans from local financial institutions to meet the cash shortages. In such cases when additional loans are to be arranged for overcoming liquidity problems, the financial analysis might be revised to take into account the effects of additional of debt, if considered to be significant.

Consequently, liquidity analysis is a quite useful methodology for computing direct cash inflows and out flow to determine in advance how and to what extent an investment project would meet its financial liabilities. Moreover, in cases of revealing cash shortages in some years, the project manager would search for solutions in advance how to solve them and thus make some financial plans. Such financial plans sometimes entail changes in capital structure and revisions in financial analysis. Needless to indicate, in liquidity analysis positive cash balances are usually desired in order not to face any financial problems in the future. Furthermore, some project managers even require cumulative cash balances to be over a predetermined "security margin" as a kind of safeguard against liquidity problems. In all cases, the efficiency of the financial system of the host country is always taken into account in terms of providing opportunities to obtain or raise funds when needed during the operating period of the investment project.

EVALUATION OF INVESTMENT PROJECTS AT HOME COUNTRY (PARENT COMPANY) LEVEL

As explained in the foregoing section, if an investment project promises profit at the host country (project) level, that is, if the project is a profitable investment proposal within the existing conditions of the country selected for direct investment, then, the investment project should be evaluated from the viewpoint of the parent company at the home country level. The final acceptance or rejection of an investment project depends on the results obtained at this level in terms of profits and/or dividends to be remitted to the home country. That is to say a project, which was found profitable at the host country level as a desirable investment proposal, may be rejected at the home country level when it is evaluated from the viewpoint of the parent company.

Some countries have strict regulations and deterrent taxation policies on transferring funds and/or remitting dividends to the home countries of parent companies. Therefore, as explained earlier, when selecting a country for a direct investment, the project manager should be aware of these restrictions concerning remittances and take them into account at this stage of project evaluation. Indeed, the evaluation of a direct investment project is essentially based on the income transferred and/or dividends remitted to the parent company in the home country. Therefore, the cash inflows and outflows associated with the investment project as estimated at the host country level are taken as the base of the evaluation process and, then, adjustments are made in terms of the amount of cash inflows to be remitted to the parent company. Finally, the investment project is evaluated through the classical methods of payback, net present value, and internal rate of return on the basis of the adjusted and transferable net cash inflows as explained in the following pages.

Determining the Amounts of Dividends and the Related Income to Be Transferred to the Parent Company

The procedure to evaluate a foreign direct investment project from the viewpoint of the parent company also uses the financial data and information previously used for evaluating an investment project at host country level, because the amount of dividends and/or income to be transferred to the parent company depends on the amount of sales revenues. Therefore, for evaluating the WGMBH's investment project in Turkey at the *host country level* we need the costs and revenues data given previously in Tables 3, 5, and 9 from Chapter 5. These tables are given below again to recall easily and use the relevant data for the evaluation at home country level.

As seen in the tables, having reviewed the financial structure, the payments of debt in terms of principal and interest, and the net cash flows associated with the investment project as estimated at the host country level; the first thing to do for evaluating an investment project from the viewpoint of the parent company at the home country level is to prepare a financial table showing the amounts of dividends and the related income to be transferred to the parent company. The preparation of such a financial table requires the adjustment of the related data shown in Tables 6, 7, and 8 as explained below step by step:

Table 6. Financial Structure of the Investment Project

Cost Items	Foreign Currency (000 EUR)		Local Currency (000 TL)	
	t_0	t_1	t_0	t_1
I. Initial Investment				
1. Fixed Capital 2. Working Capital[(a)]	100,000 ----	50,000 50,000	380,000 ----	206,500 206,500
Total Annual	100,000	100,000	380,000	413,000
II. Financing				
1. Owners' Equity 2. Long Term Loan	100,000	---- 100,000	380,000 ----	413,000

[(a)]Working capital is required in the last year of the establishment period.

Table 7. Principal and Interest Payments of the Loan in Both Currencies (000 for both EUR and TL)

Years (Operating Period)	1	2	3	4	5
Principal (EUR)	16,380	18,018	19,820	21,802	23,982
Interest (EUR)	10,000	8,362	6,560	4,578	2,398
TOTAL (EUR)[(a)]	26,380	26,380	26,380	26,380	26,380
Exchange Rate TL/EUR = 3.80	4.13	4.49	4.88	5.30	5.76
Principal (TL)	67,649	80,901	96,722	115,551	138,136
Interest (TL)	41,300	37,545	32,013	24,263	13,812
TOTAL (TL)[(a)]	108,949	118,446	128,735	139,814	151,948

[(a)]As seen, due to the high inflation rate expected in Turkey equal installments in EUROs are not equal in TL in the future years.

1. The amount of the annual net operating profit that is allowed to be remitted to the home country is determined. Concerning our example of WGMBH's project in Turkey it should be stated that there is no restrictions or deterrent tax applications in Turkey with regard to transferring profits or income to the home country of the parent company. That is, income or dividends could easily be remitted to the parent company. However, for the sake of explanation to complete the procedure, let us assume that only 70% of the annual net operating profit is allowed to be remitted. Therefore, 70% of the annual net operating profits given in the 6th row of Table 1 are computed and stated as *dividends* in Table 9. Values in

Table 8. Pro Forma Net Cash Flows by Years (000 TL)

	Life Cycle of the Project (Years) (Establishment Period + Operating Period)						
	t_0	t_1	t_2	t_3	t_4	t_5	t_6
1. Sales Revenues (**R**)	-	-	450,000	637,000	750,000	750,000	1,712,500
2. Initial Investment (**I**)	380,000	413,000	-	-	-	-	-
3. Operational Costs (**C**) (Interest and depreciation charges are not included)	-	-	150,200	185,700	207,000	207,000	207,000
4. Depreciation Charges(*) (**D**)	-	-	20,000	20,000	20,000	20,000	20,000
5. Taxes (R – I – C – D) T			55,960	86,260	104,600	104,600	297,100
6. Net Operating Profit (**P**) (R – I – C – D) (1 – T)	-	-	223,840	345,040	418,400	418,400	1,188,400
7. Net Cash Flows (**NCF**) (R – I – C – D) (1 – T) + D	-380,000	-413,000	243,840	365,040	438,400	438,400	1,208,400

Table 9. Transfer of Dividends and Income to the Parent Company (000)

Exchange Rates (TL / EUR)	t_0 **--**	t_1 **3.80**	t_2 **4.13**	t_3 **4.49**	t_4 **4.88**	t_5 **5.30**	t_6 **5.76**
1.Initial Invest.(EUR)	-100,000	-100,000					
Dividends(70%P)[a] TL			*156,688*	*241,528*	*292,880*	*292,880*	*831,880*
2. Dividends (EUR)			37,939	53,792	60,016	55,260	144,424
LicenseFees(2%R)[b]TL			*9,000*	*12,740*	*15,000*	*15,000*	*34,250*
3.License Fees(EUR)			2,179	2,837	3,074	2,830	5,946
4.Principal (EUR)			16,380	18,018	19,820	21,802	23,982
5. Interest (EUR)			10,000	8,362	6,560	4,578	2,398
TOTAL (EUR) (1+2+3+4+5)	-100,000	-100,000	66,498	83,009	89,470	84,470	176,750

(a) 70% of annual net operating profits in TL and then converted to Euros by the exchange rates given in the first row.
(b) 2% of annual revenues in TL and then converted to Euros by the exchange rates given in the first row.

Turkish Liras (TL) are converted to Euros (EUR) by the exchange rates estimated with the purchasing power parity (PPP) method as explained previously.

2. As stated earlier, parent companies investing abroad usually charge a *running royalty* as a certain percentage of the estimated production value or the sales revenues of the investment project for the know-how provided to the project. The running royalties are allowed to be remitted to the parent company quite easily. Moreover, the tax rate (withholding tax) on running royalties when transferred to the parent company is lower

than that on the remittances of dividends. In practice, parent companies generally charge a ratio between 2 and 4 percent of annual sales revenues along the operating period as *license fees* (*running royalty*) for the know-how provided for the project. In brief, after tax license fees should be computed and included in Table 9. For our example of the WGMBH project, 2% of the sales revenues in Table 1 are taken as the after tax license fees to be transferred.

3. From the viewpoint of parent companies one of the most important sources of income from a direct investment is the *principal and interest payments* made by the project (the subsidiary) for the debt or term loans obtained from the parent company. Transfer of these payments does not create any problem in the sense of legal regulations and/or permissions required. Additionally, just like transferring license fees or running royalties, the tax rate (withholding tax) on transferring the principal and interest payments is relatively low compared to dividends. Hence, when parent companies make direct investments abroad, they use significant amounts of external financing in terms of debt from the parent company. As for our example of the WGMBH project, 50% of the initial investment is assumed to be financed through a five-year term loan with 10% annual interest rate. The principal and interest payments as computed previously and repeated in Table 2 are shown in Table 9, as income to be transferred to the home country of the parent company.
4. In transferring dividends and the related income to the home country of the parent company, no corporate tax payment on behalf of the home country was considered because no *double taxation* is assumed. Thus, there is no corporate tax payment in Table 9. However, in countries where double taxation is practiced or as in the case of USA when the corporate tax rate in the host country is lower than that of USA and thus the difference is paid in USA; the corporate taxation should be taken into account. Additionally, the amounts of dividends, license fees, and principal and interest payments to be transferred are taken as after tax (withholding tax) values in Table 9. In countries where withholding tax rates are different for the items to be transferred, the tax computations should take into account such differences. In brief, all transfers or remittances to the home country of the parent company should be computed as after tax values.
5. Finally, as indicated earlier, in converting local currency into foreign currency, the exchange rates are estimated by the purchasing power parity (PPP) method for practical reasons. No doubt that one may use

any other method that is deemed appropriate for estimating or forecasting the exchange rates along the operating period of the investment project.

Evaluating the Profitability of the Investment Project

Once the total annual income to be transferred to the parent company is determined, as indicated in Table 9, the profitability of the investment project from the viewpoint of the parent company can be evaluated through the classical methods of payback period, net present value, and internal rate of return as explained earlier. Here, the simple rate of return method is purposefully left out since this method would not help any further at this stage of evaluation. In conclusion, the evaluation of the WGMBH's direct investment project in Turkey may be carried from the viewpoint of WGMBH Company on the basis of the data in Table 9 as follows.

The Payback Period

According to the total annual income figures transferred to the main company, as shown in the last row of Table 9, the payback period (PBP) is shown in Box 4.

$$100{,}000+100{,}000 \Leftrightarrow 66{,}498+83{,}009+\frac{[(100,000+100,000)-(66,498+83,009)]}{89,470}$$

PBP = 1+1+0.56

PBP = 2.56 years.

This means that the direct investment projects pays back the total initial investment of (100.00.000+100.000.000=) 200.000.000 EUR in 2.56 years or approximately (2.56 x 12 = 30.72) 31 months. Recalling that the payback period required by the WGMBH Company was, M = 3 years, the investment project should be accepted since;

Box 4.

TOTAL (EUR) (1+2+3+4+5)	-100,000	-100,000	66,498	83,009	89,470	84,470	176,750

PBP = 2.56 < M = 3.

The critical points to be considered when using the payback period method in evaluating investment projects were elaborated earlier. Accordingly, there is no need to repeat them here once more.

The Net Present Value

For computing the net present value (NPV) of the direct investment project, as explained previously, the total annual income to be transferred to the parent company, as computed in the last row of Table 9, should be discounted by the average cost of capital. The average cost of capital for evaluating the investment project at the parent company level is the cost of capital specifically for the WGMBH Company not that in the local market (host country) conditions as calculated in the foregoing section. In brief, the computation of NPV at parent company (home country) level necessitates the estimation of the cost of the capital particularly for the WGMBH Company.

Naturally, the cost of the capital to be invested in a project depends on the sources of funds. If the project is going to be financed through owner's equity, the cost of capital would be different than that of using external financing such as issuance of debt securities. Moreover, in cases of using both sources of funds at varying ratios the cost of capital would be the weighted average of the costs of sources of funds. Therefore, the costs of capital for equity and debt is first computed separately and then, on the basis of the capital structure of the project, that is, the share of each source of financing, an average cost of capital would be calculated as explained below.

1. **The Cost of Equity:** The cost of the equity invested in a foreign direct investment project is estimated differently depending on the type of the parent company being a public company or not. If the parent company is *not* a public company, that is, it is a closed firm whose stocks are not traded publicly in securities markets or exchanges; the only way of estimating the cost of equity is to find out its "*opportunity cost*" since there is no relevant data to compute it. The opportunity cost is *the earnings foregone* for tying up the equity in the project in question rather than investing it in somewhere else. Accordingly, the opportunity cost will vary for business firms depending on their investment opportunities. Thus, the returns that might have been obtained from such opportunities are

estimated and then regarded as the cost of equity financing. Nevertheless, in practice, when there are difficulties to estimate the opportunity cost, the annual interest rate is often taken as a proxy.

It should also be added here that a closed firm may try to find a similar public firm resembling its financial outlook and operational characteristics. If there is any such resembling public company, then by using the securities market data of this similar public firm, the cost of equity capital may be estimated according to the *capital assets pricing model* (CAPM) or *Gordon's growth model*, as will be explained shortly. Of course, here the problem would be to find a similar public company whose securities market data and operational characteristics resemble the closed firm's financial data and operational features. Therefore, if a closed firm resembles a public company in terms of financial and operational characteristics, the cost of equity could be computed through these models as explained below.

For a public company whose common stocks are traded publicly in securities markets and/or exchanges, the cost of equity is computed as the *rate of return required* by the stockholders according to the *capital asset pricing model* (CAPM) as given below. The CAPM and Gordon's growth models are well known in the field of finance; however, their theoretical backgrounds will not be explained here but there are good sources in the literature (Welch, 2014; Gitman & Zutter, 2014; Brealey, Myers, & Allen, 2016). The capital asset pricing model (CAPM) is stated as:

$$k_e = k_{RF} + ß_i (k_M - k_{RF})$$

where;

k_e: Denotes the rate of return required by stockholders,
k_{RF}: Risk-free interest rate (e.g., interest rate on treasury bonds),
k_M: The annual rate of return in the capital market,
$ß_i$: The (Beta) coefficient of the systematic risk for the stock of the ith company.

For instance, let's assume that the WGMBH Company is a public company with a systematic risk coefficient of $\beta = 1.62$ and that in its home country (Germany) $k_{RF} = 2\%$ and $k_M = 8\%$, then, the rate of return required by stockholders, that is, the cost of equity would be:

$$k_e = 0.02 + 1.62\ (0.08 - 0.02)$$

$k_e = 0.117$ or

$k_e = 11.7\%$

According to the capital asset pricing model (CAPM), this rate is the minimum rate of return that the stockholders require of their investment; otherwise, they would sell their shares or stocks and leave the company. As such, this rate of return required by stockholders may be accepted as the cost of equity.

On the other hand, for a public company the cost of equity may also be estimated by the so-called *Gordon's growth model* as given below:

$$k_e = \frac{D_0(1+g)}{P_0} + g$$

where;

k_e: The rate of return required by stockholders as before,
D_0: The dividend per share paid in the previous year,
g: The constant growth rate expected in dividends,
P_0: The present market price for a stock.

For example, let us consider a public company different than the GMBH Company whose stocks are presently trading in the securities market each for 5 USD. If this company paid 0.45 USD last year as dividend per share and that the dividends are expected to increase by 10% in the future, the rate of return required by stockholders; that is, the cost of capital for equity would be:

$$k_e = \frac{0.45(1+0.10)}{5} + 0.10$$

$k_e = 19.90\%$

At this point it should also be added that if equity is going to be raised by issuing new common stocks, the so-called *flotation costs* (the costs of issuing new shares) should be deducted from the market price of the stock. Then the above given formula would become as:

$$k_s = \frac{D_0(1+g)}{P_0(1-f)} + g$$

where;

f: Represents percentage flotation cost per share or stock and
k_s: The cost of equity raised by new stock issues.

For example, if the flotation cost per stock is 0.5%, that is, $f = 0.005$, then the cost of equity raised by new stock issues (k_s) would be:

$$k_s = \frac{0.45(1+0.10)}{5(1-0.005)} + 0.10$$

$$k_s = 19.95\%$$

2. **The Cost of Debt:** In general, the cost of external financing is the rate of interest paid for obtaining debt or long term loans, irrespective of the type of the company being public or not. However, since interest payments are tax deductible, the cost of debt is computed after tax as;

$$K_d\,(1 - V)$$

where;

K_d: Stands for the interest rate on debt and
V: The corporate tax rate.

For example, if the interest rate on debt is 10% and the corporate tax rate is 20%, the true cost of debt is;

$$0.10\,(1 - 0.20) = 0.08$$

Finally, once the costs of equity and debt are computed as explained above, the weighted average cost of capital should be calculated according to the ratio of each source of finance in the firm's capital structure.

For instance, let us consider our example of the WGMBH's direct investment project in Turkey whose initial investment was estimated to be 200,000,000 EUR and that 100,000,000 EUR is decided to be financed by owner's equity while the remaining 100,000,000 EUR is to be financed through a term loan of 5 years with an interest rate of 10%. That is to say, 50% of the initial investment is to be financed with a long term loan whose interest rate was determined at 10%, ($K_d = 0.10$), and the remaining 50% of the initial investment is to be financed with the owner's equity whose cost of capital, as computed above through the capital asset pricing model (CAPM), is 11.7%, ($k_e = 0.117$).

Therefore, assuming that the corporate tax rate in Germany is 20% excluding municipality taxes, the weighted average cost of capital for the GMBH Company may be calculated as follows:

$$k_o = w_e k_e + w_d k_d (1 - V)$$

where:

k_o: The weighted average cost of capital,
w_e: The portion or weight of equity in the capital sources (50%),
w_d: The portion or weight of debt in the capital sources (50%),
k_e: The cost of equity capital (11.7%),
k_d: The interest rate of debt (10%),
V: The corporate tax rate (20%).

Thus,

$$k_o = 0.50(0.117) + 0.50(0.10)(1 - 0.20)$$

$$k_o = 0.0585 + 0.04$$

$$k_o = 0.0985$$

This formulation may be stated more directly as given below, where Q and L represent the amounts of equity and loan (debt), respectively:

$$k_o = \left(\frac{Q}{Q+L}\right) k_e + \left(\frac{L}{Q+L}\right) k_d (1 - V)$$

$$k_o = \left(\frac{100,000}{100,000 + 100,000} \right) 0.117 + \left(\frac{100,000}{100,000 + 100,000} \right) 0.10\,(1 - 0.20)$$

$$k_o = 0.50(0.117) + 0.50(0.10)\,(1 - 0.20)$$

$$k_o = 0.0585 + 0.04$$

$$k_o = 0.0985$$

Consequently, the average cost of capital for the WGMBH project in Turkey is 9.85 percent. That is, $k_0 = r = 9.85\%$, and this rate is used as a discount rate to compute the NPV of the project on the basis of the total annual transferable income given in the last row of the Table 9 as shown in Box 5.

$$NPV = \frac{-100,000}{(1+0.0985)^0} + \frac{-100,000}{(1+0.0985)^1} + \frac{66,498}{(1+0.0985)^2} + \frac{83,009}{(1+0.0985)^3} + \frac{89,470}{(1+0.0985)^4} + \frac{84,470}{(1+0.0985)^5} + \frac{176,750}{(1+0.0985)^6}$$

NPV = -100,000 – 91,033 + 55,107 + 62,620 + 61,445 + 52,807 + 100,592

NPV = 141,538(000) EUR.

Since NPV > 0, the project should be accepted as an investment proposal. Furthermore, the profitability index (PI) could be computed as:

$$PI = \frac{NPV}{\sum_{t=0}^{m} I_t / (1+r)^t}$$

Box 5.

TOTAL (EUR) (1+2+3+4+5)	-100,000	-100,000	66,498	83,009	89,470	84,470	176,750

Since the values of initial investment (I) are 1000.000.000 EUR in both the year t_0 and t_1, and the cost of capital is r = 0.0985, then;

$$PI = \frac{141,538,000}{100,000,000 + 100,000,000 \,/\, (1 + 0,098)}$$

PI = 0.74

Therefore, the investment project is profitable since its profitability index is larger than zero, that is, 0.74 > 0.

The Internal Rate of Return

The internal rate of return (IRR) of the investment project by definition is the discount rate that makes the sum of the discounted annual income values given above equal to zero. That is, the IRR value that makes the left side of the below given equation equal to zero:

$$\frac{-100,000}{(1+IRR)^0} + \frac{-100,000}{(1+IRR)^1} + \frac{66,498}{(1+IRR)^2} + \frac{83,009}{(1+IRR)^3} + \frac{89,470}{(1+IRR)^4} + \frac{84,470}{(1+IRR)^5} + \frac{176,750}{(1+IRR)^6} = 0$$

The discount rate that makes the value of the above given equation equal to zero is;

IRR = 0.28

Since the internal rate of return is higher than the average cost of capital; that is,

$IRR = 28\% > k_0 = 9.85\%$

the investment project should be accepted. That is, it is a profitable direct investment opportunity for the WGMBH Company.

CONCLUSION

In conclusion, the evaluation of the WGMBH's direct investment project through the methods of payback period, net present value, and internal rate of return clearly indicates that it is a profitable investment proposal. Therefore, it may be realized according to the details indicated in the feasibility study if the risk associated with it is at a tolerable level which the investor WGMBH Company would be willing to take over. The concept of risk and the related risk analysis are the subjects of the next chapter.

However, before concluding this section, it must be pointed out that, as it is commonly known, business companies use these three classical methods together to evaluate investment projects because each method sheds light on one dimension of the profitability of an investment project. The payback period method measures how quickly an investment project pays back its initial investment and the net present value method shows the magnitude of the net cash inflow as an indicator of the overall profit volume while the internal rate of return reveals the specific unit profitability rate of the investment project. Therefore, altogether they would provide comprehensive and valuable information for appraising the overall profitability of an investment project. If these methods indicate that the direct investment project is a profitable investment proposal, then, a risk analysis should be conducted to evaluate the riskiness of the foreign direct investment project as explained in the following chapter.

REFERENCES

Brealey, R. A., Myers, S. C., & Allen, F. (2016). *Principles of Corporate Finance*. New York: McGraw-Hll Education.

Eithman, D. K., Stonehill, A. I., & Moffet, M. H. (2015). *Multinational Business Finance* (14th ed.). Boston: Pearson Education Inc.

Gitman, L., & Zutter, C. (2014). *Principles of Managerial Finance* (14th ed.). Boston: Pearson Education, Inc.

Mao, J. C. T. (n.d.). *Quantitative Analysis of Financial Decisions*. New York: Macmillan Publishing Co., Inc.

Van Horne, J. C., & Wachowicz, J. M. Jr. (2009). *Fundamentals of Financial Management* (13th ed.). New York: Pearson Education Limited.

Welch, I. (2014). *Corporate Finance*. Boston: Pearson Education, Inc.

Chapter 7 Risk Analysis in Project Evaluation

ABSTRACT

This final chapter is devoted to the analysis of the risks associated with foreign direct investments, namely business (commercial) risk, political risk, and currency exchange rate risk. Each risk factor is considered as a separate evaluation criterion. That is, an investment project may be rejected due to having a high level of any one of these three risk factors. For instance, a profitable investment proposal may not have a significant business risk but might have a high level of political risk requiring its rejection. Risk analysis is conducted only if a foreign investment project is profitable from the viewpoint of the parent company. Otherwise, there is no need for a risk analysis since a direct investment project that does not create profit for the parent company would be rejected anyway.

DOI: 10.4018/978-1-5225-7696-9.ch007

THE CONCEPT OF RISK AND APPROACHES FOR IDENTIFYING RISK

As it is clear from the foregoing explanations, evaluating an investment project is based on the pro forma net cash flows statement which was prepared according to the data obtained in the base year as the best estimates of the project manager. That is, the estimated net cash flows and thus the resulting profitability is a value which is expected from the investment project in the future. For instance, as it is indicated in the preceding section, the net present value of 141,538,000 EUR, which was computed according to the estimated annual net cash flows, is an anticipated value to happen in the future. However, later on, when the project is realized and starts its operation, net cash flows may change and thus the resulting net present value will change accordingly. For example, the realized NPV might be computed as 200,000,000 EUR or 250,000,000 EUR or even a loss of – 75,000,000 EUR, depending on the changes in cash flows. Why do net cash flows change? Because the future is dynamic and everything changes, nothing stays the same: sales, costs, prices, taxation laws, interest rates, exchange rates all change in the future, so do the realized NPVs.

This inevitable change is called *risk* in the field of finance in general and capital budgeting in specific. Thus, risk refers to the gap or discrepancy between the expected and the realized values of the investment project. The larger the gap the riskier the project would be. The existence of risk in an investment project does not only refer to a loss situation, it equally refers to a gain situation as well. That is to say, if the expected NPV of 141.5 million EUR is actually realized as 200 million EUR, this positive change is also considered a risky event, since such changes also prevent decision makers to take right decisions. Therefore, the dispersion of the end results of an investment project in either negative or positive side is generally considered risk.

Risk as a degree of change in the expected values is inevitable in all capital investment projects since those projects cover a long life span in the future. Therefore, this change or risk should be taken into account clearly and be dealt with carefully when evaluating investment projects. For this reason, in order to make more correct decisions regarding the evaluation of investment projects, the existence and, if possible, the magnitude of the risk should be identified and assessed for each investment project and then the profitability of the risky investment be analyzed in detail. Depending on the factors or variables leading to changes or creating risk, the risk related to a foreign direct investment project might be classified in three categories as *business (commercial) risk, political risk,* and *currency risk,* as elaborated in the following subsections.

Business (Commercial) Risk

The risk resulting from changes in the market values of variables, such as sales or sales revenues, all costs of production factors and capital goods, product and input prices, etc., but except those related to foreign currency and political changes, is named as *business* or *commercial risk.* Accordingly, this risk is related to the commercial activities of business firms and thus affects their economic profitability. For example, the sales estimated during the project feasibility study, later on in the operating period of project may rise by 15% and thus as a result of increses in revenues the realized profitability of the business will go up, or vice versa. Similarly, the raw material prices in the future may go up by, say, 20% or the price per unit may go down 25% and, thus, the profitability of investment would be significantly affected.

Several approaches and/or methods are used to identify or determine the business or commercial risk associated with investment projects; namely, sensitivity analysis, probability analysis, breakeven analysis, degrees of operating and financial leverages, and simulation techniques as explained in the following pages.

Sensitivity Analysis

This analysis aims at finding out the most critical factors or variables to which the profitability of an investment project is very sensitive to by raising and answering some "*what if*" type questions. For example, "what if the unit price of the product rises by 10% or drops by 20%?" "What if the sales or the quantity sold increases by 25%?" After each question the profitability of the investment such as NPV is computed and whichever variable changes NPV more drastically is labeled or selected as the "critical" variable. Critical variables are the most important factors in a project such that any change in their values will bring about significant changes in the NPV of the investment project.

Therefore, once the critical variables are determined, the project analysts will pay due attention to such variables and thus will do their best to gather appropriate data and information to make correct estimates of them as much as possible. Since errors in estimating the values of those critical variables will significantly affect the profitability of the project or even lead to a wrong decision regarding the selection of the investment project, project analysts always conduct some kind of sensitivity analysis to raise their awareness regarding critical factors and, if possible, to take some measures in advance.

Conducting a sensitivity analysis to determine critical variables does not require any standardized model or technique. Any kind of model or even any equation relating some variables to the profitability of the investment project may be used to conduct a sensitivity analysis. For example, the NPV method as a discounting cash flow method may be used by specifying some variables in the evaluation equation. For instance, revenues of the investment project (R) may be defined as the quantity of the products sold (Q) times the product unit price (f), that is:

$$R = (Q) \text{ x } (f)$$

Then, this statement will be used instead of (R) in the formula of computing net cash flows as given earlier;

$$NCF_t = (R_t - I_t - C_t - D_t)\,(1 - V) + D_t$$

Thus,

$$NCF_t = ((Q_t \text{ x } f_t) - I_t - C_t - D_t)\,(1 - V) + D_t$$

Finally, on the basis of these NCF_t values the NPV of the project is:

$$NPV = \sum_{t=0}^{n} NCFt \,/\, (1+r)^t$$

That is,

$$NPV = \sum_{t=0}^{n} \frac{\left((Q_t\, x\, f_t) - I_t - C_t - D_t\right)(1-V) + D_t}{(1+r)^t}$$

As seen, seven variables, namely, quantity sold (Q_t), price per unit (f_t), initial investment (I_t), operating costs (C_t), depreciation charges (D_t), corporate tax rate (V), and average cost of capital (r) are specified in this NPV evaluation model. Once the NPV is computed on the basis of the best estimates (base values) of these variables, for instance a value of NPV = 141,538,000 EUR, then the impact of any assumed change in one of these variables on NPV is evaluated by raising "what if" type questions. For instance "what if the unit price of the product (f) rises by 10%?" Then the base value (the best estimate) of the unit price is increased by 10% and an NPV is computed while keeping the base values of all the other variables constant. In the same manner, similar questions are raised. For example, "what if the unit price decreases by 15%"? Then an NPV value is computed by decreasing the base value of (f_t) by 15% and keeping the base values of all the other variables constant. So, repeating the process several times for a variable, the degree of the change (sensitivity) in terms of the relationship between the variable in question and the NPV can be determined.

Consequently, conducting the same analysis for all variables and then comparing their degrees of change (sensitivity) with relation to NPV, those variables with high degrees of change (sensitivity) are considered as critical variables. Needless to indicate that there are many variables in an investment project and thus conducting sensitivity analyses for all of them would be a very much time consuming activity for project analysts. Nevertheless, such a comprehensive sensitivity analysis is indeed redundant since some variables such as most of the variables related to the initial investment are certain in the base year of the establishment period and do not change in the future. Furthermore, some variables such as tax rates, depreciation charges, and interest rates on contractual long term loans do not change in the short run. On the other hand, lots of variables such as the costs of indirect materials and supplies, maintenance and repair, and general administrative expenses will have negligible impact on the profitability of the investment project because of their small shares in the total operating expenditures.

Accordingly, the number of variables that needs to be included in a sensitivity analysis is not so large. In practice, project analysts usually consider the quantity sold (Q), the price per unit (f), the cost of capital (r), and in some cases the price of the essential input of the production as the most critical variables. In fact, the practical experience has proved that the profitability of an investment project is essentially sensitive to those variables. Consequently, an investment project is considered to be risky if small changes in these critical variables bring about magnified changes in its NPV. Similarly, when examining the riskiness of alternative investment projects through changes in critical variables, the project that would have the largest changes in its NPV is labeled as the riskiest project.

Finally, it should be pointed out that in sensitivity analysis changes in variables are made haphazardly. That is, changes in variables are made without any logical reasoning because the purpose of the sensitivity analysis is just to identify the critical variables to which an investment project is sensitive, not to make correct estimates of changes in the variables. Estimating the degree of changes in critical variables is the purpose of the probability analysis which is explained below.

Probability Analysis

The sensitivity analysis is not concerned with the estimates of the values of changes in critical variables. In contrast, the probability analysis aims at estimating the magnitude of the changes in the critical values as well as assigning probabilities of occurrence to those estimates. For this purpose lots of past and present data and information is gathered and analyzed in addition to collecting the advice and judgmental evaluations and predictions from colleagues as well as the experts on the subject. Therefore, for each critical variable a probability distribution is developed. For developing a probability distribution the procedure often followed is a judgmental method that is sometimes called the "step rectangular" approach.

This method, firstly, requires determining the lowest and the highest values that a variable may have in the future and, then, dividing the range between the lowest and the highest values into intervals to which judgmental probabilities are attributed. Finally, each critical variable will have a probability distribution dispersing around the base value (the best estimate) as well as with the lowest and the highest values indicating that the critical variable will not take any value below or above them. For example, the project analyst who considers the quantity to be sold (Q) and the price per unit (f) as critical variables in an investment project may develop probability distributions for these variables as given in Box 1.

As seen, the project manager envisages that the best estimates which are made at present time (base values) may change in the future according to the probabilities indicated above. Additionally, as noticed, the best estimate (the base value) of the quantity to be sold (Q_i = 60,000 units) is believed to have a probability of 55% while the lowest and the highest values are estimated to

Box 1.

Quantity (Q_i)	Probability (p_i)	Price (f_i)	Probability (p_i)
50,000	10%	325 TL	5%
55,000	10%	400 TL	15%
60,000 (Base)	55%	450 TL (Base)	50%
80,000	20%	550 TL	25%
95,000	5%	650 TL	5%
	100%		100%

be 50,000 and 95,000 units with probabilities of 10% and 5%, respectively. On the other hand, the base value of the price per unit (f_i = 450 TL) has a probability of occurrence of 50%. The lowest and the highest values of the price per unit are estimated to be 325 TL and 650 TL, respectively, with equal chances of occurrence of 5%. The other values of the probability distributions are as given above.

For now, the project analysts will compute the weighted averages of these distributions and then use them to calculate the profitability of the investment project through the NPV method as indicated below. Therefore, rather than simply using the best point estimates of 60,000 units and 450 TL price per unit to calculate sales revenues and then compute the NPV of the project, the weighted averages of the probability distributions as the expected values of the critical variables are used instead. The weighted averages of the above given statistical distributions as expected values are calculated as follows:

The expected value for the quantity to be sold, E(Q), is:

$$E(Q) = \sum_{i=1}^{k} (Q_i)(p_i)$$

E(Q) =(50,000x0.10)+(55,000x0.10)+(60,000x0.55)+(80,000x0.20)+(95,000x0.05)

E(Q) = 64,250 units.

Similarly, the expected value for the price per unit, E(f), is:

$$E(f) = \sum_{i=1}^{k} (f_i)(p_i)$$

E(f) =(325x0.05)+(400x0.15)+(450x0.50)+(550x0.25)+(650x0.05)

E(f) = 471.25 TL.

As it is seen, the probability analysis is a complementary method to the sensitivity analysis in the sense that the possible changes in the critical variables in the future will now be taken into account according to the related probabilities and, thus, the magnitude of the resulting variations in NPVs would indicate the existence of the risk inherent in the project. Therefore, the probability analysis adds a meaningful reasoning to the "what if" type questions of the sensitivity analysis. That is, the "what if" questions now are not raised haphazardly but rather are based on the probable changes in the future. Accordingly, the magnitude of variations in NPV values would indicate the existence of the risk associated with the investment project. That is, the larger the variations in the NPV the riskier the investment project would be.

Breakeven Analysis

The purpose of the breakeven analysis is to find out the quantity of production that makes the total sales revenues equal to the total production costs. Therefore, there is no profit at the breakeven quantity of the production process. Assuming that upon production the products are immediately sold and that the relationship between the sales revenues and the amount of production as well as that between the variable costs and the amount of production are linear, the breakeven quantity can be found by equating the total revenues to the total costs of production as follows:

$$(Q \times f) = S + (Q \times d)$$

where;

Q: The amount of production,
f: Price per unit of production,
S: The total fixed costs, and
d: The amount of variable cost per unit.

The left side of the equation defines the total amount of sales revenues simply multiplying the amount of production by the unit price. Similarly, the right side of the equation defines the total costs of the production by adding fixed costs to the total amount of variable costs. Now, the breakeven quantity, that is, the amount of the production (Q) that equates the total amount of sales revenues to the total costs of the production can be found by solving the equation as follows:

$$(Q \times f) = S + (Q \times d)$$

$$(Q \times f) - (Q \times d) = S$$

$$Q\,(f - d) = S$$

$$Q = \frac{S}{(f - d)}$$

The relationship between the amounts of production and sales revenues as well as the costs may also be shown graphically as given in Figure 1. Here the vertical axis shows the sales revenues and/or costs of production whereas the horizontal axis indicates the amount of production. As seen, the fixed costs are parallel to the horizontal axis indicating the amount of production at all levels of production even when there is no (zero) production since they are independent of the amount of the production. The essential items of fixed costs are the rent paid for the long term rented production facilities (financial leases), insurance and maintenance costs of machinery and equipment, depreciation charges, salaries of key personnel and/or labor, etc. As such, whatever the level of the production is, even if it is zero, the amount of fixed costs would not change to a certain level of the production capacity.

On the other hand, the variable costs start from the point of the origin of the graph (where there is neither production nor variable costs) and increase proportionally with the amount of production. That is, a linear relationship is assumed between the variable costs and production quantity. The line for the total costs is simply obtained by adding variable costs to fixed costs. That means the line for the variable costs is just placed or put on the top of the line for the fixed costs. That is why the lines for the total costs and the variable costs are parallel to each other with a difference equal to the total fixed costs.

Figure 1. Breakeven Point

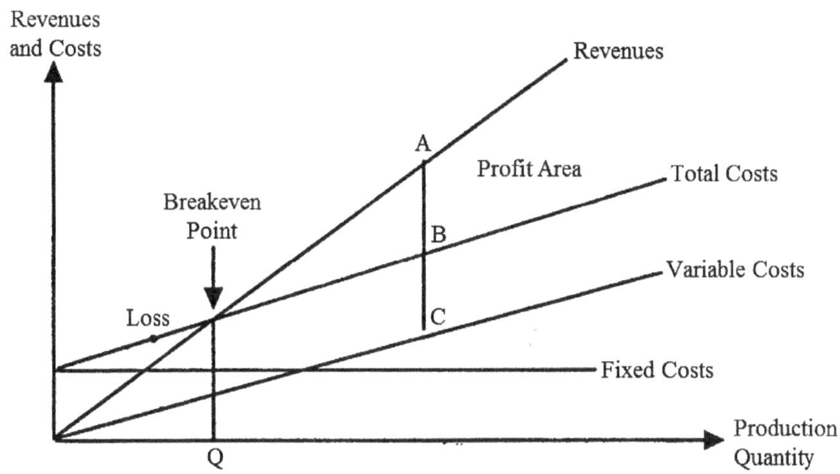

The line for the total sales revenues also starts from the origin of the graph just like the line for the variable costs. When there is no production and/or sales, the revenues are zero at the point of origin. However, when production and/or sales start the amount of total sales revenues rises proportionately with the amount of production and sales, again assuming a linear relationship. Finally, when the line for the total sales revenues intersects with the line for the total costs (that is, where they are equal), the amount of production at this point (Q) is the breakeven point of the production where the total revenues are equal to the total costs. The production quantity above this point will lead to a profit and that one below it will incur a loss. As seen in Figure 1, when the production quantity is above the breakeven point, the distance between the points A and C indicates the operating profit before fixed costs while that one between the points A and B shows the operating profit after fixed costs.

As it will be explained shortly, the larger the amount of production at the breakeven point the riskier a firm or an investment project would be. Accordingly, when evaluating alternative investment projects in terms of their business risks, the investment project whose breakeven quantity (Q) is the smallest one is regarded to be the least risky one. Similarly, the investment project with the largest breakeven quantity is the riskiest one. For example, consider two business firms X and Y in the same economic sector and producing similar products with the data shown in Box 2.

The breakeven points for the two firms are:

Box 2.

	Firm X	Firm Y
Fixed Costs	S= 5,000,000 TL	S= 7,000,000 TL
Price per Unit	f= 750 TL	f= 800 TL
Unit Variable cost	d= 400 TL	d= 450 TL

$$Q_X = \frac{5,000,000}{(750 - 400)} = 14,286 \text{ units for the firm X and}$$

$$Q_Y = \frac{7,000,000}{(800 - 450)} = 20,000 \text{ units for the firm Y.}$$

Therefore, it can be stated that the firm Y is riskier than X since it has a larger breakeven quantity. The reasoning for this conclusion is quite clear: The firm Y has to sell more products than X to reach the breakeven point to start making profit. That is, when the firm X reaches the sales level of 14,286 units for making profit, the firm Y still has a long way to reach the breakeven point of 20,000 units for making profit. In another word, the firm Y has to sell more to start making profit. As known, in competitive markets selling a product is not an easy job to be accomplished and, thus, creates risk for a firm. As such, the breakeven analysis provides indirect information regarding the riskiness of a firm or an investment project as a potential firm.

However, when there is no alternative to compare it with, that is, when a single firm is in question, the quantity of the breakeven point would not be much meaningful since the breakeven points of competitors or the average in the industry is not known. So, the firm's breakeven quantity cannot be evaluated for judging its riskiness because there is no value available to compare it with. In such single cases, where there is only a breakeven quantity for a single firm, the ratio of the breakeven quantity to the total production capacity of the firm may be computed and, then, this ratio can be compared with the nationwide published annual capacity utilization rates of the industrial sector in which the firm operates.

For instance, let us assume that an investment project planned in Turkey has estimated total fixed costs of 10,000,000 TL, a price per unit of 1,500 TL, and a variable unit cost of 700 TL. Additionally, the total production capacity of the investment project is determined to be 40,000 units in the technical analysis stage of the feasibility study. If the overall capacity utilization rate for the industry in which the investment project would operate in is 76% as published by the Statistical Institution of Turkey (TUİK), how can the riskiness of this investment project be evaluated?

The breakeven point for the project is:

$$Q = \frac{S}{(f - d)}$$

$$Q = \frac{10,000,000}{(1,500 - 700)} = 12,500 \text{ units.}$$

The ratio of the breakeven point to the total production capacity is:

12,500 / 40,000 = 0,357

This means that if this project uses 35.7% of its production capacity, it would reach to the breakeven point where there is neither profit nor loss; that is, the total sales revenues are equal to the total costs of production. Now, comparing this ratio with the published capacity utilization rate of 76% for the industry,

35.7% < ==> 76%

one may say that the commercial risk associated with this investment project is not high. Because, when the project is realized, it would possibly operate at a capacity utilization rate around the industry average of 76% and this rate is far above the breakeven ratio of the total production capacity. That is, this investment will use 35.7% of its established production capacity to reach the breakeven point and, then, there is a good chance to make a profit since it would not be so difficult to go above 35.7% of its production capacity in an industrial sector where the capacity utilization rate is 76%. However, if the ratio of the breakeven point to the total production capacity was something around, say, 65% rather than 35.7%, then, one may say that this project has a high level of business risk to be taken into consideration.

Before concluding this section it should also be added that the formula for computing the breakeven quantity may also be used for sensitivity analysis. By changing three basic variables (fixed costs, price per unit, and the variable cost per unit) one at a time and keeping the other two variables constant, the impact of changes in these variables on the breakeven quantity and thus on the riskiness of an investment project may be evaluated. It should not be that much difficult to indicate that the amount of fixed costs is the most critical factor since the price per unit and the variable cost per unit are more or less similar for business firms in a competitive industry or market. So firms will focus on fixed costs to reduce their commercial risk level. In the practice of the risk analysis for project evaluation, usually a "normal" year in which neither revenues nor costs differ significantly is selected and the breakeven analysis is conducted, since this analysis is done at a certain point in time.

Degrees of Operating and Financial Leverages

The Degree of Operating Leverage

In a competitive market environment all business firms are subject to changes in the market dynamics in terms of the supply and demand conditions that lead to variations in sales volumes, revenues, costs, and profits of business companies. Moreover, all firms are equally subject to technological breakthroughs, creative and innovative strategies of competitors that bring about changes in the market shares of firms as well. No doubt that all such market related changes create uncertainties and risks that will definitely affect the economic activities and thus the profitability of business firms. This risk which is inherent in the business activities of all firms is called *business risk*. It should also be added that business risk is not related to the financing decisions of business firms. A firm that does not even use any external financing or debt may face high business risk.

The degree of business risk varies according to the economic sectors as well as individual business firms. For example, firms like iron and steel companies operating in capital intensive industries are considered to have high degrees of business risk while firms in food industry are regarded as less risky. The reason is mainly related to the stability in sales and the magnitude of fixed costs due to the investment in heavy machinery and equipment. Iron and steel industry is partly seasonal and requires a great deal of fixed investment in machinery and equipment. On the contrary, the demand in food industry is more stable and the sector is less capital intensive compared to the iron and steel industry.

Additionally, the business risk differs from firm to firm operating in the same economic sector. Some firms in the same industry or economic sector are more adversely affected by the same changes in the market conditions whereas some passes through them quite easily. That is, the business firms operating in the same industry and facing the same changes are affected differently because they have different levels of business risk. One of the essential reasons for the differences in business risk is the varying magnitude of fixed costs that firms have. Some firms either prefer or, in some cases, have to establish large-scaled production systems that are usually capital intensive. Such large-scaled firms eventually will have large amounts of fixed costs and thus do not react appropriately to the decreases in demand and prices because they cannot lower their fixed costs accordingly. That is, they have to incur those large amounts of fixed costs any how despite of shrinking sales revenues since those costs are independent of the sales volume. How long a firm can tolerate such conditions is a matter of another discussion.

The firms with large amounts of fixed costs are said to have high levels of *operating leverage*. In another word, it is said that firms having large amounts of fixed costs are using high levels of operating leverage. Operating leverage in this context refers to incurring fixed costs in order to increase the amounts of production and profit. That is, firms incur fixed costs expecting that large amounts of production and thus sales volume will create revenues much more than the total of all fixed and variable costs. Thus, the level of operating leverage indicates the magnitude of the fixed costs in a business firm. The higher operating leverage the larger fixed costs would be or the larger fixed costs the higher operating leverage, *ceteris paribus*.

Consequently, *the degree of operating leverage* would be a good indicator of the business risk which is associated with the level of the fixed costs of business companies. For a business company, at a certain level of production, *the degree of operating leverage* (DOL) is defined as the ratio of the operating profit before fixed costs to the operating profit after fixed costs:

$$\text{DOL} = \frac{OperatingProfitBeforeFixedCosts}{OperatingProfitAfterFixedCosts}$$

If we define (Q) as the sales volume, (f) price per unit, (d) variable cost per unit, and (S) the amount fixed costs, the profit before and after fixed costs and the degree of operating leverage (DOL) may be formulated as follow:

The Operating Profit before Fixed Costs = (Q x f) – (Q x d) = Q (f – d)

The Operating Profit after Fixed Costs = (Q x f) – (Q x d) – S = Q (f – d) – S

As noticed, the operating profit after fixed costs is the same as the earnings before interest and tax (EBIT). Thus, the formula for the degree of operating leverage (DOL) would be:

$$\text{DOL} = \frac{Q(f-d)}{Q(f-d)-S}$$

This equation for computing degree of operating leverage may be more clearly stated as given below:

$$\text{DOL} = \frac{SalesRevenues - TotalVariableCosts}{SalesRevenues - TotalVariableCosts - FixedCosts}$$

As seen in the above formula, the degree of operating leverage is directly related to the amount of fixed costs. The larger fixed costs the higher the degree of operating leverage (DOL) would be. From this viewpoint the degree of operating leverage is similar to the breakeven analysis in the sense that they both relate the business risk to the fixed cost of business firms. However, as it is stated below, the degree of operating leverage provides a specific value concerning the existence of the business risk[1]. As such, the degree of operating leverage is complementary to the breakeven analysis for determining the business risk. For this reason they are generally used together to evaluate the riskiness of a business firm.

Paying attention to the above given formula, it would be easy to state that DOL will take on values between 1 and infinity (∞). Because, when there is no fixed cost (zero fixed cost), the numerator and the denominator of the equation for DOL would be equal and thus the DOL value will be found as 1. As fixed costs starts increasing, DOL would increase as well; theoretically up to infinity (∞) when the fixed costs get equal to the operating profit before the fixed costs. That is, when the denominator of the equation becomes zero the result of the division will be infinite (∞). On the other hand, in practice, a value of DOL between 2 and 3 is considered an ideal position while the larger values are considered as indicators of increasing business risk.

Now, let us assume that a company or an investment project as a potential business firm has the following data regarding its production activity at a certain period of time (in project work an assumed "normal" year is selected for computation):

Q = 35,000 units,

f = 1,250 TL,

d = 900 TL,

S = 10,000,000 TL.

Therefore, the degree of the operating leverage (DOL) would be:

$$\text{DOL} = \frac{Q(f-d)}{Q(f-d)-S}$$

$$\text{DOL} = \frac{35,000(1,250-900)}{35,000(1,250-900)-10,000,000}$$

DOL = 5.4

This is a quite large value indicating a higher level of business risk. More specifically, the degree of the operating leverage indicates the impact of a percentage change in sales on the firm's operating profit (EBIT). Thus, DOL = 5.4 states that a 1 percent change in sales (above or below of Q = 35,000 units) will cause a 5.4 percent change in the firm's operating profit (EBIT). Accordingly, if the sales volume of this firm decreases by 10 percent, the firm's EBIT will drop by (5.4 x 10 =) 54 percent or vice versa. That is, if the sales increase by 10 percent, EBIT will go up by 54 percent. As seen, a small change, which is quite common in business life, brings about a magnified impact on the operating profit of the firm, hence indicating a high business risk for the firm in question.

The Degree of Financial Leverage

The financial leverage involves the use of external financing with fixed cost or interest payment. Thus, firms using long term loans or issuing long term bonds with fixed interest rates are said to be using financial leverage both to grow and to take advantage of tax shield effect of interest payments which are tax deductible. The use of financial leverage is generally by choice. However, the operational leverage is often dictated by the physical requirements of production systems.

Financial leverage is related to the financial risk of business firms in terms of meeting their financial obligations on time. Firms that use relatively high amounts of debt may not pay the regular interest payments on time when sales revenues drop to a certain level. This cash insolvency is an important cause of financial risk. Hence, it may be stated that business firms that are heavily in debt are also subject to high levels of financial risk. The degree of financial risk for business firms is measured by *the degree of financial leverage* (DFL) which is simply the ratio of the earnings before interest and tax (EBIT) to the earnings after interest (EBIT – I) as given below. Here, EBIT (the earnings before interest and tax) also refers to the operating profit after fixed costs in the case of the degree of the operating leverage.

$$\text{DFL} = \frac{EBIT}{EBIT - I}$$

Thus, with our previous notation, the degree of the financial leverage (DFL) is:

$$\text{DFL} = \frac{Q(f - d) - S}{Q(f - d) - S - F}$$

Where; F stands for the amount of interest payments as we defined in the previous sections and all the other variables are the same as defined earlier. The formula further indicates that, as in the case of the degree of the operating leverage, the value of DFL would be between 1 and infinity (∞), because when a firm uses no debt (zero interest payment) the value of the equation will be 1. However, if a firm borrows a lot and pays large amounts of interest such that uses up all of its operating profit before interest and tax (EBIT), the value of DFL will be infinite (∞) since the denominator of the equation would be zero. Practical experience shows that values around 2 for DFL are ideally desired values while larger ones indicate increasing financial risk for a business firm.

Now let us assume again that our example whose data given above to compute the operating leverage has also an interest payment of 1,750,000 TL, that is:

Q = 35,000 Units,

f = 1,250 TL,

d = 900 TL,

S = 10,000,000 TL,

F = 1,750,000 TL.

Therefore, the degree of the financial leverage (DFL) would be:

$$DFL = \frac{35,000(1,250 - 900) - 10,000,000}{35,000(1,250 - 900) - 10,000,000 - 1,750,000}$$

DFL = 4.5

This value points to a moderately high level of financial risk compared with ideal values around 2. Furthermore, this value of DFL specifically indicates that a unit percent change in earnings before interest and tax (EBIT) would affect earnings per share (EPS) by 4.5 times. Thus, if EBIT decrease by 15%, earnings per share (EPS) will decrease by (4.5 x 15% =) 67.5% or if EBIT increases by 10% then dividend per share will go up by (4.5 x 10% =) 45%.

The Degree of Total Leverage

The total leverage refers to using both operating leverage and financial leverage. As such, at a particular level of sales for a firm or in a "normal" year for an investment project, it focuses on the total risk of a company resulting from incurring a large amount of fixed costs and using a great deal of external financing with fixed interest rates. Therefore, the degree of the total leverage (DTL) is a combination of the degrees operating and financial leverages computed by multiplying (not adding) both values. The reason is that the degree of financial leverage (DFL) magnifies the effect of the degree of operating leverage (DOL).Thus, the degree of the total leverage (DTL) is:

DTL = (DOL) x (DFL)

If the formulas for DOL and DFL are placed in the above equation, then;

$$\text{DTL} = \frac{Q(f-d)}{Q(f-d)-S} \text{ x } \frac{Q(f-d)-S}{Q(f-d)-S-F}$$

Here, the denominator of the first and the numerator of the second statement on the right side of the equation will cancel each other, therefore, the degree of the total leverage would be:

$$\text{DTL} = \frac{Q(f-d)}{Q\ (f-d)-S-F}$$

Accordingly, for our example given above, since DOL = 5.4 and DFL = 4.5, the degree of the total leverage (DTL) is:

DTL = (DOL) x (DFL)

DTL = (5.4) x (4.5)

DTL = 24.3

Similarly;

$$\text{DTL} = \frac{35,000(1,250-900)}{35,000\ (1,250-900)-10,000,000-1,750,000}$$

DTL = 24.5 (the same value if we disregard rounding errors).

As seen, the total risk (as a combination of business and financial risks) is very high. The financial risk magnifies the business risk tremendously. The degree of the total leverage indicates the impact of a unit percentage change in sales on the firm's earnings per share (EPS). Furthermore, a financial analyst wishing to decrease the level of the total risk has to deal with variables involved in DOL and DFL and search for ways to keep them at desirable levels. For instance, possibilities for decreasing fixed and variable costs as well as lowering interest payments by using less debt should be looked for when designing the production system and financing the business operations.

The Simulation Technique

Simulation is an experimental methodology or a technique that requires the development of a quantitative model which necessitates the use of computer programs or software packages. Various assumptions and/or "what if" type questions are evaluated on a computer based mathematical model to see the effects of different alternative courses of action. In other words, simulation is a computerized mathematical modeling technique that tries to represent a system through defining its behaviors mathematically. Experimental characteristics of simulation modeling make the use of computers inevitable which, in turn, makes the simulation model dynamic in the sense of including a real time flow in the model.

Moreover, logical statements of computers enable analysts to develop dynamic models that run on a real time basis such as hours, days, months, and years in addition to controlling the flow of the model through logical checking points such as "IF … GREATER THAN … OR EQUAL TO … THEN …", "IF … LESS THAN … THEN …", and "IF EQUAL TO …. THEN ..." Accordingly, the simulation technique or simulation modeling is considered as an experimental study that enables decision makers to conduct various trials or experiments on a mathematical model to see the effects of alternative courses of action in advance before they are implemented.

There are two common ways of using the simulation technique in the field of finance; namely, *System Simulation* and *Monte Carlo Simulation.* In *the system simulation* models trials or experiments for evaluating alternative courses of action are made on the real system through the use of real data obtained about the operation of the real system or the related surrounding environment. However, in *the Monte Carlo Simulation* the data used is obtained through statistical sampling from the probability distributions resembling the behaviors of the real system. Obtaining or generating data from the probability distributions through statistical sampling requires the use of *random numbers*. Previously, random numbers were obtained by throwing a pair of dice (as gambling in the city of Monte Carlo) to make the numbers really random statistically. However, presently "random functions" in computers generate numbers through some mathematical procedures that are assumed to be random and thus are called "pseudo-random numbers".

The Monte Carlo simulation is largely used in the risk analysis for real capital investment projects both to determine the degree of risk associated with an investment project and to evaluate the profitability of the risky investment. The use of the Monte Carlo simulation as a method for determining the riskiness of an investment project will be dealt with in the next subsection titled "Evaluating Risky Investment Projects" since the simulation technique is also a method for evaluating risky investments. Thus, simulation will be used as a technique for both determining the riskiness and evaluating the profitability of a risky investment project in the next subsection.

Political Risk

The concept of political risk and its various types as well as the factors leading to it were discussed in an earlier section with respect to "Country Evaluation and Selection for Foreign Direct Investments". As stated earlier, political risk refers to any political change that worsens the working conditions for international companies. Various types of political risk might be distinguished depending on the factors causing the political risk. As such, three types of political risk are specified; namely, *operational political risk*, *differentiating risk*, and *takeover risk*.

Operational risk includes all legal changes in laws or rules governing businesses that affect all companies as well as interventions by host countries in transactional and operational activities of foreign firms. Direct and indirect interventions that affect business operations of firms most often include increasing taxes and customs duties, restricting imports and monetary transfers, and even intervening in wages of employees of foreign companies. As such, this type of political risk in developing countries is generally related to the economic instability in terms of adherence to the rules and regulations of market mechanism as an economic system. The important point with regard to operational risk is that legal changes that are made after the investment is realized may deteriorate the position of foreign companies. That is, if those changes had been done before the investment was realized, that country would not have been selected. For example, consider a country which was selected for a foreign direct investment because of having a liberal monetary transfer policy. However, two years later after the investment was realized, the country restricts the transfer of dividends from an allowable upper limit of 80% to 50%. This would certainly be a shock for foreign companies.

On the other hand, *differentiating risk* refers to the behaviors of host countries treating foreign companies differently and unfairly. Changes in laws or regulations are prepared and implemented in favor of host countries. In many cases, the same laws and/or regulations are enforced differently with respect to foreign companies or are not enforced at all when foreign firms are concerned. For example, in some cases, the existing laws protecting the rights of business companies in general may just exist on paper when foreign companies are of concern. For instance, intellectual property regulations such as those related to trademarks are often not enforced or inadequately enforced to protect the rights of foreign firms.

Additionally, protectionism is a more common way of differentiating risk. Most of developing countries protect their local firms in certain industries from the competition caused by foreign firms for the purpose of creating a favorable economic environment for the so-called "infant" industries to prosper. Similarly, some developing countries define some industries such as agriculture, telecommunication, and defense as "strategic" industries and do not permit foreign companies to operate in them. This designation depends on what the politicians consider strategic according to their political opinions. Accordingly, the governmental intervention in business life excessively with the objective of protecting "baby" and/or "strategic" industries would be a significant political risk for foreign companies, since foreign companies are not to be allowed to operate in such industries, even though they might have been entered earlier. Therefore, a *takeover risk* of losing businesses and property completely, such as expropriation or confiscation and even nationalization, may arise.

Furthermore, in some countries political thoughts and opinions related to political ideologies might work against foreign companies if they become widespread. For instance, some power groups and politicians or political parties of a country may believe that foreign companies are exploiting their national resources and that their home countries are operating against the interests of their own country. In such cases, when these politicians or political parties take power in the national government and/or local municipalities, they may discriminate against foreign firms in various ways to disturb them so as to have them leave the country. The reasons for such differentiating conduct against foreign firms are various; however, the basic motive is to disturb foreign companies to leave the host country. Undoubtedly, in such cases, take over risk is always a threat for foreign companies if they would not leave willingly.

As explained previously, the reasons and/or causes creating political risk vary from changes in political ideology and policies of governments to regime changes by force. Some other significant sources of political risk are; severe differentiation in opinions of political leaders and parties, frequent interventions and/or legal changes in laws or rules governing businesses, social and political unrest, widespread crime, human right violations, nationalism and xenophobia, animosity between the host and home countries, and military interventions or coup d'états. Any change in these or similar factors would certainly deteriorate the operational conditions of foreign firms in terms of raising operational costs, losing sales in some market segments, forcing them to accept lower profit levels, and even losing their whole businesses (expropriation or nationalization).

However, what is important then to note here is the fact that political risks often occur after the foreign direct investments are realized. Needless to indicate that if project managers notice the existence of a significant political risk during the country evaluation study, undoubtedly, they will eliminate that country as an alternative. Accordingly, the project manager's task in this case is to predict the probabilities of confronting a political risk during the operation period of the investment; that is, after the investment is realized and starts its operations. Therefore, predicting political risk is perhaps the most important aspect of political risk analysis. It requires carefully and neatly designed studies to gather and analyze lots of data and information regarding the possible scenarios for the political developments of host countries as stated below (Wild & Wild, 2015; Daniels, Radebaugh, & Sullivan, 2015):

1. Analyzing the past patterns of the political development as well as the historical stability of the country in question to see and evaluate how the political system operated in the past, what important political events and major changes took place, and how the society reacted to those political changes. This analysis mainly based on the political history of the country analyzed tries to figure out general political trends and, then, to foresee possible political tendencies and changes that may create political risk in the future.

2. Gathering and analyzing the opinions of influential people, such as well-known politicians and academicians, local and foreign businessmen, ambassadors, and leaders of labor unions of the country being analyzed. For this purpose, neatly designed interviews, organizing as well as participating in social events, paying visits to embassies of the countries having intensive economic and political relations with the country in question, requesting help and support of local business community and friends would be quite helpful to visualized possible anticipated political and economic changes that may lead to political risk.
3. Analyzing the political and economic conditions of the country in terms of political and economic instability analysis, including statistical analysis of social and economic indicators leading to instability. Here the objective is to find out the reasons for economic and political instability that had been witnessed in the past, if there was any, and then to predict the possibility of encountering them in the future as a source of political risk[2].

Such analyses will definitely provide valuable information to predict the likelihood of facing political risks during the operating period of the investment in the country being evaluated. At this point it should also be added that there are many commercial risk-assessment services in addition to a variety of *country reports* published by international institutions; such as IMF (International Monetary Fund), World Bank, WTO (World Trade Organization), OECD (Organization for Economic Co-operation and Development), UN (United Nations), ICC (International Chamber of Commerce), as well as socio-political reports of Transparency International and Amnesty International. Recently, international companies have been relying more on such services and reports. Nonetheless, if project managers are not satisfied with them in terms of the information provided, they should visit the countries they are interested in and conduct their own political risk analysis through the methods specified above. Eventually, a site visit would be planned to the country in question anyhow. Thus, the value of available information would be judged for analyzing the political risk for a decision. If the existing and/or acquired information is not found sufficient, a political risk analysis will be conducted during the country visits.

Consequently, project managers should take into account the possible existence of political risk, especially when they plan to invest in emerging economies and/or developing countries. However, predicting political risk is not an easy job. As it is asserted, the political risk analysis in a country generally extrapolates from economic, political, and social reports to generate meaningful insights about which politicians and/or political parties will govern the county in question, what policies would possibly be followed, and how these kinds of political changes would affect the business activities of foreign companies (Deuchars, 2017). No doubt that these insights are meaningful to understand the political environment and the related risks, nevertheless, by no means are sufficient to predict the political risk in the future, since the political world is complex and changes quickly.

Finally, before concluding this section it should be pointed out that there is, indeed, not much to protect a firm against political risk even if it is predicted. In practice, when evaluating an economically very profitable investment project in a country where political risk is believed to be considerably high; either the cost of capital is increased by adding a high risk premium to make its acceptance difficult or the possibility of purchasing a political risk insurance or a guarantee program is searched for. For instance, Overseas Private Investment Corporation (OPIC) offers political risk insurance for U.S. investment projects overseas and also some private insurance companies underwrite political risk protection. Nevertheless, political risk insurance or guarantee programs are not easily available.

In conclusion, if project managers are quite skeptical about the existence of political risk in the future, perhaps, the most plausible way is to quit the project and not to invest in that country since there is not much to do when confronted with political risk after the investment is realized. Nevertheless, in cases where foreign companies confront with political risk after investment, the following methods are recommended for managing political risk (Wild & Wild, 2015):

1. **Adapting to Local Conditions:** Foreign companies are often advised to adapt to local conditions, especially when political risks are prevailing, through various strategies such as; finding an adequate local partner to share the risks and deal with social and political problems, assisting the host country or the nearby regional community to develop living standards of the surrounding environment by ways of helping with building schools, bridges, roads, play grounds for children, etc., implementing business strategies to develop close relations with the locals such as commemorating national holidays, promoting national values, even modifying the company's name to local preferences, etc.

2. **Gathering Information:** Foreign companies should collect the necessary data and gather information to foresee possible political risk and, if possible, take precautions in advance to manage it. In addition to the above mentioned information sources, the local employees of operating foreign companies are of great importance for obtaining relevant information.
3. **Influencing Local Politics:** Developing close relations with politicians to deal with lawmakers in order to get undesirable legislation rejected is an objective that is always sought by business community in general and foreign companies in specific. Foreign companies usually accomplish this objective through lobbying activities that involve hiring influential persons to defend views of foreign companies on political matters to prevent unfavorable legislation changes and get the favorable ones enacted.

Foreign Exchange Risk: Exposure

Foreign exchange risk is defined as the degree of variations in the economic profitability of an investment project due to the changes in exchange rates. It is generally measured as the sensitivity of cash flows and value of a firm to exchange rate movements. Foreign exchange risk is usually referred to as *the foreign exchange exposure* in order to identify a measure for the possibility of change in the profitability, net cash flows, and market value of a business firm due to a change occurring in exchange rates (Eiteman, Stonehill, & Moffett, 2015). So, an important task for a project manager is to take into account foreign exchange exposure when evaluating the potential profitability of an investment project[3].

From the viewpoint of the effects of exchange rate changes on the profitability, net cash flow, and market value of a firm, three main types of foreign exchange risk or exposure are generally identified; namely, *transaction*, *operating*, and *translation exposures.*

1. *Transaction exposure* refers to the effects of changes in exchange rates on the value of financial obligations contracted previously before a change in exchange rates occurred. That is, transaction exposure measures the degree of variations in cash flows of contractual obligations resulting from exchange rate changes. The most common examples of transaction exposure are when companies purchase or sell on credit and that the prices are stated in foreign currencies, as well as borrow or lend funds with repayments to be made in foreign currencies. For example, consider

a Turkish company which bought a machine last year in Holland from a Dutch company for 100,000 EUR to be paid 12 month (a year) later. Accordingly, at that time, a contract indicating the financial obligation of the Turkish firm was prepared and signed by both parties. When the contract was signed the exchange rate for Turkish Lira (TL) and Euro (EUR) was 3.10TL/EUR. Thus, the Turkish firm regarded its obligation as if it was (100,000 x 3.10 =) 310,000 TL.

Now the time has come and the financial obligation is due so the Turkish company is planning to purchase 100,000 EUR in the Turkish money market to pay its debt to the Dutch firm in Holland. However, from the last year up to today exchange rates in Turkey changed significantly so that the present day exchange rate has reached to a level of 4.15TL/EUR. Ultimately, the Turkish company paid (100,000 x 4.15 =) 415,000 TL to purchase 100,000 EUR in the Turkish money market. Therefore, the cash outflow expected at the beginning of the contract changed from (100,000 x 3.10 =) 310,000 TL to (100,000 x 4.15 =) 415,000 TL. Thus, exchange rate changes brought about an additional cash outflow, that is, an extra payment of (415,000 - 310,000 =) 105,000 TL for the Turkish company. This change is due to transaction exposure.

2. *Operating exposure* indicates the changes in the market value of a firm measured by the net present value of the expected future cash flows resulting from the changes in foreign exchange rates. In other words, operating exposure states that the market value of a firm changes because of the changes in sales, prices, and costs in the future due to the changing exchange rates. More specifically, exchange rate changes will affect the future prices, sales, and costs of a firm that, in turn, lead to changes in the cash flows of the firm. No doubt, changing cash flows due to unexpected exchange rate changes mean variations in the market value of the firm which is measured by the net present value of cash flows. Operating exposure is sometimes referred to as *economic exposure* or *competitive exposure*.

As seen, operating exposure deals with expected future operating cash flows that may be changing since unexpected changes in exchange rates may affect market conditions in terms of increases or decreases in prices, costs, and, sales volume. However, unlike the transaction exposure which deals with the contracted and thus certain future cash flows resulting from changes in exchange rates, the operating exposure would be the result of expected changes. In another word, in the case of operating exposure, changes in exchange rates may not bring about changes in future cash flows if they do not alter market conditions in terms of increases or decreases in prices, costs, and, sales volume. However, in the case of transaction exposure changes in exchange rates definitely cause changes in future cash flows since they are contractually tied up with exchange rates. As such, devaluation of a currency would have different effects on operating and transaction exposures.

3. *Translation exposure* is related to preparing the consolidated financial statements of the parent company to include the investment made (the subsidiary established) abroad. For this reason it is also called *accounting exposure*. As it is known, a company or a factory established abroad as a direct investment is generally a subsidiary of a parent company which is often a multinational corporation. Therefore, when a parent company or a multinational corporation prepares its consolidated financial statements for some reasons (e.g., declarations to shareholders, the public, governmental authorities for taxation, and so on), it has to translate the financial statements of its foreign subsidiaries prepared in local currency into a single reporting currency to prepare consolidated financial statements.

Accordingly, changes in the exchange rates occurred before preparing the consolidated financial statements would certainly affect the owner's equity in terms of an increase or a decrease in the parent company's net worth. Needless to say, the management of the parent company would also assess the performance of foreign subsidiaries on the basis of their effects on the consolidated financial statements. Nevertheless, when exchange rate changes are different for items in financial statements, difficulties would arise in preparing consolidated financial statements. In such cases, the method for translating the subsidiary's financial statements into the consolidated financial statements becomes important. In practice, accountants generally use two translation methods called "the current rate" and "the temporal" methods. The current method is stated to be the most widely used method for preparing consolidated financial statements (Eiteman, Stonehill, & Moffett, 2015).

Consequently, a project manager has to be aware of such foreign exchange exposures or risks and, if possible, should take necessary precautions in advance to manage them. However, the measures to be taken in advance are limited since the operating periods of investment projects are too long to deal with the effects of exchange rate changes on the operational cash flows of an investment project. Hence, the general approach that is recommended during the operating period to deal with *operating exposure* is the so-called *natural-hedging* of matching foreign currency cash outflows with cash inflows associated with operational activities of a business firm. Unfortunately, structuring the operation of an investment project for matching the cash flows in terms of foreign currency is not an easy job, if not possible at all.

On the other hand, contractual hedging techniques such as *forward, option, futures*, and *swap* are recommended for business firms to manage foreign exchange risk of *transaction exposure* (Eiteman, Stonehill, & Moffett, 2015; Fabozzi, Modigliani, & Jones, 2010; Smart, Gitman, & Joehnk, 2016). These hedging techniques are actually financial contracts enabling an individual or a company to purchase or sell a given amount of a foreign currency at a certain future date and at a specified exchange rate determined in advance. That is, the exchange rate is fixed when the agreement is made and the delivery of the foreign currency is made in the future at a specified time. Accordingly, forward, option, futures, and swap are surely useful hedging techniques for business firms to manage transaction exposure. Nevertheless, with respect to investment projects they may not be so attractive in the sense that they might only be used for transactions to be made during the establishment period of a project and that this period is not so long to create exchange rate risk.

Furthermore, the use of these hedging techniques for managing *translation exposure* is considered too costly and speculative. For this reason, the only method recommended for minimizing translation exposure is the so-called *balance sheet hedge* which requires an equal amount of exposed foreign currency assets and liabilities in balance sheets (Eiteman, Stonehill, & Moffett, 2015).

Options and futures as stated above are standardized and exchange-traded contracts[4] whereas forwards and swaps are customized according to the needs of contracting parties and thus are not traded on exchanges. Options give the purchaser the right (not the obligation), that is, the option of buying or selling a given amount of foreign currency. The option that gives the right to purchase is named the "*call option*" whereas the one that gives the right of selling is labeled as the "*put option*". This optional right of purchasing or selling is obtained through paying a price called "the option premium". Thus, until the contract expires the purchaser may use his/her option if it is desired. Otherwise, the option will not be used (exercised) and the purchaser bears the cost of "the premium". In contrast to options; forwards and futures contracts are obligations to be fulfilled. That is, the foreign currency in question has to be delivered to the related party at the specified time, at the specified amount, and at the specified exchange rate. Forwards are not traded on exchanges and they are regular agreements usually made among banks and business firms to enable companies to purchase foreign currency in advance for future delivery.

Swaps are a bit different in the sense that they involve simultaneous purchase and sale of foreign exchanges between two firms usually through an intermediary bank at a certain time, at a given amount, and at a predetermined exchange rate. This process of purchasing and selling foreign exchanges between two parties through a bank is repeated several times during a certain period of time. Generally, one firm sells its own local currency through a bank to another company which, in turn, pays its obligation with its own local currency at a specified exchange rate at a certain time in the future. For example, a German and an American company are in need of foreign exchanges to pay their foreign debts denominated in USD and EUR, respectively. To meet their foreign exchange needs as well as to hedge against foreign exchange risk, they get together through the help of a bank to make foreign exchange deal called "currency swap". Thus, the German firm agrees to sell 1,000,000 EUR to the American company at an agreed exchange rate of 1.2 USD/EUR and that the American company also agrees to pay in turn 1,200,000 USD to the German firm, and that this process is going to be repeated for several years through the bank charging a commission for its swap services.

At this point, it should be kept in mind that foreign exchange exposure is not always against the advantage of a firm. Depending on the appreciation or depreciation trend of the foreign currency in question, exchange rate risk or exposure may be for the advantage of a firm as well. Thus, hedging or not hedging is a matter of careful analysis of the changing trends of foreign currency in question. Furthermore, if the analysis of the past trends of the foreign currency in question reveals high volatility matched with a significant level of instability, the economic policies and the potential political risk of the host country have to be carefully reevaluated so as to decide whether or not to accept a profitable investment project. No doubt that if the foreign exchange exposure or risk level is such that it cannot be tolerated, the investment project has to be rejected even if it seems profitable.

EVALUATING RISKY INVESTMENT PROJECTS

Having explained the methods and approaches to analyze and determine the risk associated with an investment project, the investment project considered risky should be reevaluated for its economic profitability from the viewpoint of the risk involved in it. Several approaches; such as *risk adjusted discount rate method, certainty equivalent method, expected net present value method, expected net cash flows method, decision tree*, and *simulation technique*, are often utilized for evaluating risky investment projects. Some of these methods are quite similar so it would suffice to explain the methods of: (1) *the risk adjusted discount rate*, (2) *the expected net present value*, (3) *the expected net cash flow, and (4) the simulation technique* in the following pages.

The Risk Adjusted Discount Rate Method

This method aims at determining a risk premium that stands for the risk assumed to be associated with over all cash flows of a project and then adding it to the discount rate which represents the weighted average cost of capital. Once a risk adjusted discount rate is estimated, this discount rate is then used to compute the net present value of the investment project or to compare with the internal rate of return of the project.

The risk premium is generally based on the judgmental evaluation of the project managers and/or analysts conducting the feasibility study, although consultations with colleagues and specialists in the field are always searched for. Accordingly, the discount rate for a risky investment project is stated as:

$(1 + r + e)^t$

where;

r: The cost of capital or the expected minimum rate of return,
e: The risk premium conceived, and
t: Year in the life cycle of the investment project.

However, it should be kept in mind that the average cost of capital (r) implicitly includes a risk premium already. Thus, when trying to estimate a risk premium (e), double counting the risk premium should always be remembered. For this reason, sometimes the risk adjusted discount rate is stated as:

$(1 + R + e)^t$

where; R refers to the risk free cost of capital.

Now, assuming that the average cost of capital for an investment project is estimated to be 12% and that the risk premium deemed to be appropriate is 8%, the net present value (NPV) can be calculated as follows:

$$\text{NPV} = \sum_{t=0}^{n} \frac{NCF_t}{(1+r+e)^t}$$

NCF_t stands for net cash flow in year (t).

$$\text{NPV} = \sum_{t=0}^{n} \frac{NCF_t}{(1+0.12+0.08)^t}$$

$$\text{NPV} = \sum_{t=0}^{n} \frac{NCF_t}{(1+0.20)^t}$$

Since this method is both simple and practical, it is widely used by multinational corporations in practice. For instance, when a project manager is a bit suspicious about the political risk conditions surrounding a project, the risk premium is almost automatically increased to a level that decreases the net worth of the project significantly. Project managers and analysts preparing comprehensive feasibility studies and conducting detailed analyses throughout all the stages as well as evaluating business, political, and currency risks associated with investment projects would feel comfortable to assign a risk premium to the cost of capital or the discount rate.

Nonetheless, this method is still largely criticized for being judgmental. Furthermore, in practice, the risk premium conceived appropriate at the beginning of the project is kept constant throughout the whole life cycle of the investment project. This practical implementation is criticized on the grounds that the risk prevailing at the beginning of the project may decrease later on when the project succeeds in the beginning years. In fact, if a project survives the first few years of the operating period successfully, the risk for failure will definitely decrease in the years to come. Thus, changing the degree of risk premium level according to the stages of the life cycle of the project might be an answer to this criticism. Consequently, as seen, this method deals with the risk associated with an investment project by simply decreasing its net worth so that risky investment projects may be rejected because of increased discount rates.

The Expected Net Present Value Method

The method of the expected net present value requires that if a project manager believes that an investment project is risky, he or she then should develop a probability distribution about the net present value computed according to the best estimates of the net cash flows. For this purpose the project manager develops a probability distribution for the best estimate (base value) of the net present value (NPV) on the bases of the analyses done throughout the feasibility and risk evaluation studies, personal experience, and judgment as well as consultations with colleagues and specialists in the field.

As explained in the subsection on “The Probability Analysis”, a commonly used approach for developing a probability distribution is the so-called “step rectangular approach” that calls for determining the highest and lowest possible values of NPV above and below the best estimate (the base value) of the NPV. Then, the ranges around the base value of the NPV are divided in several intervals and probabilities of occurrence are assigned to those values including the base value of the NPV. The possible distribution of NPV values may also be developed as the estimates of “excellent”, “good”, “bad”, and “worse” economic conditions if desired.

For now, as an illustrative example let us assume that a project manager has computed an NPV of 45 million USD as the best estimate of the feasibility study conducted. However, the project seems to be risky as the result of the risk analysis methods used so far. Thus, the project manager believes that the NPV will change in the future. But he/she is confident enough that the NPV in the future would be neither higher than 60 million USD nor lower than 25 million USD. It is further believed that values of 55 million USD and 30 million USD around the best estimate of 45 million USD are also possible. Moreover, the probability (P_i) for the best estimate (the base value) to occur is deemed to be 60% while the probabilities assigned to the other values are as given in Table 1.

The expected net present value E(NPV) of this distribution can be computed as follows:

$$\text{E(NPV)} = \sum_{i=1}^{k} NPV_i \times P_i$$

$$\text{E(NPV)} = 60(0.05) + 55(0.10) + 45(0.60) + 30(0.05) + 25\,(0.20)$$

Table 1. Net Present Value Distribution (Million USD)

NPV_i	P_i
60	0.05
55	0.10
45 (base)	0.60
30	0.05
25	0.20
	1.00

E(NPV) = 42 million USD.

E(NPV) is still positive and thus the project would be accepted since it is economically profitable. However, the riskiness of the project should be separately examined. Because the risk is defined as the variability or dispersion of the value of a variable, *the standard deviation* of the above given probability distribution for the net present value (NPV_i) would be the best measure for the riskiness of the investment project. Statistically, *standard deviation* indicates the amount of unit change around the expected value or deviations from the weighted average of the distribution. Thus, the standard deviation of a distribution would be the best measure for its variability or riskiness. The standard deviation (s) of the above given probability distribution of (NPV_i) is computed as given below:

$$s = \sqrt{\sum_{i=1}^{k} (NBD_i - E(NBD))^2 P_i}$$

$$s = \sqrt{\begin{matrix}(60-42)^2(0.05)+(55-42)^2(0.10)+(45-42)^2(0.60) \\ +(30-42)^2(0.25)+(25-42)\end{matrix}}(0.20)$$

$$s = \sqrt{16.2 + 16.9 + 5.4 + 36.0 + 57.8}$$

s = 11.5 million USD.

No doubt, the larger the standard deviation the riskier the project would be. For example, if there is an alternative project with a standard deviation of, let's say, 8.6 million USD, this alternative project should be considered less risky since it has a smaller standard deviation.

However, it would be difficult to judge the riskiness of a single project through its single standard deviation value since there is no yardstick to compare it with. Thus, we are not so sure whether the standard deviation value of 11.5 million USD indicates a higher or lower risk level, especially for the projects with very large numbers of net cash flows. In such cases of evaluating the riskiness of a single project through its standard deviation as well as comparing alternative projects that have very close standard deviations, the *coefficient of variation* of a probability distribution would be a much better risk indicator.

The coefficient of variation is simply the ratio of the standard deviation (s) to the expected net present value, E(NPV). That is, coefficient of variation (CV) is:

$$\text{DK} = \frac{s}{E(NBD)}$$

$$\text{DK} = \frac{11.5}{42}$$

$$\text{DK} = 0.27$$

This value of the coefficient of variation may be evaluated as a percentage of the expected value so that the riskiness of a single project might be judged through it. As such, a 27% change over the expected value indicates a moderate level of risk for the project in question. No doubt that when comparing alternative projects, the project with the lowest value of the coefficient of variation is the least risky one. For example, if project A has a coefficient of variation of 0.27 while project B has one with 0.38, then it can be stated that the project A is less risky that the project B.

However, perhaps the best way to evaluate the riskiness of a single project when there is no alternative to compare its standard deviation and coefficient of variation with is to assume that the NPV distribution is a *normal* distribution (if there is no strong argument against it) and then to convert it to the *standard normal probability distribution*. As such, the probability of the E(NPV) value being greater or smaller than a certain X value may be computed through the formula of the standard normal distribution for Z scores as follows:

$$Z = \frac{X - E(NBD)}{s}$$

where:

Z: indicates how many standard deviations X is from the expected net present value, E(NPV),
X: denotes a certain value for comparison,
s: is the standard deviation for the probability distribution of NPV_i.

For example, for the above given probability distribution of (NPV_i) with an expected value of E(NPV) = 42 million TL and a standard deviation of s = 11.5 million TL, what is the probability of the expected net present value being less than 20 million TL. That is, the probability of E(NPV) < 20 million TL?

$$Z = \frac{20 - 42}{11.5}$$

Z = - 1.91

So, this figure indicates that a net present value of 20 million TL lies 1.91 standard deviations to the "left" of the expected value of the probability distribution of possible net present values (NPV_i). (The negative Z score value tells us that we should be looking to the left of the mean or the expected value.)

Thus, according to the Table for Standard Normal Distribution given in Appendix 1, the probability of the area for Z = - 1.91 is 0.4719. Since the probability areas above (to the right of) and below (to the left of) the expected value are 0.50, the probability of the expected value being less than 20 million TL is (0.50 - 0.4719 =) 0.0281. That is, the probability for E(NPV) < 20 million TL is 2.81%. Of course, the probability of E(NPV) > 20 million TL is (0.50 + 0.4719 =) 97.17%. Now one may say that this project is not risky.

Similarly, the probability of E(NPV) > 50 million TL is:

$$Z = \frac{50 - 42}{11.5}$$

Z = 0.69

The probability of the area for Z = 0.69 in the Table for Standard Normal Distribution in Appendix 1 is 0.2549. Since the probability of the area above the expected value is 0.50, the probability of E(NPV) being greater than 50 million TL would be (0.50 - 0.2549 =) 0.2451, that is, 24.51%. As seen, Z scores are quite helpful to evaluate the riskiness of a single investment project per se.

Finally, before concluding this subsection it should be added that when comparing alternative projects with standard deviations and/or coefficient of variation equal or close to each other, the coefficients of *skewness* and *kurtosis* of the alternative distributions may be computed to judge the riskiness of alternative projects. For instance, let's consider a hypothetical yet instructive example of a multinational corporation that is hesitant about deciding on the final location of its plant in either country X or country Y. The multinational corporation that is planning a market seeking direct investment conducted a detailed feasibility study which revealed the fact that both country X and Y are equally desirable. Hence, they are considered as parallel alternatives in the sense that the feasibility study would be repeated in both countries and finally whichever country leads to larger profit is to be selected as the host country.

For now, having completed the market and technical analyses with regard to both countries, at this stage of the financial evaluation concerning the risk analysis, interestingly enough, both countries showed very close measures of risk in terms of standard deviations and coefficients of variation as calculated on the basis of the data given below in Table 2 and Table 3. The project analyst, once computed an NPV value for each country in the financial evaluation stage as explained earlier, develops probability distributions (P_i) for these NPV values (NPV_i) depending on the economic outlook of each country.

For example, in Table 2, the NPV computed for country X under "normal" conditions is estimated to be 40(000) USD and it has a probability of 50% to happen. The chance for the economy of country X to be "good" in the future is estimated to be 30%. If the economic outlook becomes good, NPV would be 50(000) USD. However, there is a probability of 20% that the economic outlook of county X may be "bad" and, in this case, NPV would be 30(000) USD. Similar comments apply to country Y in Table 3.

$$E(NPV) = 30(0.20) + 40(0.50) + 50(0.30)$$

$$E(NPV) = 41(000)\ USD$$

Table 2. Investment in Country X (000 USD)

Economic Outlook	P_i	NPV_i
Bad	0.20	30
Normal	0.50	40
Good	0.30	50
	1.00	

s = 7(000) USD

CV = 7/41= 0.17

E(NPV) = 35(0.30) + 45(0.50) + 55(0.20)

E(NPV) = 44 USD

s = 7(000) USD

CV = 7/44 = 0.16

As noticed, the projects X and Y have equal standard deviation (s) and very close coefficient of variation (CV) values as risk measures. That is, the standard deviations for both countries are the same (s = 7,000 USD) and the coefficients of variation are very close with values 0.17 and 0.16 for country X and Y, respectively. The difference of (0.17 – 0.16 =) 0.01 might quite possibly be an estimation error as well.

Table 3. Investment in Country Y (000 USD)

Economic Outlook	P_i	NPV_i
Bad	0.30	35
Normal	0.50	45
Good	0.20	55
	1.00	

Consequently, when standard deviation and coefficient of variation values as risk measures do not provide sufficient information regarding the riskiness of the investment projects because of being very close or equal to each other, the coefficients of *skewness* and *kurtosis* of the alternative distributions may be of help to assess the riskiness of alternatives. The coefficients of *skewness* and *kurtosis* may be computed quite easily through *the third moment* and *the fourth moment*, respectively, as follows (remember that the variance of a distribution is *the second moment*):

$$M_3 = \sum_{i=1}^{k} (NPV_i - E(NPV))^3 \times P_i$$

$$M_4 = \sum_{i=1}^{k} (NPV_i - E(NPV))^4 \times P_i$$

where:

k = Refers to the values of NPV_i in the distribution, (i =1, 2, 3),
M_3 = The third moment,
M_4 = The fourth moment.

Accordingly, the coefficient of skewness (G_1) is computed as the ratio of the third moment to the third power (cube) of standard deviation (s^3) as given below:

$$G_1 = \frac{M_3}{s^3}$$

While the coefficients of *kurtosis* (G_2) is calculated as the ratio of the fourth moment to the fourth power of standard deviation (s^4) as;

$$G_2 = \frac{M_4}{s^4}$$

On the basis of the data and the related computed statistics for the countries X and Y as given in Tables 2 and 3, the coefficient of skewness may computed as follows:

For Country X:

$$G_1 = \frac{M_3}{s^3}$$

$$M_3 = \sum_{i=1}^{k}(NPV_i - E(NPV)^3) \times P_i$$

$$M_3 = (30 - 41)^3 \text{ x } 0.20 + (40 - 41)^3 \text{ x } 0.50 + (50 - 41)^3 \text{ x } 0.30$$

$$M_3 = -48$$

$$G_1 = \frac{-48}{7^3} = -0.14$$

For Country Y:

$$M_3 = (35 - 44)^3 \text{ x } 0.30 + (45 - 44)^3 \text{ x } 0.50 + (55 - 44)^3 \text{ x } 0.20$$

$$M_3 = 47$$

$$G_1 = \frac{47}{7^3} = 0.137$$

Probability distributions with positive values of coefficients of skewness ($G_1 > 0$) are said to be skewed to the right and thus the larger the coefficient of skewness the less risky an investment project is considered to be. The reason for this is quite clear because there are larger positive values of NPV_i than the expected value of E(NPV) when taking the cubes (the third power) values of $(NPV_i - E(NPV))^3$ for the third moment (M_3). On the other hand, in contrast, the projects with smaller, especially negative, values of coefficients of skewness ($G_1 < 0$) are lft skewed and considered more risky. Needless to indicate that a coefficient of skewness being equal to zero (0) means that the distribution is symmetrical.

Consequently, with regard to our hypothetical examples given above, it may be stated that country X is more risky than country Y since its coefficient of skewness is negative and smaller than that of country Y, ($G_{1X} = -0.14 <$

G1Y = 0.137). Therefore, the American multinational corporation should chose country Y for its direct investment. In cases of equality of coefficients of skewness, the coefficients of kurtosis may be computed as stated above. The coefficient of kurtosis measures the steepness of a distribution and it is equal to 3 for the normal distribution. Thus, projects with coefficients of kurtosis greater than three (3) are regarded less risky and steeper than the normal distribution. Similarly, in comparing alternatives those with larger values of coefficients of kurtosis are considered less risky. However, the coefficient of kurtosis is just used as a supporting statistic with other risk measures. That is, it is not taken as a single factor to judge the riskiness of a distribution since the steepness of a distribution may not prevent the dispersion of a distribution as an indicator of risk.

The Expected Net Cash Flow Method

As noticed above, the expected net present value is a kind of *top-level methodology* that requires the development of a probability distribution for the overall profitability of an investment project as a whole in terms of the net present value (NPV). This, indeed, is not an easy task for a project manager since it needs a great deal of experience and wisdom to foresee the functioning and interaction of all individual variables leading to changes in an investment project. For this reason, only well experienced project managers who have conducted various similar projects in the past are expected to employ the expected net present value method. However, not all project managers would have such experience, knowledge, and information to develop a probability distribution about the final result of an investment project as an NPV.

Accordingly, an alternative procedure labeled as the expected net cash flow model is used in evaluating risky investment projects when it is difficult to develop an overall net present value distribution. The expected net cash flow model is a *mid-level methodology* that requires developing probability distributions for the annual net cash flow estimated as the best point estimates. That is, a probability distribution is developed for the net cash value in each year of the operating period by taking the previously estimated best value as the base value. Then, the expected net cash values in each year of the operating period are computed. Finally, the expected net cash flow of the operating period is discounted to find the expected net present value of the investment project.

Therefore, in contrast to the expected net present value method - E(NPV); the expected net cash flow method - E(NCF) - does not focus on the changes in the net present value at the top level rather on the changes in the annual net cash values leading to changes in the net present value. Probability distributions are not developed for the cash outflows of the years in the establishment period since the establishment period is very short (one or two years) and that estimates of cash outflows for building the plant are almost certain.

Now, in order to illustrate this methodology let's assume that the computed net cash flows for an investment project are as given below (for the sake of simplifying computations the lengths of the establishment and operating periods are taken as 1 and 3 years, respectively) (see Box 3).

However, further studies revealed that the project is risky and so the project manager, through his experience and analyses, believes that the net cash flows which were computed as his/her best estimates have the following chances (probabilities) of occurrence (Box 4).

In addition, the project manager also believes that the above given best estimates of NCFs (base values) would change as according to the probabilities stated next to them (Box 5).

As seen, the project manager takes into account changes in the annual net cash flows and develops a probability distribution for each year of the operating period. For example, in the year t_1, the probability of the best estimate of the NCF being $350,000 is 60%. Additionally, there are probabilities of 30% and 10% that NCFs would be $400,000 and $200,000, respectively. The profitability and the riskiness of the investment project may now be evaluated according to the expected net cash flow method – E(NCF) – as follows:

Box 3. Net Cash Flows (000 USD)

	t_0	t_1	t_2	t_3
NCF	-380,000	350,000	390,000	420,000

Box 4. Probabilities of Net Cash Flows (000 USD)

	t_0	t_1	t_2	t_3
NCF	-380,000 100%	350,000 60%	390,000 60%	420,000 50%

Box 5. Probabilities of Changes in Net Cash Flows (000 USD)

t_0		t_1		t_2		t_3	
NCF_i	**P_i**	**NCF_i**	**P_i**	**NCF_i**	**P_i**	**NCF_i**	**P_i**
-380,000	100%*	400,000	30%	410,000	20%	470,000	10%
		350,000	60%	390,000	60%	420,000	50%
		200,000	10%	300,000	20%	350,000	40%

* Cash outflow in the base year (establishment period) is assumed to be certain.

$$E_t(NCF) = \sum_{i=1}^{k} NCF_{it} \times P_{it} \text{ (i = 1, 2, ..., k) (For all t's, t= 0, 1, ..., n)}$$

Therefore, the expected net present value – E(NPV) – would be computed as:

$$E(NBD) = \sum_{t=0}^{n} \frac{E_t(NCF)}{(1+R)^t}$$

where:

NCF_{it}: The ith net cash flow in year t,
P_{it}: Probability of ith net cash flow in year t,
$E_t(NCF)$: Expected net cash flow in year t,
E(NBD): Expected net present value of the project,
R: Risk free cost of capital.

The risk free cost of capital is the discount rate which does not include any risk premium since the changes in the net cash flows in terms of risk are taken into account by the probability distributions developed. Therefore, the risk premium added to the current cost of capital as it was indicated previously should be deducted when the E(NCF) method is used. Otherwise, there would be a double counting of the risk assumed to be associated with the investment project. For now, assuming that the risk free cost of capital is 10%, that is, (R = 0.10), the expected net present value of the project - E(NBD) – could be computed as given below:

E_0 (NCF) = -380,000 (1) = -380,000 USD

E_1(NCF) = 400,000 (0.30) + 350,000 (0.60) + 200,000(0.10)

E_1 (NCF) = 350,000 USD,

E_2(NCF) = 410,000 (0.20) + 390,000 (0.60) + 300,000(0.20)

E_2(NCF) = 376,000 USD,

E_3(NCF) = 470,000 (0.10) + 420,000 (0.50) + 350,000(0.40)

E_3(NCF) = 397,000USD.

Thus, if R = 0.10, the expected net present value of the investment project is;

$$E\ (NPV) = -380{,}000 + \frac{350000}{(1+0.10)} + \frac{376000}{(1+0.10)^2} + \frac{397000}{(1+0.10)^3}$$

E(NPV) = 547,198 USD.

Since the expected net present value is positive, that is;

E(NPV) = 547,198 USD > 0

this project is an acceptable investment proposal in terms of its profitability.

However, in order to evaluate the overall riskiness of the investment project, the standard deviation of the project as a whole has to be computed on the basis of the distributions of the net cash flows given above. But the probability distributions are developed according to the annual net cash flows separately. Therefore, what has to be done is to compute the standard deviations of the annual net cash flows separately first and, then, to combine them to find out the standard deviation of the project as a whole. Needles to indicate that if the standard deviations of net cash flows are large, the standard deviation of the investment project would be large as well, meaning that the project is risky; or vice versa.

Nevertheless, when combining the standard deviations of annual net cash flows to get the overall risk or the standard deviation of the investment project, interdependency (autocorrelation) of net cash flows is an important point to consider since it inflates the value of the standard deviation computed. For this reason, computing the standard deviation of an investment project as a whole is based on the assumption of *independency* or *interdependency* of annual net cash flows as stated below:

Independency

If annual net cash flows are independent of each other, that is, if the net cash flow in a year is assumed to be not affected by the net cash flow of the previous year, the overall standard deviation of the investment project (S) is computed (Van Horne, 1980) on the basis of the standard deviations of annual net cash flows (s_t) as given below:

$$S = \sqrt{\sum_{t=0}^{n} \frac{s_t^2}{(1+R)^{2t}}} \quad (t = 0, 1, 2, \ldots\ldots, n)$$

and

$$s_t = \sqrt{\sum_{i=1}^{k} (NCF_{it} - E(NCF))^2 \times P_{it}} \quad (i = 1,2,\ldots,k) \text{ For all t's } (t = 0, 1, 2, \ldots, n)$$

Therefore, the annual standard deviations (s_t) are:

$s_0 = 0$ (Since the cash flow in year t_0 is assumed to be certain with100% probability),

$s^2_1 = (400{,}000 - 350{,}000)^2 (0.30) + (350{,}000 - 350{,}000)^2 (0.60) + (200{,}000 - 350{,}000)^2 (0.10)$

$s_1 = 54{,}772$ USD.

Similarly;

$s_2 = 38{,}781$ USD.

$s_3 = 41{,}000$ USD.

Consequently, recalling that the risk free cost of capital for the investment project was 10%, the overall standard deviation of the investment project when the annual net cash flows are assumed to be independent is:

$$S = \sqrt{0 + \frac{(54772)^2}{(1+0.10)^{2x1}} + \frac{(38781)^2}{(1+0.10)^{2x2}} + \frac{(41000)^2}{(1+0.10)^{2x3}}}$$

S = 66,373 USD.

Additionally, the coefficient of the variation (CV) for the investment project is:

$$CV = \frac{S}{E(NPV)} = \frac{66373}{547198}$$

CV = 0.12

Thus, one may say that this investment project is not risky since the variation of the outcome of the investment is not high as the coefficient of the variation indicated. On the other hand, since the expected net present value of the project was positive,

E(NPV) = 547,198 USD > 0

this project may be accepted as an investment proposal.

Interdependency

If the assumption of the independency of annual net cash flows is not acceptable, then the case of interdependency comes to mind. In fact, the assumption of "independency" is very questionable in reality since large sales in a year would most likely affect the next year's sales. That is, the marketing success in a year would possibly have a considerable influence on the following year's marketing activities. Therefore, there is always a situation of interdependency between annual net cash flows. When an interdependency condition between consecutive net cash flows is eventually considered, the overall standard deviation of the investment project is computed as:

$$S = \sum_{t=0}^{n} \frac{s_t}{(1+R)^t} \text{ (t= 0, 1, 2, ..., n)}$$

$$S = 0 + \frac{54772}{(1+0.10)} + \frac{38781}{(1+0.10)^2} + \frac{41000}{(1+0.10)^3}$$

S = 112,647 USD.

As seen, in the case of interdependency, the standard deviation increased drastically, indicating the effect of autocorrelation. So the coefficient of variation for the project in this case would be,

$$CV = \frac{S}{E(NPV)} = \frac{112647}{547198}$$

CV = 0.20

still not a high level of risk for the project in question.

At this point, it should be stated that although interdependency is a more plausible condition in realty, however, a full interdependency condition as formulated above might be an extreme case. That is, full interdependency or independency conditions are extreme cases. The truth is somewhere in between in the sense that annual net cash flows are neither independent nor interdependent completely. If a "where in between" question is raised, the answer would be the judgment and experience of the project manager. For example, for our above given example the range of standard deviation with regard to independency and interdependency cases was computed to be;

66,373 < ----------- > 112,647 USD.

So, depending on the outcomes of the market analysis and his/her personal experience, the project manager might take a value of, say, 85.000 USD as a "moderate level" of the standard deviation and then compute the coefficient of variation to evaluate the riskiness of the investment project. Nevertheless, those project managers that stay away from judgmental decisions but enjoy working with probabilities may even calculate *conditional* and/or *joint* probabilities for annual net cash flows and then calculate standard deviations.

But such cumbersome probabilistic analyses are best dealt with the simulation technique as explained in the next section.

The Simulation Technique

As explained earlier in the subsection concerning the techniques for determining the project risk, the simulation technique is an experimental methodology that requires the development of a quantitative model which necessitates the use of a computer based software. In other words, simulation is a computerized mathematical modeling technique that tries to represent a system through defining its behaviors mathematically. As such, various assumptions and/or "what if" type questions are evaluated on an interactive mathematical model to see the effects of different alternative courses of action. Hence, simulation is a valuable technique for evaluating changing behaviors of investment projects in the future. Particularly, the so-called *Monte Carlo simulation* modeling technique is the most common simulation method used for risk analysis in real capital investment projects.

Monte Carlo simulation that generates data from the probability distributions resembling the behaviors of a real system through statistical sampling[5] is used both to determine the degree of risk associated with an investment project and to evaluate the profitability of the risky investment. The use of Monte Carlo simulation for the risk analysis in investment projects goes through the following steps:

1. Critical variables are determined, preferably through a sensitivity analysis. For the sake of explanation, let us assume that sales volume (Q) and price per unit (f) are selected as critical variables.
2. The probability distributions are developed for the critical variables by the method of probability analysis as explained previously. Later on, in order to generate random values (variates) from these probability distributions, *random number intervals* are determined on the basis of the *cumulative distribution* which is obtained by summing up individual probabilities associated with each variable. As an example, the probability distribution, the cumulative distribution, and the random number intervals for the critical variable of sales volume or the quantity sold (Q_i) are given below in Table 4.

Table 4. The Distribution of Sales Volume (Quantity Sold)

Quantity	Probability	Cumulative Probability	Random Number Interval
50,000	0.20	0.20	00 - 19
60,000	0.55	0.75	20 - 74
95,000	0.25	1.00	75 - 99

Since zero (0) is a number, random number interval starts from zero (00) and goes till 99, thus, covering the total of 100% probability. No doubt that for each critical variable selected a probability distribution and the associated random number intervals similar to Table 4 has to be prepared. For example, if there are five critical variables, five distribution tables as given in Table 4 are needed.

3. At this stage, the investment evaluation model, such as the net present value (NPV) model, has to be formulated in detail so as to include specifically the critical variables. For instance, for our explanation given above, the sales volume or quantity produced (Q) and the price per unit (f) were selected as critical variables. Therefore, in the valuation model of NPV method given below, since sales revenues (R) are the product of sales volume or quantity produced (Q) times the price per unit (f), sales revenues (R_t) will be firstly computed by the equation,

$$R_t = (Q_t \text{ x } f_t)$$

and then the value of sales revenues (R_t) computed would be used in the valuation model to calculate the NPV value.

$$\text{NPV} = \sum_{t=0}^{n} \frac{(R_t - I_t - C_t - D_t)(1 - V_t) + D_t}{(1 + r)^t}$$

Therefore, the investment valuation model is composed of two consecutive equations and that the NPV would be calculated at two steps through two simultaneous equations:

$R_t = (Q_t \text{ x } f_t)$

$$NPV = \sum_{t=0}^{n} \frac{(R_t - I_t - C_t - D_t)(1 - V_t) + D_t}{(1 + r)^t}$$

where, as indicated before;

R_t: Sales revenues in year t,
Q_t: Sales volume or quantity sold in year t,
f_t: Price per unit in year t,
I_t: The total of initial investment,
C_t: Operational costs in year t,
D_t: Depreciation charges in year t,
V_t: Corporate tax rate in year t,
r : The discount rate (should be taken as risk free cost of capital),
t : Years (t=0,1,2,3,……,n),
n = Life cycle of the project as the number of years.

Needless to state that the content of the valuation model or the number of simultaneous equations for computing NPV will depend on the number of critical variables as well as the functions defining them.

4. Upon determining the valuation model covering critical variables and the probability distributions for the critical variables, simulation trials (or experiments) will be started to generate random values (variates) from the probability distributions of critical variables. For this purpose, for each critical variable in question, a random number is selected and then this random number is compared with the random number intervals of the critical variable to find the corresponding value of the critical variable for that simulation trial. For example, in order to generate a random value for the critical variable of the sales volume (quantity sold) whose probability distribution is given above, let us assume that at the first trial the number of 86 is selected as a random number (perhaps through a lottery among 100 numbers labeled from 00 to 99).

According to the random number intervals in Table 4, the corresponding quantity sold for the random number 86 would be 95,000 units. Thus, for the first simulation trial (experiment) the value of quantity sold (Q) is assumed to be 95,000 units. The same process is repeated for all critical variables to generate random values. Let's further assume that in a similar manner, a random value of 400 TL is generated in the same simulation trial for the critical variable of the price per unit (f). Accordingly, sales revenues will be (95,000 x 400 =) 38,000,000 TL for the first trial, excluding the surplus value of the project in the last year of the operating period (H_n). That is, the sales revenues for the first trial would be:

$$R = (Q \times f)$$

$$R = (95{,}000 \times 400)$$

Hence, keeping the values (best point estimates) of all the other variables constant and inputting in the model of,

$$\text{NPV} = \sum_{t=0}^{n} \frac{(R - I_t - C_t - D_t)(1 - V_t) + D_t}{(1+r)^t}$$

a value of NPV could be computed for the first trial. Let us label this value as NPV_1.

5. The process at the 4th stage is repeated for many times, say 500 times. Each repeat (run) is a trial (or an experiment) for generating a random value for the quantity sold (Q_i) and the price per unit (f_i) and, then, keeping the best estimate values of all the other variables constant, an NPV value is computed. More specifically, in each trial (experiment) a random number is selected and thus a random value (variate) for the quantity sold (Q_i) is generated; and the same is done to generate a random value (variate) for the price per unit (f_i). Then, keeping all the other variables in the model constant an NPV is computed.

Consequently, if this process is repeated 500 times or 500 trials are made, 500 NPV values would be computed. However, all these 500 values would be in only nine different groups since each critical variable (quantity sold and unit price) has a three step (possible) probability distribution. So for each random value of a variable there would be only three possible values of the other critical variable. Therefore, because each critical variable has a three step (possible) probability distribution, the computed NPV_i values would be only in (3 x 3 =) 9 groups. More specifically, according to the given probability distribution for each value of Q_i there would be only three (3) possible values of f_i. Since there are three possible values for Q_i, there would be only (3x3=) 9 possible combinations of Q_i and f_i as possible sales revenues. As such, at the end of 500 trials or experiments the computed 500 NPV values will be composed of 9 different values since the values of all the variables are kept constant during simulation trials or experiments as shown in Table 5.

For the sake of simplicity, let us assume that 500 hypothetical trials are made and that the computed 500 hypothetical NPV_i values have a distribution in 9 groups as given in Table 5. The size of each group is the *frequency* value of the group and that the *relative frequency* of each group may also be considered as the *probability* of occurrence for each group in the total trials of 500. According to our hypothetical data in Table 5, among 500 simulation trials 50 times NPV is computed to be 35,000 TL, so the relative frequency or the probability of this group (group 1) is (50/500=) 0.10. Similarly, the 4th group of NPV= 20,000 TL has frequency of 40 times among 500 trials

Table 5. Frequency (Probability) Distribution for NPV Values

Group	Frequency	NPV_i	Relative Frequency (Probability P_i)
1.	50	35,000	50/500=0.10
2.	30	45,000	30/500=0.06
3.	80	15,000	80/500=0.16
4.	40	20,000	40/500=0.08
5.	140	25,000	140/500=0.28
6.	30	42,000	30/500=0.06
7.	60	21,000	60/500=0.12
8.	45	44,000	45/500=0.09
9.	25	33,000	25/500=0.05
Total	**500**		**1.00**

and thus has a probability of (40/500=) 0.08, whereas NPV=25,000 TL (group 5) was computed 140 times and so its probability is (140/500=) 0.28. Consequently, the frequency or the probability distribution for the hypothetical 500 NPV_i values would be developed as given in Table 5.

6. Finally, once the probability distribution for the simulated NPV values is determined as given in Table 5, the expected net present value - E(NPV), the standard deviation (s), and the coefficient of variation (CV) of the NPV distribution could be computed to evaluate the economic profitability and the riskiness of the investment project, just as explained earlier:

The expected net present value E(NPV) can be computed as follows (NPV_i values are in thousands – 000);

$$E(NPV) = \sum_{i=1}^{k} NPV_i \times P_i$$

$$E(NPV) = 35(0.10) + 45(0.06) + 15(0.16) + 20(0.08) + 25(0.28) + 42(0.06) + 21(0.12) + 44(0.09) + 33(0.05)$$

E(NPV) = 27.85 (000) TL

E(NPV) = 27,850 TL

Since E(NPV) is positive, the hypothetical project would be accepted. The standard deviation (s) is:

$$s = \sqrt{\sum_{i=1}^{k} (NBD_i - E(NBD))^2 P_i}$$

$$s = \sqrt{5.11 + 17.64 + 26.42 + 4.93 + 2.27 + 12.01 + 5.63 + 23.47 + 1.33}$$

s = 9.94 (000) TL

s = 9,940 TL

Finally, the coefficient of variation (CV) is:

$$\text{DK} = \frac{s}{E(NBD)}$$

$$\text{DK} = \frac{9,940}{27,850}$$

$$\text{DK} = 0.36$$

Consequently, as seen, the simulation technique is in fact developing a probability distribution for possible NPV_i values through statistical analysis based on the probability distributions of critical variables. Notice that the net present value method explained before does this subjectively on the basis of judgmental evaluation of the project manager and/or project analysts.

Needless to state that all simulation trials, that is, the generation of random numbers and values as well as the related computations are all done through computer programs quite easily; no matter what the numbers of critical variables and the range of the related probability distributions are. So, what is important to pay attention in the simulation technique is to observe and comply with the statistical sampling rules so that simulation trials (experiments) would be statistically meaningful[6]. For instance, the random number selection should be really random. That is, the random numbers should have a uniform distribution with equal probabilities so that the values generated from probability distributions may be representing the reality.

The random number generation presently is done through *random functions* (RND) of computer software programs. When these random functions (RND) are called, the computer software programs generate the needed random numbers for generating random values for critical variables. The random numbers generated by computer's random functions are called *pseudo-random numbers* since they are produced though some mathematical methods. However, they are tested and proved to be random.

Additionally, the number of trials or runs of the simulation model should be sufficiently large enough so as to have statistical samples with optimal sizes. Furthermore, the last but not the least important point to observe in simulation experiments is to obey the principles of the economic theory when generating economic values such as sales volumes and unit prices, etc. That is, randomness should not lead to a conflict between the generated economic values and the principles of economic theory. For example, when a high price value is generated, a high sales volume should not be generated since high prices would not lead to high sales volumes. It should also be added that in using the Monte Carlo simulation technique for risk analysis, the project manager either develops his/her own computer simulation model or make use of various computer spread sheets or package programs that are easily available. *Excel* spread sheet and the package program called @RISK are two widely used computer applications for Monte Carlo simulation modeling[7].

CONCLUSION

In conclusion, as seen in the foregoing pages, the subject of the risk analysis in foreign direct investment projects is conceived of two dimensions: *(1)* identifying the risk associated with the investment project in terms of business (commercial), political, and foreign exchange risks and; *(2)* evaluating the risky investment projects. No doubt that the risk analysis in this content is conducted only if an investment project is accepted by the parent company on the economic profitability grounds. Thus, an economically profitable investment project is first analyzed through the use of the methods called sensitivity analysis, probability analysis, breakeven analysis, degree of operating leverage, and simulation analysis in order to determine whether or not the investment project is commercially risky. Finally, taking in to account the commercial, political, and currency risk components together, if the foreign direct investment project is considered risky, the investment project is reevaluated for its economic profitability from the viewpoint of the risk involved in it. For this purpose the approaches named *the risk adjusted discount rate method, the expected net present value method, the expected net cash flow methods, and the Monte Carlo simulation technique* are explained and discussed for evaluating risky investment projects.

REFERENCES

Alexandrova-Kabadjova, B., Martinez-Jaramillo, S., Garcia-Almanza, A. L., & Tsang, E. (2013). *Simulation in Computational Finance and Economics: Tools and Emerging Applications*. Hershey, PA: IGI Global. doi:10.4018/978-1-4666-2011-7

Arnold, G. (2012). *Modern Financial Markets and Institutions: A Practical Perspective*. Boston: Pearson Education Limited.

Brink, C. H. (2017). *Measuring Political Risk: Risks to Foreign Investment*. London: Routledge.

Daniels, J. D., Radebaugh, L. H., & Sullivan, D. P. (2015). *International Business: Environments and Operations (15th ed.)*. Harlow, UK: Pearson Education, Ltd.

Deuchars, R. (2017). *The International Political Economy of Risk: Rationalism, Calculation and Power*. London: Routledge.

Eithman, D. K., Stonehill, A. I., & Moffet, M. H. (2015). *Multinational Business Finance* (14th ed.). Boston: Pearson Education Inc.

Fabozzi, F. J., Modigliani, F., & Jones, F. J. (2010). *Foundations of Financial Markets and Institutions* (4th ed.). Boston: Pearson Education Inc.

Gitman, L., & Zutter, C. (2014). *Principles of Managerial Finance* (14th ed.). Boston: Pearson Education, Inc.

Hubbard, G. R., & O'Brien, A. P. (2012). *Money, Banking, & the Financial System*. Boston: Pearson Education Inc.

Hull, J. C. (2011). *Fundamentals of Futures and Options Markets* (7th ed.). Boston: Pearson Education Inc.

Law, A. M. (2015). *Simulation Modeling and Analysis* (5th ed.). New York: McGraw-Hill Education.

Ross, S. M. (2013). *Simulation* (5th ed.). Amsterdam: Elsevier.

Rubinstein, R. Y., & Kroese, D. P. (2008). *Simulation and the Monte Carlo Method* (2nd ed.). Hoboken, NJ: John Wiley & Sons, Inc.

Smart, S., Gitman, L., & Joehnk, M. (2016). *Fundamentals of Investing* (13th ed.). Boston: Pearson Education Inc.

Solakoglu, N. M., & Demir, N. (2009). Exchange-Rate Exposure and the Financial sector. *Journal of Economic and Social Research, 11*(2), 29–42.

Van Horne, J. (1980). *Financial Management and Policy* (5th ed.). London: Prentice - Hall Inter., Inc.

Wagner, D. (2012). *Managing Country Risk: A Practitioner's Guide to Effective Cross-Border Risk Analysis*. New York: Productivity Press. doi:10.1201/b11601

Wild, J., & Wild, K. (2015). *International Business: The Challenges of Globalization* (8th ed.). Boston: Pearson Education.

Winston, W. L., & Albright, C. S. (2018). *Practical Management Science* (6th ed.). Mason, OH: Cengage Learning.

ENDNOTES

1 For uses of operating and financial leverages in operating companies, see Gitman and Zutter (2014).

2 For some models and approaches developed for identifying, measuring, and managing political risk, see Brink (2017) and Wagner (2012).

3 Concerning exchange rate changes and foreign exchange market operations, see Arnold (2012). For measuring and calculating exchange rate exposure, see Solakoglu and Demir (2009).

4 Concerning market operations of options and futures, see Hull (2011) and Hubbard and O'Brien (2012).

5 For more about simulation technique and Monte Carlo simulation method, see Ross (2013) and Rubinstein and Kroese (2008).

6 For more about statistical sampling rules in simulation trials (experiments), see Law (2015) and Alexandrova-Kabadjova, Martinez-Jaramillo, Garcia-Almanza, and Tsang (2013).

7 For simulation modeling with @RISK, see Winston and Albright (2018).

Appendix

APPENDIX 1: TABLE FOR STANDARD NORMAL DISTRIBUTION

(**Z Scores:** Areas of normal distribution that is Z standard deviations to the left or right of the mean. The Z column shows ten decimal points while rows indicate hundred decimal points.)

(For example, the value of Z = 0.7 + 0.04 = 0.74 is 0.2704)

Table 1.

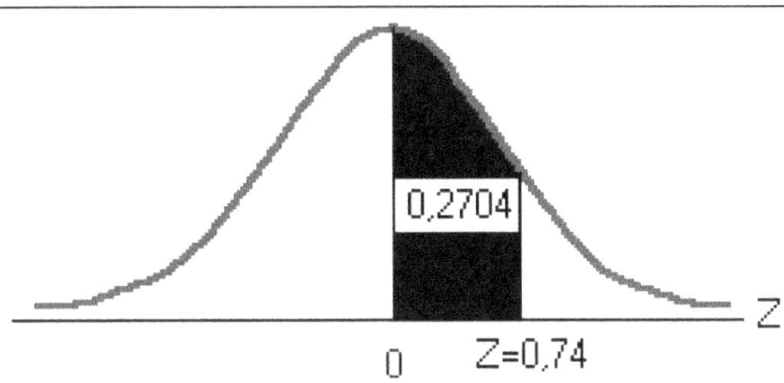

Z	0	0.01	0.02	0.03	0.04	0.05	0.06	0.07	0.08	0.09
0.0	0.0000	0.0040	0.0080	0.0120	0.0160	0.0199	0.0239	0.0279	0.0319	0.0359
0.1	0.0398	0.0438	0.0478	0.0517	0.0557	0.0596	0.0636	0.0675	0.0714	0.0753
0.2	0.0793	0.0832	0.0871	0.0910	0.0948	0.0987	0.1026	0.1064	0.1103	0.1141
0.3	0.1179	0.1217	0.1255	0.1293	0.1331	0.1368	0.1406	0.1443	0.1480	0.1517
0.4	0.1554	0.1591	0.1628	0.1664	0.1700	0.1736	0.1772	0.1808	0.1844	0.1879
0.5	0.1915	0.1950	0.1985	0.2019	0.2054	0.2088	0.2123	0.2157	0.2190	0.2224
0.6	0.2257	0.2291	0.2324	0.2357	0.2389	0.2422	0.2454	0.2486	0.2517	0.2549
0.7	0.2580	0.2611	0.2642	0.2673	**0.2704**	0.2734	0.2764	0.2794	0.2823	0.2852

continued on following page

Table 1. Continued

0.8	0.2881	0.2910	0.2939	0.2967	0.2995	0.3023	0.3051	0.3078	0.3106	0.3133
0.9	0.3159	0.3186	0.3212	0.3238	0.3264	0.3289	0.3315	0.3340	0.3365	0.3389
1.0	0.3413	0.3438	0.3461	0.3485	0.3508	0.3531	0.3554	0.3577	0.3599	0.3621
1.1	0.3643	0.3665	0.3686	0.3708	0.3729	0.3749	0.3770	0.3790	0.3810	0.3830
1.2	0.3849	0.3869	0.3888	0.3907	0.3925	0.3944	0.3962	0.3980	0.3997	0.4015
1.3	0.4032	0.4049	0.4066	0.4082	0.4099	0.4115	0.4131	0.4147	0.4162	0.4177
1.4	0.4192	0.4207	0.4222	0.4236	0.4251	0.4265	0.4279	0.4292	0.4306	0.4319
1.5	0.4332	0.4345	0.4357	0.4370	0.4382	0.4394	0.4406	0.4418	0.4429	0.4441
1.6	0.4452	0.4463	0.4474	0.4484	0.4495	0.4505	0.4515	0.4525	0.4535	0.4545
1.7	0.4554	0.4564	0.4573	0.4582	0.4591	0.4599	0.4608	0.4616	0.4625	0.4633
1.8	0.4661	0.4649	0.4656	0.4664	0.4671	0.4678	0.4686	0.4693	0.4699	0.4706
1.9	0.4713	0.4719	0.4726	0.4732	0.4738	0.4744	0.4750	0.4756	0.4761	0.4767
2.0	0.4772	0.4778	0.4783	0.4788	0.4793	0.4798	0.4803	0.4808	0.4812	0.4817
2.1	0.4821	0.4826	0.4830	0.4834	0.4838	0.4842	0.4846	0.4850	0.4854	0.4857
2.2	0.4861	0.4864	0.4868	0.4871	0.4875	0.4878	0.4881	0.4884	0.4887	0.4890
2.3	0.4893	0.4896	0.4898	0.4901	0.4904	0.4906	0.4909	0.4911	0.4913	0.4916
2.4	0.4918	0.4920	0.4922	0.4925	0.4927	0.4929	0.4931	0.4932	0.4934	0.4936
2.5	0.4938	0.4940	0.4941	0.4943	0.4945	0.4946	0.4948	0.4949	0.4951	0.4952
2.6	0.4953	0.4955	0.4956	0.4957	0.4959	0.4960	0.4961	0.4962	0.4963	0.4964
2.7	0.4965	0.4966	0.4967	0.4968	0.4969	0.4970	0.4971	0.4972	0.4973	0.4974
2.8	0.4974	0.4975	0.4976	0.4977	0.4977	0.4978	0.4979	0.4979	0.4980	0.4981
2.9	0.4981	0.4982	0.4982	0.4983	0.4984	0.4984	0.4985	0.4985	0.4986	0.4986
3.0	0.4987	0.4987	0.4987	0.4988	0.4988	0.4989	0.4989	0.4989	0.4990	0.4990

APPENDIX 2: TABLE FOR "F" DISTRIBUTION

Table 2. For α = 0.05 $df_1 = 8$ and $df_2 = 10$ $F_{0.05;\,8,\,10} = 3.07$

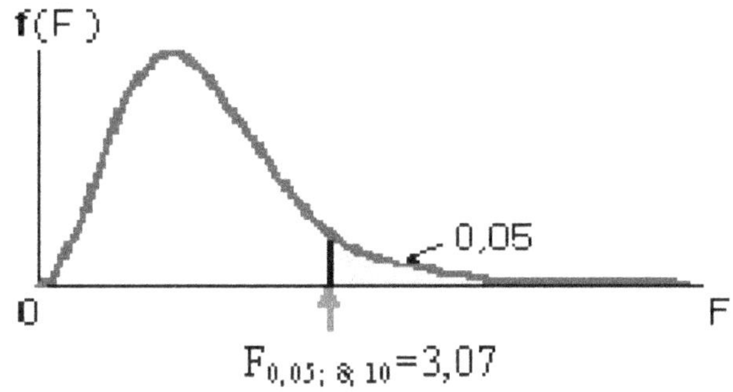

df_2 \ df_1	1	2	3	4	5	6	7	8	9	10	12	15	20	24	30	40	60	120	300
1	161	200	216	225	230	234	237	230	241	242	244	246	248	249	250	251	252	253	254
2	18.50	19.0	19.2	19.2	19.3	19.3	19.4	19.4	19.4	19.4	19.4	19.4	19.4	19.5	19.5	19.5	19.5	19.5	19.5
3	10.10	9.55	9.28	9.12	9.01	8.94	8.89	8.85	8.81	8.79	8.74	8.70	8.66	8.64	8.62	8.59	8.57	8.55	8.53
4	7.71	6.94	6.59	6.39	6.26	6.16	6.09	6.04	6.00	5.96	5.91	5.86	5.80	5.77	5.75	5.72	5.69	5.66	5.64
5	6.61	5.79	5.41	5.19	5.05	4.95	4.88	4.82	4.77	4.74	4.68	4.62	4.56	4.53	4.50	4.46	4.43	4.40	4.38
6	5.99	5.14	4.76	4.53	4.39	4.28	4.21	4.15	4.10	4.06	4.00	3.94	3.87	3.84	3.81	3.77	3.74	3.70	3.68
7	5.59	4.74	4.35	4.12	3.97	3.87	3.79	3.73	3.68	3.64	3.57	3.51	3.44	3.41	3.38	3.34	3.30	3.27	3.25
8	5.32	4.46	4.07	3.84	3.69	3.58	3.50	3.44	3.39	3.35	3.28	3.22	3.15	3.12	3.08	3.04	3.01	2.97	2.95
9	5.12	4.26	3.86	3.63	3.48	3.37	3.20	3.23	3.18	3.14	3.07	3.01	2.94	2.90	2.86	2.83	2.79	2.75	2.72
10	**4.96**	4.10	3.71	3.48	3.33	3.22	3.14	**3.07**	3.02	2.98	2.91	2.85	2.77	2.74	2.70	2.66	2.62	2.58	2.56
11	4.84	3.98	3.59	3.36	3.20	3.09	3.01	2.95	2.90	2.85	2.79	2.72	2.65	2.61	2.57	2.53	2.49	2.45	2.42
12	4.75	**3.89**	3.49	3.26	3.11	3.00	2.91	2.85	2.80	2.75	2.69	2.62	2.54	2.51	2.47	2.43	2.38	2.34	2.31
13	4.67	3.81	3.41	3.18	3.03	2.92	2.83	2.77	2.71	2.67	2.60	2.53	2.46	2.42	2.38	2.34	2.30	2.25	2.23
14	4.60	3.74	3.34	3.11	2.96	2.85	2.76	2.70	2.65	2.60	2.53	2.46	2.39	2.35	2.31	2.27	2.22	2.18	2.15
15	4.54	3.68	3.29	3.06	2.90	2.79	2.71	2.64	2.59	2.54	2.48	2.40	2.33	2.29	2.25	2.20	2.16	2.11	2.09
16	4.49	3.63	3.24	3.01	2.85	2.74	2.66	2.59	2.54	2.49	2.42	2.35	2.28	2.24	2.19	2.15	2.11	2.06	2.03
17	4.45	3.59	3.20	2.96	2.81	2.70	2.61	2.55	2.49	2.45	2.38	2.31	2.23	2.19	2.15	2.10	2.06	2.01	1.98
18	4.41	3.55	3.16	2.93	2.77	2.66	2.58	2.51	2.46	2.41	2.34	2.27	2.19	2.15	2.11	2.06	2.02	1.97	1.94
19	4.38	3.52	3.13	2.90	2.74	2.63	2.54	2.48	2.42	2.38	2.31	2.23	2.16	2.11	2.07	2.03	1.98	1.93	1.90
20	4.35	3.49	3.10	2.87	2.71	2.60	2.51	2.45	2.39	2.35	2.28	2.20	2.12	2.08	2.04	1.99	1.95	1.90	1.87
21	4.32	3.47	3.07	2.84	2.68	2.57	2.49	2.42	2.37	2.32	2.25	2.18	2.10	2.05	2.01	1.96	1.92	1.87	1.83
22	4.30	3.44	3.05	2.82	2.66	2.55	2.46	2.40	2.34	2.30	2.23	2.15	2.07	2.03	1.98	1.94	1.89	1.84	1.80
23	4.28	3.42	3.03	2.80	2.64	2.53	2.44	2.37	2.32	2.27	2.20	2.13	2.05	2.01	1.96	1.91	1.86	1.81	1.78
24	4.26	3.40	3.01	2.78	2.62	2.51	2.42	2.36	2.30	2.25	2.18	2.11	2.03	1.98	1.94	1.89	1.84	1.79	1.76
25	4.24	3.39	2.99	2.76	2.60	2.49	2.40	2.34	2.28	2.24	2.16	2.09	2.01	1.96	1.92	1.87	1.82	1.77	1.73

continued on following page

Table 2. Continued

26	4.22	3.37	2.97	2.74	2.58	2.47	2.38	2.32	2.26	2.21	2.14	2.07	1.98	1.94	1.90	1.85	1.80	1.75	1.71
27	4.21	3.35	2.96	2.72	2.57	2.45	2.37	2.30	2.25	2.20	2.13	2.06	1.97	1.93	1.88	1.84	1.79	1.73	1.70
28	4.19	3.34	2.94	2.71	2.55	2.44	2.35	2.29	2.24	2.19	2.11	2.04	1.96	1.91	1.87	1.82	1.77	1.71	1.68
29	4.18	3.32	2.93	2.70	2.54	2.43	2.34	2.28	2.22	2.18	2.10	2.02	1.94	1.90	1.85	1.80	1.75	1.70	1.66
30	4.17	3.31	2.92	2.69	2.53	2.42	2.33	2.27	2.21	2.16	2.09	2.01	1.93	1.89	1.84	1.79	1.74	1.68	1.65
40	4.08	3.23	2.84	2.61	2.45	2.34	2.25	2.18	2.12	2.08	2.00	1.92	1.84	1.79	1.74	1.69	1.64	1.58	1.54
60	4.00	3.15	2.76	2.53	2.37	2.25	2.17	2.10	2.04	1.99	1.92	1.84	1.75	1.70	1.65	1.59	1.53	1.47	1.42
120	3.92	3.07	2.68	2.45	2.29	2.18	2.09	2.02	1.96	1.91	1.83	1.75	1.66	1.61	1.55	1.50	1.43	1.35	1.30
300	3.87	3.02	2.64	2.40	2.24	2.13	2.04	1.97	1.91	1.86	1.79	1.70	1.60	1.55	1.49	1.43	1.36	1.27	1.21

APPENDIX 3: TABLE FOR T DISTRIBUTION

Table 3. For α = 0.05, thus for (α/2 = 0.025) and df = 12; $t_{0.025;12} = 2.1788$

Confidence Int. Two-Tailed One-Tailed	0.10 0.45 0.90	0.30 0.35 0.70	0.50 0.25 0.50	0.70 0.15 0.30	0.80 0.10 0.20	0.90 0.05 0.10	0.95 0.025 0.05	0.98 0.01 0.02	0.99 0.005 0.01
				df Critical Values of t					
1	0.1584	0.5095	1.0000	1.9626	3.0777	6.3137	12.7062	31.8210	63.6559
2	0.1421	0.4447	0.8165	1.3862	1.8856	2.9200	4.3027	6.9645	9.9250
3	0.1366	0.4242	0.7649	1.2498	1.6377	2.3534	3.1824	4.5407	5.8408
4	0.1338	0.4142	0.7407	1.1896	1.5332	2.1318	2.7765	3.7469	4.6041
5	0.1322	0.4082	0.7267	1.1558	1.4759	2.0150	2.5706	3.3649	4.0321
6	0.1311	0.4043	0.7176	1.1342	1.4398	1.9432	2.4469	3.1427	3.7074
7	0.1303	0.4015	0.7111	1.1192	1.4149	1.8946	2.3646	2.9979	3.4995
8	0.1297	0.3995	0.7064	1.1081	1.3968	1.8595	2.3060	2.8965	3.3554
9	0.1293	0.3979	0.7027	1.0997	1.3830	1.8331	2.2622	2.8214	3.2498
10	0.1289	0.3966	0.6998	1.0931	1.3722	1.8125	2.2281	2.7638	3.1693
11	0.1286	0.3956	0.6974	1.0877	1.3634	1.7959	2.2010	2.7181	3.1058
12	0.1283	0.3947	0.6955	1.0832	1.3562	1.7823	**2.1788**	2.6810	3.0545
13	0.1281	0.3940	0.6938	1.0795	1.3502	1.7709	2.1604	2.6503	3.0123
14	0.1280	0.3933	0.6924	1.0763	1.3450	1.7613	2.1448	2.6245	2.9768
15	0.1278	0.3928	0.6912	1.0735	1.3406	1.7531	2.1315	2.6025	2.9467
16	0.1277	0.3923	0.6901	1.0711	1.3368	1.7459	2.1199	2.5835	2.9208
17	0.1276	0.3919	0.6892	1.0690	1.3334	1.7396	2.1098	2.5669	2.8982
18	0.1274	0.3915	0.6884	1.0672	1.3304	1.7341	2.1009	2.5524	2.8784
19	0.1274	0.3912	0.6876	1.0655	1.3277	1.7291	2.0930	2.5395	2.8609
20	0.1273	0.3909	0.6870	1.0640	1.3253	1.7247	2.0860	2.5280	2.8453
21	0.1272	0.3906	0.6864	1.0627	1.3232	1.7207	2.0796	2.5176	2.8314
22	0.1271	0.3904	0.6858	1.0614	1.3212	1.7171	2.0739	2.5083	2.8188
23	0.1271	0.3902	0.6853	1.0603	1.3195	1.7139	2.0687	2.4999	2.8073
24	0.1270	0.3900	0.6848	1.0593	1.3178	1.7109	2.0639	2.4922	2.7970
25	0.1269	0.3898	0.6844	1.0584	1.3163	1.7081	2.0595	2.4851	2.7874
26	0.1269	0.3896	0.6840	1.0575	1.3150	1.7056	2.0555	2.4786	2.7787
27	0.1268	0.3894	0.6837	1.0567	1.3137	1.7033	2.0518	2.4727	2.7707
28	0.1268	0.3893	0.6834	1.0560	1.3125	1.7011	2.0484	2.4671	2.7633
29	0.1268	0.3892	0.6830	1.0553	1.3114	1.6991	2.0452	2.4620	2.7564

continued on following page

Table 3. Continued

Confidence Int. Two-Tailed One-Tailed	0.10 0.45 0.90	0.30 0.35 0.70	0.50 0.25 0.50	0.70 0.15 0.30	0.80 0.10 0.20	0.90 0.05 0.10	0.95 0.025 0.05	0.98 0.01 0.02	0.99 0.005 0.01
df Critical Values of t									
30	0.1267	0.3890	0.6828	1.0547	1.3104	1.6973	2.0423	2.4573	2.7500
40	0.1265	0.3881	0.6807	1.0500	1.3031	1.6839	2.0211	2.4233	2.7045
50	0.1263	0.3875	0.6794	1.0473	1.2987	1.6759	2.0086	2.4033	2.6778
60	0.1262	0.3872	0.6786	1.0455	1.2958	1.6706	2.0003	2.3901	2.6603
70	0.1261	0.3869	0.6780	1.0442	1.2938	1.6669	1.9944	2.3808	2.6479
80	0.1261	0.3867	0.6776	1.0432	1.2922	1.6641	1.9901	2.3739	2.6387
90	0.1260	0.3866	0.6772	1.0424	1.2910	1.6620	1.9867	2.3685	2.6316
100	0.1260	0.3864	0.6770	1.0418	1.2901	1.6602	1.9840	2.3642	2.6259
250	0.1258	0.3858	0.6755	1.0386	1.2849	1.6510	1.9695	2.3414	2.5956
500	0.1257	0.3855	0.6750	1.0375	1.2832	1.6479	1.9647	2.3338	2.5857

Glossary

Acceleration Principle: The macroeconomic principle which indicates that an increase in real capital investments accelerates new investments in the long run which, in turn, leads to further economic growth.

Actual Capacity: The amount of production that is actually realized at the end of the production process in a given period of time.

Annual Operating Period: The number of *days* in a year during which an investment project manufactures and sells a product.

Breakeven Analysis: The analysis aiming at finding out the quantity of production that makes the total sales revenues equal to the total production costs.

Coefficient of Kurtosis: The ratio of the fourth moment to the fourth power of the standard deviation of a probability distribution.

Coefficient of Multiple Determination: The degree and/or power of independent variables explaining the changes in the dependent variable.

Coefficient of Skewness: The ratio of the third moment to the third power (cube) of the standard deviation of a probability distribution.

Coefficient of Variation: The ratio of the standard deviation to the expected net present value of a risky investment project.

Commercial Risk: Also called *business risk* that results from changes in the market dynamics and values of market variables such as sales, costs of production factors, and product prices.

Cost-Plus Pricing Strategy: The price strategy followed when a company adds a certain profit margin to its manufacturing costs.

CPM (Critical Path Method): A method that project managers use for programming project activities when they prepare an implementation plan. It requires just one normal time estimate for the completion of each activity in a project.

Critical Path: The longest path of the CPM or PERT network prepared for implementing a project.

Critical Variables: The most important factors in a project such that any change in their values will bring about significant changes in the profitability of an investment project.

Current Account Deficit: The gap or discrepancy between all kinds of foreign currency inflows and outflows related to the balance of payments of a national economy.

Degree of Financial Leverage: The ratio of the earnings before interest and tax (EBIT) to the earnings after interest.

Degree of Operating Leverage: The ratio of the operating profit before fixed costs to the operating profit after fixed costs:

Delphi Technique: A qualitative forecasting method based on the personal estimates of a group of experts who are not aware of each other.

Depreciation Charges: The charges made annually to represent the costs of investment made earlier in machinery, equipment, tools, and production facilities.

Design Capacity: The maximum output that can be attained under ideal operational conditions of a company. Design capacity is also called *technical* or *theoretical* capacity.

Desk Survey: The search for and review of all published documents related to secondary data sources.

Differentiated Marketing Strategy: A strategy that differentiates between the preferences and tastes of consumers and, thus, designs and produces different types of the same product for each group of consumers.

Direct Distribution: The distribution policy that a production factory distributes products directly to consumers and incurs all distribution costs.

Distribution Channel: The number of levels that products move through and, thus, the length of a distribution channel depends on the levels of intermediaries.

Economies of Scale: The scale of production based on the principle of *increasing returns to scale* in which the average unit cost of production decreases as the volume of production increases.

Effective Capacity: It is also called *practical capacity* and refers to a production volume that considers normal or regular disruption in the production process for maintenance and common breakdowns in machinery and equipment.

Effective Demand: The part of the existing demand that would be able and thus most likely purchases a product to be manufactured by an investment project.

Enlargement Investment: The type of real capital or fixed investments directed towards increasing the production capacities of existing factories or plants by adding further production lines in terms of machinery, equipment, and labor.

Envelope Curve: The long run average unit cost curve which encompasses short run average unit cost curves of alternative capacities and that touches them on their minimum points.

Establishment Period: Duration of the activities required to build a factory as defined by the implementation plan.

Feasibility Study: A comprehensive economic study that it involves lots of detailed and interrelated studies, analyses, and decisions to determine in advance whether or not to undertake a real capital investment project in terms of its profitability and risk associated with it.

Field Survey: Collection of primary data and information through specific methods such as observations, interviews, and questionnaires.

Financial Investments: Purchasing of financial instruments and securities of all kinds whose expected profits are generally obtained when they are sold, if there is a profit.

Fisher's Rate of Return Over Cost: The discount rate that makes the net present values of two mutually exclusive investment projects equal to each other.

Fixed Costs: Expenditures required for establishing or building a factory to produce the desired goods.

Fixed Investment: This type of investment is also called real capital investment (see; real capital investment).

Force Majeure: Uncontrollable events such as natural disasters, nationwide general strikes, wars, civil wars, etc. that may interrupt the business operations so that the licensee may not pay license fees on time.

Foreign Direct Investments: Production oriented fixed or real capital investments that give international investors a controlling power to manage and control the areas in which the investments are made.

Foreign Exchange Risk: The degree of variations in the economic profitability of an investment project due to the changes in exchange rates.

Functional Specifications: The technical requirements of a product to be produced in the sense that the product will accomplish its essential objective of meeting the need for which it is purchased.

Greenfield Investments: New investments in terms of building new plants or factories in foreign countries in order to manufacture goods which the investors plan to sell and maximize their profits.

Hedging Techniques: Financial contracts enabling an individual or a company to purchase or sell a given amount of a foreign currency at a certain future date and at a specified exchange rate determined in advance.

Home Country: The country of the parent company; that is, the county of an international investor.

Host Country: The country selected for a foreign direct investment.

Indirect Distribution: The distribution policy in which producers use the services of intermediaries to move their products to the market places and make available for consumers.

Initial Investment: The total amount of investment for a project, which is composed of the sum of the fixed costs (fixed capital) plus the working capital.

Internal Rate of Return: The discount rate that makes the net present value of an investment project equal to zero.

International Portfolio Investments: Business activities of international investors that are in search of increasing their earnings through interest payments and returns on their funds invested in financial assets, such as securities of business corporations and governmental debt instruments in other countries of the world.

Investment: In general, expenditures made today for the purpose of making profit in the future.

Joint Ventures: The type of foreign direct investments through which two or more companies (at least one is a foreigner) share the ownership of a new company created for a specific business.

Know-How: The technical knowledge required for manufacturing a product.

License Agreement: A legal and binding contract between a *licensor* (the one providing know-how) and a *licensee* (the one obtaining know-how) for using a specific know-how or technology to produce a product.

Life Cycle Costing: Cost considerations in terms of purchasing, operation, maintenance, and replacement costs.

Linear Regression Models: Causal models that aim at explaining the variations in a variable through some factors by assuming a linear relationship.

Liquidity Analysis: A cash flow analysis aiming at determining if a profitable investment project would continue its operation smoothly without confronting any liquidity shortages during its operating period.

Loss-Leader Price Strategy: The practice of pricing a product below its cost with the intention of attracting consumers to buy the other products of the company.

Lump-Sum Royalty: The license fee paid at once in total when the license agreement is signed.

Market Segmentation: Determining a target market according to some specific features of consumers and/or market characteristics.

Marketing Plan: See, (marketing strategy).

Marketing Strategy: The task of preparing a marketing plan or the so-called marketing mix which requires deciding on four basic factors simultaneously for marketing a product; namely, product, price, promotion, and place (i.e., distribution) policies of a company.

Modernization (Technological) Investment: The type of fixed investments which is made for keeping up with the pace of technological development in terms of changing those obsolete machinery and equipment of a production facility with those technically modern ones.

Monetary Risk: The risk related to the *mobility of funds* out of the host country such as *transfer of dividends* as well as the possibility of the convertibility of local currency.

Monopolistic Market: A market dominated and completely controlled by a single firm so that there is almost no competition in the market.

Monte Carlo Simulation: A type of simulation technique that generates data from the probability distributions resembling the behaviors of a real system through statistical sampling.

Multiplier Effect: The macroeconomic concept indicating that a unit of spending in real capital investment brings about a magnified increase or change in economic growth in terms of gross national product equilibrium. According to the macroeconomic theory, the multiplier effect is equal to the reciprocal of the marginal propensity to save, *ceteris paribus*.

Mutually Exclusive Investment Projects: Investment projects when the selection of a project necessarily requires the rejection of all the other alternatives because they become redundant.

Net Present Value: The sum of the net cash flows discounted by the cost of capital over the life cycle of the investment project.

Network Analysis: Preparing an implementation plan through either CPM or PERT by breaking down a project into its essential activities or jobs to be done.

Normal (Conventional) Net Cash Flows: The net cash flows of an investment project that are negative during the *establishment period* and positive along the *operating period* of the project.

Oligopolistic Market: A market or an industry controlled by a limited number of large companies, such as three companies controlling 85% of a national market of a country.

Operating Cycle: The length of time between the time a firm originally purchases its raw materials and the time it sells the products and receives the cash back.

Operating Exposure: Change in the market value of a firm that is resulting from changes in foreign exchange rates.

Operating Period: The number of *years* during which an investment project manufactures and sells a product.

Operational Expenditures: All manufacturing costs incurred by a company to produce a product at a certain level of production, excluding interest expenditures and depreciation charges.

Operational Risk: The type of political risk that encompasses legal changes in laws or rules governing businesses which affect all companies including foreign ones.

Optimal Capacity: An ideal or a desired scale of production that minimizes average unit cost of production in the long run. Optimal capacity is a strategically ideal goal that each company strives to realize in the future.

Payback Period: The number of years for which the project pays back its initial investment through its expected net profits or net cash flows during the operating period.

Penetration Price Strategy: The strategy for determining a lower price than those of competitors to enter a competitive market.

PERT (Project Evaluation and Review Technique): A method used for preparing an implementation plan through programming essential activities involved in a project. It requires three different estimates of time for each activity; namely, *optimistic time, most likely time,* and *pessimistic time.*

Political Risk: Any political change that worsens the working conditions of foreign companies.

Practical Capacity: See (effective capacity).

Predatory Pricing Strategy: The price strategy that aims at wiping out competitors from the market as well as preventing new comers to enter in by setting prices significantly below their prices.

Price Leadership Strategy: The pricing strategy based on the price of the firm leading the market. In other words, firms follow and set their prices equal or quite close to the price of the leader(s) of the market.

Probability Analysis: The analysis for estimating the magnitude of changes in the values of critical variables as well as assigning probabilities of occurrence to those changes.

Product Life Cycle: The life span of an industrial product that is conceived to go through the stages named *introduction*, *growth*, *maturity*, and *decline*.

Profitability Index: The ratio of the net present value of an investment project to the amount of initial investment.

Promotion: All kinds of efforts such as advertising, personal selling, sales promotion, and public relations that aim at increasing the sales of a product.

Purchasing Power Parity (PPP) Method: The method used for estimating foreign currency exchange rates on the basis of inflation rates.

Real Capital Investments: Investments directed towards production of goods or services in terms of building plants or constructing factories, buying new machinery and equipment, enlarging and modernizing existing production capacities.

Replacement Investment: The type of real capital or fixed investments related to renewing the old and/or worn-out machinery and equipment of production facilities to maintain the existing production capacity of a business firm.

Risk Adjusted Discount Rate: The discount rate that includes a risk premium standing for the risk assumed to be associated with the overall cash flows of a project.

Risk: The gap or discrepancy between the expected and the realized profit values of an investment project.

Royalty: The license fee paid for using a licensed "know-how" or a technology in general.

Running Royalty: The license fee paid either as a percentage of the value of the production or the sales realized along the operating period of a project.

Sales Specifications: The attractive characteristics that a product should have in order to appeal to consumers.

Salvage Value: The liquidation value of all capital assets at the end of operating period upon physical deterioration of the plant and equipment.

Sensitivity Analysis: The analysis for finding out the most critical factors or variables to which the profitability of an investment project is very sensitive to by raising and answering some "*what if*" type questions.

Simple Rate of Return: The rate of return which is simply the ratio of the average annual profit to the total initial investment made during the establishment (set-up) period.

Simulation: An experimental methodology or a technique that requires the development of a mathematical model which necessitates the use of computer programs or software packages for evaluating the effects of different alternative courses of action.

Skimming Price Strategy: Setting a very high price for a high quality product to capture the richest segment of a target market.

Surplus Value: Sometimes called *terminal* or *continuation* value that represents the market value of the flow of sales revenues from the project at all remaining future dates after the length of the operating period decided.

Takeover Risk: Political changes that occur seldom but end up in catastrophic consequences leading to losing the whole business and/or property completely. As a result of such political changes, foreign companies might be expropriated or confiscated.

Target Market: A market segment specified and defined in terms of the needs, preferences, attitudes, and purchasing behaviors of consumers as well as geographic, demographic, and socio-economic characteristics.

Technical (Theoretical) Capacity: The production level realized by an existing company without any downtime and/or disruption in the production process due to failure, defect, and malfunction of machinery and equipment.

Technology: The total of knowledge, skills, and experience available in a society for producing a good or a service. The concept of technology is sometimes regarded as *the state of the art* of a society in terms of its production capabilities.

Time Series Analysis: A forecasting methodology based on the series of data observed in the past years in that the trend of the past series of data is determined through a statistical technique called *trend analysis*.

Transaction Exposure: The effects of changes in exchange rates on the value of financial obligations contracted previously before a change in exchange rates occurred.

Translation Exposure: The foreign exchange risk related to preparing the consolidated financial statements of the parent company to include the investment made (the subsidiary established) abroad. It is also called *accounting exposure*.

Undifferentiated Marketing Strategy: The marketing strategy that overlooks the differences in the characteristics of consumers and targets the whole market with one product.

Vertical Integration: Business operations in which a company manufacturing a product also controls procurement (supply of production factors) as well as distribution activities related to the same product.

Working Capital: The amount of the extra funds needed for financing the production process to run smoothly without any interruption and delay; that is, extra funds required to finance receivables, inventories of finished goods and raw materials, and unexpected expenditures during the operating period of an investment project.

Related Readings

To continue IGI Global's long-standing tradition of advancing innovation through emerging research, please find below a compiled list of recommended IGI Global book chapters and journal articles in the areas of risk assessment, project management, and portfolio management. These related readings will provide additional information and guidance to further enrich your knowledge and assist you with your own research.

Aboutalebi, R. (2016). Strategies for Effective Worldwide Supply Chains. In B. Christiansen (Ed.),. *Handbook of Research on Global Supply Chain Management* (pp. 1–14). Hershey, PA: IGI Global. doi:10.4018/978-1-4666-9639-6.ch001

Afonso, P., & Jiménez, V. J. (2016). Costing Systems for Decision Making under Uncertainty Using Probabilistic Models. In D. Jakóbczak (Ed.), *Analyzing Risk through Probabilistic Modeling in Operations Research* (pp. 221–245). Hershey, PA: IGI Global. doi:10.4018/978-1-4666-9458-3.ch010

Agarwal, R., & Virine, L. (2017). Integration of Project Risk Management (PRM) into Enterprise Risk Management (ERM). In Y. Raydugin (Ed.), *Handbook of Research on Leveraging Risk and Uncertainties for Effective Project Management* (pp. 294–317). Hershey, PA: IGI Global. doi:10.4018/978-1-5225-1790-0.ch014

Agarwal, R., & Virine, L. (2017). Monte Carlo Project Risk Analysis. In Y. Raydugin (Ed.), *Handbook of Research on Leveraging Risk and Uncertainties for Effective Project Management* (pp. 109–129). Hershey, PA: IGI Global. doi:10.4018/978-1-5225-1790-0.ch005

Agostino, D., Arnaboldi, M., & Azzone, G. (2016). Performance Measurement in Public Networks: Developing a PMS for Network Actors and Network Managers. In A. Ferreira, G. Azevedo, J. Oliveira, & R. Marques (Eds.), *Global Perspectives on Risk Management and Accounting in the Public Sector* (pp. 298–319). Hershey, PA: IGI Global. doi:10.4018/978-1-4666-9803-1.ch015

Aiello, L., & Gatti, M. (2017). Project Portfolio Management and Organization: An Integrated and Circular Model. In L. Romano (Ed.), *Project Portfolio Management Strategies for Effective Organizational Operations* (pp. 288–309). Hershey, PA: IGI Global. doi:10.4018/978-1-5225-2151-8.ch012

Alfirević, N., Šešić, M. D., & Čačija, L. N. (2017). The Fundraising Patterns and the Management Professionalization in Independent Arts Organizations in SEE. In V. Potocan, M. Üngan, & Z. Nedelko (Eds.), *Handbook of Research on Managerial Solutions in Non-Profit Organizations* (pp. 400–420). Hershey, PA: IGI Global. doi:10.4018/978-1-5225-0731-4.ch019

Amaral, A. M., & Araújo, M. (2017). Project Portfolio Selection Using a D.E.A. Approach. In L. Romano (Ed.), *Project Portfolio Management Strategies for Effective Organizational Operations* (pp. 220–244). Hershey, PA: IGI Global. doi:10.4018/978-1-5225-2151-8.ch009

Aparo von Flüe, A. (2017). Are You Pondering What I Am Pondering?: Eccentric Consideration on Strategic Management. In L. Romano (Ed.), *Project Portfolio Management Strategies for Effective Organizational Operations* (pp. 81–118). Hershey, PA: IGI Global. doi:10.4018/978-1-5225-2151-8.ch004

Araya-Leandro, C., Caba-Pérez, M. D., & López-Hernandez, A. M. (2016). Modernization of Governmental Accounting Systems: Situation in the Central American Region. In A. Ferreira, G. Azevedo, J. Oliveira, & R. Marques (Eds.), *Global Perspectives on Risk Management and Accounting in the Public Sector* (pp. 90–107). Hershey, PA: IGI Global. doi:10.4018/978-1-4666-9803-1.ch005

Archibald, R. D. (2017). Inter-Relationships between an Enterprise's Strategic Management Process and Its Program/Project Portfolio Management Process. In L. Romano (Ed.), *Project Portfolio Management Strategies for Effective Organizational Operations* (pp. 39–60). Hershey, PA: IGI Global. doi:10.4018/978-1-5225-2151-8.ch002

Arsenijević, O. M., Orčić, D., & Kastratović, E. (2017). Development of an Optimization Tool for Intangibles in SMEs: A Case Study from Serbia with a Pilot Research in the Prestige by Milka Company. In M. Vemić (Ed.), *Optimal Management Strategies in Small and Medium Enterprises* (pp. 320–347). Hershey, PA: IGI Global. doi:10.4018/978-1-5225-1949-2.ch015

Aydin, E. (2017). "Problems and Suggestions": Non-Governmental Organisations of Sexual Orientation Minorities in the Context of Turkey and United Kingdom. In V. Potocan, M. Ünğan, & Z. Nedelko (Eds.), *Handbook of Research on Managerial Solutions in Non-Profit Organizations* (pp. 232–252). Hershey, PA: IGI Global. doi:10.4018/978-1-5225-0731-4.ch011

Ayyıldız, H., Akmermer, B., & Akyüz, A. M. (2017). Marketing Approach for Non-Profit Organizations. In V. Potocan, M. Ünğan, & Z. Nedelko (Eds.), *Handbook of Research on Managerial Solutions in Non-Profit Organizations* (pp. 156–181). Hershey, PA: IGI Global. doi:10.4018/978-1-5225-0731-4.ch008

Balakrishna, P., Borener, S. S., Crook, I., Durston, A., & Robinson, M. J. (2016). Applying Probabilistic Risk Assessment to Safety Risk Analysis in Aviation. In D. Jakóbczak (Ed.), *Analyzing Risk through Probabilistic Modeling in Operations Research* (pp. 321–343). Hershey, PA: IGI Global. doi:10.4018/978-1-4666-9458-3.ch013

Bali, S., & Uslu, Y. D. (2017). Enterprise Risk Management in Non-Profit Organization. In V. Potocan, M. Ünğan, & Z. Nedelko (Eds.), *Handbook of Research on Managerial Solutions in Non-Profit Organizations* (pp. 75–93). Hershey, PA: IGI Global. doi:10.4018/978-1-5225-0731-4.ch004

Baporikar, N. (2016). Business Process Management. *International Journal of Productivity Management and Assessment Technologies*, *4*(2), 49–62. doi:10.4018/IJPMAT.2016070104

Brzozowski, M., & Ferster, I. (2017). Educational Management Leadership: High School Principal's Management Style and Parental Involvement in School Management in Israel. In V. Potocan, M. Ünğan, & Z. Nedelko (Eds.), *Handbook of Research on Managerial Solutions in Non-Profit Organizations* (pp. 55–74). Hershey, PA: IGI Global. doi:10.4018/978-1-5225-0731-4.ch003

Brzozowski, M., & Keydar, E. J. (2017). Approaches towards Measuring Success in Public Elementary Schools. In V. Potocan, M. Üngan, & Z. Nedelko (Eds.), *Handbook of Research on Managerial Solutions in Non-Profit Organizations* (pp. 362–377). Hershey, PA: IGI Global. doi:10.4018/978-1-5225-0731-4.ch017

Bucero, A. (2017). Linking Organization's Strategy and Strategic Planning with Portfolio Management. In L. Romano (Ed.), *Project Portfolio Management Strategies for Effective Organizational Operations* (pp. 61–80). Hershey, PA: IGI Global. doi:10.4018/978-1-5225-2151-8.ch003

Cakar, U., & Kim, H. (2017). Experiences of Non-Profit Organizations in Korea: Development Challenges in an Emerging Economy. In V. Potocan, M. Üngan, & Z. Nedelko (Eds.), *Handbook of Research on Managerial Solutions in Non-Profit Organizations* (pp. 499–528). Hershey, PA: IGI Global. doi:10.4018/978-1-5225-0731-4.ch023

Carini, C., & Teodori, C. (2016). Potential Uses and Usefulness of Italian Local Government Consolidated Financial Reporting: The Case of the Town Council of Brescia. In A. Ferreira, G. Azevedo, J. Oliveira, & R. Marques (Eds.), *Global Perspectives on Risk Management and Accounting in the Public Sector* (pp. 68–89). Hershey, PA: IGI Global. doi:10.4018/978-1-4666-9803-1.ch004

Caron, F. (2016). A Bayesian Approach to Project Control. In D. Jakóbczak (Ed.), *Analyzing Risk through Probabilistic Modeling in Operations Research* (pp. 125–137). Hershey, PA: IGI Global. doi:10.4018/978-1-4666-9458-3.ch005

Castagnoli, E., De Donno, M., Favero, G., & Modesti, P. (2016). A Different Way to Look at Random Variables: Do Decision Makers Look at Functions or at Sets? In D. Jakóbczak (Ed.), *Analyzing Risk through Probabilistic Modeling in Operations Research* (pp. 179–199). Hershey, PA: IGI Global. doi:10.4018/978-1-4666-9458-3.ch008

Castagnoli, E., Favero, G., & Modesti, P. (2016). Price Systems for Random Amounts: A Unified Approach. In D. Jakóbczak (Ed.), *Analyzing Risk through Probabilistic Modeling in Operations Research* (pp. 354–379). Hershey, PA: IGI Global. doi:10.4018/978-1-4666-9458-3.ch015

Chandan, H. C. (2016). Implementation of Green Supply Chain Management in a Globalized Economy. In B. Christiansen (Ed.), *Handbook of Research on Global Supply Chain Management* (pp. 402–418). Hershey, PA: IGI Global. doi:10.4018/978-1-4666-9639-6.ch023

Chapman, R. J. (2017). Complexity Theory and System Dynamics for Project Risk Management. In Y. Raydugin (Ed.), *Handbook of Research on Leveraging Risk and Uncertainties for Effective Project Management* (pp. 152–176). Hershey, PA: IGI Global. doi:10.4018/978-1-5225-1790-0.ch008

Chen, E. J. (2016). Simulation Output Analysis and Risk Management. In D. Jakóbczak (Ed.), *Analyzing Risk through Probabilistic Modeling in Operations Research* (pp. 200–220). Hershey, PA: IGI Global. doi:10.4018/978-1-4666-9458-3.ch009

Chen, Y., Davutyan, N., & Ersoy, İ. (2016). A "Flying High, Landing Soft" Platform for Supplier Diversity. In B. Christiansen (Ed.), *Handbook of Research on Global Supply Chain Management* (pp. 72–84). Hershey, PA: IGI Global. doi:10.4018/978-1-4666-9639-6.ch004

Choptiany, J. M. (2017). A Holistic Multi-Criteria Decision and Risk Analysis Method for CCS and GHG Mitigation Projects. In Y. Raydugin (Ed.), *Handbook of Research on Leveraging Risk and Uncertainties for Effective Project Management* (pp. 384–405). Hershey, PA: IGI Global. doi:10.4018/978-1-5225-1790-0.ch018

Coste, A. I., & Tiron-Tudor, A. (2016). Performance Measurement Perceptions in Romanian Higher Education. In A. Ferreira, G. Azevedo, J. Oliveira, & R. Marques (Eds.), *Global Perspectives on Risk Management and Accounting in the Public Sector* (pp. 346–365). Hershey, PA: IGI Global. doi:10.4018/978-1-4666-9803-1.ch017

Çotur, Ö. K., & Öztürkoğlu, Y. (2016). Partnerships in Supply Chain Management. In B. Christiansen (Ed.), *Handbook of Research on Global Supply Chain Management* (pp. 161–185). Hershey, PA: IGI Global. doi:10.4018/978-1-4666-9639-6.ch010

Couto, M. C., & Ferreira, A. D. (2016). The Importance of Accountability Practices in the Public Sector: Literature Review. In A. Ferreira, G. Azevedo, J. Oliveira, & R. Marques (Eds.), *Global Perspectives on Risk Management and Accounting in the Public Sector* (pp. 188–201). Hershey, PA: IGI Global. doi:10.4018/978-1-4666-9803-1.ch010

Cropley, C. H. (2017). The Case for Truly Integrated Cost and Schedule Risk Analysis. In Y. Raydugin (Ed.), *Handbook of Research on Leveraging Risk and Uncertainties for Effective Project Management* (pp. 76–108). Hershey, PA: IGI Global. doi:10.4018/978-1-5225-1790-0.ch004

Csillag, S., Balázs, E., Kocsis, M., Udvarhelyi, T., & Vago, I. (2017). Eight-Point Project: Action Research, as a Development Tool for Non-Profit Organizations. In V. Potocan, M. Ünğan, & Z. Nedelko (Eds.), *Handbook of Research on Managerial Solutions in Non-Profit Organizations* (pp. 483–498). Hershey, PA: IGI Global. doi:10.4018/978-1-5225-0731-4.ch022

Cuadrado-Ballesteros, B., García-Sánchez, I. M., & Martínez-Ferrero, J. (2016). Commercialization of Local Public Services. In A. Ferreira, G. Azevedo, J. Oliveira, & R. Marques (Eds.), *Global Perspectives on Risk Management and Accounting in the Public Sector* (pp. 132–150). Hershey, PA: IGI Global. doi:10.4018/978-1-4666-9803-1.ch007

Cuadrado-Ballesteros, B., Mordán, N., & Frías-Aceituno, J. V. (2016). Transparency as a Determinant of Local Financial Condition. In A. Ferreira, G. Azevedo, J. Oliveira, & R. Marques (Eds.), *Global Perspectives on Risk Management and Accounting in the Public Sector* (pp. 202–225). Hershey, PA: IGI Global. doi:10.4018/978-1-4666-9803-1.ch011

Cunha, A., Ferreira, A. D., & Fernandes, M. J. (2016). The Influence of Accounting Information in the Re-Election of the Mayors in Portugal. In A. Ferreira, G. Azevedo, J. Oliveira, & R. Marques (Eds.), *Global Perspectives on Risk Management and Accounting in the Public Sector* (pp. 108–131). Hershey, PA: IGI Global. doi:10.4018/978-1-4666-9803-1.ch006

Ćwiklicki, M. (2017). Applying Balanced Scorecard in Non-Government Organizations. In V. Potocan, M. Ünğan, & Z. Nedelko (Eds.), *Handbook of Research on Managerial Solutions in Non-Profit Organizations* (pp. 134–155). Hershey, PA: IGI Global. doi:10.4018/978-1-5225-0731-4.ch007

Damnjanović, A. M. (2017). Knowledge Management Optimization through IT and E-Business Utilization: A Qualitative Study on Serbian SMEs. In M. Vemić (Ed.), *Optimal Management Strategies in Small and Medium Enterprises* (pp. 249–267). Hershey, PA: IGI Global. doi:10.4018/978-1-5225-1949-2.ch012

Daneshpour, H. (2017). Integrating Sustainable Development into Project Portfolio Management through Application of Open Innovation. In M. Vemić (Ed.), *Optimal Management Strategies in Small and Medium Enterprises* (pp. 370–387). Hershey, PA: IGI Global. doi:10.4018/978-1-5225-1949-2.ch017

del Mar Gálvez-Rodríguez, M., Haro-de-Rosario, A., & Caba-Pérez, M. D. (2017). The Relation between Contingency Factors and the Efficiency of NPOs. In V. Potocan, M. Üngan, & Z. Nedelko (Eds.), *Handbook of Research on Managerial Solutions in Non-Profit Organizations* (pp. 321–342). Hershey, PA: IGI Global. doi:10.4018/978-1-5225-0731-4.ch015

Dieguez, T., Conceição, O., & Fernandes, Â. (2017). The Challenges of Managing the Private Institutions of Social Solidarity: Experiences from Portugal. In V. Potocan, M. Üngan, & Z. Nedelko (Eds.), *Handbook of Research on Managerial Solutions in Non-Profit Organizations* (pp. 23–54). Hershey, PA: IGI Global. doi:10.4018/978-1-5225-0731-4.ch002

Duong, L. N., Wood, L. C., & Wang, X. (2016). Review of RFID Applications in Perishable Inventory Management. In B. Christiansen (Ed.), *Handbook of Research on Global Supply Chain Management* (pp. 139–146). Hershey, PA: IGI Global. doi:10.4018/978-1-4666-9639-6.ch008

Emel, G. G., & Petriçli, G. (2016). A Staged Supplier Pre-Evaluation Model: To Determine Risky, Potential and Preferred Suppliers. In B. Christiansen (Ed.), *Handbook of Research on Global Supply Chain Management* (pp. 419–451). Hershey, PA: IGI Global. doi:10.4018/978-1-4666-9639-6.ch024

Ercegovac, I. R., Alfirević, N., & Koludrović, M. (2017). School Principals' Communication and Co-Operation Assessment: The Croatian Experience. In V. Potocan, M. Üngan, & Z. Nedelko (Eds.), *Handbook of Research on Managerial Solutions in Non-Profit Organizations* (pp. 276–297). Hershey, PA: IGI Global. doi:10.4018/978-1-5225-0731-4.ch013

Fayezi, S., & Zomorrodi, M. (2016). Supply Chain Management: Developments, Theories and Models. In B. Christiansen (Ed.), *Handbook of Research on Global Supply Chain Management* (pp. 313–340). Hershey, PA: IGI Global. doi:10.4018/978-1-4666-9639-6.ch018

Fox, W. P. (2016). Multi-Attribute Decision Making in Risk Analysis. In D. Jakóbczak (Ed.), *Analyzing Risk through Probabilistic Modeling in Operations Research* (pp. 246–290). Hershey, PA: IGI Global. doi:10.4018/978-1-4666-9458-3.ch011

Fox, W. P. (2016). Perfect Partners of Mathematical Modeling with Technology in Risk Assessment. In D. Jakóbczak (Ed.), *Analyzing Risk through Probabilistic Modeling in Operations Research* (pp. 61–90). Hershey, PA: IGI Global. doi:10.4018/978-1-4666-9458-3.ch003

Giacomini, D., Chiaf, E., & Mazzoleni, M. B. (2017). How to Measure Performance in Cooperatives?: A Multiple Case Study. In V. Potocan, M. Ünğan, & Z. Nedelko (Eds.), *Handbook of Research on Managerial Solutions in Non-Profit Organizations* (pp. 343–361). Hershey, PA: IGI Global. doi:10.4018/978-1-5225-0731-4.ch016

Giri, B. C. (2016). Risk-Averse Newsboy Problem with Incomplete Demand Information: Risk-Averse Newsboy Problem. In D. Jakóbczak (Ed.), *Analyzing Risk through Probabilistic Modeling in Operations Research* (pp. 344–353). Hershey, PA: IGI Global. doi:10.4018/978-1-4666-9458-3.ch014

Glavee-Geo, R. (2016). The History and Development of Purchasing Management and Its Theoretical Framework: A Review of Transaction Cost Economics. In B. Christiansen (Ed.), *Handbook of Research on Global Supply Chain Management* (pp. 379–401). Hershey, PA: IGI Global. doi:10.4018/978-1-4666-9639-6.ch022

Gökgöz, F., & Atmaca, M. E. (2017). An Optimal Asset Allocation in Electricity Generation Market for the Policy Makers and Stakeholders. In V. Potocan, M. Ünğan, & Z. Nedelko (Eds.), *Handbook of Research on Managerial Solutions in Non-Profit Organizations* (pp. 448–482). Hershey, PA: IGI Global. doi:10.4018/978-1-5225-0731-4.ch021

Gökgöz, F., & Atmaca, M. E. (2017). Ranking Turkish Universities Based on Performance Evaluation via DEMATEL-AHP Approach. In V. Potocan, M. Ünğan, & Z. Nedelko (Eds.), *Handbook of Research on Managerial Solutions in Non-Profit Organizations* (pp. 421–447). Hershey, PA: IGI Global. doi:10.4018/978-1-5225-0731-4.ch020

Gomes, P., Camões, S. M., & Carvalho, J. (2016). Determinants of the Design and Use of PMS in Portuguese Government Agencies: A Complementary Theoretical Approach. In A. Ferreira, G. Azevedo, J. Oliveira, & R. Marques (Eds.), *Global Perspectives on Risk Management and Accounting in the Public Sector* (pp. 320–345). Hershey, PA: IGI Global. doi:10.4018/978-1-4666-9803-1.ch016

Gul, S., & Williams, T. (2017). Project Complexity for the Uninitiated. In Y. Raydugin (Ed.), *Handbook of Research on Leveraging Risk and Uncertainties for Effective Project Management* (pp. 202–219). Hershey, PA: IGI Global. doi:10.4018/978-1-5225-1790-0.ch010

Gumz, J. (2017). Managing Change: Strategies and Tactics to Review the Portfolio. In L. Romano (Ed.), *Project Portfolio Management Strategies for Effective Organizational Operations* (pp. 334–357). Hershey, PA: IGI Global. doi:10.4018/978-1-5225-2151-8.ch014

Hartlieb, S., & Silvius, G. (2017). Handling Uncertainty in Project Management and Business Development: Similarities and Differences. In Y. Raydugin (Ed.), *Handbook of Research on Leveraging Risk and Uncertainties for Effective Project Management* (pp. 337–362). Hershey, PA: IGI Global. doi:10.4018/978-1-5225-1790-0.ch016

Hass, K. B. (2017). Living on the Edge: Managing Project Complexity. In Y. Raydugin (Ed.), *Handbook of Research on Leveraging Risk and Uncertainties for Effective Project Management* (pp. 177–201). Hershey, PA: IGI Global. doi:10.4018/978-1-5225-1790-0.ch009

Hollmann, J. K. (2017). Complexity Risk and Modeling Disorder. In Y. Raydugin (Ed.), *Handbook of Research on Leveraging Risk and Uncertainties for Effective Project Management* (pp. 139–151). Hershey, PA: IGI Global. doi:10.4018/978-1-5225-1790-0.ch007

Hollmann, J. K. (2017). Systemic Risks and Parametric Modeling. In Y. Raydugin (Ed.), *Handbook of Research on Leveraging Risk and Uncertainties for Effective Project Management* (pp. 61–75). Hershey, PA: IGI Global. doi:10.4018/978-1-5225-1790-0.ch003

Hu, N., & Cheng, H. (2016). Survival Analysis and ROC Analysis in Analyzing Credit Risks: Assessing Default Risks Over Time. In D. Jakóbczak (Ed.), *Analyzing Risk through Probabilistic Modeling in Operations Research* (pp. 380–403). Hershey, PA: IGI Global. doi:10.4018/978-1-4666-9458-3.ch016

Huemann, M., & Ringhofer, C. (2016). Challenge or Potential? Risk Identification in the Context of Sustainable Development: A Case Study. In C. Bodea, A. Purnus, M. Huemann, & M. Hajdu (Eds.), *Managing Project Risks for Competitive Advantage in Changing Business Environments* (pp. 87–105). Hershey, PA: IGI Global. doi:10.4018/978-1-5225-0335-4.ch005

Hulett, D. T. (2017). Monte Carlo Simulation for Integrated Cost-Schedule Risk Analysis: Concepts, Methods, and Tools for Risk Analysis and Mitigation. In Y. Raydugin (Ed.), *Handbook of Research on Leveraging Risk and Uncertainties for Effective Project Management* (pp. 29–60). Hershey, PA: IGI Global. doi:10.4018/978-1-5225-1790-0.ch002

Ivančević, K. (2017). Insurance as an Optimization Tool for Risk Management in Small and Medium-Sized Enterprises. In M. Vemić (Ed.), *Optimal Management Strategies in Small and Medium Enterprises* (pp. 178–197). Hershey, PA: IGI Global. doi:10.4018/978-1-5225-1949-2.ch009

Jakóbczak, D. J. (2016). Data Extrapolation via Curve Modeling in Analyzing Risk: Value Anticipation for Decision Making. In D. Jakóbczak (Ed.), *Analyzing Risk through Probabilistic Modeling in Operations Research* (pp. 1–31). Hershey, PA: IGI Global. doi:10.4018/978-1-4666-9458-3.ch001

Jakóbczak, D. J. (2016). The Method of Probabilistic Nodes Combination in Decision Making and Risk Analysis: Data Extrapolation in Planning. In D. Jakóbczak (Ed.), *Analyzing Risk through Probabilistic Modeling in Operations Research* (pp. 32–60). Hershey, PA: IGI Global. doi:10.4018/978-1-4666-9458-3.ch002

Jarman, M. F., & Dreher, L. G. (2017). Missed Opportunities from Misalignment of Project and Operational Requirements. In Y. Raydugin (Ed.), *Handbook of Research on Leveraging Risk and Uncertainties for Effective Project Management* (pp. 363–383). Hershey, PA: IGI Global. doi:10.4018/978-1-5225-1790-0.ch017

Kač, S. M., Tamše, T., & Gorenak, I. (2017). Intercultural Education and Training of Slovene Police Officers for the Purpose of International Missions. In V. Potocan, M. Üngan, & Z. Nedelko (Eds.), *Handbook of Research on Managerial Solutions in Non-Profit Organizations* (pp. 298–320). Hershey, PA: IGI Global. doi:10.4018/978-1-5225-0731-4.ch014

Kafi, F., & Kafi, M. (2016). Information Quality in Supply Chain Software. In B. Christiansen (Ed.), *Handbook of Research on Global Supply Chain Management* (pp. 105–126). Hershey, PA: IGI Global. doi:10.4018/978-1-4666-9639-6.ch006

Kasemsap, K. (2016). Fostering Supply Chain Management in Global Business. In B. Christiansen (Ed.), *Handbook of Research on Global Supply Chain Management* (pp. 45–71). Hershey, PA: IGI Global. doi:10.4018/978-1-4666-9639-6.ch003

Kittilaksanawong, W. (2016). Value Creation and Appropriation in Buyer-Supplier Relationships: Governance, Competition and Cultures. In B. Christiansen (Ed.), *Handbook of Research on Global Supply Chain Management* (pp. 127–138). Hershey, PA: IGI Global. doi:10.4018/978-1-4666-9639-6.ch007

Klepac, G., Mrsic, L., & Kopal, R. (2016). Efficient Risk Profiling Using Bayesian Networks and Particle Swarm Optimization Algorithm. In D. Jakóbczak (Ed.), *Analyzing Risk through Probabilistic Modeling in Operations Research* (pp. 91–124). Hershey, PA: IGI Global. doi:10.4018/978-1-4666-9458-3.ch004

Kopp, U. (2016). Easier Identification of Risks and Uncertainties with Project Risk Constellations. In C. Bodea, A. Purnus, M. Huemann, & M. Hajdu (Eds.), *Managing Project Risks for Competitive Advantage in Changing Business Environments* (pp. 106–127). Hershey, PA: IGI Global. doi:10.4018/978-1-5225-0335-4.ch006

Kucukbay, F. (2017). Cash Management in Non-Profit Organizations. In V. Potocan, M. Üngan, & Z. Nedelko (Eds.), *Handbook of Research on Managerial Solutions in Non-Profit Organizations* (pp. 94–110). Hershey, PA: IGI Global. doi:10.4018/978-1-5225-0731-4.ch005

Kutsch, E., Hällgren, M., & Turner, N. (2016). The Internalization of Attention at 28,000 Feet: Revisiting the K2 2008 Disaster. In C. Bodea, A. Purnus, M. Huemann, & M. Hajdu (Eds.), *Managing Project Risks for Competitive Advantage in Changing Business Environments* (pp. 196–215). Hershey, PA: IGI Global. doi:10.4018/978-1-5225-0335-4.ch010

Lahmiri, S., & Gagnon, S. (2016). A Sequential Probabilistic System for Bankruptcy Data Classification. In D. Jakóbczak (Ed.), *Analyzing Risk through Probabilistic Modeling in Operations Research* (pp. 138–147). Hershey, PA: IGI Global. doi:10.4018/978-1-4666-9458-3.ch006

Lederer, M., Kurz, M., & Lazarov, P. (2017). Usage and Suitability of Methods for Strategic Business Process Initiatives: A Multi Case Study Research. *International Journal of Productivity Management and Assessment Technologies*, *5*(1), 40–51. doi:10.4018/IJPMAT.2017010103

Lee, I. (2017). A Social Enterprise Business Model and a Case Study of Pacific Community Ventures (PCV). In V. Potocan, M. Üngan, & Z. Nedelko (Eds.), *Handbook of Research on Managerial Solutions in Non-Profit Organizations* (pp. 182–204). Hershey, PA: IGI Global. doi:10.4018/978-1-5225-0731-4.ch009

Levin, G., & Pitotti, N. (2017). Program and Portfolio Management Relationship and Support. In L. Romano (Ed.), *Project Portfolio Management Strategies for Effective Organizational Operations* (pp. 310–333). Hershey, PA: IGI Global. doi:10.4018/978-1-5225-2151-8.ch013

Liu, Z. (2016). Structuring and Managing Supply Network: A Review of Current Literature and Conceptual Framework. In B. Christiansen (Ed.), *Handbook of Research on Global Supply Chain Management* (pp. 341–353). Hershey, PA: IGI Global. doi:10.4018/978-1-4666-9639-6.ch019

Lokuwaduge, C. S. (2016). Exploring the New Public Management (NPM)-Based Reforms in the Public Sector Accounting: A Sri Lankan Study. In A. Ferreira, G. Azevedo, J. Oliveira, & R. Marques (Eds.), *Global Perspectives on Risk Management and Accounting in the Public Sector* (pp. 49–67). Hershey, PA: IGI Global. doi:10.4018/978-1-4666-9803-1.ch003

Lorber, M., Treven, S., & Mumel, D. (2017). Leaders' Behavior in Association with Job Satisfaction and Organizational Commitment. In V. Potocan, M. Üngan, & Z. Nedelko (Eds.), *Handbook of Research on Managerial Solutions in Non-Profit Organizations* (pp. 111–133). Hershey, PA: IGI Global. doi:10.4018/978-1-5225-0731-4.ch006

Maciejczak, M., & Słodki, A. (2017). Initial Price Strategies of Polish Micro and Small Enterprises: An Application of Game Theory for Industrial Organization of the SME Sector. In M. Vemić (Ed.), *Optimal Management Strategies in Small and Medium Enterprises* (pp. 126–143). Hershey, PA: IGI Global. doi:10.4018/978-1-5225-1949-2.ch007

Magalhães, F. R., & Santos, C. (2016). Online Financial Transparency: Local Governments of the MERCOSUR Member Countries. In A. Ferreira, G. Azevedo, J. Oliveira, & R. Marques (Eds.), *Global Perspectives on Risk Management and Accounting in the Public Sector* (pp. 252–273). Hershey, PA: IGI Global. doi:10.4018/978-1-4666-9803-1.ch013

Malega, P. (2017). Small and Medium Enterprises in the Slovak Republic: Status and Competitiveness of SMEs in the Global Markets and Possibilities of Optimization. In M. Vemić (Ed.), *Optimal Management Strategies in Small and Medium Enterprises* (pp. 102–124). Hershey, PA: IGI Global. doi:10.4018/978-1-5225-1949-2.ch006

Malek, N. A., & Takala, J. A. (2017). Regression Analysis for Environmental Practices: Participation among Finnish SMEs. In M. Vemić (Ed.), *Optimal Management Strategies in Small and Medium Enterprises* (pp. 44–59). Hershey, PA: IGI Global. doi:10.4018/978-1-5225-1949-2.ch003

Malewska, K. M. (2017). Intuition in Decision-Making on the Example of a Non-Profit Organization. In V. Potocan, M. Üngan, & Z. Nedelko (Eds.), *Handbook of Research on Managerial Solutions in Non-Profit Organizations* (pp. 378–399). Hershey, PA: IGI Global. doi:10.4018/978-1-5225-0731-4.ch018

Malik, M. S. (2017). Risk Based Contingency in Project Cost Estimates. In Y. Raydugin (Ed.), *Handbook of Research on Leveraging Risk and Uncertainties for Effective Project Management* (pp. 130–138). Hershey, PA: IGI Global. doi:10.4018/978-1-5225-1790-0.ch006

Mendes, H. C., Santos, C., Ferreira, A. D., Marques, R. P., Azevedo, G. M., & Oliveira, J. D. (2016). Local Authorities and the Disclosure of Financial Information via the Internet: The Portuguese Case. In A. Ferreira, G. Azevedo, J. Oliveira, & R. Marques (Eds.), *Global Perspectives on Risk Management and Accounting in the Public Sector* (pp. 274–297). Hershey, PA: IGI Global. doi:10.4018/978-1-4666-9803-1.ch014

Miller, T., de Matta, R., & Xu, M. (2016). High Level Inventory Network Modeling Approaches. In B. Christiansen (Ed.), *Handbook of Research on Global Supply Chain Management* (pp. 15–44). Hershey, PA: IGI Global. doi:10.4018/978-1-4666-9639-6.ch002

Milošević, O. (2017). Critical Review of SME Regulation Optimization in Serbia: A Reflection on Harmonization with the EU Acquis. In M. Vemić (Ed.), *Optimal Management Strategies in Small and Medium Enterprises* (pp. 79–101). Hershey, PA: IGI Global. doi:10.4018/978-1-5225-1949-2.ch005

Mogos, R., Bodea, C., Stancu, S., Purnus, A., & Dascalu, M. (2016). Educating Project Managers to Deal with Project Risks: Improvement of the Educational Programmes Design by Using Curriculum Management Systems. In C. Bodea, A. Purnus, M. Huemann, & M. Hajdu (Eds.), *Managing Project Risks for Competitive Advantage in Changing Business Environments* (pp. 231–257). Hershey, PA: IGI Global. doi:10.4018/978-1-5225-0335-4.ch012

Molnar, R. M. (2017). Structural Change Management for Sustainable SME Development: Applying Classical Management Tools. In M. Vemić (Ed.), *Optimal Management Strategies in Small and Medium Enterprises* (pp. 348–369). Hershey, PA: IGI Global. doi:10.4018/978-1-5225-1949-2.ch016

Nandonde, F. A., & Nguni, W. (2016). Relationship Establishment in SCM in a Market with Enforcement and Regulation Challenges: Case of Tanzania. In B. Christiansen (Ed.), *Handbook of Research on Global Supply Chain Management* (pp. 354–365). Hershey, PA: IGI Global. doi:10.4018/978-1-4666-9639-6.ch020

Nedelko, Z., & Potocan, V. (2017). Management Solutions in Non-Profit Organizations: Case of Slovenia. In V. Potocan, M. Üngan, & Z. Nedelko (Eds.), *Handbook of Research on Managerial Solutions in Non-Profit Organizations* (pp. 1–22). Hershey, PA: IGI Global. doi:10.4018/978-1-5225-0731-4.ch001

Nersesian, R. L. (2017). Incorporating Simulation in Project Scoping. In Y. Raydugin (Ed.), *Handbook of Research on Leveraging Risk and Uncertainties for Effective Project Management* (pp. 406–434). Hershey, PA: IGI Global. doi:10.4018/978-1-5225-1790-0.ch019

Nesbitt, R., & Kotb, A. (2016). Governance in NHS Foundation Trusts: Insights from Company Secretaries. In A. Ferreira, G. Azevedo, J. Oliveira, & R. Marques (Eds.), *Global Perspectives on Risk Management and Accounting in the Public Sector* (pp. 167–187). Hershey, PA: IGI Global. doi:10.4018/978-1-4666-9803-1.ch009

Nonino, F. (2017). Project Selection Frameworks and Methodologies for Reducing Risks in Project Portfolio Management. In L. Romano (Ed.), *Project Portfolio Management Strategies for Effective Organizational Operations* (pp. 245–263). Hershey, PA: IGI Global. doi:10.4018/978-1-5225-2151-8.ch010

Olson, B. (2017). Optimizing Portfolio Value through Comprehensive Project Metrics. In L. Romano (Ed.), *Project Portfolio Management Strategies for Effective Organizational Operations* (pp. 178–201). Hershey, PA: IGI Global. doi:10.4018/978-1-5225-2151-8.ch007

Parth, F. R. (2017). Preparing the Organization for Portfolio Management: Overcoming Resistance and Obstacles. In L. Romano (Ed.), *Project Portfolio Management Strategies for Effective Organizational Operations* (pp. 119–152). Hershey, PA: IGI Global. doi:10.4018/978-1-5225-2151-8.ch005

Parth, F. R. (2017). Project Portfolio Management Growth and Operation: Portfolio Management Structure, Operations, Risk, and Growth. In L. Romano (Ed.), *Project Portfolio Management Strategies for Effective Organizational Operations* (pp. 264–287). Hershey, PA: IGI Global. doi:10.4018/978-1-5225-2151-8.ch011

Pečarič, M. (2016). The Awareness of Mentality in Public Administration as the Key for the Management of Its Complexity. In A. Ferreira, G. Azevedo, J. Oliveira, & R. Marques (Eds.), *Global Perspectives on Risk Management and Accounting in the Public Sector* (pp. 1–24). Hershey, PA: IGI Global. doi:10.4018/978-1-4666-9803-1.ch001

Peng, H. (2016). Condition-Based Maintenance: Capital Goods Industry. In D. Jakóbczak (Ed.), *Analyzing Risk through Probabilistic Modeling in Operations Research* (pp. 292–320). Hershey, PA: IGI Global. doi:10.4018/978-1-4666-9458-3.ch012

Pereira de Campos, C. M., Rodrigues, L. L., & Jorge, S. M. (2016). The Role of Management Accounting Systems in Public Hospitals and the Construction of Budgets: A Literature Review. In A. Ferreira, G. Azevedo, J. Oliveira, & R. Marques (Eds.), *Global Perspectives on Risk Management and Accounting in the Public Sector* (pp. 366–389). Hershey, PA: IGI Global. doi:10.4018/978-1-4666-9803-1.ch018

Pham, T. S., Darabi, F., & Wilmot, N. V. (2016). International Supply Chain Case Study. In B. Christiansen (Ed.), *Handbook of Research on Global Supply Chain Management* (pp. 205–226). Hershey, PA: IGI Global. doi:10.4018/978-1-4666-9639-6.ch012

Pinho, M., & Santos, C. (2016). Plan for Prevention of Risks of Corruption and Related Infractions: The Application of FMEA Methodology. In A. Ferreira, G. Azevedo, J. Oliveira, & R. Marques (Eds.), *Global Perspectives on Risk Management and Accounting in the Public Sector* (pp. 390–412). Hershey, PA: IGI Global. doi:10.4018/978-1-4666-9803-1.ch019

Plumery, R. C. (2017). Risk-Centric Performance Measurement: Deriving Best Value from Performance Management Systems. In Y. Raydugin (Ed.), *Handbook of Research on Leveraging Risk and Uncertainties for Effective Project Management* (pp. 318–336). Hershey, PA: IGI Global. doi:10.4018/978-1-5225-1790-0.ch015

Postăvaru, N., & Leonte, B. (2016). Project Portfolio Risk Management: Managing Risk in Case of Investment Portfolio. In C. Bodea, A. Purnus, M. Huemann, & M. Hajdu (Eds.), *Managing Project Risks for Competitive Advantage in Changing Business Environments* (pp. 279–300). Hershey, PA: IGI Global. doi:10.4018/978-1-5225-0335-4.ch014

Qi, A., & Zheng, L. (2016). Project Risk Management: A Chinese Perspective. In C. Bodea, A. Purnus, M. Huemann, & M. Hajdu (Eds.), *Managing Project Risks for Competitive Advantage in Changing Business Environments* (pp. 45–69). Hershey, PA: IGI Global. doi:10.4018/978-1-5225-0335-4.ch003

Raue, S., & Klein, L. (2016). Systemic Risk Management: A Practice Approach to the Systemic Management of Project Risk. In C. Bodea, A. Purnus, M. Huemann, & M. Hajdu (Eds.), *Managing Project Risks for Competitive Advantage in Changing Business Environments* (pp. 70–85). Hershey, PA: IGI Global. doi:10.4018/978-1-5225-0335-4.ch004

Raydugin, Y. (2017). Integrated Risk-Based and Economic-Based (IRBEB) Methodology for Selection of Project Alternatives. In Y. Raydugin (Ed.), *Handbook of Research on Leveraging Risk and Uncertainties for Effective Project Management* (pp. 459–469). Hershey, PA: IGI Global. doi:10.4018/978-1-5225-1790-0.ch021

Raydugin, Y. (2017). Project Risk Management: Popular Fallacies and Overlooked Best Practices. In Y. Raydugin (Ed.), *Handbook of Research on Leveraging Risk and Uncertainties for Effective Project Management* (pp. 1–28). Hershey, PA: IGI Global. doi:10.4018/978-1-5225-1790-0.ch001

Rinderu, P., Voiculescu, C. I., & Visanescu, D. L. (2016). Risks in Implementing EU-Funded Projects in Romanian Public Higher Education System: Measures for Better Institutional Response. In A. Ferreira, G. Azevedo, J. Oliveira, & R. Marques (Eds.), *Global Perspectives on Risk Management and Accounting in the Public Sector* (pp. 413–441). Hershey, PA: IGI Global. doi:10.4018/978-1-4666-9803-1.ch020

Romano, L. (2017). Adaptive Portfolio Management. In L. Romano (Ed.), *Project Portfolio Management Strategies for Effective Organizational Operations* (pp. 153–177). Hershey, PA: IGI Global. doi:10.4018/978-1-5225-2151-8.ch006

Romano, L. (2017). Portfolio Management as a Step into the Future. In L. Romano (Ed.), *Project Portfolio Management Strategies for Effective Organizational Operations* (pp. 1–38). Hershey, PA: IGI Global. doi:10.4018/978-1-5225-2151-8.ch001

Romano, L., Grimaldi, R., & Colasuonno, F. S. (2017). Demand Management as a Success Factor in Project Portfolio Management. In L. Romano (Ed.), *Project Portfolio Management Strategies for Effective Organizational Operations* (pp. 202–219). Hershey, PA: IGI Global. doi:10.4018/978-1-5225-2151-8.ch008

Rostek, K. B. (2016). Risk Management: Role and Importance in Business Organization. In D. Jakóbczak (Ed.), *Analyzing Risk through Probabilistic Modeling in Operations Research* (pp. 149–178). Hershey, PA: IGI Global. doi:10.4018/978-1-4666-9458-3.ch007

Sá, F., Rocha, Á., & Pérez-Cota, M. (2016). A Literature Review on Quality Models for Online E-Government Services. In A. Ferreira, G. Azevedo, J. Oliveira, & R. Marques (Eds.), *Global Perspectives on Risk Management and Accounting in the Public Sector* (pp. 151–166). Hershey, PA: IGI Global. doi:10.4018/978-1-4666-9803-1.ch008

Sanchez-Ruiz, L., & Blanco, B. (2017). Process Management for SMEs: Barriers, Enablers, and Benefits. In M. Vemić (Ed.), *Optimal Management Strategies in Small and Medium Enterprises* (pp. 293–319). Hershey, PA: IGI Global. doi:10.4018/978-1-5225-1949-2.ch014

Schoper, Y., Böhle, F., & Heidling, E. (2016). Coping Better with the Project's Unknown Unknowns: New Competences for Overcoming Uncertainty in Projects. In C. Bodea, A. Purnus, M. Huemann, & M. Hajdu (Eds.), *Managing Project Risks for Competitive Advantage in Changing Business Environments* (pp. 1–22). Hershey, PA: IGI Global. doi:10.4018/978-1-5225-0335-4.ch001

Serpell, A. F., Ferrada, X., & Rubio, L. (2016). Using a Knowledge-Based Approach to Foster the Use of Risk Management in Construction. In C. Bodea, A. Purnus, M. Huemann, & M. Hajdu (Eds.), *Managing Project Risks for Competitive Advantage in Changing Business Environments* (pp. 258–278). Hershey, PA: IGI Global. doi:10.4018/978-1-5225-0335-4.ch013

Shang, K. (2017). Improving Objectivity in Project Risk Management. In Y. Raydugin (Ed.), *Handbook of Research on Leveraging Risk and Uncertainties for Effective Project Management* (pp. 248–265). Hershey, PA: IGI Global. doi:10.4018/978-1-5225-1790-0.ch012

Sharma, S. K., Bhat, A., Kumar, V., & Agarwal, A. (2017). Path Analysis Model for Supply Chain Risk Management. *International Journal of Information Systems and Supply Chain Management, 10*(2), 21–41. doi:10.4018/IJISSCM.2017040102

Shih, C. P., & Orochena, O. D. (2016). Analyzing the Effect of Transformational Leadership on Innovation and Organizational Performance. *International Journal of Productivity Management and Assessment Technologies, 4*(2), 11–27. doi:10.4018/IJPMAT.2016070102

Silvius, G. (2016). Integrating Sustainability into Project Risk Management. In C. Bodea, A. Purnus, M. Huemann, & M. Hajdu (Eds.), *Managing Project Risks for Competitive Advantage in Changing Business Environments* (pp. 23–44). Hershey, PA: IGI Global. doi:10.4018/978-1-5225-0335-4.ch002

Soniewicki, M. (2017). The Importance of Market Orientation in Creating a Competitive Advantage of Micro, Small, and Medium-Sized Companies in the Internationalization Process. In M. Vemić (Ed.), *Optimal Management Strategies in Small and Medium Enterprises* (pp. 1–21). Hershey, PA: IGI Global. doi:10.4018/978-1-5225-1949-2.ch001

Sönmez, R. (2017). Value Creation through Social Alliances: Theoretical Considerations in Partnership Relationships. In V. Potocan, M. Üngan, & Z. Nedelko (Eds.), *Handbook of Research on Managerial Solutions in Non-Profit Organizations* (pp. 205–231). Hershey, PA: IGI Global. doi:10.4018/978-1-5225-0731-4.ch010

Sowa, F., & Staples, R. (2016). Public Administration in the Era of Late Neo-Liberalism: Placement Professionals and the NPM Regime. In A. Ferreira, G. Azevedo, J. Oliveira, & R. Marques (Eds.), *Global Perspectives on Risk Management and Accounting in the Public Sector* (pp. 25–48). Hershey, PA: IGI Global. doi:10.4018/978-1-4666-9803-1.ch002

Stancu, S. (2016). Managing Risks in the Innovation Projects in the Services Sector: A Case Study for the Mobile Communication. In C. Bodea, A. Purnus, M. Huemann, & M. Hajdu (Eds.), *Managing Project Risks for Competitive Advantage in Changing Business Environments* (pp. 174–195). Hershey, PA: IGI Global. doi:10.4018/978-1-5225-0335-4.ch009

Stefanova, J. S., & Wenner, Z. (2017). Entrepreneurship and Enterprise Value Creation in Support of Smart, Sustainable, and Inclusive Growth in the European Union. In M. Vemić (Ed.), *Optimal Management Strategies in Small and Medium Enterprises* (pp. 268–292). Hershey, PA: IGI Global. doi:10.4018/978-1-5225-1949-2.ch013

Stoian, M., & Stoian, R. (2016). Financial Risk Management: An Introduction. In C. Bodea, A. Purnus, M. Huemann, & M. Hajdu (Eds.), *Managing Project Risks for Competitive Advantage in Changing Business Environments* (pp. 301–311). Hershey, PA: IGI Global. doi:10.4018/978-1-5225-0335-4.ch015

Tavares, M. D., & Rodrigues, L. L. (2016). The Determinants of Sustainability Reporting of the Portuguese Public Sector Entities. In A. Ferreira, G. Azevedo, J. Oliveira, & R. Marques (Eds.), *Global Perspectives on Risk Management and Accounting in the Public Sector* (pp. 226–251). Hershey, PA: IGI Global. doi:10.4018/978-1-4666-9803-1.ch012

Timilsina, B. (2017). Overcoming the Barriers of Strategic Planning, Implementation, and Monitoring in Turbulent Business Environment: A Qualitative Study on Finnish SMEs. In M. Vemić (Ed.), *Optimal Management Strategies in Small and Medium Enterprises* (pp. 226–248). Hershey, PA: IGI Global. doi:10.4018/978-1-5225-1949-2.ch011

Tongiani, M. G., & Zhao, S. (2017). Traditional Italian Food Products on the Chinese Market: Best Practices for Italian Small and Medium Enterprises. In M. Vemić (Ed.), *Optimal Management Strategies in Small and Medium Enterprises* (pp. 22–43). Hershey, PA: IGI Global. doi:10.4018/978-1-5225-1949-2.ch002

Toth, T., & Sebestyen, Z. (2016). Project Risk Management Process for Professionals: A Value-Based Approach. In C. Bodea, A. Purnus, M. Huemann, & M. Hajdu (Eds.), *Managing Project Risks for Competitive Advantage in Changing Business Environments* (pp. 128–149). Hershey, PA: IGI Global. doi:10.4018/978-1-5225-0335-4.ch007

Townley, T. W. (2017). Modeling Risk and Opportunity Reality. In Y. Raydugin (Ed.), *Handbook of Research on Leveraging Risk and Uncertainties for Effective Project Management* (pp. 435–458). Hershey, PA: IGI Global. doi:10.4018/978-1-5225-1790-0.ch020

Trickey, G. (2017). Getting to Grips with Behavioural Bias: How Projects Fail and What To Do About It. In Y. Raydugin (Ed.), *Handbook of Research on Leveraging Risk and Uncertainties for Effective Project Management* (pp. 220–247). Hershey, PA: IGI Global. doi:10.4018/978-1-5225-1790-0.ch011

Tudor, C., & Tudor, M. (2016). On Using Monte Carlo Simulations for Project Risk Management. In C. Bodea, A. Purnus, M. Huemann, & M. Hajdu (Eds.), *Managing Project Risks for Competitive Advantage in Changing Business Environments* (pp. 150–173). Hershey, PA: IGI Global. doi:10.4018/978-1-5225-0335-4.ch008

Turner, R. (2016). Risks in Project Marketing. In C. Bodea, A. Purnus, M. Huemann, & M. Hajdu (Eds.), *Managing Project Risks for Competitive Advantage in Changing Business Environments* (pp. 217–230). Hershey, PA: IGI Global. doi:10.4018/978-1-5225-0335-4.ch011

Vaiappuri, S. K., Kamarulzaman, N. H., Vijayan, G., & Mukherjee, A. (2016). An Empirical View of Knowledge Management. In B. Christiansen (Ed.), *Handbook of Research on Global Supply Chain Management* (pp. 452–465). Hershey, PA: IGI Global. doi:10.4018/978-1-4666-9639-6.ch025

Vecchi, A., & Vallisi, V. (2016). Supply Chain Resilience. In B. Christiansen (Ed.), *Handbook of Research on Global Supply Chain Management* (pp. 147–160). Hershey, PA: IGI Global. doi:10.4018/978-1-4666-9639-6.ch009

Vemić, M. B. (2017). A Further Look at Working Capital Optimization in Medium-Sized Firms: Concepts and Evidence. In M. Vemić (Ed.), *Optimal Management Strategies in Small and Medium Enterprises* (pp. 144–177). Hershey, PA: IGI Global. doi:10.4018/978-1-5225-1949-2.ch008

Vemić, M. B. (2017). Financial Innovation in Medium-Sized Enterprises Optimizes Their Gravitation Towards Capital Markets: Financial Future in Perspective. In M. Vemić (Ed.), *Optimal Management Strategies in Small and Medium Enterprises* (pp. 198–224). Hershey, PA: IGI Global. doi:10.4018/978-1-5225-1949-2.ch010

Vijayan, G., Kamarulzaman, N. H., Mukherjee, A., & Vaiappuri, S. K. (2016). Strategic Value Creation in a Supply Chain. In B. Christiansen (Ed.), *Handbook of Research on Global Supply Chain Management* (pp. 186–204). Hershey, PA: IGI Global. doi:10.4018/978-1-4666-9639-6.ch011

Wodecka-Hyjek, A. (2017). Co-Operation between the Public Administration and Non-Profit Organisations as a Condition of the Development of Public Entrepreneurship: On the Example of the Selected World Solutions. In V. Potocan, M. Üngan, & Z. Nedelko (Eds.), *Handbook of Research on Managerial Solutions in Non-Profit Organizations* (pp. 253–275). Hershey, PA: IGI Global. doi:10.4018/978-1-5225-0731-4.ch012

Yordanova, S. D. (2017). Optimizing Virtual Communities in Tourism to Facilitate Development of Small and Medium-Sized Enterprises. In M. Vemić (Ed.), *Optimal Management Strategies in Small and Medium Enterprises* (pp. 60–78). Hershey, PA: IGI Global. doi:10.4018/978-1-5225-1949-2.ch004

Yumurtacı, I. Ö., & Oflaç, B. S. (2016). Supply Chain Management Practices in Retail-The Trends and Future Perspective. In B. Christiansen (Ed.), *Handbook of Research on Global Supply Chain Management* (pp. 366–378). Hershey, PA: IGI Global. doi:10.4018/978-1-4666-9639-6.ch021

Zhang, Y. (2016). An Empirical Investigation of the Role of E-Communication in International Collaborations. In B. Christiansen (Ed.), *Handbook of Research on Global Supply Chain Management* (pp. 85–104). Hershey, PA: IGI Global. doi:10.4018/978-1-4666-9639-6.ch005

Zomorrodi, M. (2016). Supply Chain Risk Management: A Review of the Literature. In B. Christiansen (Ed.), *Handbook of Research on Global Supply Chain Management* (pp. 516–530). Hershey, PA: IGI Global. doi:10.4018/978-1-4666-9639-6.ch029

About the Author

Halil Sarıaslan is presently a professor of financial and quantitative analysis in the Department of International Business at Baskent University, Ankara, Turkey. Dr. Sarıaslan was formerly a full professor in the Department of Management, Faculty of Political Sciences, at University of Ankara, where he started his academic career as an assistant professor. Professor Halil Sarıaslan received his B.A. degree from Ankara University in 1972 and his M.S. and Ph. D. degrees from the Florida State University, USA, in 1975 and 1978, respectively. He is presently the Chairman of the Department of International Trade (Business), College of Commercial Sciences, Baskent University, and the author of eight books, five research reports published in Turkey, Sweden, and USA, and more than twenty articles published in refereed and peer-reviewed journals. His publications are mostly in the field of finance and quantitative analysis for business management.

In addition to his academic career at Ankara and Baskent universities, Professor Sarıaslan also served the Union of Chambers and Commodity Exchanges of Turkey (TOBB) between the years 1993 and 2000 as an economic consultant to the Presidents of the Union of Chambers (TOBB). Furthermore, he participated in and submitted papers and/or reports to many different meetings, panels, and conferences held by Euro-chambers, UN, and OECD, as the delegate of TOBB. Moreover, he also conducted and authored several economic research reports on Small and Medium - Sized Enterprises (SMEs) and privatization activities in the Turkish economy that where published nation-wide by TOBB as the basis of the economic policy of TOBB. Later on, being nominated by the Union of Chambers and Commodity Exchanges of Turkey (TOBB), Professor Sarıaslan was appointed by the Government at that time to the Capital Markets Board of Turkey as a commissioner (a board member) and he served the Capital Markets Board between the years of 2000 – 2006. Professor Sarıaslan also served on the executive board of several large financial and industrial firms in Turkey as an independent board member.

Index

N

P

R

S

T

U

W

www.ingramcontent.com/pod-product-compliance
Lightning Source LLC
LaVergne TN
LVHW080020210926
848481LV00011B/3065
* 9 7 8 1 5 2 2 5 8 6 7 2 2 *